Thinking through the Body

This book provides a richly rewarding vision of the burgeoning interdisciplinary field of somaesthetics. Composed of fourteen wide-ranging but finely unified essays by Richard Shusterman, originator of the field, *Thinking through the Body* explains the philosophical foundations of somaesthetics and applies its insights to central issues in ethics, education, cultural politics, consciousness studies, sexuality, and the arts. Integrating Western philosophy, cognitive science, and somatic methodologies with classical Asian theories of body, mind, and action, these essays probe the nature of somatic existence and the role of body consciousness in knowledge, memory, and behavior. Deploying somaesthetic perspectives to analyze key aesthetic concepts (such as style and the sublime), Shusterman offers detailed studies of embodiment in drama, dance, architecture, and photography. The book also includes somaesthetic exercise for the classroom and explores the use of *ars erotica* for the art of living.

Richard Shusterman is the Dorothy F. Schmidt Eminent Scholar in the Humanities and Professor of Philosophy at Florida Atlantic University, where he also directs the Center for Body, Mind, and Culture. He is the author of numerous books, including *Body Consciousness: A Philosophy of Mindfulness and Somaesthetics* (Cambridge, 2008), *Performing Live* (2000), and *Pragmatist Aesthetics* (1992, 2nd ed. 2000, and published in fifteen languages).

Thinking through the Body

Essays in Somaesthetics

RICHARD SHUSTERMAN

CAMBRIDGE
UNIVERSITY PRESS

CAMBRIDGE UNIVERSITY PRESS
Cambridge, New York, Melbourne, Madrid, Cape Town,
Singapore, São Paulo, Delhi, Mexico City

Cambridge University Press
32 Avenue of the Americas, New York, NY 10013-2473, USA

www.cambridge.org
Information on this title: www.cambridge.org/9781107698505

© Richard Shusterman 2012

This publication is in copyright. Subject to statutory exception
and to the provisions of relevant collective licensing agreements,
no reproduction of any part may take place without the written
permission of Cambridge University Press.

First published 2012

Printed in the United States of America

A catalog record for this publication is available from the British Library.

Library of Congress Cataloging in Publication Data
Shusterman, Richard.
Thinking through the body : essays in somaesthetics / Richard Shusterman.
p. cm.
Includes index.
ISBN 978-1-107-01906-5 (hardback)
1. Humanities – Philosophy.   2. Human body (Philosophy)   3. Humanities – Study
and teaching (Higher)   4. Aesthetics – Philosophy.   I. Title.
AZ101.S58   2012
128'.6–dc23   2011052117

ISBN 978-1-107-01906-5 Hardback
ISBN 978-1-107-69850-5 Paperback

Cambridge University Press has no responsibility for the persistence or accuracy of URLs
for external or third-party Internet Web sites referred to in this publication and does not
guarantee that any content on such Web sites is, or will remain, accurate or appropriate.

For Peng Feng

献给彭锋

Contents

Preface	page ix
Introduction	1

PART I. SOMATIC BEING, KNOWING, AND TEACHING

1 Thinking through the Body: Educating for the Humanities	25
2 The Body as Background	47
3 Self-Knowledge and Its Discontents: From Socrates to Somaesthetics	68
4 Muscle Memory and the Somaesthetic Pathologies of Everyday Life	91
5 Somaesthetics in the Philosophy Classroom: A Practical Approach	112

PART II. SOMAESTHETICS, AESTHETICS, AND CULTURE

6 Somaesthetics and the Limits of Aesthetics	125
7 Somaesthetics and Burke's Sublime	145
8 Pragmatism and Cultural Politics: From Textualism to Somaesthetics	166
9 Body Consciousness and Performance: Somaesthetics East and West	197

PART III. THE ARTS AND THE ART OF LIVING

10 Somaesthetics and Architecture: A Critical Option	219
11 Photography as Performative Process	239

12 Asian *Ars Erotica* and the Question of Sexual Aesthetics   262
13 Somaesthetic Awakening and the Art of Living: Everyday Aesthetics in American Transcendentalism and Japanese Zen Practice   288
14 Somatic Style   315

Select Bibliography   339
Index   355

Preface

From our earliest days of life, we are nourished by the pleasures of bodily beauty. Enchanting visions of loving bodies that feed and care for us are deliciously blended with beautiful feelings the body enjoys through its other senses and own inner experiences. My interest in aesthetics emerged, I believe, from such childhood raptures of radiant bodily charms and blissful somatic fulfillment that branded me with a continuous yearning for beauty, long before I knew of any distinction between body and soul. That yearning has always inspired my ideals and my studies, despite philosophy's body-negating tradition and the troubling ways in which bodily beauty and desire have been distorted, exploited, and abused in contemporary culture. Ever present – though often only in sublimated form – this loving enchantment with somatic beauty haunted my philosophical research on other topics until it finally emerged as an explicit theme in the concluding chapters of *Pragmatist Aesthetics: Living Beauty, Rethinking Art* (1992), awakened into full consciousness through renewed engagement with the beauties of dance and through my philosophical conversion to a body-respecting, experience-oriented, melioristic pragmatism.

Adopting pragmatism as my new philosophical direction meant rediscovering the pressing existential issue that first drew me to philosophy and that first defined philosophy in ancient times: the question of how one should live. The idea of philosophy as an art of living aimed at realizing beauty through creative intelligence and critical reflection (involving both aesthetic and ethical sensitivity) thus formed the topic of my subsequent book, *Practicing Philosophy: Pragmatism and the Philosophical Life* (1997), the first English publication in which I proposed the idea of somaesthetics. The project of somaesthetics evolved as the logical consequence of my arguments advocating pragmatist aesthetics and the philosophical life. As art cannot be created or appreciated without using our bodily senses, actions, and experience, so our lives must inevitably be lived somatically. If we wish to improve our lives (and not only by improving the arts and aesthetic experience that enrich our lives), then one important way to do so would be to improve our understanding and mastery of our bodies – the fundamental, indispensable instrument or medium through which we perceive, act, and live this life on earth. As there seemed to be no field explicitly designed to develop this improved somatic understanding and mastery, somaesthetics thus emerged for me as an essential project, one to which I have since dedicated most of my research efforts.

Recognizing that a traditional field like philosophy might find the proposal of this new body-centered discipline a condemnable act of arrogant audacity, I first tentatively introduced the notion of somaesthetics in a German book, *Vor der Interpretation* (1996), where I argued for cultivating the body and appreciating its role in nondiscursive forms of understanding that lie beneath our interpretive efforts. Though somaesthetics quickly caught the attention of the influential daily *Frankfurter Algemeine Zeitung* (November 28, 1996), the reviewer savagely ridiculed the project. Betraying the exclusively text-centered bias so typical of philosophy, he misrepresented somaesthetics as a mere method of reading, "as something like whipping oneself while reading Kant, mountain-climbing while reading Nietzsche, and doing breathing exercises while reading Heidegger." This absurd and hurtful caricature stung me into articulating the somaesthetic project with sufficient detail to combat such distortions.

Fortunately, subsequent reactions to somaesthetics have been far more thoughtful and positive than that shocking first review. Many fine scholars in different fields have developed the somaesthetic project in intriguing and rewarding ways, through penetrating criticism and imaginative application to a variety of disciplines both within and beyond philosophy. Too numerous to mention here, their contributions are listed on the somaesthetics bibliography I maintain at *http://www.fau.edu/humanitieschair/Somaesthetics_Bibliography_Others.php*.

That first painful newspaper review of somaesthetics taught me an important lesson: the value of trying riskier ideas in international venues and foreign languages where one's errors, transgressions, or embarrassments are not so clearly exposed to one's home community, whose continued respect and support for one's work is especially crucial. That is why I also initiated my practical somaesthetics workshops in Europe, beyond the borders of the Anglo-American academic world I happily call home. This greater freedom to experiment in distant lands and foreign languages has a somaesthetic parallel in anatomy. One has more ease and range of movement in distal than proximal body parts; we can move our hands and feet much better than we can move our pelvis or torso.

Exploratory experiments in foreign languages require skilled translation, however, so I here express my gratitude to the many excellent scholars who translated my texts on somaesthetics and from whose penetrating questions and comments I have greatly learned. Among them, I am particularly indebted to Jean-Pierre Cometti, Peng Feng, Wojciech Małecki, Heidi Salaverria, Nicolas Viellescazes, Kim Jinyup, Cheng Xiangzhan, Lee Hyijin, Robin Celikates, Higuchi Satoshi, Giovanni Matteucci, Barbara Formis, Thomas Mondémé, Christophe Hanna, Krystyna Wilkoszewska, Alina Mitek, Aoki Takao, Sebastian Stankiewicz, Emil Visnovsky, Oishi Masashi, and Liliana Coutinho.

Foreign institutions of learning have been wonderfully receptive to somaesthetics. Among them, I should particularly note those universities that officially hosted me as a visiting professor during the years (2005–2011) in which I wrote the texts that form this book: the University of Paris (1 and 3), the University of Lyon, the University of Oslo, the University of Rome, the Technical University of Vienna, Renmin University (Beijing), and Shandong University. I am especially grateful to the Royaumont Foundation's dance research program ("Transforme," directed by Myriam Gourfink) and to Maguy Morin's dance training program at the Centre Chorégraphique National de Rillieux-la-Pape for inviting me to give three-day practical workshops in somaesthetics, and to the University of Paris 1 for inviting me to adapt that workshop for its graduate students and faculty in visual arts. Sibelius Academy in Finland and the University of Copenhagen (kinesiology) were also welcoming in arranging shorter workshops; and I cannot forget the kindness of Paris's École Normale Supérieure and Peking University's Center for Aesthetics and Aesthetic Education for hosting special conferences on somaesthetics, respectively organized (in February and July 2011) by Mathias Girel and Peng Feng.

Several of the book's essays originated in invited keynote lectures at other conferences. "Self-Knowledge and Its Discontents" was the 2007 Kneller Lecture for the Society of Philosophy and Education, while "Somaesthetics at the Limits" opened the annual conference of the Nordic Society for Aesthetics (in Aarhus, 2007). More recently, "Somaesthetics and Architecture: A Critical Option" was first given as a keynote lecture at the 11th International Bauhaus-Kolloquium (Weimar, 2009);

"Muscle Memory and the Somaesthetic Pathologies of Everyday Life" had a similar role in the annual conference of the Polish Physiotherapy Association (Wroclaw, 2010); while "Somatic Style" served that function at two conferences: the 18th International Congress for Aesthetics (Beijing, 2010) and the Kyung Hee Peace Bar Festival (Seoul, 2010). The title paper of this book was prepared for a particularly important occasion in my academic career – my inaugural lecture as the Dorothy F. Schmidt Eminent Scholar in the Humanities at Florida Atlantic University. This extraordinary interdisciplinary position, handsomely endowed through the great generosity of the Schmidt family, has provided me with superb resources for pursuing my somaesthetic research and stimulating that of others through the Center for Body, Mind, and Culture that I direct at FAU. I take this opportunity to express my profound thanks to Dick and Barbara Schmidt for their munificence and vision.

Grants from the Alexander von Humboldt Foundation and from the Japan Society for the Promotion of Science have also supported research for this book, whose essays have often profited from the keen critical eyes of first-rate journal editors. I especially wish to thank Susan Feagin, editor of *The Journal of Aesthetics and Art Criticism*, and Pradeep Dhillon of *The Journal of Aesthetic Education* for being receptive to papers on somaesthetics. Many colleagues offered helpful comments on earlier drafts of individual chapters. Unable to list them all, I should particularly acknowledge Arthur Danto, Roger Ames, Rita Felski, Jacob Lund, Morten Kyndrop, Hans-Peter Krüger, Martin Seel, Susan Laird, David Granger, Shaun Gallagher, John Protevi, Martin Jay, Dom Lopes, Diarmuid Costello, Andrea Kenkmann, Zdravko Radman, Martin Seel, Denis Cerclet, Kari Jormakka, Olaf Pfeiffer, Galen Cranz, Curtis Carter, Aoki Takao, Winfried Fluck, Wolfgang Welsch, Jurgen Streek, Christophe Kihm, Else Marie Bukdahl, Mark Johnson, Mathias Girel, Ken-ichi Sasaki, and David Zerbib.

Special thanks go to Professor Wojciech Małecki, who not only translated two of the book's essays into Polish but generously read the entire manuscript and suggested many improvements. My research assistants, Megan Fryer and Joel Wilson, were very helpful in preparing the final manuscript and verifying references. Working with Beatrice Rehl of Cambridge University Press has been a continuing pleasure for which I am very grateful. Erica Ando and our daughter Talia Emi have lived with my somaesthetic project for many years, providing exemplary lessons of beauty, critique, and patience to nourish my life and thought. They deserve much more than the thanks I offer here. This book is dedicated to Professor Peng Feng of Peking University, who first introduced the project of somaesthetics to China by superbly translating three of my books – *Pragmatist Aesthetics, Practicing Philosophy,* and *Performing Live* – and who then ingeniously applied somaesthetics to contemporary art in curating the Chinese Pavilion at the 2011 Venice Biennale. Peng Feng not only made my name in China, he also gave me my Chinese name. For his creative intelligence and his continued friendship, I am profoundly grateful.

Though most of these essays have already appeared in preliminary versions, I have revised all of them, often very substantially, for publication in this volume. I gratefully acknowledge the permission of the original publishers to revise and reprint this material. Here is a list of the original sources: "Thinking Through the Body, Educating for the Humanities: A Plea for Somaesthetics," *Journal of Aesthetic Education* 40 (2006): 1–21; "Self-Knowledge and Its Discontents: From Socrates to Somaesthetics," the Kneller Lecture, in *Philosophy and Education Yearbook* (2007): 25–37; "Muscle Memory and the Somaesthetic Pathologies of Everyday Life," *Human Movement* 12 (2011): 4–15; "Somaesthetics in the Philosophy Classroom: A Practical Approach," in Andrea Kenkmann (ed.), *Teaching Philosophy* (New York, NY: Continuum Press, 2009): 57–68; "Somaesthetics at the Limits," *The Nordic Journal of Aesthetics* 35 (2008): 7–23; "Somaesthetics and Burke's Sublime," *British Journal of Aesthetics* 45 (2005): 323–341; "Pragmatism and Cultural Politics: From Rortian Textualism to Somaesthetics," *New Literary History*, 41 (2010), 69–94; "Body Consciousness and Performance: Somaesthetics East and West," *Journal of Aesthetics and Art Criticism* 67 (2009) 133–145; "Somaesthetics and Architecture: A Critical Option," in K. Faschingeder and K. Jormakka et al. (eds.), *Architecture in the Age of Empire: 11th International Bauhaus-Colloquium* (Weimar: Verlag der Bauhaus-Universität Weimar, 2011); "Asian *Ars Erotica* and the Question of Sexual Aesthetics," *Journal of Aesthetics and Art Criticism* 65 (2007): 55–68; and "Somatic Style," *Journal of Aesthetics and Art Criticism,* 69 (2011), 147–149.

Introduction

I

Initially conceived as a branch of aesthetics within the larger discipline of philosophy, somaesthetics reflects my pragmatist efforts to reshape both these fields. But it has blossomed into a truly interdisciplinary enterprise. Many fine scholars in diverse disciplines have developed the somaesthetic project in fascinating and useful ways. Before introducing the essays that constitute this collection, I should note some of these developments along with the major criticisms somaesthetics has received and the challenges it needs to address in future work. First, however, I should briefly sketch how somaesthetics seeks to reorient its original disciplinary domain of aesthetics and philosophy. The ensuing chapters of this book flesh out this sketch in much greater detail.

Art enchants us through its richly sensuous dimensions, perceived through the bodily senses and enjoyed through embodied feelings. Yet philosophical aesthetics largely neglects the body's role in aesthetic appreciation. No theorist could ignore the frequent focus of painting and sculpture on beautiful bodily forms, nor deny the obvious fact that artworks are made through bodily efforts and skill; but philosophers generally disregard the body's broader aesthetic importance, conceiving it as a mere physical object for artistic representation or a mere instrument for artistic production. Even when Alexander Baumgarten, in the mid-eighteenth century, first defined modern aesthetics explicitly as a science of sensory perception (deriving its name from the Greek word for such perception, $\alpha\iota\sigma\theta\eta\sigma\iota\varsigma$), the body played no part in his theory, despite the bodily nature of our senses. Although Kant continued to treat aesthetic appreciation in the sensory terms of "judgment of taste" and "feeling of pleasure," the body remained excluded from its determining "a priori grounds" of form. Truly aesthetic judgments of taste are distinguished from bodily "judgments of sense" in that they involve "not what gratifies in sensation but merely by what pleases by its form," and are thus untainted with the "merely empirical delight" from somatic feelings, charm, and emotion.[1]

With Hegel's idealist, conceptual turn that essentially set the subsequent direction of modern aesthetics, the body is still more firmly dismissed because the focus on sensory perception, pleasure, and judgment is replaced by the project of defining fine art. Such art, he argues, should not be "servile" by satisfying "the ends of pleasure," but rather achieve its freedom (paradoxically) by its service in revealing and expressing spiritual truth, particularly "the most comprehensive truths of the mind." No longer the Baumgartian science of perception, aesthetics becomes "the *science* of art," a project not for increasing "our immediate enjoyment" or "stimulating art production, but in order to ascertain scientifically what art is."[2] Even analytic philosophy, which originally cut its teeth by rejecting Hegelian views, has now long been wedded to the project of defining aesthetics through the key issue of defining art. Some analytic aestheticians combine this project with Kantian ideas that define art in terms of aesthetic experience and judgment as disinterested, nonfunctional, and concerned with pleasure and beautiful form; others instead reject Kantian concerns with beauty and pleasure as inessential for art.[3]

As pragmatist aesthetics rejects the essential Kantian opposition of the aesthetic to the practical by insisting that art and aesthetic experience can serve life's interests without losing their status as worthy ends, so it also opposes Hegel's idealist scientism by celebrating the value of immediate enjoyment and of the body as a central locus where life's interests, pleasures, and practical purposes are realized. If pragmatist aesthetics likewise resists the traditional aesthetic attitude of distanced, disinterested contemplation by advocating an aesthetics of active, creative engagement, then it also should recognize that all action (artistic or political) requires

---

[1] Immanuel Kant, *The Critique of Judgment*, trans. J.C. Meredith (Oxford: Oxford University Press, 1986), 57, 63, 65, 67.
[2] G.W.F. Hegel, *Introductory Lectures in Aesthetics*, trans. Bernard Bosanquet (London: Penguin, 1993), 9, 13.
[3] This was not always the case. On the contrary, early analytic aesthetics often strongly resisted the project of defining art because of art's great diversity and open, dynamic character. For more details on this transformation, see Richard Shusterman, "On Analytic Aesthetics: From Empiricism to Metaphysics," in *Surface and Depth: Dialectics of Criticism and Culture* (Ithaca: Cornell University Press, 2002), 15–33.

the body, our tool of tools.[4] Building on the pragmatist insistence on the body's central role in artistic creation and appreciation, somaesthetics highlights and explores the soma – the living, sentient, purposive body – as the indispensable medium for all perception.

Somaesthetics thus redirects aesthetics back to the core issues of perception, consciousness, and feeling, which are embodied in the root meaning of "aesthetic" and its familiar contrast – "anaesthetic." Freed from the limiting focus on philosophy of language and metaphysics – the preoccupation with deriving definitions for the field of fine art and describing the ontology of its objects or artworks – aesthetic inquiry emerges enriched through somaesthetics as an exploratory orientation for new research in philosophy of mind. Aesthetic experience in the special sense of art can thus be better understood through a better grasp of its underlying ground in more basic forms of perceptual experience that are also essentially and actively embodied. If experiences of art and beauty are distinctive for the powerfully gratifying ways they absorb our attention, unify our consciousness, and engage our emotions, then increasing our powers of awareness, focus, and feeling through better mastery of their somatic source could render more of our experience similarly rewarding in such ways. Not only art's creation and appreciation would be enhanced through this heightening of consciousness; the attractive shaping of our lives as an art of living could also be enriched by greater perceptual awareness of aesthetic meanings, feelings, and potentials in our everyday conduct of life.

Beyond reorienting aesthetic inquiry, somaesthetics seeks to transform philosophy in a more general way. By integrating theory and practice through disciplined somatic training, it takes philosophy in a pragmatic meliorist direction, reviving the ancient idea of philosophy as an embodied way of life rather than a mere discursive field of abstract theory. As embodiment becomes an increasingly trendy theme in academia, the idea of embodied philosophy is often affirmed, but nonetheless remains ambiguous. Minimally, it signifies a philosophy that (unlike idealism) takes the material body seriously as a valuable dimension of human experience and knowledge. Embodied philosophy means something stronger in phenomenologies like Maurice Merleau-Ponty's, in which the body forms a central perspective that structures the philosophical system and

---

[4] Pragmatism's engaged stance includes the recognition that social forces significantly shape art's aesthetic experience and its social and political visions, but also that art reciprocally can inspire social and political transformation.

is celebrated as a sentient, intelligent, purposive, skilled subjectivity that likewise helps construct the world rather than being a mere physical object in it.

My somaesthetics differs from such phenomenologies in a number of ways. First, rather than seeking to reveal an alleged primordial, foundational, and universal embodied consciousness that (in Merleau-Ponty's words) is "unchanging, given once and for all," and "known by all men" in all cultures and times, I claim that somatic consciousness is always shaped by culture and thus admits of different forms in different cultures (or in different subject positions within the same culture).[5] Second, somaesthetics is interested not merely in describing our culturally shaped forms of somatic consciousness and modes of somatic practice, but also in improving them. Third, to effect such improvements, it also includes practical exercises of somatic training rather than mere philosophical discourse.[6]

In short, for somaesthetics, embodied philosophy is more than the theoretical affirmation and articulation of the body's crucial role in all perception, action, and thought; it is more than the elaboration of this theme in the familiar discursive forms of writing, reading, and discussing texts. Embodied philosophy also means giving real body to thought through somatic style and behavior, demonstrating one's philosophy through one's own bodily example, expressing it through one's manner of living. Adapting more colloquial idioms, it means putting one's body where one's mouth is; to really walk the walk, not just talk the talk. Building on pragmatic insights and ancient philosophical traditions (of both East and West), somaesthetics advocates somatic training as a worthy dimension of philosophical cultivation and expression. Confucius clearly affirmed somatic cultivation as a crucial dimension of philosophical education, once informing his disciples that he could cease speaking and simply teach, as nature does, by embodying his philosophy in his bodily behavior. Greek and Roman thinkers often likewise advocated this ideal, sometimes by contrasting true philosophers who lived their philosophy to those who merely wrote philosophy and thus were denigrated

---

[5] See Maurice Merleau-Ponty, *Phenomenology of Perception*, trans. Colin Smith (London: Routledge, 1962), xiv; and Maurice Merleau-Ponty, *In Praise of Philosophy and Other Essays*, trans. John Wild, James Edie, and John O'Neill (Evanston: Northwestern University Press, 1970), 63.

[6] What precisely constitutes improvement is not a question that admits of a single, general, definitive answer. Different contexts and problems will demand different solutions. Moreover, one dimension of somaesthetic inquiry involves the debate over somatic norms, methods, and values that eventually determine how to understand improvement in particular contexts.

as mere "grammarians."[7] The idea of philosophy as an embodied art of living found renewed expression in American thinkers like Emerson and Thoreau who inspired both pragmatism and somaesthetics, underlining the distinction between mere "professors of philosophy" and real philosophers who truly embody or live their thought.[8]

Invoking this ancient tradition, I introduced somaesthetics "as a new name for some old ways of thinking," borrowing the shrewd formulation William James used to subtitle his first book on pragmatism. I wanted a new name to represent the new project of somatic philosophy I envisaged, because new names can be helpful both in stimulating new thinking and in reorganizing and reanimating older insights. Established terms such as "aesthetics of the body" or "philosophy of the body" were too rife with problematic associations that provoke misunderstanding. First, the definite article in these expressions suggests a dangerous essentialism or uniformity about our embodiment, as if we are dealing with only one single thing – "the body" – rather than doing justice to the diversity of our bodies (in terms of gender, age, and ethnicity, for example) and the different ways of experiencing them. Moreover, familiar expressions such as "body aesthetics" evoke our culture's persistent preoccupation with superficial stereotypes of bodily beauty (our unhappy domination by somatic norms focused on external bodily appearance and derived from supermodels, beauty queens, and body builders), while I wish to promote a much broader palette of somatic forms of aesthetic experience. Besides, because of our culture's deeply entrenched body/mind dualism, the very notion of body suggests mere material mass and mindlessness, which makes "philosophy of body" seem a contrast to philosophy of mind. I seek to overcome such dualisms by recognizing the body as a site of active perception and subjectivity.

The term "soma" (a less familiar expression deriving from the Greek word for body) struck me as a useful way of designating embodiment but without all the problematic associations of the terms "body" or "flesh." I chose soma to insist that my project concerns the sentient lived body rather than merely a physical body.[9] It can thus incorporate dimensions of bodily subjectivity and perception that I regard as crucial to the aesthetics

---

[7] For more on these points, see Richard Shusterman, *Practicing Philosophy: Pragmatism and the Philosophical Life* (London: Routledge, 1997); and "Pragmatism and East-Asian Thought," in Richard Shusterman (ed.), *The Range of Pragmatism and the Limits of Philosophy* (Oxford: Blackwell, 2004), 13–42.

[8] Henry David Thoreau, *Walden*, in Brooks Atkinson (ed.), *Walden and Other Writings* (New York: Modern Library, 2000), 14.

[9] Homer is the exception among ancient Greeks in using σῶμα to designate the corpse, using instead δέμας (frame) for the living body of a person. For more details, see H. G.

of embodiment and to aesthetic experience in general (since all experience, at least for us humans, is embodied). So "somaesthetics" (a simple splicing of "soma" and "aesthetics") seemed an apt name for my new project, which sought to give the body more careful aesthetic attention not only as an object that externally displays beauty, sublimity, grace, and other aesthetic qualities, but also as a subjectivity that perceives these qualities and that experiences attendant aesthetic pleasures somatically.

Admittedly, the term is not without problems. It lacks the vivid imagery of "washboard abs" or "buns of steel"; phonetically, it is more ugly than mellifluous, and its unfamiliar character can cause confusion. (The first time I gave "Somaesthetics" as the title of an invited lecture outside North America, the conference organizers misread my handwritten fax and announced the title as "Some Aesthetics" in their program). By and large, however, the term is immediately understood as relating to the aesthetics of embodiment (including embodied perception), and I am very pleased that many scholars in diverse fields have adopted it. Some critics have worried that "soma" ambiguously refers to a divine ritual drink described in the Vedic tradition and has served to designate a hallucinogenic, pleasure-producing drug in some twentieth-century fiction.[10] These spiritual and literary associations strike me as far less troubling than today's commercial use of "soma" as the brand name of an addictive, perception-dulling muscle relaxant often prescribed for backache. For such musculoskeletal ailments, I would prefer to recommend somaesthetic cultivation of heightened body awareness and control.

Philologists have sometimes complained that the term "somaesthetics" is a morphologically misconstructed compound whose proper form should instead be "somatoaesthetics" (as in the somatosensory system). But I can defend the construction by noting its established use in neurophysiology, where it typically appears without the "a" (as "somesthetic") to designate the somatosensory. In neuroscience, the somaesthetic system refers most specifically to bodily senses other than those of sight, hearing, smell, and taste; that is, it designates feelings of skin (touch), proprioception, kinaesthesia, bodily temperature, balance, and pain. I was not aware of this usage when I chose the term "somaesthetics" for the field I envisaged, but its existence is encouraging because it suggests how somaesthetics can usefully intersect with neuroscience and philosophy

---

Liddell and Robert Scott (eds.), *A Greek-English Lexicon* (Oxford: Clarendon Press, 1996), 378.

[10] Kathleen Higgins, "Living and Feeling at Home: Shusterman's Performing Live," *Journal of Aesthetic Education*, 36 (2002): 84–92.

of mind in exploring a common concern with bodily perceptions. Moreover, it signals the interdisciplinary nature of somaesthetics, guided by my premise that philosophical thinking thrives better through collaborative engagement with other disciplines than through a purist policing of disciplinary borders. While my own somaesthetic theorizing is principally in the philosophical genre (because of my academic training), somaesthetic research can be pursued through other disciplines in the humanities, arts, and social and natural sciences.

My choice of the term "somaesthetics," I should confess, was also motivated by its elegant way of mitigating an orthographical problem that increasingly perturbed me: Should the discipline Baumgarten founded be rendered in English as "aesthetics" or more simply as "esthetics"? Although the question seems trivial, it is as stubbornly pervasive as the written use of the term (and its cognates); it cannot be evaded, and for me it posed some deeper issues of identity. My analytic philosophical education at Jerusalem and Oxford taught me to use the more sophisticated Greek-styled diphthong "ae" that was standard in English literature, but having become an advocate of American pragmatism, should I not adopt the simpler, more streamlined spelling "esthetic" that John Dewey insisted on using? The "ae" was more familiar and more elegant, but the plain "e" seemed clearly more honest and economically functional, and thus more in keeping with pragmatism.

The "ae"-versus-"e" dilemma is thematized in a cartoon that Saul Steinberg created for the poster celebrating the fiftieth anniversary of the American Society for Aesthetics, in which a thick, monumental-sized "E," solidly planted on the earth and towering over surrounding trees, imagines itself as a slim, elegant "Æ" in an ethereal cloud-like cartoon bubble above its head. In discussing Steinberg's poster, Arthur Danto describes this "aesthetics" / "esthetics" difference as one merely "in font" and visual appearance, with no semantic or phonetic significance.[11] Though the difference of a letter is surely more than a difference of font, Danto is right that the "a" in "aesthetics" does no real semantic or phonetic work, so that "aesthetics" and "esthetics" are phonetically and referentially the same. Principles of functional economy that are central to philosophical reasoning and especially to pragmatism should then convince a pragmatist to drop the unnecessary, nonfunctional "a" as Dewey did. Nonetheless, I remained charmed by the more visually elegant dipthong. The term

---

[11] Arthur Danto, "Minding His A's and E's," *Art News* (November 2006): 112, 114; quote on 114.

"somaesthetics" resolves this discomfort by giving the "a" a real semantic function through its use in "soma" but preserving the visual form and pronunciation of "aesthetics" within its longer lexical frame, while also enriching the field of aesthetics by highlighting the vital bodily dimension of creating, perceiving, and appreciating works of art and other objects of aesthetic experience.

II

Engaging a wide variety of knowledge forms and disciplines that structure our somatic experience or can improve it, somaesthetics is a framework to promote and integrate the diverse range of theorizing, empirical research, and meliorative practical disciplines concerned with bodily perception, performance, and presentation. While originally rooted in my philosophical research, it is not a single theory or method advanced by a particular philosopher, but rather an open field for collaborative, interdisciplinary, and transcultural inquiry. Its applications already extend beyond philosophy to a broad array of topics ranging from the arts, product design, and politics to fashion, health, sports, martial arts, and the use of hallucinogenic drugs in education.[12] Somaesthetics' most notable developments thus far can be grouped into three general areas: arts, politics, and design technology.

Although dance may be the most paradigmatic of somatic arts, somaesthetics has been likewise applied to theatre in analyzing the somatic styles of movement and posture of actors on stage.[13] Eric Mullis does this with

---

[12] See, for instance, Titti Kallio, "Why we choose the more attractive looking objects: somatic markers and somaesthetics in user experience," *Proceedings of the 2003 International Conference on Designing Pleasurable Products and Interfaces* (New York: ACM, 2003), 142–143; N.W. Loland, "The Art of Concealment in a Culture of Display: Aerobicizing Women's and Men's Experience and Use of Their Own Bodies," *Sociology of Sport Journal*, 17 (2000): 111–129; J.G. Forry, "Somaesthetics and Philosophical Cultivation: An Intersection of Philosophy and Sport," *Acta Universitatis Palackianae Olomucensis. Gymnica*, 36 (2006): 25–28; Michael Surbaugh, "'Somaesthetics,' Education, and Disabilty," *Philosophy of Education*, (2009): 417–424; S.J. Smith and R.J. Lloyd "Promoting Vitality in Health and Physical Education," *Qualitative Health Research*, 16 (2006): 249–267; Ken Tupper, "Entheogens and Education," *Journal of Drug Education and Awareness*, 1 (2003): 145–161.

[13] For applications to dance, see, for example, Peter Arnold, "Somaesthetics, Education, and the Art of Dance," *Journal of Aesthetic Education*, 39 (2005): 48–64; Lis Engel, "The Somaesthetic Dimension of Dance Art and Education – a Phenomenological and Aesthetic Analysis of the Problem of Creativity in Dance," in E. Anttila, S. Hämäläinen, T. Löytönen & L. Rouhiainen (eds.), *Ethics and Politics Embodied in Dance: Proceedings of the*

respect to some Western theories of acting, while I analyze (in Chapter 9) the somaesthetic training and ideals of movement and posture in Japanese Nō theatre. Somaesthetic concepts and theories have been just as extensively deployed for understanding music and music education.[14] Beyond concepts and theories, practical somaesthetic training in heightened body consciousness has also found a place in the performing arts, particularly in music and dance education.[15]

In visual arts, somaesthetics has been used to explain not only how artists use their bodies in making artworks, but also how observers deploy themselves somatically to perceive such works. Many works of visual art (whether paintings, sculptures, photographs, or installations) consciously presuppose and play with the viewers' somatic standpoint, so that the soma can be powerfully thematized in a work without a body being visually represented in it.[16] As I explain in Chapter 10, the body (with its multiple senses and movement through space) likewise plays a formative role in architectural design and experience. Performance art presents a distinctive case in which the body is not only a tool of creation and means of perception, but also the expressive medium and visual end product or art object. Building on my somaesthetic theory, Martin Jay shows the political import of body-centered performance works that challenge the prevailing norms of bodily form and comportment with their attendant sociopolitical hierarchies of domination. Drawing on my analysis of hip hop's integration of somatic energy and political protest,

---

International Dance Conference, December 9–12, 2004 (Helsinki: Theatre Academy, 2005), 50–58; Patricia Vertinsky, "Transatlantic Traffic in Expressive Movement: From Delsarte and Dalcroze to Margaret H'Doubler and Rudolf Laban," *The International Journal of the History of Sport*, 26 (2009): 2031–2051; and Isabelle Ginot, "From Shusterman's Somaesthetics to a Radical Epistemology of Somatics," *Dance Research Journal*, 42 (2010): 12–29. For applications to acting, see Eric Mullis, "Performative Somaesthetics: Principles and Scope," *Journal of Aesthetic Education*, 40 (2006): 104–117.

[14] See, for example, the special issue on somaesthetics (focused on my book *Body Consciousness*) in the journal *Action, Criticism, and Theory for Music Education* 9 (2010): http://act.maydaygroup.org/php/archives_v9.php#9_1.

[15] I have given practical somaesthetic workshops for choreographers and dancers in France (in the training programs of Myriam Gourfink at Royaumont and Maguy Morin at Lyon) and for musicians at the Sibelius Academy in Finland. Clips from the workshop at Royaumont can be viewed at the somaesthetics site https://sites.google.com/site/somaesthetics/

[16] See, for example, David Zerbib, "Soma-esthétique du corps absent," in Barbara Formis (ed.), *Penser en corps: Soma-esthetique, art, et philosophie* (Paris: L'Harmattan, 2009), 133–159; Aline Caillet, "Emanciper le corps: sur quelques applications du concept de la soma-esthétique en art," in Formis (ed.), *Penser en corps*, 99–112.

Jay helpfully extends its Deweyan democratic message to a visual art of high culture (albeit one that often deploys a style of crude lowness as part of its critical, provocative purpose).[17]

Somaesthetics has begun to have an impact not only on the analysis of visual art but on its practice as well. One prominent example is its use as a generative theoretical background for Peng Feng's curatorial project for the Chinese Pavilion of the 2011 Venice Biennale. Entitled *Pervasion*, this show of five installation pieces (including clouds with tea fragrance; pipes dripping with Chinese schnapps; fragrant porcelain pots of herb medicine; fog of incense; and lotus-scented virtual snow) sought to emphasize that our appreciation of even visual art is always much more than visual, and to highlight the soma's role as a transmodal perceiving subjectivity by engaging the pleasures of other bodily senses as well.[18] Somaesthetics has also been used as a creative framework for a series of photographic and cinematic works that Parisian artist Yann Toma has realized in close collaboration with me. Here, I assume the role of performance artist, somatically reshaped (and somewhat challenged) by a tight-fitting gold latex body stocking through which I encounter the camera, the artist, and the wider world. If this artistic series of *SOMAFLUX* embodies one particular role that somaesthetics can play in contemporary art, it likewise exemplifies the more general aim of pragmatist aesthetics to narrow the gap between theory and practice, between philosophy and art, by inserting the philosopher – in the flesh – into active artistic practice. I elaborate some of the theoretical lessons learned from this creative adventure in Chapter 11, with a discussion of photography as performative process.[19]

Among political applications of somaesthetics, feminist interventions loom large. This should not be surprising, for women are traditionally identified with body and thus negatively contrasted with what our culture deems to be the superior male principle of mind. As Shannon Sullivan uses somaesthetic ideas to critique the devalorization of bodily practices associated with women and to insist (through notions of somaesthetic teaching, caring, and dialogue) that working on the body is not a merely

---

[17] See Martin Jay, *Refractions of Violence* (New York: Routledge, 2003), 163–176.

[18] For a brief account of this show and its relation to somaesthetics, see my discussion with curator Peng Feng in *Art Press* 379 (June 2011): Venice Biennale Supplement, 24–25.

[19] A more personal, colorful account of this experience (including images) can be found in Richard Shusterman, "A Philosopher in Darkness and in Light: Practical Somaesthetics and Photographic Art," in Anne-Marie Ninacs (ed.), *Lucidité. Vues de l'intérieur/Lucidity. Inward Views: Le Mois de la Photo à Montréal 2011* (Montréal: Le Mois de la Photo à Montréal, 2011), 280–287.

selfish, unsocial project, so Cressida Heyes deploys somaesthetics as a model enabling "political resistance to corporeal normalization" that subjugates women and men as well. Because race – like gender – is perceived through somatic appearance, racism provides another political issue in which somaesthetic strategies have been proposed both as explanations and as therapeutic remedies.[20]

The most surprising extension of somaesthetics has been in the arena of high-tech design. I expected no interest from this field because somaesthetics was largely inspired by ancient ideas of the embodied philosophical life and by traditional Asian somatic practices (such as yoga and *zazen*) or contemporary Western counterparts (such as Alexander Technique or Feldenkrais Method) that preserve a similar organic character by not treating the body with electronic appliances. Although my work addressed the new media's challenge to embodiment, I did so mainly by arguing two key points. First, no technological invention of virtual reality will negate the body's centrality as the focus of affective, perceptual experience through which we perceive and engage the world. Second, cultivating better skills of body consciousness can provide us with enhanced powers of concentration to help us overcome problems of distraction and stress caused by the new media's superabundance of information and stimulation. I made no effort, however, to envisage positive ways that our newest technologies might reshape somatic experience. How, for example, could future developments in genetic engineering, nanotechnology, robotics, and experimental drugs yield significant changes in our somatic powers either by changing the bodies that nature gives us or complementing them with prosthetic or chemical enhancements that dramatically augment the soma's perceptual, cognitive, and motor capabilities? How should somaesthetics prepare to deal with these changes and their corresponding new capacities for somatic self-cultivation, self-stylization, and social interaction?

---

[20] See Shannon Sullivan, "Transactional Somaesthetics: Nietzsche, Women, and the Transformation of Bodily Experience," in *Living Across and Through Skins: Transactional Bodies, Pragmatism, and Feminism* (Bloomington: University of Indiana Press, 2001), 111–132; Cressida Heyes, "Somaesthetics for the Normalized Body," in *Self-Transformations: Foucault, Ethics, and Normalized Bodies* (Oxford: Oxford University Press, 2007), 111–132, quotation p. 124; David Granger, "Somaesthetics and Racism: Toward an Embodied Pedagogy of Difference," *Journal of Aesthetic Education* 44 (2010): 69–81. For an instructive discussion of some of these strategies, see Wojciech Małecki, *Embodying Pragmatism: Richard Shusterman's Philosophy and Literary Theory* (Frankfurt: Peter Lang, 2010), ch. 4.

Philosopher Jerrold Abrams has helpfully responded to this omission by exploring such futuristic issues of what some might call posthuman somaesthetics.[21] Although the human soma (already a product of considerable evolution) seems plastic enough to absorb significant change and prosthetic devices without losing its human identity, questions about the human soma's limits and whether or how should we should speak of nonhuman somas are surely interesting topics for somaesthetic analysis. I cannot, however, properly address them here, and they may indeed preclude a definitive answer that survives the rapid transformations of our technological future.[22] For the present, I feel fortunate to find researchers of computer technology currently using somaesthetic ideas in tackling actual problems in human-computer interaction (HCI) and design. Such research includes both theoretical models and more concrete productions. One noteworthy theoretical effort (developed by Youn-Kyung Lim and Erik Stolterman) proposes a model that integrates the basic sensory and affective experience of the computer user with the physical properties of the tools deployed in computer interaction, and then explains how these and other factors produce higher, emergent qualities of interactive aesthetic Gestalt that belong to the overall interactive situation or experience.[23] Particularly intriguing is Thecla Schiphorst's HCI research, in which she "argues for the value of exploring design strategies that employ a somaesthetic approach" not simply through theory but by fashioning a series of interactive, networked artworks based on sensory interactions involving touch and breathing. Some of these works are "interactive wearable art," in which the garments react not only to the wearer's movements or breath but also to tactile or breathing inputs from other participants interacting through the computer network, which includes iPhone inputs.[24]

---

[21] J.J. Abrams, "Pragmatism, Artificial Intelligence, and Posthuman Bioethics: Shusterman, Rorty, and Foucault," *Human Studies* 27 (2004): 241–258; and "Shusterman and the Paradoxes of Posthuman Self-Styling," in Dorota Koczanowicz and Wojciech Małecki (eds.), *Shusterman's Pragmatism: Between Literature and Somaesthetics* (Amsterdam: Rodopi, 2012), 145–61.

[22] With respect to nonhuman animals, I have argued that higher animals have somas but lack the status of selves or persons. For elaboration of these points, see Richard Shusterman, "Soma and Psyche," *Journal of Speculative Philosophy* 24 (2010): 205–223.

[23] Youn-Kyung Lim et al. "Interaction Gestalt and the Design of Aesthetic Interactions," *Proceedings of the 2007 Conference on Designing Pleasurable Products and Interfaces* (New York: ACM, 2007), 239–254. See also P. Sundström, K. Höök, et al., "Experiential Artifacts as a Design Method for Somaesthetic Service Development," *Proceedings of the 2011 ACM Symposium on the Role of UbiComp Research* (New York: ACM, 2011), 33–36.

[24] Thecla Schiphorst, "soft(n): Toward a Somaesthetics of Touch," *Proceedings of the 27th International Conference on Human Factors in Computing Systems* (New York: ACM, 2009),

III

If the wide-ranging pluralism of somaesthetics contributes to its richness, it likewise provides a steady source of confusion and critique. As a general field of research, somaesthetics involves the theoretical study of our somatic perception, functioning, and forms of self-stylization, but it further includes the analysis, comparative critique, and actual practice of body disciplines designed to improve our somatic experience and performance. My advocacy of somaesthetics is sometimes misconstrued as uncritically recommending the concrete performance of all the different body practices falling within the field's general purview, even practices (and their attendant ideologies) that I critique rather than endorse. As this misunderstanding is easily avoided by attending to my actual arguments and the distinction between theoretical and practical branches of the field, so the structural source of such confusion is not peculiar to somaesthetics but rather equally present in other fields involving both comparative theoretical critique and actual practice. We can advocate the practice of philosophy while criticizing many of the philosophies theoretically proposed or concretely practiced. We can assert the value of religious studies without affirming the concrete practice of the religions that are studied.

A contrasting confusion arises because the somaesthetic field is too complexly diverse to be exhaustively covered in one synoptic treatment; it calls for piecemeal analysis of its different dimensions in terms of different purposes and exploratory contexts. Because my specific arguments often focus on some aspects rather than others, critics sometimes assume that my somaesthetic project is much narrower than it actually is. Critics friendly to somaesthetics thus occasionally take me to task for being one-sided in neglecting other aspects or practices of somaesthetics whose value they (rightly) feel should be highlighted as well. I welcome such criticism for repeatedly underlining the variety that somaesthetics in fact embraces and that I have always recognized. But for purposes of clarity, efficiency, and depth of analysis, it has seemed most useful to concentrate – with each research sortie – on a limited part of the vast somaesthetic field; just as a penetrating mental body scan requires focusing

---

2427–2438, quotation p. 2427; and Thecla Schiphorst, Jinsil Seo, and Norman Jaffe, "Exploring Touch and Breath in Networked Wearable Installation Design," *Proceedings of the International Conference on Multimedia* (New York: ACM, 2010), 1399–1400, quotation p. 1399. See also the application of somaesthetics to computer games in H.S. Nielsen, "The Computer Game as a Somatic Experience," *Eladamus. Journal for Computer Game Culture* 4 (2010): 25–40.

attention successively on only one part of the body at a time rather than trying to grasp the whole in its totality in a single moment.

My earliest advocacy of somatic aesthetics highlighted the body's role in immediate, nondiscursive understanding and pleasures in order to challenge the hermeneutic hegemony that confined legitimate aesthetic appreciation to intellectual interpretation. So when I later introduced the project of somaesthetics, it was initially criticized as reflecting today's commercialized obsession with mindless physical delights and superficial stereotypes of good looks, while exacerbating this problematic trend by giving it theoretical backing as well. I thus had to emphasize the reflective and cognitive dimensions of somaesthetics, its concern with acutely discriminating bodily perceptions and with meditative experiences of beautiful inner feelings. This reflective, inward turn only led other critics to worry that the project was too coldly intellectual and insufficiently respectful of somatic spontaneity, emotion, or the beauty of bodily surfaces.[25] Somaesthetics in fact affirms the reflective and the nonreflective, the cognitive and the affective, dimensions of somatic behavior while insisting on their intimate relations. In the same way, it engages both inner somatic experience and external somatic representations.

Because it emerged from my work in pragmatist aesthetics, whose sympathetic study of hip-hop culture aroused the most attention and controversy, scholars first identified somaesthetics with rap's somatic styles: flamboyant dress, emphatic gesture, and vigorous, boisterous body motions engaged with the social performativity of music, dance, and the raising of collective consciousness. I saw it was necessary to underline the field's plurality by emphasizing more silent, meditative, and restrained personal disciplines such as *zazen*, yoga, or Alexander Technique. Likewise, when early critics too narrowly identified somaesthetics with the muscularity of bodybuilding and therefore questioned why somatic cultivation should be relevant for appreciating art that merely involves seeing and hearing, I felt obliged to insist on the very subtle (and typically unnoticed) use of muscles in refined aesthetic perception. Besides the larger muscles needed for locomotion and erect posture of the head in order to view

---

[25] For critical discussions that focus on somaesthetics' alleged uncritical hedonism and unreflective sensualism, see Antonia Soulez (who also wittily brands my democratic ethics and politics as "con-sensualist"), "Practice, Theory, Pleasure, and the Problems of Form and Resistance: Shusterman's *Pragmatist Aesthetics*," *Journal of Speculative Philosophy* 16 (2002): 1–9; Simo Säätelä, "Between Intellectualism and 'Somaesthetics'," *Filozofski Vestnik* 2 (1999): 151–62; Casey Haskins, "Enlivened Bodies, Authenticity, and Romanticism," *Journal of Aesthetic Education* 36 (2002): 92–102; and for contrasting critiques of intellectualism, see, for example, Higgins, "Living and Feeling at Home," 89–90.

paintings and sculptures from the proper standpoints or angles, the visual arts require subtler muscles of the eye. We need, for example, the eye's ciliary muscles to adjust its lens for noticing close details, just as we need the eye's extrinsic muscles and those of the eyelids to focus one's vision and to move one's gaze to scan a painting.[26] But highlighting such subtle "gymnastics of the eye" does not mean somaesthetics finds no value in more robust muscle movement and vigorous gross motor action such as we find in sports, sex, rap, and other forms of popular dance music.

Some critics, however, mistakenly draw that conclusion, assuming my advocacy of subtle, gentle, meditative somatic disciplines means denying or demeaning those other, more forceful forms of somatic culture, even when I explicitly note their importance in the somaesthetic field.[27] Because such robust forms of bodily expression (along with practices of beautifying body appearance) constitute the overwhelmingly dominant mode of somatic cultivation in contemporary culture, I thought that giving them special attention was unnecessary and would only strengthen their dominance to the continued neglect of other, more meditative, somaesthetic disciplines. Disciplines of meditative awareness are especially useful for showing the soma's subtle, sensing subjectivity and the value of enhanced body awareness for knowing oneself and improving one's habits.

Highlighting such practices to demonstrate the cognitive and spiritual aspects of somaesthetics should not be misconstrued as a general somaesthetic privileging of solitary, gentle disciplines of personal focusing while implying that vigorous group practices such as team sports are unsuitable for developing somatic awareness. The undeniable value of team (and other) sports for developing body consciousness and cognition should never be forgotten. Nor should we overlook, however, that so-called personal disciplines of meditative awareness are frequently done in groups whose communal energy greatly enhances not only the individual's meditative power but also social solidarity among practitioners. I know this from my New York Feldenkrais training, but especially from my

---

[26] For this critique of somaesthetics and my detailed response, see respectively, Thomas Leddy, "Shusterman's *Pragmatist Aesthetics*," *Journal of Speculative Philosophy* 16 (2002): 10–15; and Richard Shusterman, "Pragmatism and Criticism: A Response to Three Critics of *Pragmatist Aesthetics*," *Journal of Speculative Philosophy* 16 (2002): 26–38.

[27] For such criticisms, see K.P. Skowronski, *Values and Powers: Re-reading the Philosophical Tradition of American Pragmatism* (Amsterdam: Rodopi, 2009), 124–130; Ginot, "From Shusterman's Somaesthetics," 20–22; and Eric Mullis, "Review of *Body Consciousness: A Philosophy of Mindfulness and Somaesthetics*," *Journal of Aesthetic Education* 45 (2011): 123–127.

Japanese training in *zazen*, whose communal somaesthetic dimensions I explore in Chapter 13. In any case, now that the key role of meditative, spiritual somatic disciplines has been firmly established in somaesthetics, greater attention can be directed to more vigorous forms of somaesthetic practice, such as the art of lovemaking analyzed in Chapter 12. This practice, in which pleasure comes both from letting go and from disciplined control, usefully highlights another pluralistic dimension of somaesthetic cultivation – its diverse forms of freedom and constraint.

IV

The complex diversity of somaesthetics aptly reflects that of the soma itself: its richly intricate variety of body parts, systems, senses, feelings, motor schemata, and habits of action; its different modes of experience, consciousness, and knowledge that are differently shaped by both nature and culture. The book's first group of essays, "Somatic Being, Knowing, and Teaching," thus begins with an exploration of the soma's complex existence (as sentient subjectivity and material thing, agent and instrument) before probing more deeply into the different forms of somatic knowing (including their respective benefits and risks for action) and examining how such knowledge can be sharpened through the teaching of somatic awareness. In tackling such issues, these essays relate the somaesthetic project to central topics in ontology, ethics, epistemology, and philosophy of mind and action, thus illustrating how somaesthetics extends far beyond the standard domain of aesthetics.

The opening, title essay, "Thinking through the Body: Educating for the Humanities," introduces the general structure and aims of somaesthetics in order to advocate a greater role for somatic cultivation in the humanities, while also explaining how the soma's complex ontology has discouraged this. In expressing the fundamental ambiguity of human existence – as both subject and object, powerful and frail, knowing and ignorant, free and constrained, dignified and brutish – the body reminds us of essential human weaknesses that humanists prefer to forget by focusing their efforts on the mind or soul, which they see as fundamentally free of such limitations salient in the soma. The essay goes on to examine a similar error of one-sidedness in which the crucial instrumentality of the body leads humanists to conceive it narrowly as a merely menial means for achieving other ends of life, forgetting that the soma is also a lived subjectivity whose experiences, perceptions, and activities are worth cultivating and appreciating as enjoyable, worthy ends. German phenomenology distinguishes between two senses of the human body: *Körper* (the physical body as object) and *Leib* (the body as subjectively lived experience). The concept of soma includes both these senses or dimensions, and somaesthetics ambitiously aims to improve them both by rendering external physical form and inner perceptual experience more aesthetically satisfying while adding grace and efficacy to our somatic performance.

Turning from ontology to epistemology and philosophy of action, Chapter 2 develops the increasingly prominent theme that perception, language, understanding, and behavior all necessarily rely on a contextual background (a network of factors not present in foregrounded consciousness) in order to achieve their effective meaning and direction. "The Body as Background" explores this theme in the different traditions of analytic philosophy (with Ludwig Wittgenstein and John Searle), phenomenology (with Merleau-Ponty), and pragmatism (with William James and John Dewey), but also in Pierre Bourdieu's influential social theory. It demonstrates the body's central background role, focusing especially on how our entrenched sensorimotor skills and other somatic habits provide the smooth efficacy of spontaneous action that allows us to focus foregrounded attention on the goals of action and understanding. But the chapter goes on to argue (against most of these important background theorists) that the body sometimes needs to be foregrounded in order to improve our understanding of its background functioning, so we can also improve its effective performance through the reconstruction of poor habits. Such somatic self-knowledge is not easily acquired because our perceptual habits and interests direct us instead to focus on our goals and purposes in the outside world. But if this probing into the background somatic self demands discipline and effort, then such askesis aptly embodies one of philosophy's oldest and most crucial aims – the quest for self-knowledge.

The next chapter, "Self-Knowledge and its Discontents: From Socrates to Somaesthetics," takes a close critical look at this quest by examining the most influential ways it has been portrayed during its long philosophical history and the different charges that have been leveled against it. These attacks on self-examination include such charges as selfish self-absorption, impoverishing narrowness of perspective, impediment to action, obsessive rumination, melancholy, depression, and hypochondria. Somatic self-examination has been especially targeted for such critique, so one task of the chapter is to distinguish between helpful and harmful kinds of self-examination and then explain how enhanced skills of body consciousness can empower us toward better forms of self-knowledge and self-care.

One way that better somatic awareness can improve our lives is by freeing us from problematic but unnoticed bodily habits that impair our quality of experience and performance by generating unnecessary pain, inefficiency, or error. Such harmful habits involve varieties of implicit memory that are colloquially called "muscle memory" because they are thoroughly grounded in the body and function without explicit consciousness. But implicit muscle memory is equally present (and necessary) in our most effective habits; it is what guides our unconscious stream of thought and automatic skilled behavior with smooth spontaneity uninterrupted by the hesitating deliberations of explicit reflective consciousness. Chapter 4, "Muscle Memory and the Somaesthetic Pathologies of Everyday Life," first demonstrates the body's essential role in the major forms of implicit memory, ranging from one's sense of self, place, social role, and interpersonal recognition to the unreflective performance of motor tasks and finally to the unintentional traces of implicit post-traumatic memory expressed through somatic symptoms. After showing how even the most helpful forms of implicit muscle memory generate various pathologies in everyday life, the chapter argues that these pathologies can be treated by bringing these implicit somatic memories into explicit consciousness through better skills of somaesthetic attention and awareness.

Chapter 5 then tackles the crucial practical question of how in fact to develop such skills through somaesthetic training in heightened body consciousness. The standard philosophy classroom is surely not the best place for such practical training. But after explaining the challenges such a setting poses, I provide a script for teaching a fundamental lesson in somatic awareness that is expressly adapted to the typical classroom context of sitting. Readers can, of course, deploy this seated body-scan lesson outside the classroom at their own convenience, and the chapter concludes with an explanation of how the logic of the lesson is structured through basic psychological principles that shape all perception.

The book's second part, "Somaesthetics, Aesthetics, and Culture," explores issues that situate somaesthetics both in its native field of philosophical aesthetics and in the wider cultural arena, where its transdisciplinarity, multicultural sources, and practical activist orientation make it a promising tool for cultural politics aimed at forging a new soma-centered dialogue between East and West. Such a dialogue engages not only ancient and contemporary philosophy and physiology but also practical disciplines of body training. Chapter 6, "Somaesthetics and the Limits of Aesthetics," begins by explaining the logical path that led me from analytic aesthetics to pragmatism and then to somaesthetics as a way of realizing the pragmatist aesthetic agenda. In tracing the arguments that motivated this trajectory, the chapter illustrates how somaesthetics' attempt to overcome traditional limits in aesthetics actually reflects a fundamental logic of transcending limits that lies at the origin of modern aesthetics (in Baumgarten's founding initiative) and continues to shape its historical tradition.

Although philosophy's dominant idealism and rationalism largely marginalize the body in aesthetics, there are notable exceptions (such as Nietzsche) that prefigure the project of somaesthetics by insisting on the essential physiological dimension of aesthetic experience. Examining Edmund Burke as another important advocate of the body's central role in aesthetics, Chapter 7 argues that this dimension of his aesthetic theory has been neglected not only because of the anti-somatic bias that Burke bravely challenges but also because of his theory's overly simplified, one-sidedly mechanistic physiological explanations of our feelings and judgments of the beautiful and sublime. "Somaesthetics and Burke's Sublime" shows why he was right to highlight the bodily dimension of aesthetic experience (and other mental phenomena) in order to improve both our theoretical understanding and our practical capacities for such experience. But it likewise reveals the reductionist errors in the way he applied this insight and how modern physiology and psychology can provide better resources for current somaesthetic research to attain these melioristic goals.

Chapter 8 examines a radical challenge to the whole project of somaesthetics, pointedly raised by pragmatism's most influential contemporary thinker, Richard Rorty. "Pragmatism and Cultural Politics: From Textualism to Somaesthetics" first provides a detailed analysis of the major differences between Rorty's and my versions of pragmatism on key issues of metaphysics, interpretation, ethics, and politics in order to frame our debate about the relevance and viability of somaesthetics. Rorty's prime objection to somaesthetics is its trafficking with nonlinguistic experience. Claiming that philosophy (and indeed all understanding) should be entirely limited to language, he argues that philosophically invoking experience inevitably commits the fallacy of "the myth of the given," an epistemological appeal to prove our beliefs by something more basic and certain than any reasons we can formulate in language. Refuting Rorty's specific critiques of my position (including its alleged commitment to the myth of the given), this chapter further demonstrates how Rorty's own final vision of philosophy as melioristic, pluralistic cultural politics – an enterprise of suggesting new ideas or vocabularies or practices that aim to make a difference to the way people live – should indeed compel recognition of somaesthetics' relevance and value.

The final chapter of Part II, Chapter 9, introduces the important transcultural dimension of somaesthetics by demonstrating how its theme of heightened body consciousness for better knowledge and performance is expressed in East-Asian culture. "Body Consciousness and Performance: Somaesthetics East and West" examines how ancient Chinese philosophy (like recent Western philosophy) debates the precise value of body consciousness, especially the question of whether unthinking spontaneity or studied, reflective awareness is most conducive to better performance. Exploring the contrasting arguments of Confucian and Daoist thinkers on these issues, this chapter shows how their differing views can be reconciled and integrated through a logic of interchanging phases or stages designed to promote superior performance. The chapter concludes by examining the use of explicit, heightened body consciousness in the training of performers in a classic East-Asian art – Japanese Nō theatre – as advocated by its greatest theorist and practitioner, Zeami Motokiyo (1363–1443) and then explains this use in terms of contemporary neuroscience.

Somaesthetics' application to the arts is developed in the final group of essays that comprise Part III, some of which focus on arts of living that are situated far beyond the institutional borders of fine art but are nonetheless extremely rich in aesthetic potential and power. Chapter 10, "Somaesthetics and Architecture: A Critical Option," begins by illustrating how the body fundamentally shapes some of architecture's most basic concepts (such as space, mass, volume, proportionate form, and directionality) and then draws on somaesthetic insights to address two important issues in the much-discussed decline in architecture's critical function. The first concerns critical distance: How can architecture really be critical of the established social order when it so deeply relies on that order to produce its work; how can it criticize the system in which it is already implicated and from which it cannot fully detach itself? After explaining how the body provides a helpful model for immanent critique, this chapter turns to the second issue: the rise of experiential, multisensory atmosphere as an important architectural value that (unlike visual form or tectonic structure) seems too elusive to capture for critical reflection. Here, heightened body consciousness provides a strategy for sharpening our critical perception of atmosphere by making us more aware of the bodily feelings that atmosphere evokes and that indeed help constitute part of what is experienced as atmosphere.

Chapter 11 employs somaesthetic perspectives to revise the standard view of photographic art as essentially reducible to the photograph. Focusing on photographic portraiture, "Photography as Performative Process" explores the different forms of somatic artistry that the photographer and the posing subject should display in their communicative interaction to create the good shot that results in the good photograph. This communicative interaction (involving a dialogical play of somatic gestures and postures) has distinctly creative, dramatic, and expressive dimensions that can make the lived process of photographic mise-en-scène and shooting an aesthetic experience in its own right. I elaborate these aesthetic dimensions by discussing my work in photography and film with the Parisian artist Yann Toma, a collaboration that also illustrates the productive interchange between creative efforts in the art of living and the making of fine art.

Chapter 12 moves beyond the conventional realm of art to examine the field of *ars erotica*. Lovemaking is a distinctly somatic activity (involving the soma as both a perceiving, desiring subject and a perceived, desired, fondled object); and it surely provides experiences of intense beauty and pleasure. But since it is obviously not one of the conventional fine arts, how can we speak of it as an art in the truly aesthetic sense? After tracing how the dominant Western philosophical tradition has long defined the aesthetic by contrast with sexual desire and other bodily appetites, "Asian *Ars Erotica* and the Question of Sexual Aesthetics" invokes classical Chinese and Indian erotic theory to make an argument for the rich aesthetic potential of lovemaking and its important value as an art of living. When studied and practiced with careful mindfulness and sensitivity as part of one's project of melioristic self-cultivation, the art of lovemaking can bring rewarding cognitive, ethical, and interpersonal improvements that transcend the limits of momentary sexual pleasure, thus promoting the somaesthetic projects of augmenting our perceptual and performative powers and enriching our work of self-creation.

Continuing the transcultural dialogue between Western and Asian approaches to aesthetic embodiment, the book's final two chapters go further in exploring how cultivating somatic practices of everyday life can enhance one's art of living and creative self-fashioning. Recalling the ancient idea of philosophy as an art of living, Chapter 13 examines a historically recurrent yet much neglected vision of such art – one of awakening alertness in living that provides a far richer, clearer, critical awareness of what one perceives, performs, and experiences.

"Somaesthetic Awakening and the Art of Living" examines how Emerson and Thoreau (American transcendentalists, proto-pragmatists, and prophets of somaesthetics who were also strongly influenced by Asian thought) interpret this philosophical ideal in terms of heightened consciousness that deepens or "spiritualizes" our senses. Such enhanced attentive awareness enables us to appreciate the abundant beauty surrounding us in everyday life that we are otherwise too distracted to perceive. It can transfigure the simplest acts and most menial objects into moments of spiritual wonder and delight. After explaining the role somatic disciplines and heightened body consciousness play in Emerson's and Thoreau's theories of awakened life, the chapter concludes by illustrating how their aesthetic and spiritual ideals of revealing the extraordinary in the ordinary find powerful concrete expression in the everyday embodied practices of Zen monastic life, as I experienced in my training in Japan.

The book's final chapter is devoted to style, a central feature both in fine arts and the arts of living, though often regarded as merely superficial and contrasted with real substance or character. Enlisting a variety of Western sources and Confucian arguments, "Somatic Style" challenges this view of style as mere surface dressing or external technique by exploring style's deep-rooted expression of both self and society. Somatic style forms the prime focus not merely because of its obvious connection to somaesthetics but because such style is deemed especially superficial, as the body is regarded merely in terms of representational surface. Countering this misconception by showing somatic style's role in transmitting philosophical ideas and expressing ethical character, Chapter 14 analyzes five logical ambiguities that inhabit and complicate the notion of style (including somatic style). It then explores the different ways that the body's various elements contribute to expressing somatic style and the different ways that our multiple somatic senses perceive and critically appreciate it. I conclude by examining the connection between somatic style and spirit in our efforts of self-cultivation. If this provides a useful way to end the book by underlining the soma's fundamental unity – whose material sensory surface and animating inner subjectivity constitute the two principal dimensions of somaesthetics, it conversely suggests a program for further work in developing and harmonizing these dimensions more fully and productively, in theory and in practice.

PART I

SOMATIC BEING, KNOWING, AND TEACHING

1

Thinking through the Body

Educating for the Humanities

I

What are the humanities and how should they be cultivated? With respect to this crucial question, opinions differ as to how widely the humanities should be construed and pursued. Initially connoting the study of Greek and Roman classics, the concept now more generally covers arts and letters, history, and philosophy.[1] But does it also include the social sciences, which are often distinguished from the humanities and grouped as a separate academic division with greater pretensions to scientific status? And should our pursuit of humanistic study be concentrated on the traditional methods and topics of high culture that give the humanities an authoritative aura of established nobility, or should it extend to new and funkier forms of interdisciplinary research such as popular culture or race and gender studies?

Despite such questions and controversy, it is clear (even from etymology) that the meaning of the humanities essentially relates to our human condition and our efforts to perfect our humanity and its expression. But what, then, does it mean to be human? I cannot pretend here to adequately answer such a complexly difficult question. I will, however, argue that because the body is an essential and valuable dimension of our humanity, it should be recognized as a crucial topic of humanistic study and experiential learning. Although the truth of this thesis should be obvious, it goes sharply against the grain of our traditional understanding

---

[1] *Webster's Third New International Dictionary* (Springfield, MA: Merriam Co., 1961), 1101 defines humanities as "the branch of learning regarded as having primarily a cultural character and usually including languages, literature, history, mathematics, and philosophy"; *The Random House College Dictionary* (New York: Random House, 1984), 645 defines it as "a. the study of classical Latin and Greek language and literature. b. literature, philosophy, art, etc. as distinguished from the sciences."

of the humanities. One striking example of such anti-somatic bias is the very term that German speakers use to designate the humanities – *Geisteswissenschaften* – whose literal English translation would be "spiritual (or mental) sciences," in contrast to the natural sciences – *Naturwissenschaften* – which treat physical life (with which, of course, the body is clearly linked). Hence, given the pervasive physical/spiritual opposition, the body is essentially omitted or marginalized in our conception of humanistic studies.[2]

We humanist intellectuals generally take the body for granted because we are so passionately interested in the life of the mind and the creative arts that express our human spirit. But the body is not only an essential dimension of our humanity, it is also the basic instrument of all human performance, our tool of tools, a necessity for all our perception, action, and even thought. Just as skilled builders need expert knowledge of their tools, so we need better somatic knowledge to improve our understanding and performance in the arts and human sciences, and to advance our mastery in the highest art of all – that of perfecting our humanity and living better lives. We need to think more carefully through the body in order to cultivate ourselves and edify our students, because true humanity is not a mere genetic given but an educational achievement in which body, mind, and culture must be thoroughly integrated. To pursue this project of somatic inquiry, I have been working in the interdisciplinary field called somaesthetics, whose disciplinary connections extend beyond the humanities to the biological, cognitive, and health sciences, which I see as valuable allies for humanistic research.[3]

---

[2] There is considerably more interest in the body in social sciences, especially sociology. The humanist neglect of the body is reflected even in basic arts education, where obviously body-centered arts like dance and theatre get far less attention in the curriculum. On this point, see Liora Bressler, "Dancing the Curriculum: Exploring the Body and Movement in Elementary Schools," in Liora Bressler (ed.), *Knowing Bodies, Moving Minds* (Dordrecht: Kluwer, 2004), 127–151.

[3] Though I first introduced the idea of somaesthetics in *Vor der Interpretation* (Wien: Passagen Verlag, 1996) and *Practicing Philosophy* (London: Routledge, 1997), I only later articulated its structure in Richard Shusterman, "Somaesthetics: A Disciplinary Proposal," *Journal of Aesthetics and Art Criticism* 57 (1999): 299–313, revised and reprinted in the second edition of *Pragmatist Aesthetics* (New York: Rowman & Littlefield, 2000). I elaborated it in *Performing Live* (Ithaca: Cornell University Press, 2000) and still further in *Body Consciousness: A Philosophy of Mindfulness and Somaesthetics* (Cambridge: Cambridge University Press, 2008). For a critical overview of somaesthetics, see Wojciech Małecki, *Embodying Pragmatism: Richard Shusterman's Philosophy and Literary Theory* (Frankfurt: Peter Lang, 2010), ch. 4, "Body Consciousness, Body Surfaces, and Somaesthetics." A detailed bibliography of writings on somaesthetics by myself and other authors can be found,

Somaesthetics, roughly defined, concerns the body as a locus of sensory-aesthetic appreciation (aesthesis) and creative self-fashioning. As an ameliorative discipline of both theory and practice, it aims to enrich not only our abstract, discursive knowledge of the body but also our lived somatic experience and performance; it seeks to enhance the understanding, efficacy, and beauty of our movements and improve the environments to which our movements contribute and from which they draw their energies and significance. Somaesthetics therefore involves a wide range of knowledge forms and disciplines that structure such somatic care or can improve it. Recognizing that body, mind, and culture are deeply codependent, somaesthetics comprises an interdisciplinary research program to integrate their study. Mental life relies on somatic experience and cannot be wholly separated from bodily processes, even if it cannot be wholly reduced to them. We think and feel with our bodies, especially with the body parts that constitute the brain and nervous system. Our bodies are likewise affected by mental life, as when certain thoughts bring a blush to the cheek and change our heart rate and breathing rhythms. The body-mind connection is so pervasively intimate that it seems misleading to speak of body and mind as two different, independent entities. The term "body-mind" would more aptly express their essential union, which still leaves room for pragmatically distinguishing between mental and physical aspects of behavior and for the project of increasing their experiential unity.[4]

But whether we speak of body-mind or body and mind, we are dealing with what is fundamentally shaped by culture. For culture gives us the languages, values, social institutions, and artistic media through which we think and act and also express ourselves aesthetically, just as it gives us the forms of diet, exercise, and somatic styling that shape not only our bodily appearance and behavior but also the ways we experience our body – whether as a holy vessel or a burden of sinful flesh; a pampered personal possession for private pleasure or a vehicle of labor to serve the social good. Conversely, culture – its institutions and humanistic achievements – cannot thrive or even survive without the animating power of embodied thought and action. And one measure of a culture's quality of

---

respectively, at http://www.fau.edu/humanitieschair/Somaesthetics_Bibliography.php and http://www.fau.edu/humanitieschair/Somaesthetics_Bibliography_Others.php.

[4] John Dewey employs the term "body-mind" in *Experience and Nature* (Carbondale: Southern Illinois University Press, 1988), 191; he later uses the term "mind-body" to designate "a unified wholeness" in his essay "Body and Mind" in John Dewey, *The Later Works*, vol. 3 (Carbondale: Southern Illinois University Press, 1988), 27.

life and humanity is the level of body-mind harmony it promotes and displays.

For continued progress to be made in somaesthetics, resistance to body-focused learning and practical training in the humanities must be overcome. That is the prime purpose of this opening chapter. So before saying more about somaesthetics, I should explain and challenge this resistance. I will argue the paradoxical thesis that the body has been rejected in the humanities precisely because it so powerfully expresses the fundamental ambiguity of being human, and because of its all-pervasive, indispensable instrumentality in our lives. In striving for a nobler, less vulnerable, and thus more one-sided vision of the human, our tradition of humanistic research implicitly shuns the body – just as our humanistic focus on valuable intellectual and moral goals tends to obscure or marginalize the study of the very somatic means necessary for achieving those goals and other worthy ends of action.

II

The living body – a sensing, sentient soma rather than a mere mechanical corpse – embodies the fundamental ambiguity of human being in several ways. First, it expresses our double status as object and subject – as something in the world and as a sensibility that experiences, feels, and acts in the world. When using my index finger to touch a bump on my knee, my bodily intentionality or subjectivity is directed to feeling another body part as an object of exploration. I both *am* body and *have* a body. In much of my experience, my body is simply the transparent source of perception or action, not an object of awareness. It is that *from which* and *through which* I perceive or manipulate the objects of the world on which I am focused, but I do not grasp it as an explicit, external object of consciousness, even if it is sometimes obscurely felt as a background condition of perception. But often I perceive my body as something that I have rather than am: something I must drag out of bed to do what I wish to do; something I must command to perform what I will but that often fails in performance; something that includes heavy limbs, rolls of fat, a sometimes aching back, and a too often unshaven, tired-looking face, all of which I recognize as mine but do not identify as who I really am.

The body further expresses the ambiguity of human existence as both shared species being and individual difference. Philosophers have emphasized rationality and language as the distinguishing essence of human kind; but human embodiment seems at least as universal and essential a condition of humanity. Try to imagine a human being, and you cannot help but call up the image of the human bodily form. If we imagine creatures displaying human language and behavior but having a very different kind of body, we would think of them not as humans but as monsters, mermaids, robots, aliens, angels, or persons whose humanity has been somewhat robbed or diminished, perhaps by some inhuman spell, as in fables such as "Beauty and the Beast."[5]

But though our bodies unite us as humans, they also divide us (through their physical structure, functional practice, and sociocultural interpretation) into different genders, races, ethnicities, classes, and further into the particular individuals that we are. We may all use legs to walk or hands to grasp, but each person has a different gait and fingerprint. Our experience and behavior are far less genetically hardwired than in other animals: A bird of the same species will sing much the same in Peking and in Paris, whereas human vocalization patterns vary quite widely because they depend on learning from the experienced environment. There are anatomical reasons for this greater role of individual experience. The pyramidal tracts – which connect the cerebral cortex to the spinal cord and are essential for all voluntary movement (including vocalization) – are not fully formed and fixed at birth, but continue to develop during infancy through the movement a baby is made to perform.[6] This means the precise makeup of an individual's nervous system (her preferred repertoire of neural pathways) is partly a product of her individual experience and cultural conditioning. The body thus shows that human nature is always more than merely natural.

The commonality and difference of our bodies are deeply laden with social meaning. We appeal to our shared somatic form, experience, needs, and suffering when charitably reaching out to people of very different ethnicities and cultures. But the body (through its skin and hair color, facial features, and even its gestural behavior), conversely, is the prime site for emphasizing our differences and for uncharitable profiling. Most ethnic and racial hostility is the product not of rational thought but of deep prejudices that are somatically marked in terms of

---

[5] Of course, given the sloppy, haphazard abundance of nature, there are always occasional human mutants, but such exceptions only confirm the bodily norm, which can be understood as an evolving form rather than a fixed, sacred, ontological essence.

[6] Evidence for this includes the so-called sign of Babinski or plantar response – the toes in infants dorsiflex and fan with stroking of the sole, similar to the response of adults with damage to the motor cortex.

vague uncomfortable feelings aroused by alien bodies, feelings that are experienced implicitly and thus engrained beneath the level of explicit consciousness. Such prejudices and feelings therefore resist correction by mere discursive arguments for tolerance, which can be accepted on the rational level without changing the visceral grip of the prejudice. We often deny we even have such prejudices because we do not realize that we feel them, and the first step to controlling them or eventually expunging them is to develop the somatic awareness to recognize them in ourselves. This cultivation of skills of enhanced awareness is a central task of somaesthetics.[7]

The body exemplifies our multiform ambivalent human condition between power and frailty, worthiness and shame, dignity and brutishness, knowledge and ignorance. We invoke the notion of humanity to urge a person toward moral excellence and rationality that transcend mere animality, but we also use the predicate "human" to describe and excuse our flaws, failures, and lapses into base or even bestial behavior: they are human weaknesses, limits linked to the frailties of the flesh we share with common beasts. Yet despite its animal nature, the body serves as a symbol of human dignity, expressed in the irrepressible desire to depict the body in art's beauteous forms and to portray even the gods in human shape.[8] Respect for the body's dignity forms part of our basic respect for personhood and human rights; it is implicit in the right to life and in our tacit sense of respecting a certain physical distance from each other to allow some free space for the body – a basic *Lebensraum* or kinesphere. But even in death is the body respected; most cultures dispatch the corpse with some dignifying ritual of burial or cremation.

Moralists often inveigh against the body as the enemy of righteousness, as when St. Paul declares, "Nothing good dwells in me, that is, in my flesh" (Romans 7:18). Although frailty of flesh often undermines our moral aspirations, we should realize that all our ethical concepts and norms (and even the very notion of humanity that underwrites them) depend on social forms of life involving the ways we experience our bodies and

---

[7] I elaborate this argument more fully in *Body Consciousness*, ch. 4.

[8] Although proscribing graven images, the ancient Hebrew bible affirmed that humans were molded in God's image, suggesting our bodies have a divine source and paradigm. If the question of God's own body remains problematically mysterious in the Old Testament, then the New Testament's human incarnation of God in Christ, though adding further mystery, nonetheless reconfirms the human form as worthy of divine inhabiting. Hegel and others have admired Greek sculpture for capturing the way the harmonious proportions of the human body express the dignity of our rational spirit.

the ways that others treat them. As Wittgenstein remarked in a strangely brutal passage of his *Notebooks*:

> Mutilate completely a man, cut off his arms & legs, nose & ears, & then see what remains of his self-respect and his dignity, and to what point his concepts of these things are still the same. We don't suspect at all, how these concepts depend on the habitual, normal state of our bodies. What would happen to them if we were led by a leash attached to a ring through our tongues? How much humanity still remains in him then?[9]

In a world where bodies were always mutilated, starved, and abused, our familiar concepts of duty, virtue, charity, and respect for others could get no purchase and make no sense. Moreover, bodily abilities set the limits of what we can expect from ourselves and others, thus determining the range of our ethical obligations and aspirations. If paralyzed, we have no duty to leap to the rescue of a drowning child. Virtue cannot require constant labor with no rest or nourishment because these needs are physical necessities.

Besides grounding our social norms and moral values, the body is the essential medium or tool through which they are transmitted, inscribed, and preserved in society. Ethical codes are mere abstractions until they are given life through incorporation into bodily dispositions and action. Any properly realized ethical virtue depends not only on some bodily act (speech acts included) but also on having the right somatic and facial expression, indicative of having the right feelings. A stiffly grudging, angry-faced offering cannot be a true act of charity or respect, which is why Confucius insisted on the proper demeanor as essential to virtue.[10]

Moreover, by being inscribed in our bodies, social norms and ethical values can sustain their power without any need to make them explicit and enforced by laws; they are implicitly observed and enforced through our bodily habits, including habits of feeling (which have bodily roots). Confucius therefore insists that exemplary virtue is somatically formed through "the rhythms of ritual propriety and music," and wields its harmonizing power not by laws, threats, and punishments but by inspiring emulation and love.[11] Michel Foucault and Pierre Bourdieu, in contrast,

---

[9] Ludwig Wittgenstein, *Denkebewegung: Tagebücher 1930–1932, 1936–1937*, ed. Ilse Somavilla (Innsbruck: Haymon, 1997), 139–140.

[10] Roger Ames and Henry Rosemont Jr. (trans.), *The Analects of Confucius* (New York: Ballantine, 1998), 2:8, 8:4.

[11] *The Analects of Confucius*, 16:5, and see 4:1, 4:17, 12:24. For more detailed discussion of Confucian somaesthetics, see my "Pragmatism and East-Asian Thought," in Richard Shusterman (ed.), *The Range of Pragmatism and the Limits of Philosophy* (Oxford: Blackwell, 2004), 13–42.

highlight the oppressive aspects of social embodiment. Entire ideologies of domination can be covertly materialized and preserved by encoding them in somatic norms that, as bodily habits, are typically taken for granted and so escape critical consciousness. The norms that women of a given culture should only speak softly, eat daintily, sit with closed legs, walk behind the men, and only look with veiled, bowed heads and lowered eyes both embody and reinforce such gender oppression. Domination of this subtle sort is especially hard to challenge, because our bodies have so deeply absorbed it that they themselves revolt against the challenge – as when a young secretary involuntarily blushes, trembles, flinches, or even cries when trying to raise a voice of protest toward someone she has been somatically trained to respect as her superior. Any successful challenge of oppression should thus involve somaesthetic diagnosis of the bodily habits and feelings that express that domination so that they, along with the oppressive social conditions that generate them, can be overcome.

Our ethical life is grounded in the body in a still more basic way. Ethics implies choice, which in turn implies freedom to choose and act on that choice. We cannot act without bodily means, even if these means are reduced (through the wonders of technology) to pressing a button or blinking an eye to implement our choice of action. The body may even be the prime source of our very ideas of agency and freedom. What could be a better, more fundamental paradigm of voluntary or willed action[12] than the way we move our bodies to do what we will – raise a hand, turn the head? What could provide a clearer, more immediate sense of freedom than the freedom to move our bodies, not merely in locomotion but in opening our eyes and mouth or regulating our breathing? Life implies some sort of animating movement, and the freedom to move is perhaps the root of all our more abstract notions of freedoms. On the other hand, true to its essential ambiguity, the body also clearly symbolizes our unfreedom: the bodily constraints on our action; the corporeal bulk, needs, and failures that weigh us down and limit our performance; the relentless degeneration of aging and death.

If we turn from ethics and action to epistemology, the body remains emblematic of human ambiguity. As both an indispensable source of perception and an insurmountable limit to it, the body epitomizes the human condition of knowledge and ignorance. Because, as a body, I am

---

[12] Even mere willing itself (i.e., willing that fails to issue in performing the willed action) will still involve – especially if it is effortful willing – bodily means and be expressed in patterns of muscular contraction. For more detailed argument on the bodily nature of will, see *Body Consciousness*, ch. 5-6.

a thing among things in the world in which I am present, that world of things is also present and comprehensible to me. Because the body is thoroughly affected by the world's objects and energies, it incorporates their regularities and thus can grasp them in a direct, practical way without needing to engage in reflective thought. Moreover, to see the world, we must see it from some point of view: a position that determines our horizon and directional planes of observation, that sets the meaning of left and right, up and down, forward and backward, inside and outside, and that eventually shapes the metaphorical extensions of these notions in our conceptual thought. The soma supplies that primordial point of view through its location both in the spatiotemporal field and the field of social interaction. As William James remarks, "The body is the storm centre, the origin of co-ordinates, the constant place of stress in [our] experience-train. Everything circles round it, and is felt from its point of view." "The world experienced," he elaborates, "comes at all times with our body as its centre, centre of vision, centre of action, centre of interest."[13]

But every point of view has its limitations, and so must that provided by the body, whose sensory teleceptors all have limits of sensory range and focus. Our eyes are fixed forward in the head, so that we cannot see behind it or even see our own face without the aid of reflecting devices; nor can we simultaneously focus our gaze forward and backward, left and right, up and down. Philosophy is famous for radically critiquing the body and its senses as instruments of knowledge. Ever since the Socrates of Plato's *Phaedo* defined philosophy's aim as separating the knowing mind from its deceptive bodily prison, the somatic senses and desires have been repeatedly condemned for both misleading our judgment and distracting our attention from the pursuit of truth. But according to Xenaphon (another of his close disciples), Socrates affirmed a much more body-friendly view, recognizing that somatic cultivation was essential because the body was the primordial, indispensable tool for all human achievement. "The body," Socrates declared, "is valuable for all human activities, and in all its uses it is very important that it should be as fit as possible. Even in the act of thinking, which is supposed to require least assistance from the body, everyone knows that serious mistakes often happen through physical ill-health."[14]

---

[13] See William James, "The Experience of Activity," in *Essays in Radical Empiricism* (Cambridge, MA: Harvard University Press, 1976), 86.

[14] See Diogenes Laertius, *Lives of Eminent Philosophers*, trans. R.D. Hicks (Cambridge, MA: Harvard University Press, 1991), vol. 1, 153, 163; Xenophon, *Conversations of Socrates*, trans. Hugh Tredennick and Robin Waterfield (London: Penguin, 1990), 172.

The basic somaesthetic logic here (also affirmed by other Greek thinkers) is that rather than rejecting the body because of its sensory deceptions, we should try to correct the functional performance of the senses by cultivating improved somatic awareness and self-use, which can also improve our virtue by giving us greater perceptual sensitivity and powers of action.[15] The advocacy of somatic training for wisdom and virtue is even more striking in Asian philosophical traditions, where self-cultivation includes a distinctive bodily dimension developed through ritual and artistic practice (both conceived in highly embodied terms) and through specifically somatic training (such as disciplines of breathing, yoga, Zen meditation, and martial arts) that aim to instill better body-mind harmony, proper demeanor, and superior skill for appropriate action.[16] As Mencius insists, care of the body is the basic task without which we cannot successfully perform all our other tasks and duties. "Though the body's functions are the endowment of nature

---

[15] Aristippus, founder of the Cyrenaic school, insisted, "that bodily training contributes to the acquisition of virtue," since fit bodies provide sharper perceptions and more discipline and versatility for adapting oneself in thought, attitude, and action. Zeno, founder of Stoicism, likewise urged regular bodily exercise, claiming that "proper care of health and one's organs of sense" are "unconditional duties." Cynicism's founder, Diogenes, was even more outspoken in advocating bodily training as essential for the knowledge and discipline needed for wisdom and the good life. He also experimented with a striking range of body practices to test and toughen himself: extending from eating raw food and walking barefoot in the snow to masturbating in public and accepting the blows of drunken revelers. Of Diogenes the Cynic, it is said: "He would adduce indisputable evidence to show how easily from gymnastic training we arrive at virtue." Even the pre-Socratic Cleobulus, a sage "distinguished for strength and beauty," "advised men to practise bodily exercise" in their pursuit of wisdom. The citations in this paragraph come from Diogenes Laertius, *Lives of Eminent Philosophers*, vol. 1, 91, 95, 153, 221; vol. 2, 71, 73, 215.

[16] See, for example, Xunzi's emphasis on embodiment in "On Self-Cultivation" "Discourse on Ritual Principles," and "Discourse on Music," in John Knoblock, trans., *Xunzi* (Stanford: Stanford University Press, 1988), respectively vol. 1, 143–158; and vol. 3 48–73; 74–87; Zhuangzi and Guanzi on breathing in "The Great and Venerable Teacher," in *Chuang-Tzu*, trans. Burton Watson (New York: Columbia University Press, 1968), 77–92; "Nei Yeh" in *Kuan-Tzu*, trans. W.A. Rickett (Hong Kong: Hong Kong University Press, 1965), vol. 1, 151–168; and D.T. Suzuki on swordsmanship in his *Zen and Japanese Culture* (Princeton: Princeton University Press, 1973), ch. 5 and 6. The contemporary Japanese philosopher Yuasa Yusuo insists that the concept of "personal cultivation" or *shugyo* (which is presupposed in Eastern thought as "the philosophical foundation") has an essential bodily component, since "true knowledge cannot be obtained simply by means of theoretical thinking," but only "through 'bodily recognition or realization' (*tainin* or *taitoku*)." See Yuasa Yusuo, *The Body: Towards an Eastern Mind-Body Theory*, trans. S. Nagatomo and T.P. Kasulis (Albany: SUNY Press, 1987), 25.

[or heaven, 天 *tian*], it is only the Sage who can properly manipulate them."[17]

If the body captures the ambiguous human condition of subject and object, power and vulnerability, dignity and indignity, freedom and constraint, commonality and difference, knowledge and ignorance, why does modern humanistic philosophy tend to take the positive sides of this ambiguity for granted and negatively marginalize the body by emphasizing its weaknesses? Part of the reason is our profound reluctance to accept our human limitations of mortality and frailty that the body so clearly symbolizes. Though the field of humanities was first introduced in contrast to theological studies termed divinity,[18] humanist thinkers do not seem content to be human; they secretly want to transcend mortality, weakness, and error and to live like gods. Because bodily life does not allow this, they focus on the mind.

Transcendence, as the urge to reach beyond oneself, may be basic to human existence and is certainly central to pragmatist meliorism, but it need not be interpreted in supernatural terms. Our very being is a flux of becoming something else, which can be constructively construed in moral terms of self-improvement. Like other aspects of our humanity, transcendence has a distinctive bodily expression in the soma's basic urge for locomotion; in its reaching out to the world for nutrition, reproduction, and a field of action; in its natural normativity of developmental growth and self-transformations of its physiological systems. Essentially top-heavy when erect, the living body finds it easier to sustain dynamic equilibrium through movement than to stay in place.[19] Even at rest, however, the soma is not a motionless thing but a complex field of multiple movement, a surge of life, a projection of energy that Bergson described as *élan vital*.

III

The body's instrumental function is etymologically indicated in words such as "organism" and "organ" that derive from the Greek word *organon*, meaning "tool." So when humanists defend the body and advocate its

---

[17] *Mencius: A New Translation*, trans. W.A.C.H. Dobson (Toronto: Toronto University Press, 1969), 144. He also writes, "Whichever trust I fail to fulfil, it must not be that of keeping my body inviolate, for that is the trust from which all others arise," 138.

[18] See *Oxford English Dictionary*, 2nd ed. (Oxford: Clarendon Press, 1989), vol. 7, 476.

[19] Most of our body weight (head, shoulders, torso) is on top, while our legs and feet are much lighter. This anatomical structure, which contrasts with the stability of a pyramid, mechanically encourages us to move in reaction to gravitational pressure to make us fall.

cultivation, they usually do so in terms of its instrumentality, its necessary role in sustaining life and its service to higher functions of humanity identified with the soul. Rousseau, for instance, insists that "The body must be vigorous in order to obey the soul," because "a good servant ought to be robust.... The weaker the body, the more it commands," thus "a frail body weakens the soul." Strengthening the body helps develop the mind, which it nourishes and informs through its senses: Thus, "it is only with a surplus of strength beyond what [man] needs to preserve himself that there develops in him the speculative faculty fit to employ this excess of strength for other uses.... To learn to think, therefore, it is necessary to exercise our limbs, our senses, our organs, which are the instruments of our intelligence."[20] "The human body," Emerson later reaffirms, is the source of all invention: "All the tools and engines on earth are only extensions of its limbs and senses."[21]

To be recognized as humanity's primal and indispensable tool should constitute an unequivocal argument for humanistic cultivation of the body. But unfortunately, in humanistic culture, the very notion of instrumentality retains strong connotations of inferiority, as noble ends are contrasted to the mechanical means that serve them. This negative nuance can be seen in Rousseau's image of the body as servant to the soul, a familiar analogy from ancient Greek philosophy and traditional Christian theology that continues into modern times. Moreover, the analogy of instrumental servant to higher functions is often coupled with "gendering" the body in a way that underscores its inferior, serving status while also reinforcing and naturalizing the second-class status of the gender with which it is associated – woman. Thus even Montaigne – a sincere lover of women and fervent advocate of embodiment – lapses into this devaluing figure in his very effort to affirm the body, urging that we "order the soul... not to scorn and abandon the body... but to rally to the body, embrace it, cherish it, assist it, control it, advise it, set it right and bring it back when it goes astray; in short, to marry it and be a husband to it, so that their actions may appear not different and contrary, but harmonious and uniform."[22]

---

[20] Jean-Jacques Rousseau, *Emile* (New York: Basic Books, 1979), 54, 118, 125.

[21] Ralph Waldo Emerson, "Works and Days," in *Society and Solitude, Works of Ralph Waldo Emerson*, vol. 2 (Boston: Houghton, Osgood Company, 1880), 129.

[22] See Michel de Montaigne, *The Complete Essays of Montaigne*, trans. Donald Frame (Stanford: Stanford University Press, 1965), 484–485. Montaigne condemned as "inhuman" any philosophy "that would make us disdainful enemies of the cultivation of the body" (ibid., 849).

Here we face the second of the two paradoxical reasons why somatic studies are demoted in humanistic education. Its indispensable instrumentality ironically relegates it to the devalued realm of service (associated with servants and women and the mere mechanics of material means), while the humanities are instead identified with the pursuit of the highest and purest of spiritual ends – venerated forms of knowledge concerning classics, philosophy, literature, and the arts. Why, then, (goes the argument) should we humanists busy ourselves with studying the body (as the *means*) when we can concentrate directly on enjoying the *ends*, on studiously appreciating our spiritual and artistic achievements?

One answer, inspired by the pragmatist philosophy that shapes somaesthetics, is that if we truly care about the ends, we must care about the means necessary to realize those ends. The body deserves humanistic study to improve its use in the various artistic and scholarly pursuits it underlies and serves. Musicians, actors, dancers, and other artists can perform better and longer, with less attendant pain and fatigue, when they learn the proper somatic comportment for their arts: how to handle their instruments and themselves so as to avoid unwanted, unnecessary muscle contractions that result from unreflective habits of effort, detract from efficiency and ease of movement, and ultimately generate pain and disability. A famous case in point concerns the somatic theorist-therapist F.M. Alexander, who first developed his acclaimed technique to address his own problems of hoarseness and loss of voice in theatrical acting that were generated by faulty positioning of his head and neck. Such learning of intelligent somatic self-use is not a matter of blind drill in mechanical techniques but requires a careful cultivation of somatic awareness.

Philosophers and other humanities scholars can likewise improve their functioning as thinkers by improving their awareness and regulation of their somatic instrument of thought. Wittgenstein frequently insists on the crucial importance of slowness for good philosophical thinking. Philosophers often err in rashly jumping to wrong conclusions by hastily misinterpreting the surface structure of language. To unravel and avoid such errors, philosophy needs painstaking linguistic analysis that requires slow, patient labor and thus demands a sort of practiced, disciplined slowness and calm. Hence Wittgenstein's appreciation of tranquil slowness, urging, "The salutation of philosophers to each other should be: 'Take your time!'" and advocating an "ideal [of] a certain coolness," a state of tranquility where "conflict is dissipated" and one achieves "peace in one's thoughts." Wittgenstein's own manner of reading and writing aims at attaining this calming slowness. "I really want my copious punctuation marks to slow down the speed of reading. Because I should like to be read slowly. (As I myself read.)"[23]

But a more basic, versatile, and time-proven method for attaining the tranquility needed for slow, sustained thinking is focused awareness and regulation of our breathing. Because breathing has a profound effect on our entire nervous system, by slowing or calming our breathing, we can bring greater tranquility to our minds. In the same way, by noticing and then relaxing certain muscle contractions that are not only unnecessary but distractive to thinking (because of the pain or fatigue they create), we can strengthen the focus of our mental concentration and build its patient endurance for more sustained philosophical meditations. We can then afford to take our time.

Philosophers, however, often argue that thinking of our bodily means harmfully distracts attention from our ends and thus is more likely to cause problems. Despite the general thrust of his pragmatist and body-respecting philosophy, William James insists that bodily actions are more certain and successful when we focus on "the end alone" and avoid "consciousness of the [bodily] means." Given the parsimonious economy of consciousness, we should concentrate its limited attention on the most important features of action – namely our goals – and leave the bodily means to our established unreflective habits of somatic use: "We walk a beam the better the less we think of the position of our feet upon it. We pitch or catch, we shoot or chop the better the less" we focus on our own bodily parts and feelings, and the more exclusively on our targets. "Keep your *eye* on the place aimed at, and your hand will fetch it; think of your hand, and you will very likely miss your aim."[24]

Immanuel Kant further warns that somatic introspection "takes the mind's activity away from considering other things and is harmful to the head." "The inner sensibility that one generates through one's reflections is harmful.... This inner view and self-feeling weakens the body and diverts it from animal functions."[25] In short, somatic reflection harms both body and mind, and the best way to treat one's body is to ignore as much as possible the sensations of how it feels, while using it actively

---

[23] Ludwig Wittgenstein, *Culture and Value*, bilingual ed. (Oxford: Blackwell, 1980), 2, 9, 43, 68, 80. I sometimes use my own translation from the German original.

[24] William James, *The Principles of Psychology* (Cambridge, MA: Harvard University Press, 1983), 1128.

[25] Immanuel Kant, *Reflexionen zur Kritische Philosophie*, ed. Benno Erdmann (Stuttgart: Frommann-Holzboog, 1992), 68–69. Kant later critically remarks that "man is usually full of sensations when he is empty of thought," 117; my translations.

in work and exercise. As James put the point in his *Talks to Teachers*, we should focus on "what we do...and not care too much for what we feel."[26] Astutely recognizing that "action and feeling go together," James urged (in both public lectures and private advice) that we should just control our feelings by focusing on the actions with which they are linked. To conquer depression, we should simply "go through the *outward movements*" that express cheerfulness, willfully making our body "act and speak as if cheerfulness were already there." "Smooth the brow, brighten the eye, contract the dorsal rather than the ventral aspect of the frame, and speak in a major key." "My 'dying words,'" he exhorted (more than thirty years before his actual death), "are, 'outward acts, not feelings!'"[27]

The Kantian-Jamesian rejection of somatic introspection is, I think, misguided (and largely a product of their avowed fears of hypochondria[28]). But their arguments do rest on a significant truth. In most of our usual activities, attention is and needs to be primarily directed not to our inner feelings but to the objects of our environment in relation to which we must act and react in order to survive and flourish. Thus for excellent evolutionary reasons, nature positioned our eyes to be looking out rather than in. The error of Kant and James is in confusing ordinary primacy with exclusive importance. Though attention should be directed mostly outward, it is nevertheless often very useful to examine one's self and sensations. Consciousness of breathing can inform us that we are anxious or angry when we might otherwise remain unaware of these emotions and thus more vulnerable to their misdirection. Proprioceptive awareness of one's muscle tension can tell us when our body language is expressing a timidity or aggression that we wish not

---

[26] William James, *Talks To Teachers on Psychology and To Students on Some of Life's Ideals* (New York: Dover, 1962), 99.

[27] James, *Principles of Psychology*, 1077–78; *Talks To Teachers*, 100; *The Correspondence of William James*, vol. 4 (Charlottesville: University Press of Virginia, 1995), 586.

[28] Noting his "disposition to hypochondria," Kant felt that heightened attention to inner somatic sensations resulted in "morbid feelings" of anxiety. See his book *The Contest of the Faculties*, trans. M.J. Gregor (Lincoln: University of Nebraska Press, 1992), 187–189. On James's hypochondria, see Ralph Barton Perry, *The Thought and Character of William James*, (Nashville: Vanderbilt University Press, 1996), who also cites James's mother's complaints of his excessive expression of "every unfavorable symptom" (361). On the "philosophical hypochondria" of "introspective studies," see James's letter to brother Henry of August 24, 1872, in *The Correspondence of William James*, vol. 1 (Charlottesville: University Press of Virginia, 1992), 167. James repeatedly confessed, in private correspondence, to being "an abominable neurasthenic." See, for example, his letters to F.H. Bradley and George H. Howison in *The Correspondence of William James*, vol. 8, 52, 57.

to display, just as it can help us avoid unwanted, parasitic muscular contractions that constrain movement, exacerbate tension, and eventually cause pain. In fact, pain itself – a somatic consciousness that informs us of injury and prompts a search for remedy – provides clear evidence of the value of attention to one's somatic states and sensations. Care of the self is improved when keener somatic awareness advises of problems and remedies before the onset of pain's damage.[29]

Although James rightly affirms it is generally more efficient to focus on the end and trust the spontaneous action of established habits to perform the bodily means, there are many times when those habits are too faulty to be blindly trusted and require somatic attention for their correction. For example, a batter will normally hit the ball better if she is concentrating on the ball, not on the stance of her feet, the posture of her head and torso, or the grip of her hands on the bat. But a poor or slumping batter may learn (often from a coach) that her stance, posture, and grip tend to put her off balance or inhibit movement in the ribcage and spine in a way that disturbs her swing and impairs her vision of the ball. Here conscious attention must, for a time, be directed to the somatic feelings of the problematic postures so that these postures can be proprioceptively identified and thus avoided while new, more productive habits of posture (and their attendant feelings) are developed and attended to. Without such proprioceptive attention, the batter will spontaneously relapse to (and thus reinforce) the original, problematic postural habits without even being aware of this.

Once an improved habit of swinging is established, the somatic means and feelings of swinging should no longer claim our primary attention, as the ultimate end remains hitting the ball. However, achieving that end requires treating the means as a temporary end and focus, just as hitting the ball – itself only a means to get on base or score a run or win the game – is treated as a temporary end in order to achieve those further ends. Direct seeking of ends without careful attention to the

---

[29] In advocating the cultivation of somatic awareness, I am not suggesting that our bodily feelings are infallible guides to practice and self-care. On the contrary, I recognize that the average individual's somatic self-perception is often quite inaccurate (not noticing, for instance, excessive and harmful chronic muscular contractions). This is precisely why somatic awareness needs to be cultivated in order to make it more accurate and discriminating, and why such cultivation typically requires the aid of a teacher. I also do not want to suggest that our somatic self-awareness could ever be complete in a way that we become totally transparent to ourselves. For the limits and difficulties of somatic introspection, see *Body Consciousness*, ch. 2, 5, 6.

needed means will only bring frustration. Consider the batter who wills herself with all her might to hit the ball with distance, yet fails because her eagerness to attain the end prevents her from concentrating on the required bodily means, such as simply maintaining the proper head posture needed to keep her eye on the ball. Likewise, scholars whose creative productivity is constrained by recurrent headaches and writing pains resulting from bad bodily habits of self-use at their work stations cannot remedy or overcome these problems by mere willpower; the bodily habits and their attendant consciousness need to be examined before they can be properly transformed. We must know what we actually do in order to correct it reliably, into doing what we want.

Although wise to advocate the value of somatic actions for influencing our feelings, James fails to recognize the corresponding importance of somatic feelings for guiding our actions. We cannot properly know how to smooth the brow if we cannot feel that our brow is furrowed or know what it feels like to have one's brow smooth. Similarly, since most of us have been habituated to faulty posture, the ability to hold ourselves straight in a way that avoids excessive rigidity requires a process of learning that involves sensitive attention to our proprioceptive feelings. James's unfeeling insistence on vigorous dorsal contraction and stiff upright posture ("bottle up your feelings... and hold yourself straight," he exhorted) is thus a sure prescription for the kind of back pain he indeed suffered throughout his life, just as it is surely an expression of his puritan ethics more than a product of careful clinical research. If "action and feeling go together," as James remarked, they *both* warrant careful consideration for optimal functioning, just as both ends and means require our attention. Though knives are most clearly means for cutting rather than ends of sharpening, we sometimes need to focus on improving their sharpness and other aspects of their use in order to improve their effectiveness. Such means-respecting logic underlies the project of somaesthetics as a meliorative study of the use of our bodily instrument in perception, cognition, action, aesthetic expression, and ethical self-fashioning that together constitute humanistic research, artistic creation, and the global art of perfecting our humanity through better living.

IV

The question of how to improve an instrument's use helps introduce the three major branches of somaesthetics whose structure I elaborate elsewhere in more detail.[30] First, a tool is better deployed when we have a better understanding of its operational structure, established modes of use, and the relational contexts that shape them. *Analytic somaesthetics* – the most distinctively theoretical and descriptive branch of the project – is devoted to such research, explaining the nature of somatic perceptions and comportment and their function in our knowledge, action, and construction of the world. Besides traditional topics in philosophy concerning the mind-body issue and somatic aspects of consciousness and action, analytic somaesthetics is concerned with biological factors that relate to somatic self-use. How, for example, greater flexibility in the spine and ribcage can increase one's range of vision by enabling greater rotation of the head while, on the other hand, more intelligent use of the eyes can conversely (through their occipital muscles) improve the head's rotation and eventually the spine's.

This does not mean somaesthetics should be assimilated into physiology and expelled from the humanities; it only underlines the (obvious but much neglected) point that humanities research should be properly informed by the best scientific knowledge relevant to its studies. Renaissance art and art theory owe much of their success to their study of anatomy, mathematics, and the optics of perspective. Philosophers' traditional disdain for the body may be largely a product of their ignorance of physiology (as Nietzsche suggested), coupled with their pride in privileging only the knowledge that they do master.[31] Analytic somaesthetics is also deeply concerned with what the social sciences have to say about the modes and structuring contexts of somatic experience. This includes genealogical, sociological, and cultural analyses that show how the body is both shaped by social power and employed as an instrument to maintain it; how bodily norms of health, skill, and beauty and even our categories of gender are constructed to reflect and sustain social forces.

Secondly, use of a tool can be improved by studying the range of already proposed methods for improving that use. Such critical and comparative study of somatic methods constitutes what I call *pragmatic somaesthetics*. Since the viability of any such method will depend on certain facts about the body, this pragmatic dimension presupposes the analytic dimension. However, it transcends analysis not only by evaluating the facts analysis

---

[30] See, for example, Richard Shusterman, *Performing Live: Aesthetic Alternatives for the Ends of Art* (Ithaca: Cornell University Press, 2000), ch. 7-8.

[31] See Friedrich Nietzsche, *The Will to Power*, trans. W. Kaufmann and R.J. Hollingdale (New York: Vintage, 1968), 220.

describes, but also by proposing means to improve certain facts by remaking the body and the environing social habits and frameworks that shape it. A vast array of pragmatic methods have been designed to improve the experience and use of our bodies: various diets; modes of grooming and decoration; meditative, martial, and erotic arts; aerobics; dance; massage; bodybuilding; and modern psychosomatic disciplines such as the Alexander Technique and the Feldenkrais Method.

We can distinguish between holistic or more atomistic methods. While the latter focus on individual body parts or surfaces (styling the hair, painting the nails, shortening the nose through surgery), the former techniques (such as Hatha yoga, taijiquan, and the Feldenkrais Method) comprise systems of somatic postures and movements to develop the harmonious functioning and energy of the person as an integrated whole. Penetrating beneath skin surfaces and muscle fiber to realign our bones and better organize the neural pathways through which we move, feel, and think, these practices insist that improved somatic harmony is both a contributory instrument and a beneficial by-product of heightened mental awareness and psychic balance. Such disciplines refuse to divide body from mind in seeking to improve the entire person.

Somatic practices can also be classified in terms of being directed primarily at the individual practitioner herself or instead primarily at others. A massage therapist or a surgeon works on others; but in doing taijiquan or bodybuilding, one is working more on oneself. The distinction between self-directed and other-directed somatic practices cannot be rigidly exclusive, for many practices are both. Applying cosmetic makeup is frequently done to oneself and to others; erotic arts display a simultaneous interest in both one's own experiential pleasures and one's partner's by maneuvering the bodies of both self and other. Moreover, just as self-directed disciplines (like dieting or bodybuilding) often seem motivated by a desire to please others, so other-directed practices like massage may have their own self-oriented pleasures.

Despite these complexities (which stem in part from the interdependence of self and other), the distinction between self-directed and other-directed body disciplines is useful for resisting the common presumption that to focus on the body implies a retreat from the social. Experience as a Feldenkrais practitioner has taught me the importance of caring for one's own somatic state in order to pay proper attention to one's client. In giving a Feldenkrais lesson of Functional Integration, I need to be aware of my own body positioning and breathing, the tension in my hands and other body parts, and the quality of contact my feet have with the floor in order to be in the best condition to assess the client's body tension, muscle tonus, and ease of movement and to move him in the most effective way.[32] I need to make myself somatically very comfortable in order not to be distracted by my own body tensions and to communicate the right message to the client. Otherwise, when I touch him, I will be passing on to him my feelings of somatic tension and unease. Because we often fail to realize when and why we are in a state of slight somatic discomfort, part of the Feldenkrais training is devoted to teaching how to discern such states and distinguish their causes.

Somatic disciplines can further be classified by whether their major orientation is toward external appearance or inner experience. Representational somaesthetics (such as cosmetics) is concerned more with the body's surface forms while experiential disciplines (such as yoga) aim more at making us feel better in both senses of that ambiguous phrase: to make the quality of our somatic experience more satisfying and more acutely perceptive. The distinction between representational and experiential somaesthetics is one of dominant tendency rather than rigid dichotomy. Most somatic practices have both representational and experiential dimensions (and rewards) because there is a basic complementarity of representation and experience, outer and inner. How we look influences how we feel, and vice versa. Practices like dieting or bodybuilding that are initially pursued for representational ends often produce inner feelings that are then sought for their own experiential sake. The dieter may become an anorexic craving pleasurable sensations of lightness or hunger, while the body builder becomes addicted to the experiential surge of energy known as "the pump." Just as somatic disciplines of inner experience often use representational cues (such as focusing attention on a body part or using imaginative visualizations), so a representational discipline like bodybuilding deploys experiential clues to serve its ends of external form, using feelings to distinguish, for example, the kind of pain that builds muscle from the pain that indicates injury.

---

[32] The Feldenkrais Method deploys an educational rather than therapeutic-pathological model. Clients are regarded as students rather than patients, and we speak of our work as giving lessons rather than therapy sessions. I analyze the Feldenkrais Method in *Performing Live*, ch.8. Functional Integration is only one of the two central modes of the Method, the other being Awareness through Movement. The latter is best described in Feldenkrais's introductory text *Awareness Through Movement* (New York: Harper and Row, 1972). A very detailed but difficult account of Functional Integration is provided in Yochanan Rywerant, *The Feldenkrais Method: Teaching by Handling* (New York: Harper and Row, 1983).

Another category of pragmatic somaesthetics – *performative somaesthetics* – may be distinguished for disciplines that focus primarily on building strength, health, or skill and that would include practices like weightlifting, athletics, and martial arts. But to the extent that these disciplines aim either at the external exhibition of performance or at one's inner feeling of power and skill, they might be associated with or assimilated into the representational or experiential categories.

Finally, a third way to improve our use of a tool is actual practice with it, as we learn to do by doing. Thus, besides the analytic and pragmatic branches of somaesthetics, we also need a branch I call *practical somaesthetics*, which involves actually engaging in programs of disciplined, reflective, corporeal practice aimed at somatic self-improvement (whether representational, experiential, or performative). This dimension of not just reading and writing about somatic disciplines but systematically performing them is sadly neglected in contemporary philosophy, though it has often been crucial to the philosophical life in both ancient and non-Western cultures.[33]

V

In arguing for the humanistic study and cultivation of the body as our primordial, indispensable instrument, we should not forget that the body – as purposeful subjectivity – is also the user of the tool it is. Moreover, we should question the body's presumed status as mere means in contrast to higher ends. This disparaging categorization rests on an implicit means-ends dichotomy that needs to be challenged. The means or instrumentalities used to achieve something are not necessarily outside the ends they serve; they can be an essential part of them.[34] Paint, canvas, representational figures, and the artist's skillful brush strokes are among the means for producing a painting, but they (unlike other enabling causes, such as the floor on which the artist stands) are also part of the end product or art object, just as they are part of the further end of our aesthetic experience in viewing the painting. In the same way, the dancer's body belongs as much to the ends as to the means of the dance work. As Yeats poetically put it (in "Among School Children"), "O body swayed to music. O brightening glance. How can we know the dancer from the

---

[33] See Richard Shusterman, *Practicing Philosophy: Pragmatism and the Philosophical Life* (New York: Routledge, 1997), 1–64.
[34] John Dewey powerfully makes this point in *Art as Experience*, (Carbondale: Southern Illinois University Press, 1987), ch 9.

dance?" More generally, our appreciation of art's sensuous beauties has an important somatic dimension, not simply because they are grasped through our bodily senses (including the sense of proprioception that traditional aesthetics has ignored) but, in addition, because art's emotional values, like all emotion, must be experienced somatically to be experienced at all.

Beyond the realm of art, somatic experience belongs to higher ends, not merely menial means. Athletic exercise may be a means to health, but we also enjoy such exercise in itself, as part of what health actually signifies – the ability to enjoy strenuous movement. And bodily health itself is enjoyed not just as a means to enable laboring for other ends; it is enjoyed intrinsically as an end in its own right. Happiness and pleasure are often prized as highest ends, but somatic experience clearly forms part of them. What are the joys of love without desiring and fulfilled emotions that are always experienced bodily, no matter how pure or spiritual one's love is claimed to be? How can we appreciate even the pleasures of thought without recognizing their somatic dimensions – the pulsing of energy, flutters of excitement, and rush of blood that accompany our impassioned flights of contemplation? Knowledge, moreover, is sturdier when incorporated into the muscle memory of skilled habit and deeply embodied experience.[35] As human thought would not make sense without the embodiment that places the sensing, thinking subject in the world and thereby gives her thought perspective and direction, so wisdom and virtue would be empty without the diverse, full-bodied experience on which they draw and through which they manifest themselves in exemplary embodied speech, deeds, and radiating presence.

We thus conclude with another double feature of the living body. Not only instrumentally valuable for perfecting our humanity, the soma is also part of this valued end. In educating and cultivating the sensibility of somaesthetic awareness to improve our thinking through the body, we not only enhance the material means of human culture but also our capacities as subjects to enjoy it.[36]

---

[35] Hence, Montaigne wisely urged that "we must not [merely] attach learning to the mind, we must incorporate it; we must not sprinkle, but dye," (Montaigne, *Complete Essays*, 103).

[36] Heightened awareness enables us to increase our pleasures by making them more consciously savored and deepening them with the pleasures of reflection. As Montaigne writes, "I enjoy [life] twice as much as others, for the measure of enjoyment depends on the greater or lesser attention that we lend it," (Montaigne, *Complete Essays*, 853).

2

The Body as Background

I

The notion of background has moved progressively into the foreground of philosophical discussion. Over the past century, philosophers have increasingly recognized that our conscious mental life cannot adequately function without relying on a background of which we are not properly conscious but which guides and structures our conscious thought and action. The notion of body, though largely disregarded or disparaged by the dominantly idealistic tradition of Western philosophy, has likewise increasingly moved toward the foreground of philosophical theory, and indeed has formed my principal axis of research for the last decade. Because the term "body" is too often contrasted with mind and applied to insentient, lifeless things, while the term "flesh" has such negative associations in Christian culture (and evokes the merely fleshy dimension of embodiment), I use the term "soma" to designate the living, sensing, dynamic, perceptive, purposive body that lies at the heart of my research project of somaesthetics.

If both background and body have moved toward the forefront of philosophical discussion, this is not mere coincidence. They are intimately connected in contemporary theories of the background that assert its crucial importance for mental life and that recognize the crucial somatic dimension of mind. This chapter examines the body's role as structuring unreflective background to conscious mental life and purposive action. But it further explains why this unreflective somatic background should be brought into the foreground of consciousness, not just theoretically but also sometimes in practical action. Such foregrounding of the somatic background in practical contexts of action goes against the received wisdom of master thinkers as different as Immanuel

Kant, William James, and Maurice Merleau-Ponty. Critically addressing their key arguments while outlining some advantages of foregrounding background body consciousness, this chapter also examines how such foregrounding can be integrated and reconciled with the persistent, productive somatic background.

Besides pragmatism, we can identify at least three different philosophical approaches that affirm the embodied background's central role: phenomenology, analytic philosophy, and social theory of the sort most clearly exemplified by Pierre Bourdieu. I will focus primarily on the pragmatist treatment of the body as background, not only because of its richness but also because its contributions have received much less attention than other philosophical theories of the embodied background, despite the fact that the pragmatist treatment preceded them and may even have influenced some of them.[1]

II

Phenomenological theories of the embodied background go back to Edmund Husserl and Martin Heidegger and extend to Hubert Dreyfus today. Their most famous formulation, however, is found in Maurice Merleau-Ponty, who powerfully foregrounds the body's value while intriguingly explaining the body as silent, structuring, concealed background: "Bodily space ... is the darkness needed in the theatre to show up the performance, the background of somnolence or reserve of vague power against which the gesture and its aim stand out." More generally, "one's own body is the third term, always tacitly understood, in the figure-background structure, and every figure stands out against the double horizon of external and bodily space."[2] The body is also mysterious as a locus of "impersonal" existence, beneath and hidden from normal selfhood. It is "the place where life hides away" from the world, where I retreat from my interest in observing or acting in the world, "lose myself in some pleasure or pain, and shut myself up in this anonymous life which subtends my personal one. But precisely because my body can shut itself

---

[1] Wittgenstein's views on the background seem to be influenced (albeit polemically) by some of James's views on the somatic background. For a discussion of Wittgenstein's critique of the Jamesian view of bodily sensations as the defining background of mental concepts, see Richard Shusterman, *Body Consciousness: A Philosophy of Mindfulness and Somaesthetics* (Cambridge: Cambridge University Press, 2008), ch. 4.

[2] Maurice Merleau-Ponty, *Phenomenology of Perception*, trans. Colin Smith (London: Routledge, 1962), 100–101; hereafter PoP with page references cited parenthetically in the text.

off from the world, it is also what opens me out upon the world and places me in a situation there" (PoP, 164–165).

For Merleau-Ponty, the body's background role is so essential that he seems to make background status (its being kept in the background) equally necessary for our proper functioning. His most radical argument against explicit or reflective somatic observation is not merely that preoccupation with such bodily observation is unnecessary and that our focused attention to bodily sensations also interferes with spontaneous, unthematised somatic perception and action; the argument, rather, is that one simply cannot observe one's own body at all, because it is the permanent, invariant perspective through which we observe other things. Unlike ordinary objects, the body "defies exploration and is always presented to me from the same angle.... To say that it is always near me, always there for me, is to say that it is never really in front of me, that I cannot array it before my eyes, that it remains marginal to all my perceptions, that it is *with* me," as a background condition for observing other things. "I observe external objects with my body, I handle them, examine them, walk round them, but my body itself is a thing which I do not observe: in order to be able to do so, I should need the use of a second body" (PoP, 90–91). As he elsewhere claims, "I am always on the same side of my body; it presents itself to me in one invariable perspective."[3]

Turning to analytic philosophy, we should note Ludwig Wittgenstein and John Searle as influential advocates of the background who recognize its crucial somatic dimension. Wittgenstein brings a series of complex but convincing arguments (often directed at the views of William James) to show that mental concepts such as emotion, will, and personal identity cannot be reduced to bodily feelings that are closely associated with such concepts and used to explain them. Even if a person's fear of the dark is always experienced with a rapid heartbeat, even if her expression of will is always felt with a clenching of the jaw, such emotions or acts of the will cannot be identified with these mere physical sensations. Instead, Wittgenstein argues, such mental concepts can only be explained in terms of a whole surrounding context of life, aims, and practices, "the whole hurly-burly of human actions, the background against which we see any action." In the case of will, for example, what defines a movement as a voluntary action is not a particular feeling of desire or effort

---

[3] Maurice Merleau-Ponty, *The Visible and the Invisible*, trans. A. Lingis (Evanston: Northwestern University Press, 1968), 148. These arguments of Merleau-Ponty are criticized in detail in *Body Consciousness*, ch. 2.

in making the movement but rather the background context of goals, intentions, and activities in which the movement is performed. "What is voluntary is certain movements with their normal *surrounding* of intention, learning, trying, acting."[4]

Despite his critique of reducing mental concepts to somatic sensations, Wittgenstein nonetheless affirms the body's importance as a crucial dimension of the underlying background and orientation for mental life, including the refinements of culture and aesthetics, which – like our mastery of language and other rule-governed practices – involves a basic level of motor training for mastery of habits of competency. As with Merleau-Ponty, the body serves Wittgenstein as a central instance and symbol of what forms the crucial, silent, mysterious background for all that can be expressed in language or in art, the unreflective source for all that can be consciously grasped in reflective thought or representation. "The purely corporeal can be uncanny," he declares. "Perhaps what is inexpressible (what I find mysterious and am not able to express) is the background against which whatever I could express has its meaning."[5]

Meaning relies on a network of practices, competencies, and activities that provide the necessary contextual background for making sense of things and actions and for making language meaningful; and this network of practices, competencies, and activities has a salient somatic dimension. Wittgenstein moreover suggests how our bodily background can endow extremely powerful meaning to phenomena beyond the realm of language. Music's inexpressible depth of meaning and its grand, mysterious power derive from the body's silent role as creative ground and intensifying background. That is how a surface of ephemeral sounds can touch the very depths of human experience. "Music, with its few notes & rhythms, seems to some people a primitive art. But only its surface [its foreground] is simple, while the body which makes possible the interpretation of this manifest content has all the infinite complexity that is suggested in the external forms of other arts & which music conceals. In a certain sense it is the most sophisticated art of all."[6]

---

[4] Ludwig Wittgenstein, *Zettel*, trans. G.E.M. Anscombe (Oxford: Blackwell, 1967), 567, 577.

[5] Ludwig Wittgenstein, *Culture and Value*, trans. P. Winch (Oxford: Blackwell, 1980), 16, 50; hereafter CV.

[6] The parenthetical term "foreground" refers to the German *Vordergrund*, which was a textual variant to "surface" (*Oberfläche*) in the manuscripts. See the revised second edition of Ludwig Wittgenstein, *Culture and Value* (Oxford: Blackwell, 1998), 11, from which I cite here.

Wittgenstein further argues that background kinesthetic feelings help us derive a greater fullness, intensity, or precision in our experience of art because (at least for some of us) aesthetic imagination or attention is facilitated or heightened by certain bodily movements that somehow feel as if they correspond to the work, even if these feelings remain in the background and not in our explicit consciousness. He writes:

> When I imagine a piece of music, as I often do every day, I always, so I believe, grind my upper and lower teeth together rhythmically. I have noticed this before though I usually do it quite unconsciously. What's more, it's as though the notes I am imagining are produced by this movement. I believe this may be a very common way of imagining music internally. Of course I can imagine without moving my teeth too, but in that case the notes are much ghostlier, more blurred and less pronounced[7] (CV, 28).

John Searle acknowledges Wittgenstein as an analytic forerunner to his own theory of the background. For Searle, intentionality and linguistic meaning are not "self-interpreting" but instead require for their proper functioning and interpretation a background context that is pre-intentional, "a bedrock of mental capacities that do not themselves consist of Intentional states (representations), but nonetheless form the preconditions for the functioning of Intentional states."[8] Dubbing this "bedrock" (a term Wittgenstein famously employed) as "the Background," Searle argues, "Intentional phenomena such as meanings, understandings, interpretations, beliefs, desires, and experiences only function within a set of Background capacities that are not themselves intentional."[9] He later elucidates this as, "Any intentional state only functions, that is, it only determines conditions of satisfaction, against a set of Background abilities, dispositions, and capacities that are not of the intentional content and could not be included as part of the content."[10] Putting the point in terms of representations, "all representation, whether in language, thought, or experience, only succeeds in representing given a set of nonrepresentational capacities" (RM, 175).

---

[7] Perhaps Wittgenstein's habits as a clarinet player had something to do with these somaesthetic feelings because playing this instrument involves holding the teeth together.

[8] John R. Searle, *Intentionality: An Essay in the Philosophy of Mind* (Cambridge: Cambridge University Press, 1983), 143.

[9] John R. Searle, *The Rediscovery of the Mind* (Cambridge, MA: MIT Press, 1992), 175; hereafter RM.

[10] John R. Searle, *The Construction of Social Reality* (New York: Free Press, 1995), 131–32; hereafter CSR.

Searle articulates seven enabling roles of the background to show precisely how it must be presupposed for the proper functioning of our mental life. Guiding the interpretation of linguistic meaning and perceptual content (which requires a framing and disambiguating context), the background also structures consciousness and gives experience a meaningful narrative organization. The background, moreover, underlies the coherence of our motives and attitudes, our readiness to deal with certain situations rather than others, and our behavioural dispositions. In Searle's words (and italics):

> *First,* ... *the Background enables linguistic interpretation to take place.* ... *Second, the Background enables perceptual interpretation to take place.* ... *Third, the Background structures consciousness.* ... *Fourth* [because of the Background], *temporally extended sequences of experiences come to us with a narrative or dramatic shape. They come to us under what for want of a better word I will call "dramatic" categories* [that are constituted from the Background of capacities and activities and institutions or forms of life]. ... *Fifth, each of us has a set of motivational dispositions* [of which we may not be consciously aware of, hence existing in the Background], *and these will condition the structure of our experiences.* ... *Sixth, the Background facilitates certain kinds of readiness.* ... *Seventh, the Background disposes me to certain sorts of behavior* (CSR, 132–136).

Searle departs from Wittgenstein (and Merleau-Ponty) in explaining the Background as essentially causal, biological, and confined to the brain. Defining the Background in terms of "neurophysiological structures that function causally in the production of certain sorts of intentional phenomena" (CSR, 130), Searle insists: "It is important to see that when we talk about the Background we are talking about a certain category of neurophysiological causation. Because we do not know how these structures function at a neurophysiological level, we are forced to describe them at a much higher level" (CSR, 129). So we should think of the Background's "abilities, capacities, tendencies, and dispositions ontologically speaking as a set of brain structures. Those brain structures enable me to activate the system of intentionality and to make it function, but the capacities realized in the brain structures do not themselves consist in intentional states."[11]

Searle's theory has at least three problematic aspects. First, it presumes that the Background exists only as a neurophysiological cause rather than including any other kind of motivation or guiding, stimulating orientation. Second, it claims that the Background exists only within the

---

[11] John R. Searle, *Rationality in Action* (Cambridge, MA: MIT Press, 2001), 58.

individual subject or agent rather than extending beyond that individual to the natural and social environments that structure her capacities, tendencies, and dispositions. Finally, even if it is indeed only neurophysiological and wholly within the single individual, Searle apparently regards the Background's causality as confined to brain structures rather than involving other aspects of the individual's nervous system and physiology. That seems both an impoverished background and an eviscerate sense of the human body.

Rather than linger on these deficiencies in Searle's account, we should turn to another thinker he acknowledges as having a substantive theory of the Background – Pierre Bourdieu, the French sociologist whose theory is clearly free of these Searlean problems. Originally trained in philosophy, Bourdieu absorbed a wide range of philosophical influences. These include not only the phenomenological tradition against which he rebelled because of what he saw as its insufficient attention to the social world that profoundly conditions the phenomenologist's experience, but also structuralist and Marxist thought and the analytic philosophy of Wittgenstein and John L. Austin. (Austin, we should note, was also an especially strong influence on Searle and likewise emphasized the need of background contexts for understanding linguistic meaning).[12] Bourdieu's theory of the background is conceptualized through his technical notion of *habitus*, which he explains as "a structured and structuring structure" that is *structured* by background social conditions beyond the individual agent or particular social group while *structuring* the individual's (or group's) dispositions, perceptions, behavior, and beliefs by constituting an organized background *structure* or grid of categories of understanding, value, and action through which the world is perceived, understood, and engaged.[13]

Bourdieu repeatedly insists on the bodily dimension of habitus and the way its somatic incorporation of social categories, norms, beliefs,

---

[12] For Bourdieu's relationship to Wittgenstein and Austin, see my "Bourdieu and Anglo-American Philosophy," in Richard Shusterman (ed.), *Bourdieu: A Critical Reader* (Oxford: Blackwell, 1999), 14–28. Searle's debt to Austin is perhaps most evident in his book *Speech Acts* (Cambridge: Cambridge University Press, 1969), which elaborates Austin's ideas of "illocutionary acts" and "performative utterances" that emphasized that properly understanding the meaning of a sentence depends on understanding it as a "total speech act in the total speech situation" in which it appears. This total situation implies, of course, a complex social as well as linguistic background. See J. L. Austin, *How to Do Things with Words* (Oxford: Oxford University Press, 1962), 148.

[13] Pierre Bourdieu, *Distinction: A Social Critique of the Judgment of Taste*, trans. Richard Nice (Cambridge, MA: Harvard University Press, 1984), 171.

and values determines the unconscious but guiding background of perception, action, and thought. "The social order inscribes itself in bodies," and it is through "the incorporation of social structures in the form of dispositional structures, of objective chances in the form of expectations or anticipations" in our bodies that we acquire the implicit practical sense and unreflective modes of dealing with the social world, including those vast dimensions of the physical world that society helps structure – from our constructed environments to the markings of calendar time with routines of night and day, work and rest. Shaped by the social background, habitus in turn forms the background that shapes our experience and thought. "Habitus, understood as an individual or a socialized biological body, or as the social, biologically individuated through incarnation in a body" constitutes a background set of dispositions that "impose presuppositions and limitations on thought which, being embedded in the body, are beyond the reach of consciousness." These socially formed dispositions constitute an "immediate," "*corporeal knowledge* that provides a practical comprehension of the world quite different from the intentional act of conscious decoding that is normally designated by the idea of comprehension," an immanent bodily understanding that is not a "representation" explicitly grasped by "a self-conscious perceiving subject."[14]

Bourdieu was, of course, also deeply influenced by the French sociological tradition of Émile Durkheim, who censured pragmatism as "irrationalism" and "an attack on reason," despite his respect for John Dewey.[15] Bourdieu admits that his theory of habitus bears "quite striking" affinities with Dewey's pragmatist account of habit, which (like most of Dewey's philosophy of mind and action) is largely influenced by William James.[16] Both pragmatists strongly insist on habit's bodily dimension and vital role in the structuring background of consciousness, and we now turn to their theories of the background.

---

[14] Pierre Bourdieu, *Pascalian Meditations*, trans. Richard Nice (Stanford: Stanford University Press, 2000), 130, 135, 141, 142, 157, 182. Similar affirmations of the body's central role in habitus can be found throughout his work; for example, "Belief in the Body," in Pierre Bourdieu, *The Logic of Practice*, trans. Richard Nice (Stanford: Stanford University Press, 1990), 66–79.

[15] Emile Durkheim, *Pragmatism and Sociology*, trans. J.C. Whitehouse (Cambridge: Cambridge University Press, 1983), 1.

[16] Bourdieu acknowledges his affinities with Dewey in Pierre Bourdieu and Loic Wacquant, *An Invitation to Reflexive Sociology* (Chicago: University of Chicago Press, 1992), 122. I explore some of their similarities and differences in "Bourdieu and Anglo-American Philosophy," in Richard Shusterman (ed.), *Bourdieu: A Critical Reader* (Oxford: Blackwell, 1999), 14–28.

III

We can distinguish two kinds of embodied background theory in the pragmatist philosophy of James and Dewey. The first can be described as *qualitative* or phenomenal because its key concept is a background quality of experience that is felt but not known or thematized or represented as an intentional object of the mind but that the theory asserts is essential for the proper functioning of all coherent thought and action. The second pragmatist theory of the background is wider. Rather than focusing on experienced qualities, the background is here defined in terms of entrenched habits, environing conditions, and purposes that not only go beyond felt qualities of experience but also beyond the particular experience and the experiencing subject. Habit is the dominant concept in this background theory through which the other components are connected to explain the background. Dewey elaborates both strains of the theory more systematically than James, whose trailblazing *Principles of Psychology* Dewey, however, acknowledged as the strongest influence on his philosophy of mind.[17] We will consider the broader, habit-centered theory first because it offers perhaps the clearest way to introduce their advocacy of the bodily background in mental life.

"Mind," Dewey writes, "is more than consciousness, because it is the abiding even though changing background of which consciousness is the foreground."[18] Through experience, one acquires habits, "attitudes and interests" that "become a part of the self" as "funded and retained meanings" that constitute mind's background resources and orientation. As "mind forms the background upon which every new contact with surroundings is projected," so such background is not "passive," but rather formatively "active" (AE, 269). Dewey elaborates: "This active and eager background lies in wait and engages whatever comes its way so as to absorb it into its own being. Mind as background is formed out of modifications of the self that have occurred in the process of prior interactions with environment." It is directed "toward further interactions," and its environments for interaction are social as well as natural. Just as habits always incorporate conditions from the environments in which they are

---

[17] William James, *The Principles of Psychology* (1890; Cambridge: Harvard University Press, 1983), 308. For Dewey's explicit recognition of this book's influence on him, see Jane Dewey, "Biography of John Dewey" in P. Schilpp and L. Hahn, eds., *The Philosophy of John Dewey* (LaSalle, IL: Open Court, 1989), 23.

[18] John Dewey, *Art as Experience* (Carbondale: Southern Illinois University Press, 1987), 270; hereafter AE.

formed, so do the habits that constitute the background of mind. "Since it is formed out of commerce with the world and is set toward that world," mind should never be regarded as "something self-contained and self-enclosed." Even in its acts of meditative withdrawal from the world, "its withdrawal is only from the immediate scene of the world during the time in which it turns over and reviews material gathered from the world" (AE, 269).

In the vast bulk of our voluntary behaviour, our unreflective habits spontaneously execute our will and direct our thought and action. Because "habits are demands for certain kinds of activity," they form the mind's will even if they remain in the background and unnoticed by conscious thought. As formative, active background, their "projectile power" of "predisposition ... is an immensely more intimate and fundamental part of ourselves than are vague, general, conscious choices." In constituting the background of mind, habits "form our effective desires and they furnish us with our working capacities. They rule our thoughts," without our even recognizing their power because they rule implicitly, unthinkingly, through their incorporation in our bodies.[19]

For this reason, Dewey ardently advocates the somatic work of F. Matthias Alexander as a means of improving thought, will, and action by reconstructing our habits to be more effective. For William James (who earlier described people and minds as "bundles of habits"), habit likewise provides the background that enables our perceptions and actions to proceed automatically or unreflectively without demanding any attention of the mind's "higher thought-centres" or foreground consciousness.[20] James, moreover, firmly grounds habit in our bodily being, affirming as his "first proposition" that "*the phenomena of habit in living beings are due to the plasticity of the organic materials of which their bodies are composed*" (PP, 110). Like Bourdieu, James recognizes that such background habits are both socially formed and socially utilized to shape and constrain not only the action but also the thoughts, tastes, and desires of different professional and social classes. "Habit is thus the enormous fly-wheel of society, its most precious conservative agent," writes James. "It alone prevents the hardest and most repulsive walks of life from being deserted by those brought up to tread therein. It keeps the fisherman and the deck-hand

---

[19] John Dewey, *Human Nature and Conduct* (Carbondale: Southern Illinois University Press, 1983), 21; hereafter HC.

[20] William James, *The Principles of Psychology* (Cambridge, MA: Harvard University Press, 1983), 109, 120; hereafter PP.

at sea through the winter; it holds the miner in his darkness.... It keeps different social strata from mixing" (PP, 125).

Alongside this view of entrenched, embodied, and environmentally and socially conditioned habits as a structuring, guiding mental background, Dewey and James also propose a qualitative, phenomenal form of mental background defined in terms of qualities that are felt in the unattended-to background of consciousness and that structure or orient consciousness but are not part of the explicit content, focus, or foreground of consciousness. Dewey describes this qualitative background as "the 'subconscious' of human thinking," because its background status removes it from explicit consciousness; he affirmed its essential somatic dimension by characterizing its qualities as expressed in the "immediate organic selections, rejections, welcomings, expulsions, appropriations, withdrawals, shrinkings, expansions, elations and dejections, attacks, wardings off" that the embodied human organism spontaneously makes.[21] Although we generally "are not aware of the qualities" involved in such reactions and "do not objectively distinguish and identify them ... they exist as feeling qualities, and have an enormous directive effect on our behavior." Dewey explains that, "[e]ven our most highly intellectualized operations depend upon them as a 'fringe' by which to guide our inferential movements. They give us our *sense* of rightness and wrongness, of what to select and emphasize and follow up, and what to drop, slur over and ignore, among the multitude of inchoate meanings that are presenting themselves." They indicate when we are going in a promising direction or whether we are "getting off the track" (EN, 227).

Here Dewey is borrowing directly from William James's idea (in *The Principles of Psychology*) that a qualitative background or felt "fringe" structures and guides our explicit or representational consciousness. Indeed, this idea – that each definite content, image, or representation of consciousness appears through a structuring background or fringe of feeling of which we are not properly aware but which guides the direction of our thought – is one key reason James famously refers to the *stream* of consciousness rather than the train of thought. "What must be admitted," James insists, "is that the definite images of traditional psychology form but the very smallest part of our mind" (PP, 246). Moreover, in the movement of consciousness, the successive mental content is not clearly individuated like separate cars in a train or even like

---

[21] John Dewey, *Experience and Nature* (Carbondale: Southern Illinois University Press, 1981), 227; hereafter EN.

separate pails of water, but rather forms part of a continuous interpenetrating flow. "Every definite image in the mind is steeped and dyed in the free water that flows round it. With it goes the sense of its relations, near and remote, the dying echo of whence it came to us, the dawning sense of whither it is to lead. The significance, the value, of the image is all in this halo or penumbra that surrounds and escorts it, – or rather that is fused into one with it and has become bone of its bone and flesh of its flesh" (PP, 246).

James describes this background "halo of felt relations" (PP, 247) as an unarticulated psychic "fringe of felt affinity" (PP, 251) that guides thought by giving us a sense of what belongs to and advances thought's current flow or instead distracts or hinders it. This unreflective guidance is done in terms of implicitly felt relations of "harmony and discord, of furtherance or hindrance" with that background quality "felt in the fringe." In other words, "any thought the quality of whose fringe lets us feel ourselves 'all right' is an acceptable member of our thinking" (PP, 250). For James, part of the fringe of thought's flowing stream is always a feeling of one's body. "We think; and as we think we feel our bodily selves as the seat of the thinking. If the thinking be *our* thinking, it must be suffused through all its parts with that peculiar warmth and intimacy that make it come as ours," a "warmth and intimacy" from "the feeling of the same old body always there" (PP, 235).

It is Dewey, however, who makes the most sustained and systematic argument for the qualitative background as necessary to mental life, a transcendental argument that he first articulates in an article "Qualitative Thought" published in 1930, when he was preparing the first William James Lectures at Harvard that would eventually issue in Dewey's book *Art as Experience*.[22] Perception, judgment, action, and thinking, Dewey argues in that article, are never performed in absolute isolation but only in terms of a background contextual whole, a unity of experience that he calls "a situation." He further claims that such a situation always structures our experience as a felt whole and guides or orients our understanding of it. But what, then, enables the constituting of the situation and gives it the unity, structure, and limits that define it as a particular situation or experience? Dewey's answer is a special kind of qualitative background, a directly felt "immediate quality." The situation or experience is "held together in spite of its internal complexity by the

[22] John Dewey, "Qualitative Thought," reprinted in *John Dewey: The Later Works*, vol. 5 (Carbondale: Southern Illinois University Press, 1984), 243–262; hereafter QT.

fact that it is dominated and characterized throughout by a single quality" felt as "a direct presence," though only as a background presence that is not explicit or represented as part of the content of the situation itself (QT, 246, 248). Besides this first function of the background quality, Dewey articulates four others.

In constituting the situation, this "immediate quality of the whole situation" (QT, 249) also controls the distinction of objects or terms that thinking later identifies and employs as parts (relations, elements, objects, distinctions) of that situation or experience. "The underlying unity of qualitativeness regulates pertinence or relevancy and force of every distinction and relation; it guides selection and rejection and the manner of utilization of all explicit terms" because such terms "are *its* distinctions and relations" (QT, 247–248). This underlying quality, however, is not itself an explicit term or content of the situation. For if it were or becomes so, it would no longer be in the background but would instead become an element (or representational content) of a new situation that would have its own underlying background quality. The "underlying pervasive quality" that constitutes a situation and structures the terms of that situation or experience serves yet a third function by providing a sense of what is adequate in judgment; for example, what level of detail, complexity, or precision is sufficient to render the contextual judgment valid. We could always make our judgments more detailed and precise, for instance, by giving our time of arrival not merely in terms of minutes but in terms of milliseconds. "But enough," as Dewey says, "is always enough, and the underlying quality is itself the test of the 'enough' for any particular case" (QT, 254, 255).

A fourth function of immediate quality is to determine the basic sense or direction of the situation and to sustain it over time, despite the confusing general flood of experience. Although the background quality is nondiscursively "dumb," it has "a movement or transition in some direction" which provides the unifying "background, the thread, and directive clue" for the unity and continuity of the ongoing inquiry. "This quality enables us to keep thinking about one problem without our having constantly to stop to ask ourselves what is it after all that we are thinking about" (QT, 248, 254).

Fifth, Dewey claims that a unifying background quality of immediate experience is the only adequate way to explain the association of ideas. The standard explanations of physical contiguity and similarity are insufficient, he argues, to make the associative link, because "there is an indefinite number of particulars contiguous to one another in space and time" and because everything in some respect is similar to everything else. Dewey concludes that association must be "an *intellectual* connection" produced through "an underlying quality which operates to control the connection of objects thought of...; there must be relevancy of both ideas to a situation defined by unity of quality" (QT, 257–258).

It may be true that we often feel a pervasive unifying background quality of immediate experience that performs all these five functions for our mental life: structuring our experience into a coherent whole; organizing its terms and limits; giving our thought direction; and determining adequacy and appropriateness of association. However, as I have elsewhere shown, Dewey's arguments do not decisively demonstrate that such a felt unifying background quality must *always* be present or is always necessary for coherent thought.[23] This is because other pervasive background factors of our experience could together perform all those five functions – notably such factors as the continuity and direction of habit and the practical focusing unity of purpose, factors that Dewey himself emphasizes.

Purpose binds together the situational elements enlisted in its pursuit, and habit already implies an internal organization of activity that projects itself on further organization. Habit and purpose not only shape our distinctions of objects and relations within the situation but also guide our judgments of their relevance and importance. Habit and purpose also give the situation and its experience a sustained direction. Dewey insists that "all habit has *continuity*," and is "projective" by its very nature; our thinking habits naturally continue their directional course, and tend to resist interruption of distraction (HC, 31, 168). Purpose, too, as Dewey recognizes, gives "unity and continuity" of action, because its "end-in-view" calls forth a series of coordinated means to reach it.[24] Moreover, as Dewey admits, purpose further explains what is adequate in judgment, since "any proposition that serves the purpose for which it is made is logically adequate" (QT, 255). Finally, habit and purpose can explain our association of ideas without invoking an ineffable unifying quality to link them. "When I think of a hammer," Dewey asks, "why is the idea of nail so likely to follow?" (QT, 258). The more obvious answer is not the glue of immediate, ineffable unifying quality but rather the entrenched habit of functional association for practical purposes of building.

---

[23] Richard Shusterman, *Practicing Philosophy: Pragmatism and the Philosophical Life* (New York: Routledge, 1997), ch. 6.
[24] John Dewey, *Ethics* (Carbondale: Southern Illinois University Press, 1985), 185.

Dewey's transcendental argument that coherent thought requires an immediately felt qualitative background is not entirely successful. Its weaknesses, however, only point to the necessity of another background – namely habit – that is firmly situated in the body. Moreover, the failure of his argument for the necessity of qualitative background feelings does not in any way negate that such background feelings exist, that they (frequently and significantly) help orient our thought and behavior, and that they are felt somatically even if they escape our explicit attention. Aesthetic experience is where such unifying background qualities seem particularly important and distinctively felt, and Dewey indeed suggests that the rich qualitative unity of such experience is so powerfully "manifest" as to supply the best way "to understand what experience is" in general (AE, 63, 278).

IV

James and Dewey form a united pragmatist front both in affirming the background as cognitively necessary for mental life and in highlighting the bodily dimension of this background in their theories of mind and behavior. Their views divide sharply, however, on whether the bodily background feelings should ever be brought to the foreground in practical life. James implores psychologists to cultivate heightened awareness of their somatic feelings and movements as a means to improve their theoretical observations because he thought their theories suffered from superficial introspection of such feelings; but in practical matters, he still follows the dominant tradition of urging that the somatic background be kept in the background.

James has several reasons for rejecting somaesthetic reflection in practical life. He argues that the spontaneous action of habit not only "simplifies the movements required to achieve" our ends and thus "makes them more accurate and diminishes fatigue" but also, by diminishing "the conscious attention with which our acts are performed," enables us to concentrate our limited amount of attention on other things that require it (PP, 117, 119). While recognizing, of course, that in learning a skill of performance, "the singer may need to think of his throat or breathing; the balancer of his feet on the rope," James insists that for already skilled performers the somatic must stay in the background. To foreground it in our attention "would be a superfluous complication" (PP, 1108). Just focus on the target you want to hit and pay no mind to the bodily movements you make to hit it, letting them work in the background. In short,

"Trust your spontaneity," James advises, just as his admired godfather Ralph Waldo Emerson earlier insisted that "spontaneous action is always the best."[25] Besides the faith that spontaneous habitual action was more efficient and accurate, James shared Kant's worry that somatic introspection in practical life "is either already a disease of the mind (hypochondria) or will lead to such a disease and ultimately to the madhouse," for he also shared Kant's avowed personal tendency to hypochondria.[26] Throughout his college years, James suffered extended periods of depression related to psychosomatic symptoms that he scrutinized with intense attention during his long periods of convalescence, often at European health spas.

Dewey also recognized the dangers of ruminative introspection, but his extended experience with F.M. Alexander's technique of reconstructing habits through heightened body consciousness convinced him that disciplined, intelligently focused somatic introspection was much more valuable than destructive.[27] Although spontaneous habit frequent functions most effectively, we are often subject to the formation of bad habits. As we cannot properly correct them without knowing what they are, so we cannot know what they are without paying attention to the somatic movements and feelings with which they are performed. Systematic somatic reflection is thus necessary, Dewey argues, because it is essential to improving self-use and because self-use is essential to our use of all the other tools at our disposal. "No one would deny that we ourselves enter as an agency into whatever is attempted and done by us.... But the hardest thing to attend to is that which is closest to ourselves, that which is most constant and familiar. And this closest 'something' is, precisely, ourselves, our own habits and ways of doing things" through our primal tool or agency, the body-mind or soma. To understand and redirect its workings requires attentively self-reflective "sensory consciousness"

---

[25] William James, "The Gospel of Relaxation," in *Talks To Teachers on Psychology and To Students on Some of Life's Ideals* (New York: Dover, 1962), 109; Ralph Waldo Emerson, "Intellect," in Brooks Atkinson (ed.), *The Essential Writings of Ralph Waldo Emerson* (New York: Modern Library, 2000), 264.

[26] Immanuel Kant, *Anthropology from a Pragmatic Point of View*, trans. Victor Dowdell (Carbondale: Southern Illinois University Press, 1996), 17. Kant confessed his "disposition to hypochondria" in Immanuel Kant, *The Conflict of the Faculties*, trans. M.J. Gregor (Lincoln: University of Nebraska Press, 1992), 189. For more details on James's worries about hypochondria related to his condition of neurasthenia, see *Body Consciousness*, 168–169.

[27] Confessing to a friend that "being too introspective by nature, I have had to learn to control the direction it takes," Dewey expresses particular unease about "autobiographical introspection... as it is not good for me." See his letter to Scudder Klyce, cited in Steven Rockefeller, *John Dewey: Religious Faith and Democratic Humanism* (New York: Columbia University Press, 1991), 318.

and control. Modern science has developed all sorts of powerful tools for influencing our environment. But "the one factor which is the primary tool in the use of all these other tools, namely ourselves, in other words, our own psycho-physical disposition, as the basic condition of our employment of all agencies and energies" also needs to be "studied as the central instrumentality."[28]

What James and others have advocated as spontaneous freedom, Dewey sees more critically (through his study with Alexander) as blind obedience to entrenched habit. True freedom of will, he argues, means having control of unreflective habit. This means being able to bring it into conscious critical attention in order to reconstruct or refine it so that one can actually do with one's body what one really intends to do. Such freedom is not a native gift but an acquired skill involving mastery of inhibitory control as well as positive action. As Dewey puts it: "True spontaneity is henceforth not a birth-right but the last term, the consummated conquest, of an art – the art of conscious control," an art involving "the unconditional necessity of inhibition of customary acts, and the tremendous difficulty found in not 'doing' something as soon as an habitual act is suggested."[29]

Inhibition's crucial role in freedom finds more recent support from experimental studies in neuroscience (introduced by Benjamin Libet) showing that motor action depends on neurological events that occur about 350 milliseconds before our conscious awareness of deciding to make a movement, even if we feel that our conscious decision is what initiated the movement. Libet nonetheless argues that free will remains possible because his findings show we still have an inhibitory ability to "veto" that act between its conscious awareness and actual implementation; "the final decision to act could still be consciously controlled during the 150 ms or so remaining after the specific conscious intention appears" and before its "motor performance."[30] Free will, on this account, amounts essentially to a free "won't." Although the general concept of voluntary

---

[28] See John Dewey, "Introduction," in F.M. Alexander, *Constructive Conscious Control of the Individual* (New York: Dutton, 1923); reprinted in *John Dewey: The Middle Works*, vol. 15 (Carbondale: Southern Illinois University Press, 1983), 314–315.

[29] John Dewey, "Introductory Word," in F.M. Alexander, *Man's Supreme Inheritance* (New York: Dutton, 1918); reprinted in *John Dewey: The Middle Works*, vol. 11 (Carbondale: Southern Illinois University Press, 1982), 352; and John Dewey, "Introduction," in F.M. Alexander, *The Use of the Self* (New York: Dutton, 1932); reprinted in *John Dewey: The Later Works*, vol. 6 (Carbondale: Southern Illinois University Press, 1985), 318.

[30] See Benjamin Libet, "Unconscious Cerebral Initiative and the Role of Conscious Will in Voluntary Action," *Behavioral and Brain Sciences* 8 (1985): 529–66, quotations from 529, 536; "Do We Have Free Will?," *Journal of Consciousness Studies* 6 (1999): 47–57; "Can Conscious Experience Affect Brain Activity?" *Journal of Consciousness Studies* 10 (2003): 24–28.

action and free will should not be limited to this inhibitory, experimental model (with its focus on unsituated "abstract" movements and a razor time-slice of 150 ms for decision), Libet's findings lend scientific support to Dewey's and Alexander's emphasis on the value of inhibition for exercising conscious constructive control in motor performance.[31]

Not only essential in restraining problematic habits, inhibition is also necessary for the very effectiveness of somatic reflection that allows us to foreground and thus observe our behaviour more accurately so that we can inhibit the problematic habit and replace it with a superior mode. We cannot reliably change our actions if we do not really know what we are actually doing, yet most of us are very unaware of our habitual modes of bodily behaviour, which lurk in the background of consciousness and do not come into explicit focus. Which foot do you use when taking your first step in walking; which leg bears the most weight in standing; on which buttock do you more heavily rest in sitting? We are not at all inclined to pay attention to such things because as active creatures striving to survive and flourish within an environment, our sustained attention is habitually directed primarily to other things in that environment that affect our projects rather than to our bodily parts, movements, and sensations. For good evolutionary reasons, we are habituated to respond directly to external events rather than analyze our inner feelings; to act rather than to carefully observe; to reach impulsively for our ends rather than holding back to study the bodily means at our disposal. Thus inhibitory power is needed even to break our habits of attending to other things so that we can sustain a focus on reflective somatic consciousness.

In Chapter 4 I examine a variety of everyday pathologies that result from habits of implicit muscle memory whose effective remedy calls for bringing those problem-generating background habits into the foreground of explicit consciousness so that they can be positively transformed or at least controlled. Here, however, I should briefly note two other arguments to support the Deweyan view that the bodily background can be usefully brought to the foreground in practical contexts. First, if James and other advocates of spontaneity admit that attention to bodily movements and feelings can be useful in the learning process, then we can argue that learning is never complete because we can always further refine an already learned skill. Second, there is always the possibility that we may need to correct or revise an acquired skill when it no longer

---

[31] For a detailed account of the methodical use of inhibition in the Alexander Technique, see *Body Consciousness*, ch. 6.

proves satisfactory because of new conditions: either new conditions of the performer (for example, an injury) or new environing conditions in which the task is performed (swimming in the ocean versus swimming in a pool).[32] In a world where our technological lived environment changes so rapidly, we cannot rely on entrenched habit to keep up with these changes or on satisfactory new habits to form by themselves in dealing with them. We need to be able to monitor the unreflective ways our body performs by bringing them into the foreground, at least for the time of critical reflection and possible reconstruction. Thereafter, they can be allowed to return to the background while we bring our focused, foregrounding attention to other things.

In other words, I am not urging the impossible task that the somatic background always be brought to the foreground and that all spontaneity be eschewed. Full transparency of our actions and feelings is not only unachievable but not worth achieving in practice; on most occasions, our focus is best directed elsewhere, to the world in which we must act. The very nature of the background/foreground distinction means that there must always be something in the background beyond or beneath our foregrounding focus, just as in order for interpretation to function properly it needs to be based on some prior understanding as its ground (even if it is an imperfect understanding). But for pragmatism, these distinctions are functional and flexible, not absolute. This means that some elements of the background can be brought into the foreground and that in certain practical contexts such foregrounding is valuable. Thus rather than one-sidedly urging spontaneity or reflection, my pragmatist policy would urge an intelligent reconciliation of spontaneous and reflective moments through strategies of phasing. Having elaborated these arguments elsewhere,[33] let me conclude this chapter by noting another way that foregrounding the bodily background can be useful in practical life.

The somatic habits and qualitative feelings of the background are both conditioned by the environments in which the soma is situated and from which it derives its energies and horizons of action. These environments are both physical and social. By bringing the somatic background into the foreground, we can also place that experience-structuring environmental background into clearer focus. Consider three examples. By noticing a very slight sensory discomfort in one's breathing (that might normally go unnoticed as an insignificant background feeling), one can

---

[32] I elaborate these points in Chapter 9, 205–208.
[33] See *Practicing Philosophy*, ch. 6; *Body Consciousness*, ch. 2; and Chapter 9 of this book.

be apprised of the poor quality of the air in one's environment and do something about it – whether that means opening a window in a stuffy room, cleaning an air filter or residual mold in an air conditioning system, or petitioning for restrictions on motor vehicle traffic in one's city. By noticing one's muscular discomfort at one's work station (and finding that various postural changes fail to alleviate it), one can learn that one's chair or desk are poorly suited for long-term effective and painless performance or that one's extremely demanding work routine must allow for repeated pauses so that one can rest from the uncomfortable posture one's work station induces.

Unhappy conditions of labor usually reflect social problems; so the idea that unsatisfactory working conditions can be brought into focus by foregrounding the somatic background of discomfort provides a good transition to my third example, which has deep and painful social relevance. By critically scrutinizing one's somatic feelings and bringing those background feelings into the foreground, a person may come to notice certain previously unrecognized feelings of discomfort in interaction with (or mere proximity to) people of certain races, religions, or ethnicities. By noticing such feelings, he comes to recognize having prejudices of which he was previously unaware. Such recognition could in turn lead to the quest for personal and social changes to overcome these prejudices. One reason racial prejudice and ethnic enmity are so hard to cure is that their visceral roots lie in background feelings and habits that do not come to clear, foregrounded consciousness so they can be effectively dealt with, either through merely controlling them or transforming them through more positive somatic feelings. Somaesthetics' powers of heightened consciousness and control offer a possible remedy for such problems; and once a transformation to better feelings and habits has been achieved, they can be put back into the background to structure more positive spontaneous relations with people from those races or ethnicities.

The pragmatist theory of the background and of its crucial somatic dimension is primarily a theory of psychology, philosophy of mind, and the logic of inquiry that is meant to explain the coherence of our perception, interpretation, action, and thought by means of a background that enables, frames, or structures such coherence. That we conclude with practical matters and ethical issues like environmentalism, labor conditions, and racism is not, however, inappropriate. This is because one crucial feature of pragmatist philosophy is to draw practical and ethical conclusions from its theories of mind and action, and also to assess in part the value of those theories in terms of their contribution not only to a better understanding of our world (and of ourselves) but also to the more successful pursuit of our practical and ethical lives. Grounded in pragmatism, somaesthetics shares these aims of integrating theory and practice.

3

Self-Knowledge and Its Discontents

From Socrates to Somaesthetics

I

On Apollo's ancient temple at Dephi, three Greek maxims were inscribed whose importance was reaffirmed in Roman times, by preserving their inscription in gilt letters. The most famous of these maxims – Γνῶθι σεατόν (*Gnothi seauton* or "Know thyself") – has been, by far, the most philosophically influential and forms the focus of this chapter, though my argument will ultimately converge with a second of these maxims that is also rich in historical significance.[1] Heraclitus gave the injunction to self-knowledge its earliest enduring philosophical application when he affirmed, "I dived into myself" because "All men have the capacity to come to know themselves and to have self-control" (the Greek term is *sophronein*, sometimes translated as "temperance").[2] The next known Greek usage of the maxim is more artistic yet less cryptic. In his play *Prometheus*, Aeschylus gives self-knowledge its crucial meaning of knowing one's level or limitations. When the punished but still proudly defiant Prometheus is approached by the titan god Oceanus, who offers to help him effect a reconciliation with Zeus, Oceanus urges: "Know thyself: change thy course" because Zeus now rules "o'er the Gods."[3]

Socrates, however, is the ancient thinker most strongly associated with the maxim of self-knowledge and the one who established it at the core of philosophy. Acclaimed as the wisest of all men by the Delphic oracle

---

[1] This maxim is Μηδέν άγαν ("nothing too much"). The third of the maxims was Εγγύα, πάρα δ'άτή ("Give a pledge, and trouble is at hand"). See E.G. Wilkins, *The Delphic Maxims in Literature* (Chicago: University of Chicago Press, 1929), 1–10.

[2] Daniel Graham (ed.), *The Texts of Early Greek Philosophy* (Cambridge: Cambridge UP, 2010), 147, 149.

[3] Aeschylus, *Prometheus Bound*, trans. Arthur S. Way (London: MacMillan and Co., 1907), 19.

of Apollo (the God of Truth), Socrates argued that his main wisdom was the self-knowledge of his ignorance. In contrast to the many recognized experts who wrongly believed themselves full of wisdom concerning things they did not really know, Socrates at least knew himself well enough to know he did not know what others claimed to know; his wisdom was appreciating the limits of his knowledge. Indeed, he argues that the oracle declared him the wisest so as to prompt his critical search for wiser men and thus show that the most reputed "human wisdom is worth little or nothing" (*Apology*, 23b).[4] Asserting his lack of interest in lofty speculations, he explains (in *Phaedrus*, 229e–230a), "I am still unable, as the Delphic inscription orders, to know myself; and it really seems to me ridiculous to look into other things before I have understood that." Deploying the injunction of self-knowledge to chide the arrogant Alcibiades to recognize that his "good looks, height, birth, wealth, and native intelligence" are far from enough to put him in a class with Spartan and Persian kings, Socrates affirms such knowledge of current limitations as the necessary spur for cultivating oneself for the political leadership his ambitious young lover seeks. "Trust in me and in the Delphic inscription and 'know thyself,'" Socrates tells him, for "every human being needs self-cultivation, but *especially*... us" (*Alcibiades I*, 124b–d).

But what, exactly, is the self to be known and cultivated? After some dialogical sleight of hand, Plato's Socrates leads Alcibiades to the conclusion "that the soul is the man" and "nothing other than his soul," so "the command that we should know ourselves means that we should know our souls" (130c–d) and make them the object of our self-cultivation. Hence, a man's knowing or caring for his body is merely knowing or "caring for something that belongs to him, and not [knowing or caring] for himself." Since the soul is the true governing self, Socrates claims that "being self-controlled is knowing yourself" (131b); and this association of self-knowledge with the self-control of moderate behavior is reinforced in the *Charmides*, where we read "that 'know thyself' and 'be temperate' [*sophrosyne*] are the same" (164d–165a). The connection of self-knowledge with *sophrosyne* – a Greek term of virtue implying more than our notion of temperance by including a sense of modesty in knowing one's place and respecting one's superiors – confirms the primary ancient sense of "know thyself" as an awareness of one's vulnerability, shortcomings, mortality, or inferior stature (vis-à-vis the gods or others).

---

[4] See John Cooper (ed.), *Plato: Complete Works* (Indianapolis: Hackett, 1997), 22; all references to Plato in this chapter are quoted from this source.

If the dominant thrust of the Socratic demand for self-knowledge is critical recognition of our limitations and deficiencies, such fault-finding analysis can certainly stimulate and guide our efforts at self-improvement. But it also, if rigorously pursued, risks disheartening bouts of self-doubt and self-loathing that can generate depression. In its long history, Western philosophy (including the Christian theology it helped shape) has indeed developed more positive interpretations of self-knowledge. While briefly tracing them, this chapter also shows how the original deprecatory implication of the maxim continues to resurface, often accompanied by sharp criticism of the ideal of self-examination – including complaints that real self-knowledge is impossible and that rigorous, critical self-reflection can be psychologically devastating. From these historical lessons, complemented by some contemporary findings in experimental psychology, I argue for the need to distinguish more clearly the different varieties of self-examination whose diversity can help explain the often radically differing assessments of its value, and provide a better appreciation of the most philosophically scorned form of self-examination and self-cultivation – that of our bodies and somatic self-consciousness.

II: Historical Interpretations

Acknowledging the traditional humbling sense of "know thyself" but introducing a more positive interpretation, Cicero writes (in encouraging his brother's rhetorical talents), "Don't suppose that the old maxim γνῶθι σεατόν was made only to reduce conceit; it also tells us to know our strong points."[5] Like Plato, Cicero interprets the Delphic injunction as "know your soul," while underlining the positive nature of the soul through its divine source: "For he who knows himself will realize, in the first place, that he has a divine element within him, and will think of his own inner nature as a kind of consecrated image of God; and so he will always act and think in a way worthy of so great a gift of the gods."[6] Developing the idea of

---

[5] Cicero, *Letters to Quintus*, trans. D. R. Shackleton Bailey. (Cambridge, MA: Harvard University Press, 2002), 187. Plutarch likewise affirms that self-examination and self-knowledge should involve knowing one's positive gifts, but also one's special proclivities; hence, to obey the Delphic maxim one must "use oneself for that one thing for which Nature has fitted one" rather than "dragging oneself to the emulation of... another." See Plutarch, "Tranquility of Mind," *Plutarch's Moralia: in Sixteen Volumes*, trans. W.C. Helmbold (Cambridge, MA: Harvard University Press, 1939), vol. 6, 209.

[6] Cicero, *De re publica, De legibus*, trans. Clinton Walker Keyes (Cambridge: MA: Harvard University Press, 1928), 59, 365.

knowing the self as soul, Neoplatonists like Plotinus urge us to focus self-study on the soul's highest dimension – i.e., *Nous* – which we share with higher, purer, divine spirits. "Remove all stains from yourself and examine yourself, and you will have faith in your immortality," Plotinus explains, for "the self-knowledge of the *Nous* of the soul consists in knowing itself no longer as man but as having become altogether different, in hastening to unite itself with the Higher alone."[7] Proclus likewise explains the Delphic injunction as an "ascent to the divine and the most effective path towards purification."[8]

This logic of self-knowledge as a preparatory, purgational step toward the higher contemplation and union with God is often taken up by Christian mystics. St. Catherine of Siena urges the individual "to abide forever in the cell of self-knowledge" so as to recognize one's sins and cut them off from one's better, truer self in the continuous quest for God, who provides a mirror of holiness to regard one's flaws and lead one to higher purity and divine communion. "As a man more readily sees spots on his face when he looks in a mirror, so the soul who with true knowledge of self rises with desire and gazes with the eye of the intellect at herself in the sweet mirror of God, knows better the stains of her own face by the purity which she sees in him."[9] Affirming the holiness of one's true self as soul, St. Juan d'Avila later expresses the same basic argument that "knowledge of one's self, which is certainly a holy thing, is also the path to the Holy of Holies, which is knowledge of God."[10]

We can appreciate the spiritual uplift expressed here. But is there not a risk that rigorously examining one's sins and weaknesses in the "cell of self-knowledge" could constitute a stifling and psychologically devastating form of mental self-flagellation? If the mystic's firm faith in God's saving power of grace is what ensures that such self-critical askesis leads not to the perdition of depression and despair but rather to the elevating contemplation and union with the divine, what happens when one's faith is less than supremely certain? While Socrates had already

---

[7] Plotinus, *The Enneads*, IV.vii.10; V.iii.4. I use the translation from Pierre Hadot, *Philosophy as a Way of Life* (Oxford: Blackwell, 1995), 100; and Wilkins, *The Delphic Maxims in Literature*, 66.

[8] Proclus, "Commentary on Plato's *Alcibiades I*," in Algis Uždavinys (ed.), *The Golden Chain: An Anthology of Pythagorean and Platonic Philosophy* (Bloomington, IN: World Wisdom, 2004), 202.

[9] Catherine and Algar Labouchere Thorold, "A Treatise of Discretion," in *Dialogue of St. Catherine of Siena* (New York: Cosimo Classics, 2007), 62.

[10] Juan d'Avila. *Epistolario Espiritual* (Madrid: Espasa-Calpe, 1962), vol. XII, 153.

questioned whether one could indeed truly know oneself, Renaissance thinkers increasingly expressed worries about the health and wisdom of intense self-study, recognizing the need to look away or get away from oneself.

That Montaigne makes the quest for self-knowledge the core of his life and masterwork of *Essays* ("I study myself more than any other subject") does not prevent him from asserting that the task is not only unachievable but also devastating if taken to extremes.[11] Asserting that Socrates, by seeking "to know himself... had come to despise himself" (M, 275), Montaigne argues more generally that the Delphic maxim is "a paradoxical command," as Nature wisely directs us to look beyond ourselves. This not only helps us find resources and escape dangers from the outside but also avoids predatory problems from within, since rigorous self-study must be a depressing, difficult, and dangerous exercise for creatures so full of folly, flaws, and misery as we are. "This common attitude and habit of looking elsewhere than at ourselves has been very useful for our business. We are an object that fills us with discontent; we see nothing in us but misery and vanity. In order not to dishearten us, Nature has very appropriately thrown the action of our vision outward" (M, 766). Hence Montaigne also insists on the essential restorative value of entertainment and pleasures of diversion that both relieve and strengthen the mind through alternative exercise and focus (M, 621–638).[12] In the next century, Blaise Pascal – whose brief, unhappy life was plagued with greater physical infirmity and hypochondriac fears – confirms Montaigne's thesis that we desperately need diversion from self-reflection because of our self-wretchedness: "The only good thing for men therefore is to be diverted from thinking of what they are," since even a king "becomes unhappy as soon as he thinks about himself."[13]

If despite such worries, Montaigne could still affirm the philosophical quest for self-knowledge as the key to better self-care and self-cultivation, then it is not surprising that the centrality of self-study continues into modern philosophy through Descartes' striking method of building the entire edifice of knowledge from the foundations of his mental introspection in his influential *Meditations on First Philosophy*, which has shaped so

---

[11] Montaigne. *The Complete Essays of Montaigne*, trans. Donald Frame (Stanford: Stanford University Press, 1958), 821; hereafter M.
[12] For an analysis of Montaigne's influential views on the importance of entertainment, see my "Entertainment: A Question for Aesthetics," *British Journal of Aesthetics* 2003 (43): 289–307.
[13] Blaise Pascal, *Pensées* (Harmondsworth: Penguin, 1966), 67–68.

much of the modern philosophical agenda. "There is no more fruitful exercise than attempting to know ourselves," he elsewhere argues, where he even asserts the value of knowing our bodily constitution. But by ontologically separating body from mind and locating the substance of self within the mind alone (which, he claims, unlike the body could be known directly through introspection), Descartes furthers the Platonistic trend of identifying self-study as knowing one's mind or soul with the aim to "acquire an absolute power over its passions."[14]

The contrast of mind and body allows for two radically different approaches to the project of self-examination and self-knowledge: one including introspection of our bodily feelings, habits, and comportments; the other essentially confined to our distinctively mental life of thought. With but few exceptions, modern Western philosophy has preferred the more narrowly mentalistic approach, either ignoring or repudiating somatic introspection. Kant is exemplary in this regard. In his *Metaphysics of Morals*, he claims "the First Command of All Duties to Oneself" is to "'*know* (scrutinize, fathom) *yourself*,' not in terms of your physical perfection (your fitness or unfitness for all sorts of... ends) but rather in terms of your moral perfection in relation to your duty. That is, know your heart – whether it is good or evil, whether the source of your actions is pure or impure." Recognizing that such moral self-examination "into the depths (abysses) of one's heart" is not only cognitively difficult but could also generate self-loathing or self-contempt, Kant counters by arguing that the very effort to critically examine one's moral stature provides comforting evidence of the individual's "noble predisposition to the good" that is "worthy of respect" and can lead to self-improvement. "Only the descent into the hell of self-cognition can pave the way to godliness," Kant concludes, echoing the ancient Christian logic that purgational self-criticism provides the path to divine illumination and union.[15]

In contrast to the duty to examine one's moral consciousness, Kant repudiates the project of reflecting on bodily feelings, claiming that it leads to the madness of hypochondria and morbid despondence. In *The Conflict of the Faculties*, Kant describes hypochondria as a "sort of melancholia" (*Grillenkrankheit*) defined by "the weakness of abandoning oneself

---

[14] René Descartes, "Description of the Human Body and All of its Functions" and "The Passions of the Soul," in *The Philosophical Writings of Descartes*, trans J. Cottingham, R. Stoothoff, and D. Murdoch (Cambridge: Cambridge University Press, 1985), vol. 1. 314, 348.

[15] Immanuel Kant, *The Metaphysics of Morals*, trans. M.J. Gregor (Cambridge: Cambridge University Press, 1996), 191.

despondently to general morbid feelings" that do not point to a definite bodily malfunction but are usually associated with or produced by anxious attention to bodily sensations of unease or unhealthy discomfort. Noting constipation and flatulence as such somatic conditions of discomfort, he confesses his own "natural disposition to hypochondria because of [his] flat and narrow chest, which leaves little room for the movement of the heart and lungs," thus engendering an oppressive feeling in the chest. But insisting on "the mind's power to master its pathological feelings" through a firm resolution of will, Kant claims he was able to cure this morbidity by simply refusing to pay attention to the discomforting somatic feeling that promoted it, "by diverting [his] attention from this feeling."[16] Noting more generally how hypochondria is expressed in compulsive attention to bodily feeling, Kant concludes, "Turning reflection away from the body leads to health."[17] In short, introspective somatic self-study is harmful to both mind and body; and the best way to treat one's body is to ignore as much as possible the self-knowledge of how it feels, while using it actively in work and exercise.

In the economy of mind/body dualism, mind could signify a soul of immortal power and divine purity, while the body – already deeply associated with vulnerability, sin, and limitation (not only by its aging and mortality but also by its very spatial boundaries and personal particularities) – could be ignored as bearing all the negative connotations of self-knowledge and self-examination. G.W.F. Hegel's affirmation of the Delphic maxim reflects this logic: knowing oneself is construed emphatically as knowing *Geist* (i.e., Mind or Spirit) and not "the particular capacities, character, propensities, and foibles of the single self." Self-knowledge "means that of man's genuine reality – of what is essentially and ultimately true and real – of mind as the true and essential being."[18] Moreover, Hegel's idea of self-knowledge as knowledge of Mind is given universal historical scope, in which all history is seen as Mind's "revelation of itself from its first superficial, enshrouded consciousness [to] the attainment of this standpoint of its free self-consciousness, in order that the absolute command of mind 'Know thyself,' may be fulfilled."[19]

---

[16] Immanuel Kant, *The Conflict of the Faculties*, trans. M.J. Gregor (Lincoln: University of Nebraska, 1992), 187, 189.

[17] Immanuel Kant, *Reflexionen zur Kritische Philosophie*, Benno Erdmann (ed.), (Stuttgart: Frommann-Holzboog, 1992), 68, my translation.

[18] G.W.F. Hegel *Hegel's Philosophy of Mind*, trans. William Wallace (Oxford: Clarendon, 1894), 1, 377.

[19] G.W.F. Hegel, *Lectures on the History of Philosophy: Medieval and Modern Philosophy*, trans. E.S. Haldane (Lincoln: University of Nebraska, 1995), 7.

Through its active spirituality, the mind or soul represents the self's divine, transcendent element, ensuring that careful self-examination does not degenerate into stifling immanence, narrow self-absorption, or morbid self-loathing and despair at the self's limitations, symbolized by the body's weakness and mortality. Such fear of despair through self-knowledge without a grounding of the self in the divine finds literary expression in a well-known eighteenth-century poem by Edward Young, "Night-Thoughts," where the poet contemplates the depression that self-knowledge would bring without the faith in a divine immortal soul that God both creates and inspires in us:

> To *know myself*, true wisdom? No, to shun,
> That shocking science, Parent of despair!
> Avert thy mirror: if I see, I die."
> ...
> The man is dead, who for the body lives....
> Thyself, first, know; then love: a self there is
> Of Virtue fond, that kindles at her charms.
> ...
> Who looks on that, and sees not in himself.
> An awful stranger, a terrestrial God?
> A glorious partner with the Deity
> In that high attribute, immortal life.[20]

Coleridge's advocacy of self-reflection for self-knowledge is similarly grounded in the transcendence of the soul: "There is one art of which every man should be master – the art of reflection.... There is one knowledge which it is every man's interest and duty to acquire, namely, self-knowledge."[21] Inspired both by Neoplatonism and Christianity, the poet-philosopher writes, "We begin with the I Know Myself in order to end with the absolute I *am*."[22] If paganism gave us the Delphic maxim, Coleridge continues, Christian "Revelation has provided ... new subjects for reflection and new treasures of knowledge, never to be unlocked by him who remains self-ignorant. Self-knowledge is the key to this casket: and by reflection alone can it be obtained."[23] Other English intellectuals of faith could affirm self-knowledge by emphasizing the maxim's sense of knowing our humbler place as human creatures blessed by a far superior divinity and incapable of truly understanding God's ways. As Alexander

---

[20] Edward Young, *Night Thoughts* (Holborn, London: C. Whittingham for T. Heptinstall, 1798), 75, 180, 235.
[21] Samuel T. Coleridge, *Aids to Reflection* (New York: Stanford and Swords, 1854), xlvii.
[22] Samuel T. Coleridge, *Biographia Literaria* (London: J.M. Dent & Sons, 1975), 154.
[23] Coleridge, *Aids to Reflection*, xlvii.

Pope poetically proclaims, "Know then thyself: presume not God to scan. The proper study of mankind is man," so John Ruskin insists that man's self-knowledge is "to recognize his everlasting inferiority, and his everlasting greatness; to know himself and his place; to be content to submit to God without understanding Him; and to rule the lower creation with sympathy and kindness."[24]

Turning back to continental culture, consider Leo Tolstoy's *Confession*, a moving account of the novelist's mid-life crisis of self-questioning despair, whose only remedy was religious conversion. Tolstoy charts how the "idle reflection" of rational self-examination plunged him deeper and deeper into the morbid conclusion that his life and achievements were meaningless, provoking abject melancholy and constant thoughts of suicide, until he regained faith in God's infinitude and that of his own God-given soul. Without such faith, born not of rational but emotional conviction, he argues, "It is possible to live only as long as life intoxicates us; once we are sober we cannot help seeing that it is all a delusion, a stupid delusion." The sole secure solution to nihilistic depression, Tolstoy concludes, is by believing in and "seeking God, for there can be no life without God."[25] Earlier, Kierkegaard's classic study of despair likewise insists that the only remedy is recognition of the self's divine grounding that inspires the self to elevate itself toward the vision of God. "The self is in sound health and free from despair only when, precisely by having been in despair, it is grounded transparently in God." Without such grounding, he argues, self-reflection only intensifies the morbidity: "the more consciousness, the more intense the despair." Yet self-reflection – however painful – is affirmed by Kierkegaard; for without it the self can never properly realize its essential spirit and relationship to God, and thus permanently escape from despair.[26] "The depressed person is a radical, sullen atheist," claims our contemporary Julia Kristeva in her book on melancholia, for very different (psychoanalytic) reasons.[27]

---

[24] Alexander Pope, *An Essay on Man* (London: Cheapside, 1811), 61. and John Ruskin, "Wisdom and Folly in Science II," in *The Eagle's Nest. Ten Lectures on the Relation of Natural Science to Art, given before the University of Oxford in Lent Term, 1872* (London: Smith, Elder & Co., 1872), 30.

[25] Leo Tolstoy, *Confession*, trans. David Patterson (New York: Norton, 1983), 30, 71, 72, 75.

[26] Soren Kierkegaard, *The Sickness unto Death* in *Fear and Trembling and The Sickness Unto Death*, trans. W. Lowrie (New York: Anchor, 1954), 163, 175.

[27] Julia Kristeva, *Black Sun: Depression and Melancholia*, trans. L. Roudiez (New York: Columbia University Press, 1989), 5.

III: Modern Critiques

Not surprisingly, modern intellectuals with less commitment to traditional Christian or idealist doctrines of the soul's transcendent immortality and divine connection have been more prone to question the value of self-knowledge through self-examination. Johan Wolfgang van Goethe's critique is exemplary and influential. Fearful that the Delphic maxim confines the mind to a stifling isolation that promotes ignorance, inaction, morbidity, and "psychological self-torture," he insists that the only way to approve the command to "know thyself" is to interpret it as knowing the world in which one lives and acts. This includes knowing one's relations to other selves who provide enlightening reflections that help one know one's own self. "We mustn't interpret it," Goethe warns, in what he calls the ascetic sense of "our modern hypochondriacs, humorists... and *Heautontimorumenen* [self-torturers], but [it] quite simply means: pay attention to yourself, watch what you are doing so that you come to realize how you stand *vis-à-vis* your fellows and the world in general."[28] Elsewhere, he elaborates:

> that great and important-sounding phrase *erkenne dich selbst* merits the suspicion that it was a device of secretly bound priests, who confused men with unattainable requirements and wanted to lead them away from the activities of the outer world to an inner false contemplation. Man knows himself only in so far as he knows the world,... and he becomes aware of himself only in it. Each new object, if looked at well, opens up in us a new way to see [ourselves].[29]

Rigorous self-examination is especially unwise and unhealthy, Goethe argues, because it is perversely unnatural and its goal of self-knowledge impossible. The command "that man should strive to know himself... is a singular requisition, with which no one complies or indeed ever will comply. Man is by all his senses and efforts directed to externals – to the world around him, and he has to know this so far, and to make it so far serviceable, as he requires for his own ends.... Altogether, man is a darkened being; he knows not whence he comes, nor whither he goes; he knows little of the world, and least of himself."[30]

---

[28] Johann Wolfgang Goethe, *Maxims and Reflections*, trans. Elisabeth Stopp (London: Penguin, 1988), 88; "Sprüche: Aus Makariens Archiv," in *Goethes Werke* (Frankfurt: Insel Verlag, 1966), vol. 6, 479.

[29] Johann Wolfgang Goethe, "Allgemeine Naturwissenschaft," in *Goethes Werke* (Hamburg: Christian Wegner Verlag, 1955), vol. 13, 38.

[30] Johann Wolfgang Goethe, *Gespräche mit Eckermann* (Leipzig: Insel Verlag, 1921), 490. I use the English translation from *Conversations of Goethe with Eckermann and Soret*, trans. John Oxenford (London: Smith, Elder & Co., 1850), vol. 2, 180.

Goethe's argument not only recalls Montaigne's image of our natural outward gaze (and Montaigne's humanist spirit of pragmatic fallibilism); it also looks forward to William James's critique of self-reflection in terms of what he calls the "law of parsimony" in consciousness.[31] Because we must economize our attention, the pressing demands of life and action will not allow us to focus long and intently on ourselves. Even if we succeed in grasping ourselves, we must immediately forget ourselves to direct attention to ever-new elements in the changing flux of experience. As Goethe's pithy couplet puts this point: "*Erkenne dich! – was hab'ich da für Lohn?/Erkenne ich mich, muss ich gleich davon.*"[32]

Thomas Carlyle, who translated Goethe and greatly admired him, likewise rejects "the folly of that impossible Precept *Know Thyself*... till it be translated into this partially possible one, *Know what thou canst work at.*"[33] Convinced that the impossible Delphic maxim also implies the passivity and self-torture of introspective contemplation, Carlyle rejects this futile "tormented" project for one of external action, in which one more productively knows oneself through one's deeds and works. "Think it not thy business, this of knowing thyself; thou art an unknowable individual: know what thou canst work at; and work at it, like a Hercules! That will be thy better plan."[34]

Given Friedrich Nietzsche's notorious "death of God" thesis, his mordant skepticism towards idealist notions of mind or soul, and his ferocious critique of the self-flagellation of Christian conscience, it is not surprising that he challenges the traditional injunction to self-knowledge as psychologically unhealthy, unnatural, and indeed impossible. "This digging into one's self, this straight, violent descent into the pit of one's being, is a painful and dangerous undertaking. A man who does it may easily take such hurt that no physician can heal him," Nietzsche writes in "Schopenhauer as Educator."[35] "What indeed does a man know about himself?" he continues in his essay on "Truth and Lies in an Extra-moral Sense." "Nature keeps secret from him most things, even

---

[31] William James, *The Principles of Psychology* (Cambridge, MA: Harvard University Press, 1983), 1107.

[32] Johann Wolfgang Goethe, "Sprichtwörtlich," in Eduard Scheidemantel (ed.), *Goethes Werke* (Berlin: Deutsches Verlagshaus Bong & Co., 1891), vol. 1, 366.

[33] Thomas Carlyle, *Sartor Resartus* (London: Chapman and Hall, 1831), 114.

[34] Thomas Carlyle, *Past and Present*, 2nd ed. (London: Chapman and Hall, 1845), 264.

[35] Friedrich Nietzsche, "Schopenhauer als Erzieher," in G. Colli and M. Montinari (eds.), *Friedrich Nietzsche: Sämtliche Werke*, vol. 1 (Berlin: de Gruyter, 1999), 340; my translation. For a published English translation, "Schopenhauer as Educator," in *Nietzsche: Untimely Meditations*, trans. R.J. Hollingdale (Cambridge: Cambridge UP, 1983), 129.

about his body . . . so as to banish and lock him into a proud, delusional consciousness!" Echoing Montaigne's idea that such self-ignorance is a beneficial gift of nature's providence, Nietzsche cautions, "woe to the fateful curiosity which might be able for a moment to look out and down through a crevice in the chamber of consciousness, and discover that man, indifferent to his own ignorance, is resting on the pitiless, the greedy, the insatiable, the murderous, as if hanging in dreams on the back of a tiger."[36] Here Nietzsche moves beyond the familiar worries that self-examination brings painfully destructive and paralyzing consciousness of limitation or sin, powerfully prefiguring the Freudian notion of a far more vicious and unruly unconscious from which we are helpfully protected by ignorance of self.

Like Goethe and Carlyle, Nietzsche prefers the projective activity of self-cultivation to the introspective immanence of self-examination, hence his famous injunction "to become what one is." Rejecting the very idea of a fixed essential self to be known, Nietzsche instead advocates a self that emerges through a process of perfectionist becoming: "Active, successful natures act, not according to the dictum 'know thyself,' but as if there hovered before them the commandment: 'will a self and thou shalt *become* a self' . . . whereas the inactive and contemplative cogitate on what they *have* already chosen."[37] For the bold and willful spirit of "self-cultivation," he thus concludes, "*nosce te ipsum* [i.e., know thyself] would be the recipe for destruction."[38]

Twentieth-century thinkers as different as Ludwig Wittgenstein, William James, and Michel Foucault adapt this notion of a malleable, constructed self that is always in the making together with the perfectionist ideal to become a different, better self. James's epoch-making *The Principles of Psychology* (1890) radically dispenses with the idea of a transcendental ego, while defining the self as a bundle of habits and instructing how habits could be changed. His meliorist ideal of self-development advocates a "strenuous mood" heroically exercising "active will" toward the "character of progress."[39] By his own confession, Wittgenstein went to

---

[36] Friedrich Nietzsche, "Ueber Wahrheit und Lüge im aussermoralischen Sinne," in G. Colli and M. Montinari (eds.), *Friedrich Nietzche: Sämtliche Werke*, vol. 1 (Berlin: De Gruyter, 1999), 877; my translation.

[37] Friedrich Nietzsche, *Human, All Too Human*, trans. R.J. Hollingdale (Cambridge: Cambridge UP, 1996), 294.

[38] Friedrich Nietzsche, *Ecce Homo*, trans. R.J. Hollingdale (London: Penguin, 1992), 35.

[39] See William James, *Principles of Psychology*, 1140; and *Talks to Teachers on Psychology and to Students on Some of Life's Ideals*. (New York: Dover, 1962), 143.

war in 1914 not for the sake of country but through an intense desire "to turn into a different person," and his continuous striving to improve himself and his philosophical positions helps explain why most of his works were published posthumously and why his notebooks include the injunction: "You must change the way you live."[40] Self-transformation rather than self-knowledge, Foucault insists, is the guiding goal of the philosophical life: "The main interest in life and work is to become someone else that you were not in the beginning."[41] As Wittgenstein acknowledges that self-examination can be painfully difficult ("The folds of my heart always want to stick together, and to open it I must always tear them apart"), so Foucault highlights the tormenting interrogational practices of our culture that have been inspired by the ideal of self-knowledge, and instead privileges self-cultivation as the higher ideal.[42] Knowing the dolors of depression, both philosophers seriously contemplated suicide. It had been the solution for two of Wittgenstein's impressive older brothers, and it so fascinated Foucault that he not only attempted it, but also studied it and publicly advocated for its legitimation.[43]

William James, who suffered from repeated attacks of melancholy and related psychosomatic ailments, confessed to his brother Henry that he welcomed a university teaching job because it would divert him from "those introspective studies which had bred a sort of philosophical hypochondria."[44] Although his *Principles of Psychology* urges and indeed demonstrates exquisite expertise of introspective analysis, James (as already noted in earlier chapters) nevertheless vigorously warns against its use in practical life, arguing the case more explicitly than Foucault

---

[40] Ray Monk, *Ludwig Wittgenstein: The Duty of Genius* (London: Penguin, 1990), 111–12; and Ludwig Wittgenstein, *Culture and Value*, trans. Peter Winch (Oxford: Basil Blackwell, 1980), 27.

[41] Michel Foucault, "Technologies of the Self," in Luther H. Martin, Huck Gutman and Patrick Hutton (eds.), *Technologies of the Self* (Amherst: University of Massachusetts Press, 1988), 9.

[42] See Wittgenstein, *Culture and Value*, 57; and Foucault, "Technologies of the Self," 16–49.

[43] On Wittgenstein's preoccupation with suicide and his great admiration for Otto Weininger, who theatrically killed himself in the home where Beethoven died, see Monk, *Ludwig Wittgenstein*, 19–25, 185–86. For Foucault's preoccupation with suicide, see James Miller, *The Passion of Michel Foucault* (New York: Simon and Schuster, 1993), 54–55; and for his subordination of self-knowledge to self-cultivation or self-care, see Foucault, "Technologies of the Self," 16–49.

[44] On the "philosophical hypochondria" of "introspective studies," see James's letter to brother Henry of August 24, 1872, in *The Correspondence of William James*, vol. 1, (Charlottesville: University Press of Virginia, 1992), 167.

or Wittgenstein ever did. Intense self-examination, James writes, involves

> *strong feeling about one's self* [that] *tends to arrest the free association of one's objective ideas and motor processes.* We get the extreme example of this in the mental disease called melancholia. A melancholic patient is filled through and through with intensely painful emotion about himself. He is threatened, he is guilty, he is doomed, he is annihilated, he is lost. His mind is fixed, as if in a cramp on these feelings of his own situation, and in all the books on insanity you may read that the usual varied flow of his thoughts has ceased. His associative processes, to use the technical phrase, are inhibited; and his ideas stand stock-still, shut up to their one monotonous function of reiterating inwardly the fact of the man's desperate estate. And this inhibitive influence is not due to the mere fact that his emotion is *painful*.[45]

We must, James continues, free our selves – our thoughts, volitions, and actions – "from the inhibitive influence of reflection upon them, of egoistic preoccupation about their results," of "the over-active conscience" and self-consciousness. Of course, one must prepare oneself through thoughtful study and work, but then recall his maxim for effective action, self-expression, and self-development: "trust your spontaneity and fling away all further care."[46]

IV: Contemporary Psychology and Varieties of Self-Reflection

Widely recognized as a founder of modern psychology, James could find his view widely supported by recent psychological literature on self-examination. Current studies, which analyze this behavior under the notion of rumination, not only point to its negative psychological affects but also link it in particular to the morbidity of creative people. As novelist William Styron notes in his own memoir of melancholia:

> Despite depression's eclectic reach, it has been demonstrated with fair convincingness that artistic types (especially poets) are particularly vulnerable to the disorder – which, in its graver, clinical manifestation takes upward of twenty percent of its victims by way of suicide. Just a few of these fallen artists, all modern, make up a sad but scintillating roll call: Hart Crane, Vincent van Gogh, Virginia Woolf, Arshile Gorky, Cesare Pavese, Romain Gary, Vachel Lindsay, Sylvia Plath, Henry de Montherlant, Mark Rothko, John Berryman, Jack London, Ernest Hemingway, William Inge, Diane Arbus, Tadeusz

---

[45] William James, "The Gospel of Relaxation," in *Talks To Teachers*, 108–109.
[46] Ibid., 109.

Borowski, Paul Celan, Anne Sexton, Sergei Esenin, Vladimir Mayakovsky – the list goes on.[47]

In linking creativity with depression, recent psychological research suggests that self-reflection is the underlying root of the connection. Findings have indicated not only that "negative affect leads to increased self-reflective rumination and... that inducing self-reflective rumination leads to increased negative affect," but also that self-reflecting people tend to be both more creative and more prone to morbidity. Just as the causal link with depressive feelings is usually explained through the negative judgments of imperfections that rigorous self-examination typically yields, so increased creativity is explained as resulting from the fact that self-examiners take themselves more seriously and thus have greater motivation for distinctive creative expression. Moreover, their sustained practice of reflecting on themselves develops greater fluency of thought (such fluency measured in quantity of new ideas within a given time span), which in turn promotes creativity.[48]

Although the arguments linking self-examination and self-knowledge with depression are empirically supported, I will defend the value of self-reflection by suggesting that we need a more careful parsing of its modes and uses than its detractors (or its advocates) have provided. First, we should recognize, with Socrates, that any viable program of self-cultivation and transformation needs to start with some grasp of what one is so that one can have some sense of what one wants to change and whether or how one is changing. To get where one wants to go, it helps to know where one is. The first step to correcting a bad habit is to recognize what that habit actually is. If, as James argues, the self is a malleable bundle of habits,[49] a crucial first step to self-improvement is probing the present limits of one's self in order to grasp the needed dimensions and directions

---

[47] William Styron, *Darkness Visible: A Memoir of Madness* (New York: Random House, 1990), 35–36. Styron also notes the suicide of Primo Levi, while further suggesting that the apparently accidental deaths of Randall Jarrell and Albert Camus also bore a distinct suicidal flavor (22–23, 30–32). We should recall that Camus, in defining suicide as the "one truly serious philosophical problem," also cautions that, "Beginning to think is beginning to be undermined." See Albert Camus, "The Myth of Sisyphus," in *The Myth of Sisyphus and Other Essays*, trans. Justin O'Brien (New York: Random House, 1955), 3–4.

[48] P. Verhaeghen, J. Joormann, and R. Kahn, "Why We Sing the Blues: The Relation Between Self-Reflective Rumination, Mood, and Creativity," *Emotion* 5 (2005): 226–32. See also S. Nolen-Hoeksema, "Responses to Depression and Their Effects on the Duration of Depressive Episodes," *Journal of Abnormal Psychology* 100 (1991): 569–52; and S. Nolen-Hoeksema and J. Morrow, "Effects of Rumination and Distraction on Naturally Occurring Depressed Mood," *Cognition & Emotion* 7 (1993): 561–70.

[49] James, *Principles of Psychology*, 109.

of change. As Wittgenstein advocates, "If anyone is unwilling to descend into himself, because this is too painful, he will remain superficial."[50]

If we look more carefully at Nietzsche, we see that his repudiation of self-reflection is not complete, because a certain degree of self-knowledge is implied in his ideal of self-cultivation. "Each of us bears a productive uniqueness within him as the core of his being; and when he becomes aware of it, there appears around him a strange penumbra which is the mark of his singularity," he writes in "Schopenhauer as Educator." Recognition of this uniqueness is crucial for spurring your efforts of self-cultivation toward a higher self with the aid of exemplary authors who both inspire you toward realizing this higher self (that Nietzsche calls "your own true self" or "your true nature") and help keep you from becoming "depressed and melancholic" from this lonely labor of focus on the self.[51] Even when describing self-cultivation in terms of the deceptive fabrications and concealments of self-fashioning, Nietzsche recognizes that such artful stylizing requires self-observation and self-knowledge. One must:

> survey all the strengths and weaknesses of [one's] nature and then fit them into an artistic plan until every one of them appears as art and reason and even weaknesses delight the eye. Here a large mass of second nature has been added; there a piece of original nature has been removed – both times through long practice and daily work at it. Here the ugly that could not be removed is concealed; there it has been reinterpreted and made sublime.[52]

If self-transformation must begin with clear, explicit recognition of what one already is, we can understand why Wittgenstein insists, "A confession has to be part of your new life," for "a man will never be great if he misjudges himself."[53]

Second, since many advocates and practitioners of self-reflection have apparently not suffered from melancholia to any significant extent, there does not seem to be a necessary link between self-reflection and depression. So we need to inquire more precisely about the conditions or modes in which self-examination becomes morbidly depressing. One such condition seems to be an unrelenting, uncontrollable focus on the negative – negative judgments, negative affects, hypochondriac fears of negative

---

[50] Rush Rhees, ed., *Recollections of Wittgenstein* (Oxford: Blackwell, 1984), 174. See also Wittgenstein, *Culture and Value*, 49: "A man will never be great if he misjudges himself."
[51] Nietzsche, "Schopenhauer as Educator," 127, 129, 143, 144.
[52] Friedrich Nietzsche, *The Gay Science*, trans. Walter Kaufmann (New York: Vintage, 1974), 232.
[53] Wittgenstein, *Culture and Value*, 18, 49.

futures, and a general negativity of the meaningless of one's life. Positive dimensions and hopes are totally eclipsed or obliterated in the obsessive gloom radiating from melancholy's scorching black sun.

Negativity itself, however, is perhaps not the most depressing aspect of melancholic self-reflection; the uncontrollable, compulsive nature of such rumination may be worse. Kant thus defines the melancholia of hypochondria or the hypochondria of melancholia (the two terms, as Styron notes, being used interchangeably until the nineteenth century) precisely in terms of the mind's lack of "power to master its pathological feelings" by willfully diverting attention from its "brooding" about "fictitious disease" and imagined "ills."[54] The core problem, then, is the mind's weakness of will that is powerless to stop us from unwillingly "paying attention to mental and bodily phenomena."[55] The inability to control one's direction of thought and stem its passive repetitive feeding on morbidity creates, in turn, a strong negative feeling of impotence that heightens one's already negative mood and passive inertia, thus making it ever harder to divert one's attention to positive thoughts and action that could remedy the situation.

Contemporary psychological literature underlines this passive, uncontrollable dimension of melancholic self-reflection by defining rumination in precisely such terms. Susan Noelen-Hoeksema, a leading researcher in connecting depression and rumination (and in documenting their particularly frequent and strong combination in women), defines "rumination" as "passively and repetitively focusing on one's symptoms of distress," and argues that women are more likely to exhibit this uncontrolled, excessive focus because they tend to have a more diminished sense of mastery and control than men as well as more limited scope for remedial action in the world.[56] But must self-reflection be passive and uncontrollable? Aren't there forms of self-observation that instead display and encourage active, disciplined, and heightened control of mental focus? Doesn't such sharpening of mental concentration, acuity, and willpower constitute part of the traditional philosophical argument for self-examination and self-knowledge?

Self-reflective meditative disciplines in both Asian and Western traditions have long justified and sustained themselves by providing their

---

[54] Kant, *The Conflict of the Faculties*, 187, 189; and see Styron, *Darkness Visible*, 44.
[55] Kant, *Reflexionen zur Kritische Philosophie*, 68; my translation.
[56] S. Nolen-Hoksema, J. Larson, and C. Grayson, "Explaining the Gender Difference in Depressive Symptoms," *Journal of Personality and Social Psychology* 77 (1999): 1061–1072.

diligent practitioners with enhanced mental focus, strength of will, spiritual peace, psychic happiness, and somatic well being (including great pleasure). Recent psychological research is also beginning to realize that self-examination or "personal self-consciousness" includes a wide variety of motives, styles, and foci, so that it should not be narrowly identified with passive, obsessive, depression-promoting rumination. One study shows a clear distinction between neurotic self-attentiveness (or *rumination*) and intellectually curious self-attentiveness (or *reflection*). If the former seems clearly linked to depression and motivations of fear and anxiety, the latter is instead essentially motivated by active, positive curiosity, not significantly correlated with bad feelings but instead saliently linked to "self control" and "conscientiousness" that imply willpower and mental mastery.[57]

Other recent studies in experimental psychology and neurophysiology have demonstrated that meditation training (including disciplines of self-examination) can effectively reduce symptoms of anxiety, depression, and panic, thus generating more positive affect in the meditating subjects.[58] Further experiments have established the neurological basis of this positive power. Having determined that positive feelings and a "resilient affective style" are associated with high levels of left prefrontal activation in the brain and high levels of antibody titers to influenza vaccine, scientists have shown that subjects introduced to an eight-week meditation training program display not only significantly higher levels of left-sided anterior activation than the control group of non-meditators but also significant increases in antibody titers.[59] Such studies clearly suggest that disciplined forms of meditative self-monitoring can improve our mental health and powers.

---

[57] P. Trapnell and J. Campbell, "Private Self-Consciousness and the Five-Factor Model of Personality: Distinguishing Rumination from Reflection," *Journal of Personality and Social Psychology* 76 (1999): 284–304.

[58] See, for example, J. Kabat-Zinn et al., "Effectiveness of a Meditation-Based Stress Reduction Program in the Treatment of Anxiety Disorders," *American Journal of Psychiatry* 149 (1992): 936–43; and J. Kabat-Zinn, A. Chapman, and P. Salmon, "The Relationship of Cognitive and Somatic Components of Anxiety to Patient Preference for Alternative Relaxation Techniques," *Mind/Body Medicine* 2 (1997): 101–09. The meditative disciplines used were yoga, body scan, and seated meditation.

[59] See Richard J. Davidson et al., "Alterations in Brain and Immune Function Produced by Mindfulness Meditation," *Psychosomatic Medicine* 65 (2003): 564–70; and Richard J. Davidson, "Well-Being and Affective Style: Neural Substrates and Biobehavioural Correlates," *Philosophical Transactions of the Royal Society* Series B 359 (2004): 1395–411.

Identifying the obsessive feature of rumination as key to its morbidity should help us recognize that condemnations of self-knowledge as detrimental to mental health too often wrongly assimilate such knowledge with relentless, disproportionate overuse of self-conscious self-examination. Too much of any good thing can be bad, and that is the case for self-reflection, whose value depends on using it in the appropriate circumstances and measures. Here it is worth recalling that alongside the maxim to "know thyself," Apollo's Delphic temple inscribed the maxim "nothing too much," as if to insist on the need for appropriate moderation in understanding and applying the first maxim.[60]

VI: Somatic Self-Consciousness

Besides different styles, motives, quantities, contexts, and levels of self-control in self-examining consciousness, there are also different foci to distinguish. One useful distinction is that between attending to one's own experience in contrast to thinking about how one appears to others (whether in terms of bodily appearance, character, social status, or overall identity). And within one's own experience, some might wish to distinguish examining one's mind, character, or soul from examining one's somatic feelings. Recall how Kant and the Neoplatonists contrasted the uplifting duty to reflect on one's soul with the unhealthy degeneracy of somatic reflection. As someone who has been advocating and practicing the discipline of somatic reflection for more than a decade – not only as a philosopher engaged in somaesthetics, but as a professional somatic educator in the Feldenkrais Method, I have a stake in defending somatic self-awareness and reflection against the familiar condemnations of asocial selfishness, morbid passivity, obsessive weakness of will, melancholic hypochondria, and ruination of effective action. Having already elaborated much of this defense elsewhere, let me conclude by focusing on how somatic self-awareness relates most specifically to the tradition of self-knowledge and the issue of melancholia.

First, we should note that our Western philosophical tradition does contain some advocates of reflective body consciousness, among them Montaigne, Nietzsche, and Dewey who all, in different ways, inspired my work in somaesthetics. Celebrating its use for magnifying our sensuous

---

[60] Perhaps the third Delphic maxim, "Give a pledge, and trouble is at hand," can also be interpreted as reaffirming the danger of pledging or committing oneself wholly and inflexibly to any single ideal.

pleasures through "the greater... attention that we lend" them, Montaigne urges us to "meditate on any satisfaction" so that it reverberates beyond the "senses" (M, 853, 854). Nietzsche's critique of self-examining consciousness as fruitless and unhealthy finds a distinctive contrast in his recommendation to increase our self-knowledge with respect to corporeal matters. Complaining that "man has not known himself physiologically," Nietzsche recommends taking "the body... [as] the starting point," since "the body, as our most personal possession, our most certain being, in short our ego" inspires more faith and more promising possibilities of self-knowledge than the ethereal notions of the spirit or soul.[61] Affirming the body as "an unknown sage" within you that has "more reason than in your best wisdom," he urges us to "listen... to the voice of the healthy body."[62] John Dewey, though well aware of the dangers of ruminating introspection, avidly advocated and practiced the Alexander Technique of "conscious constructive control" that involves intense focusing on certain aspects of one's body posture and movement in order to understand more clearly our habitual modes of action (and thought) and thus provide a better cognitive basis for improving them.[63]

Moreover, the meditation techniques used in recent psychological research to demonstrate the salutary benefits of disciplined self-consciousness for reducing anxiety, panic, and depression while promoting better affective resilience include techniques that rely on deploying focused body consciousness: namely, yoga, body-scanning, and seated meditation (which involves intense concentration on one's breathing so as to distract the mind from other thoughts). This should not surprise us, since if yoga, *zazen*, and other systematic disciplines of somaesthetic introspection did indeed lead to the mental weakness, morbid introversion, and hypochondria that Kant and James feared, they would never have thrived for so many centuries and in such different cultures.

---

[61] Friedrich Nietzsche, *The Will to Power*, trans. Walter Kaufmann and R.J. Hollingdale (New York: Random House, 1967), 132, 133, 271, 347, 348.
[62] Friedrich Nietzsche, "Thus Spoke Zarathustra," in *The Portable Nietzsche*, trans. Walter Kaufmann (New York: Penguin, 1976), 145, 146–147.
[63] Recall Dewey's claim that he "had to control the direction" of his introspection (cited in Chapter 2, note 27 of this book), which suggests the useful distinction between disciplined somatic reflection for self-knowledge and uncontrolled personal ruminations about one's life. For Dewey's praise and application of the Alexander Technique, see Richard Shusterman, *Body Consciousness: a Philosophy of Mindfulness and Somaesthetics* (Cambridge: Cambridge University Press, 2008), ch. 6.

My own Zen training in Japan has taught me how methodical somaesthetic reflection can strengthen one's powers of mind and will by directing intensely focused consciousness to one's breathing or to other somatic feelings (such as the contact of one's feet with the floor in walking meditation). Willpower, as James insists, involves keeping attention firmly fixed on an idea and resisting the mind's natural tendency to wander. Our evolutionary instincts as well as our habits and interests prompt us to devote attention to the outside world of flux and the ever-changing perceptions that it stimulates, not to the constant and imminent experience of breathing. Even if we momentarily focus on our breathing, our attention very quickly turns to other things. It is thus extremely difficult to compel one's attention to remain focused wholly on the experience of breathing itself or of any somatic process. Disciplines of sustained somaesthetic focusing can strengthen our will by training our attention to sustain concentration and resist the inclination to wander. Breathing and the body are ideal targets for such exercises of focusing attention because they are always there to focus on, while the mind typically ignores them in running off to more interesting or demanding objects. One's increased powers of concentration can then be shifted beyond one's breathing or other somatic focus and applied more generally to better govern our thoughts and steer them away from morbid compulsive directions.

I conclude by confronting a lingering worry about the morbidity of somatic reflection. Christian, Platonist, and idealist arguments against attention to the body are often based on its essential vulnerability and imperfection. In contrast to the inspiring nobility, immortality, or even divinity of the soul, reflective focus on one's corporeal self promotes self-diminishment and self-loathing whose only value would be to compel us to look higher to a sacred soul. But even without invoking such a soul, should not somatic self-focus necessarily tend to depress us by reminding us of the mortal flaws and limitations of our flesh? Only, I would argue, if we unrealistically expect a kind of purity and perfection that we have no right to expect and whose absence should not therefore be a depressing disappointment. Without the presumption of divinely perfect bodies (immortally invincible and free from all pain, fatigue, or blemish), there is every reason to regard our somatic selves with grateful wonder and enthusiastic curiosity for the vulnerable yet astoundingly complex and well-functioning organization of biological, social, psychological, and cultural materials that we indeed are.

Not only poets, but even philosophers as staid as John Dewey have waxed lyrical over the somatic self, describing the living, sentient human body as "the most wonderful of all the structures of the vast universe" and condemning the fallacy that serious somatic attention "would somehow involve disloyalty to man's higher life." Praising F.M. Alexander's method of intensely focused somatic self-reflection for improved self-use, Dewey concludes, that when such an attitude becomes more general, not only individuals but the societies which they compose will be healthier through greater self-knowledge and self-control, as even one's will and thought is necessarily embodied.[64]

There is a more radical and paradoxical way to counter the fear of somatic reflection revealing deficiencies that diminish self-worth and lead to melancholy. It is the Buddhist option of using such reflection for denying the ultimate reality of a substantial, autonomous individual self whose imperfections could be a cause for deep depression. In this strategy, the self's apparent permanence and individuality is – through focused body consciousness – mindfully dissolved into a porous, messy welter of different elements (liquids, solids, and gases) whose transitory and changing collaboration gives rise to the temporary, fragile construct we identify as the bodily self and falsely oppose to the rest of the world from which it is temporally constructed and without whose materials and energies it could never be. Let me close with a passage from one of the Buddha's sermons advocating heightened mindfulness of body:

> A bhikkhu reflects on this very body enveloped by the skin and full of manifold impurity, from the sole up and the hair down, thinking thus: "There are in this body hair of the head, hair of the body, nails, teeth, skin, flesh, sinews, bones, marrow, kidneys, heart, liver, midriff, spleen, lungs, intestines, mesentery, stomach, faeces, bile, phlegm, pus, blood, sweat, fat, tears, grease, saliva, nasal mucus, synovial fluid, urine." ... Thus, he lives observing the body.[65]

So concludes the Buddha, knowing that such self-knowledge is far from a recipe for melancholia but instead a release from ultimately depressing illusions of the self's substantial permanence that make us take our

---

[64] John Dewey, *The Middle Works*, vol. 11 (Carbondale: Southern Illinois University Press, 1982), 351.
[65] See Walpoa Rahula, *What the Buddha Taught*, 2nd ed. (New York: Grove Press, 1974), 111.

individual selves with too much of the wrong kind of seriousness and selfishness.[66] Nothing too much, echoes the second Delphic maxim. A good place, perhaps, to end this longish chapter.

---

[66] Selfish self-absorption remains a real risk in the quest for self-knowledge. As Dewey rightly remarks, "Many good words get spoiled when the word self is prefixed to them: Words like pity, sacrifice, control, love." He does not continue this list to include knowledge, but he does explain the reason for the poison in the prefix: "The word self infects them with a fixed introversion and isolation." His worry about self-control is that, if taken too far, it will repress beneficial "growth that comes when the self is generously released." John Dewey, *Human Nature and Conduct* (Carbondale: Southern Illinois University Press, 1983), 96–97.

4

Muscle Memory and the Somaesthetic Pathologies of Everyday Life

I

"Muscle memory" is a term commonly used in everyday discourse for the sort of embodied implicit memory that unconsciously helps us perform various motor tasks we have somehow learned through habituation, either through explicit, intentional training or simply as the result of informal, unintentional, or even unconscious learning from repeated prior experience. In scientific terminology, such memory is often designated as "procedural memory" or "motor memory" because it enables us to perform various motor procedures or skills in an automatic or spontaneous fashion, without conscious deliberation of how the procedure should be followed and without any explicit calculation of how one identifies and achieves the various steps involved in the procedure and how one proceeds from step to step. Paradigmatic of such muscle-memory motor skills of performance are walking, swimming, riding a bicycle, tying one's shoes, playing the piano, driving a car, or typing on a keyboard. To be precise, these motor skills should be described as sensorimotor, because they involve coordinating sensory perception with the movement of action. Moreover, because these skills apparently rely on schemata or patterns deeply embedded in an individual's central nervous system, the core engine of memory in so-called muscle memory is not simply the body's muscles but instead also involves the brain's neural networks.

The term "muscle memory" is nonetheless deeply entrenched, perhaps because it serves some key rhetorical functions. Muscle suggests body in contrast to mind, as muscular effort is frequently contrasted to mental effort or as muscle men are typically opposed to men of thought. Because of this common brain/brawn opposition, muscle memory conveys a sense of mindless memory.[1] Such memory is mindless, however, only if we identify mind with mindfulness in the sense of explicit, critically focused consciousness or deliberate, reflective awareness. Procedural or performative tasks of implicit motor memory often require and exhibit significant mental skills and intelligence, as, for example, when a good pianist plays with spontaneity yet also with aesthetically sensitive mindfulness. In demonstrating that intelligent mind extends beyond clear consciousness, muscle memory also makes manifest the mind's embodied nature and the body's crucial role in memory and cognition.

The idea that our normal somatic skills of performative muscle memory are intelligently deployed without explicit thought or deliberation has played an important part in the cognitive rehabilitation of body and habit in contemporary philosophy, a project we can trace back to pragmatists like William James and John Dewey and to phenomenologists like Maurice Merleau-Ponty. In celebrating the body's effectively purposive yet unthinking spontaneous performance in perception, speech, art, and other forms of action, these philosophers recognize that such intelligent spontaneity is not mere uneducated reflex but rather the acquired product of somatically sedimented habit, which often goes by the name of muscle memory. Because the somatic self is essentially expressed through this purposive intelligence, while the term "body" is too often identified with mere physicality, I use the term soma to designate the living, sentient, purposive, perceptive body that forms the focus of the interdisciplinary project of somaesthetics.

The performative procedural skills of muscle memory comprise only one of the different kinds of implicit memory that are deeply grounded in the soma. Although the habits and skills of such memory are typically very welcome and useful, we also develop bad habits of muscle memory, many of which go unnoticed not only because of their implicit character but also because their detrimental effects are usually not so extreme as to call our conscious attention to them. Such habits of muscle memory (though undetected and seemingly benign) impair our somaesthetic perception and our consequent experience and performance. Their remedy requires a disruption of implicit memory so that it can be improved

---

[1] Here I should note that another meaning of muscle memory refers to the phenomenon that when a person suspends a sustained weightlifting program for a prolonged period and then resumes it, his earlier-trained muscles are able to return to their previous levels of size and strength more quickly and easily than was necessary to reach those levels originally, as if the muscles recalled their prior levels.

through reconstruction. After exploring the soma's role in diverse modes of implicit memory, this chapter analyzes a cluster of everyday problems that arise from such memory, and then suggests how such problems can be treated through methods of heightened body consciousness that render the implicit more explicit.[2]

II

1. Perhaps the most basic implicit memory is that of oneself, the implicit sense of continuing personal identity. When I awake in the morning, even before I open my eyes, I have the implicit memory (as an implicit feeling) of being the same person that went to sleep the night before. I do not need to recall explicitly that I am the same person, nor do I even explicitly recognize or thematize the feeling of sameness; but this implicit feeling of being the same abides with me and provides a narrative ground or core for my sense of self and for my perception of the world. This implicit body memory or feeling of continuity was recognized by William James, who construed it as the foundational factor not only for personal identity but also for the unity of consciousness and thus essentially for the coherence of a person's thinking.

This implicit feeling of being the same self as one was before (even if only a split second before), James argues, is essentially a bodily feeling. As he puts it in *The Principles of Psychology*, our thoughts are united as being ours because "as we think we feel our bodily selves as the seat of the thinking. If the thinking be *our* thinking, it must be suffused through all its parts with that peculiar warmth and intimacy" with the implicit memory of being the same body, "the feeling of the same old body always there," even if the body is, strictly speaking, always changing.[3] This implicit memory of feeling the same body, James insists, helps "form a *liaison* between all the things of which we become successively aware" (PP 235) and thus serves to organize and unify the complexity of experience through its relation to "the objective nucleus of every man's experience, his own body," which he feels implicitly as "a continuous percept."[4]

---

[2] This analysis draws on my professional practice as a somatic educator and therapist in the Feldenkrais Method.
[3] William James, *The Principles of Psychology* (Cambridge, MA: Harvard University Press, 1983), 235; hereafter PP.
[4] William James, *Essays in Radical Empiricism* (Cambridge, MA: Harvard University Press, 1976), 33; hereafter RE.

2. If one basic mode of implicit memory is the self-memory of being the same person, of remembering implicitly who one is,[5] a second crucial mode is remembering *where* one is; and very often this memory includes implicitly recalling how one gets from where one is to where one wants to go. We have all had experiences of walking a familiar route – say from one's office to the bookshop a few blocks away – and suddenly realizing one has arrived at one's destination without ever having thought about or explicitly remembered the path taken. Similarly, when we arrive at the bookshop we implicitly remember its familiar feel and layout without consciously recalling it to memory. These implicit memories of location are of course deeply grounded in the soma, which essentially determines one's location and sense of place: one's perspective on the world and one's coordinates of direction in it.

As we argued in earlier chapters, we know the world largely because we inhabit it through our soma. Because, as a body, I am also a thing among things in the world, that world of things is also present and implicitly comprehensible to me. Because the soma as subjectivity is affected by the world's objects and energies, it incorporates and implicitly remembers their regularities, thus recalling features of spaces and places without needing to engage in explicit recollection or reflection. To see any place (or any thing), one must see it from some point of view, a position that defines one's directional planes of observation and determines the meaning of up and down, forward and backward, left and right, inside and outside. One's body supplies this point of view – one's center or origin of coordinates – by being what locates a person in space and gives that lived space its directionality. Moreover, it also gives us our sense of the volume of space, because this sense relies on our experience of moving through space, an experience and ability that depends on the body's powers of locomotion.

As a holistic sensorimotor subjectivity, the soma is essential to spatial memory in yet another way. Unlike some other perceptual dimensions, our sense of space does not directly depend on a specific sensory organ but is instead essentially the product of multisensory representations that build up a spatial map through a learning process, implicit or explicit.

---

[5] Such implicit memory of knowing who one is in terms of knowing one is the same person now as in the past does not, as implicit memory, require that one remembers who one is in terms of an explicit descriptive identity of being a certain person with a particular name, age, gender, and profession. The formulation of such descriptive terms involves, of course, explicit thought, but on the basis of implicit memory of self one could recall these descriptions if one were asked.

In the implicit learning process, where the forming of a spatial map does not involve special attention or explicit conscious effort, it is through the soma's unreflective perceptions of space that a space is learned and remembered. Not only can we remember spaces we have inhabited and how to negotiate our ways through them through implicit memory without consciously reflecting on representations of those spaces in explicit thought, we can even first come to know and learn to remember a space through implicit means – without consciously making an effort to remember, without engaging our explicit, voluntary attention to learn the space. Experimental studies have confirmed what we know from ordinary experience: While explicit, focused attention facilitates the forming and stabilizing of a spatial map, such maps can be formed and stabilized (though not as powerfully) through the sort of unreflective ambient attention that an animal has just by moving through or inhabiting space.[6]

The soma's potent role in understanding and remembering space is highlighted and heightened by its asymmetries. The body's front is different from its back, its top is different from its bottom; these asymmetries are reflected in differential capacities of memory. Studies show that it is harder to retrieve spatial memory of left and right (dimensions that are symmetrical in the body) than the asymmetrical dimensions of front/back and top/bottom. For the upright observer, the head/foot axis is the easiest for recalling spatial information because it is also "correlated with the only asymmetric axis of the world, the axis created by gravity." But when reclining, observers remember information fastest on the front/back axis, which roughly correlates with the axis of what can be seen versus not seen.[7]

We sometimes distinguish place from mere space, to characterize the former as a particular landmark with value or meaning (a home, school, stadium, mall, or parking lot). Place in this sense helps define the more abstract concept of space as a general area through which movement is possible (and where places represent distinct points where one might pause in that movement). Similarly, we can distinguish memory of space and place, the latter being easier and very useful for the former. For example, we implicitly remember to turn right at a certain point because we implicitly remember the corner café as the place where we need to turn right. The body plays a central role in such memory through its

---

[6] Eric R. Kandel, *In Search of Memory* (New York: Norton, 2006), 312–313.
[7] Barbara Tversky, "Remembering Spaces," in *The Oxford Handbook of Memory* (Oxford: Oxford University Press, 2000), 371.

remembered feel of certain places (the smell of the coffee, the need to navigate one's path around the outdoor tables, etc.).

Certain places leave such strong somatic imprints of feeling that it is involuntarily evoked whenever we enter them. My life as department chair was so pressured that each time I entered that office, even during vacation, I shivered with memories of hectic work and stress so that it was impossible for me to relax or think about anything but my administrative duties, even when I was in principle free to do so. My muscle memory of that place was automatically triggered, shortening my breath and tensing my posture, though also providing implicit recall of where all the necessary tools could be found to perform my job. While we're in my office, it's worth mentioning another sort of memory (implicit or explicit) that could be grouped with memory of space and place – situational memory.

My chairman's office was a place of repeated situation types – for example, interviewing a job candidate or meeting individually with junior faculty members to discuss their progress toward promotion and tenure. Implicit somatic memory of such situations allowed me to offer with smooth spontaneity (i.e., without the awkward hesitancy of deliberative thought) the appropriate greeting and comfortable chair to my interlocutor, to assume the appropriate posture, tone, and demeanor that such situations call for – where one must be kind and encouraging but at the same time represent the impersonal authority and responsibility of one's executive position. There are countless situations in which the soma enacts such implicit situational memory. Sports provide excellent examples; experienced athletes spontaneously recognize (through implicit somatic memory) those situations in which they should pass the ball and to whom and at what speed and trajectory they should pass it.

3. A third form of implicit memory with deep bodily grounding might be described as interpersonal, or more broadly as intersomatic, so as to include nonhuman companions like animals. We develop ways of being with and reacting to certain other bodies, and these modes of relationship are incorporated into our muscle memory as habitual attitudes or schemata of action that are spontaneously recalled and repeated in the presence of those other bodies, with the appropriate contextual variations. Did you ever notice that although you have shared with your spouse or longtime lover countless beds in countless bedrooms, you always seem to lie together in the same orientation, on the same side? You do not have to think about which side of the bed you should take; and if, for some reason, you find yourself lying next to your lover on the non-habitual side, it will probably feel odd or perhaps even awkward. Similarly, when walking hand in hand or with their arms around each other, couples spontaneously take up their habitual positioning. These habitual postures are assumed without thinking about them, and they establish a feeling of comfortable familiarity that typically escapes explicit recognition but nonetheless pervasively influences one's experience. The same sort of intersomatic attunement is developed between horse and rider or between a person and her pets.

Because emotions are grounded in the body, our implicit somatic memories have an affective dimension. We carry these implicit intercorporeal memories and corresponding somatic attitudes into our encounters with new people, which is why we often have an immediate, visceral feeling of comfort or discomfort when we meet someone new who is implicitly perceived as suggesting positive or negative memories. We develop such intersomatic patterns of interactions already from infancy, as Daniel Stern has shown in his extensive studies of infant interpersonal relations, and these early schemata of interaction powerfully integrate motor, cognitive, and affective dimensions.[8] By means of such somatic patterns and attunements, we learn to understand and navigate our immediate interpersonal world even before mastering linguistic expression. Although such intersomatic memories are first developed with respect to one's parents (in most cases, especially to one's mother) and other significant others, they become generalized yet also modified by later experience; and they are unreflectively woven into a complex embodied structure of habits – of affective, cognitive, social, postural, and motor dispositions that are intimately intertwined and that essentially constitute one's personality.

Such implicit affective intersomatic memories, I have argued, can help explain why ethnic and racial prejudices prove extremely resistant to rational arguments of tolerance. Because such prejudices are grounded in implicit visceral feelings and muscle memory of discomfort of which we are not fully conscious, we may not even be aware of them and of the prejudice they generate, although others will note it in our behavior. Parents can unwittingly instill such feelings in their children without saying a word and without any dramatic display of prejudice, but simply by subtle postural and facial expressions of discomfort that the sensitive child absorbs and responds to.[9]

---

[8] Daniel N. Stern, *The Interpersonal World of the Infant* (New York: Basic Books, 1985), ch. 6–7.

[9] Richard Shusterman, *Body Consciousness: A Philosophy of Mindfulness and Somaesthetics* (Cambridge: Cambridge University Press, 2008), ch. 4.

4. Our interpersonal relations take place within a larger social setting. But if interpersonal implicit memory in some way already implies the social, we can also distinguish a more distinctively social form of implicit memory, in terms of inhabiting, recalling or replaying distinctive social roles. These roles very often involve a distinctive form of embodiment. One example I remember from military service in Israel is that of the drill sergeant major at our unit's headquarters. Although typical Israeli military posture is rather relaxed, reflecting a general somatic (and more general military) ideology that advocates the supple, fluid, and flexible, our drill sergeant major had instead learned to incorporate the rigidly erect posture and very stiff, mechanical movements that define the more traditional conventions of military drill and thus of his special social role. Even when he was not performing his official duties, we could always easily recognize him on the base by his stiff posture and gait, even if we could only view him from the back and at a great distance.

Other roles have their characteristic embodiment. A policeman, a judge, a doctor all possess different forms of authority, and they differently embody them. Success in their roles requires incorporating the right bodily attitudes and comportment, whose mastery involves implicit muscle memory in spontaneously performing them.[10] Moreover, we deploy implicit memory in transitioning from one role to another. When the female police officer comes home to assume the role of a tenderly loving mother to her infant son, she does not need to explicitly remind herself to generate the different somatic dispositions and feelings appropriate to her maternal role. Muscle memory instructs her how to transition without her needing to consciously recall what it means to be a mother. Just thinking of her baby while she is driving home may initiate the proper somatic changes, even before she actually sees him and removes her uniform so her badge won't scratch him.

5. Putting on and taking off clothes are typical examples of the most obvious type of muscle memory: performative or procedural memory. Normally, we do not have to think about how to dress or undress ourselves. We typically do not notice which sock or shoe we put on first, which arm or leg is first inserted into a sleeve or trouser, which button is first buttoned, and whether in buttoning we use the index or pointer finger with the thumb. On many occasions, one decides to get ready

---

[10] In these roles, distinctive uniforms that are worn on one's body serve as bodily cues or tools to help individuals incorporate the proper somatic dispositions and comportment.

for bed and suddenly finds oneself in pajamas without remembering the various stages of undressing and then dressing for bed. Other skills of experienced mastery in performing sequential tasks range from the most common functions of walking, running, or eating with utensils to more complicated skills like swimming, dancing the tango, riding a bicycle, touch typing, driving a car, shooting a turn-around jump shot, or playing a piano sonata. These tasks include distinctively cognitive ones such as reading and writing. We perform these skills with such effortless unthinking spontaneity that we can understand why philosophers like Merleau-Ponty describe such somatic performance in terms of "marvels," "miracles," and "magic."[11]

This sort of muscle memory is certainly most efficient, by allowing us to direct our always-limited resources of explicit consciousness to other places that need it. We can thus concentrate our attention on the ideas we are writing rather than thinking of the location of the letters on the keyboard that we want to type. I can look down the basketball court to see if a teammate is open near the basket rather than having to think about how I handle the ball to dribble and then pass it to him. By freeing our consciousness to engage other things, muscle memory extends our range of attention and perception and thus enhances our freedom of action. With many complex motor skills, moreover, it is often claimed (by philosophers, psychologists, and movement experts) that if we tried to perform them by explicitly recalling and deliberating at each step, we would awkwardly stumble. As the great choreographer George Balanchine would tell his dancers, "Don't think, dear; just do."[12]

6. The last kind of implicit muscle memory I note here is an unhappy one of unfreedom – traumatic memory. Pain is implicitly remembered in the body and projected through it into future attitudes, as proverbs like "once bitten, twice shy" suggest. Many forms of education involve

---

[11] See Maurice Merleau-Ponty, *The Phenomenology of Perception*, trans. Colin Smith (London: Routlege, 1962), 94; *Signs*, trans. R.C. McCleary (Evanston, IL: Northwestern University Press, 1970), 66. For more discussion of this point, see Shusterman, *Body Consciousness*, 59–61.

[12] This frequently quoted saying of Balanchine can be found in Deborah Jowitt, *Time and the Dancing Image* (Berkeley: University of California Press, 1989), 273, but also in mass-media dance articles, such as this review found in Rachel Howard, "Ballet Polishes up Balanchine's 'Jewels,'" *San Francisco Chronicle*, April 27, 2009. Some renowned masters of dance, notably the most influential theorist and composer of Nō theater and dance, do not share this view for reasons I explain in Chapter 9 of this book, where I also explain more generally the limits of arguments that claim explicit attention to one's action is always detrimental to effective performance after the actions of performance have been learned and habituated into muscle memory.

painful disciplines of training, an approach that may have helped prompt Nietzsche's overstatement that "only what does not cease to cause pain remains in memory."[13] In productive forms of disciplinary education, if pain is deployed it is carefully controlled and framed in relationship to positive meaning and value. Traumatic memory, in contrast, is characterized by its inability to connect positively to meaning and value. Because of trauma's intense shock and pain, the victim cannot properly integrate it into a clear, conscious, meaningful memory, since the experience overwhelms one's normal sense of self, rupturing the narrative continuity that gives meaning and stability to experience, including remembered experience. Instead, as the explicit narrative memory of trauma is significantly blurred or even lost in many of its details, so the traumatic memory thrives in implicit behavioral form in terms of somatic complaints such as flashbacks (that repeatedly relive the trauma); physical symptoms such as sweating or a racing heartbeat; frightening dreams; behavioral reactions of avoiding things that might recall the traumatic experience; being easily startled, tense, or edgy or, contrastingly, emotionally numb. Such traumatic memory forms the crux of what is diagnosed as post-traumatic stress disorder (PTSD). Because traumatic memory withdraws from explicit consciousness while implicitly working through the body to preserve, reinforce, and spread its painful effects, it is very difficult to treat and overcome its devastations. Therapy thus often involves making the implicit memory more explicit in some way so it can be more clearly identified and treated.[14]

Traumatic memory is one form of implicit somatic memory that is not really advantageous. Other forms of implicit or muscle memory can prove problematic too, albeit in a milder way. When I first spoke of such problems (in a paper in French), I called them *petites pathologies*,[15] but here I wish to explore them under the category of somaesthetic pathologies of everyday life, alluding to Freud's book *Psychopathologies of*

---

[13] "Man brennt Etwas ein, damit es im Gedächtniss bleibt: nur was nicht aufhört, weh zu thun, bleibt im Gedächtniss." In Friedrich Nietzsche, *Zur Genealogie der Moral*, II.iii, in G. Colli and M. Montinari (eds.), *Friedrich Nietzsche: Sämtliche Werke*, vol. 5 (Berlin: de Gruyter, 1999), 295.

[14] For more on this topic, see B.A. van der Kolk, J. Hopper, and J. Osterman, "Exploring the nature of Traumatic Memory: Combining Clinical Knowledge with Laboratory Methods," in J. Freyd and A. DePrince (eds.), *Trauma and Cognitive Science: A meeting of Minds, Science, and Human Experience* (Philadelphia: Haworth Press, 2001), 9–31.

[15] Richard Shusterman, "Le corps en acte et en conscience," in Bernard Andrieu (ed.), *Philosophie du corps* (Paris: Vrin, 2010), 349–372.

Everyday Life, which also deals with problems far less severe than trauma, such as slips of the tongue or other minor lapses.

III

There is not space here to treat all the different ways that insufficient somaesthetic awareness (i.e., inadequate perception of our somatic comportment and feelings) leads to minor everyday problems of dysfunction, error, discomfort, pain, or decline from proper efficiency. They include unnecessary self-induced accidents like biting one's tongue when eating; tripping over one's own feet; choking by swallowing food or drink down the wrong "pipe"; hurting one's back or knee by lifting or turning in the wrong position; straining one's lower back by not noticing the discomfort experienced in having sat too long at one's workstation. Then there are everyday somaesthetic pathologies involving a variety of malfunctions in sports-related skills – such as failing to hit a ball properly (in tennis, golf, or baseball) because one is unaware that one's eyes, hands, and other body parts are not in the right position for making proper contact. We also find similar motor malfunctions in work-related activities, such as mistakenly clicking on the mouse when not really ready to send a message or other errors arising from not being sufficiently aware of one's handling of the computer keyboard or cell phone touch screen. Other common somaesthetic problems include not being able to sleep because one is not aware that one's breathing is too short and one's body too tensely held to induce a condition of repose that can induce sleep.

The various somaesthetic pathologies of everyday life could be grouped in different ways, but rather than proposing a general taxonomy here, I will discuss a few examples drawn from the five positive forms of implicit memory noted earlier, while suggesting how they may be remedied through heightened somaesthetic awareness. Organizing this discussion in terms of these different modes of muscle memory should give greater clarity and unity to our discussion.

1. In affirming an implicit abiding memory of self that provides our sense of personal identity and continuity of consciousness, James insists that it is essentially somatic, a muscle memory of feeling oneself as the same person. Even in our moments of pure thinking, "we feel the whole cubic mass of our body all the while, [and] it gives us an unceasing sense of personal existence" (PP, 316). If James describes "the past and present selves" as unified by "a uniform feeling of 'warmth,' of bodily existence... that pervades them all... and gives them a *generic* unity," he insists that "this generic unity co-exists with generic differences just as real as the unity" (PP, 318).

James's language here is not entirely clear, but I think he is not (and should not be) asserting that there is one single, isolatable, constant, and unchanging somatic "me" feeling that accompanies all my other bodily feelings and that defines my sense of unity. Rather, one's sense of being the same person is an emergent, holistic feeling of sameness based on a whole network of feelings of "warmth and intimacy" (PP, 235) between the generic pattern of one's present somatic feelings and that of one's remembered counterparts. One's actual body feelings will always change with changing conditions, although the generic pattern can remain stable while also expressing significant differences. Not all somatic feelings, according to James, have the same weight in determining one's sense of self. In *The Principles of Psychology*, he identifies the crucial somatic feelings of the core self (the innermost self of active consciousness, which he calls the "nuclear self" or "the Self of selves") with various "muscular adjustments," "*for the most part taking place within the head*" or "*between the head and throat*" (PP, 287, 288). By this he means to include adjustments of the cephalic sense organs associated with thinking, such as pressure and orientation of the eyeballs as well as muscular contractions of the brow, jaw, and glottis. It is understandable to highlight feelings in the head and neck area, which not only houses the brain, the organs of vision, hearing and taste, and the vestibular system of the inner ear (that provides stability of posture and gaze) but also the first two cervical vertebra (the atlas and axis) whose articulations and attached ligaments and muscles are what enable us to raise, lower, and rotate the head, thus affording greater scope for the head's sensory organs.

James later particularly emphasizes the bodily feelings of breathing as what gives felt unity to one's "stream of thinking," locating those feelings of breath too narrowly in the nose and throat.[16] Without insisting that

---

[16] My consciousness or "stream of thinking," James argues, relying on his own introspection, "is only a careless name for what, when scrutinized, reveals itself to consist chiefly of the stream of my breathing. The 'I think' which Kant said must be able to accompany all my objects, is the 'I breathe' which actually does accompany them." James concludes that, "breath, which was ever the original of 'spirit,' breath moving outwards, between the glottis and the nostrils, is, I am persuaded, the essence out of which philosophers have constructed the entity known to them as consciousness" (RE, 19). James surprisingly ignores both the feelings of inhalation and the fact that one very often feels one's breathing not only in the head and neck but also down into one's thoracic area, where

feelings in the head and neck area are what define our inner self-feeling, we can recognize that those feelings could be very important to one's sense of self, so that even when we do not explicitly notice these feelings they form a familiar perceptible background to our more explicit objects of consciousness and foci of attention. Such feelings can become so habitual and pervasively familiar that they form part of one's implicit sense of self. This can happen even if these particular feelings in the head and neck are neither necessary (i.e., alternative feelings are equally possible) nor beneficial.

Many individuals suffer from a somaesthetic pathology that exemplifies this situation. They have a condition of chronic excessive tension in the neck, caused by habitual reactions of muscular contraction to repeated situations of stress. Because this condition of excessive tension is habitual, it also becomes familiar as a background feeling. The affected individuals typically do not even know that they have this problem because the excessive tension feels familiar (and in that sense normal) to them; indeed, it forms part of their core feeling of who they are, even if such tension results eventually in the noticeable discomfort of headaches, neck aches, and backaches. We can recognize such people by the way they always have their shoulders quite tensed and elevated closer to the upper neck and ears than one's shoulders should normally be in a proper, adequately relaxed posture. The pressure of the raised shoulders involves muscular tensions that in turn put excessive pressure on the muscles of the neck and the cervical vertebrae; we therefore could describe this pathology as the chronically pinched neck. Besides the pain and damage to the cervical spine that this chronic contraction can eventually cause, such posture hinders the efficiency of our action, as its tensed posture inhibits movement in the neck, shoulders, and ribcage. Nonetheless, through its habituated incorporation into a familiar bodily feeling, the pinched-neck posture feels normal to those who suffer from this somaesthetic pathology, which is thus a pathology of perception (aesthesis) as well as of posture.

Clinical experience has taught me that when such a person is asked to relax his shoulders to ease his neck, he will happily assent to the request but essentially fail to comply, although he thinks he is complying (very often by making a sort of shrug that just raises the shoulders further before letting them subside to their habitual raised position). Not only

---

the movement of the lungs interacts with movements in the chest or ribcage; that same thoracic area provides the familiar background feelings of one's beating heart.

does he not realize that his elevated shoulders and neck are excessively tensed (because they feel normal to him), he also does not know how to lower or relax them because he no longer knows what that relaxed posture feels like. When, after some hands-on work with him, I induce a relaxation in his neck and shoulders, he reports that it feels a bit strange to him, that he feels somehow lazy or soft and not quite himself. He confuses the release from chronic hypertension with a loss of the familiar sense of his forceful dynamic self that has become habitually linked to his chronic feelings of excessive muscular contractions. This change of posture may thus not be psychologically comfortable for him, even if it is physiologically more comfortable and can be behaviorally more advantageous.

A patient's identity may be so intimately linked to her handicap or problem that even when she complains about the problem she may, at a deeper level, resist efforts to rid herself of it. I knew a talented, beautiful, and wealthy Parisian academic who, for many years, complained to me about being miserable because of the man she lived with. Whenever I suggested she leave him, however, she replied that this problematic relationship had become a cornerstone of her identity and her psychological coping structure, supplying her with an excuse for being unhappy and for not writing all the books she thought she should write. Without this problem, she argued, she would have no adequate excuse for her failures and would thus be even more miserable and full of self-loathing.

With respect to the somaesthetic pathology of the pinched neck, if the chronic feeling of tension is felt as an important part of the person's sense of self, then he must take the trouble of revising his familiar sense of self so that a more relaxed muscular tonus is not confused with torpor and can instead be associated with his resilient dynamism. For many individuals, to take the time and effort to make this transition may not seem worth the sacrifice, especially since the advantages of the new posture and sense of self are neither very clear nor guaranteed in advance, while the problems they currently suffer from their pinched-neck pathology seem manageably minor and familiar. That is one reason why this somaesthetic pathology remains so prevalent.

2. Muscle memory guides us in spatial orientation but it can also misguide us. One space-related somaesthetic pathology of everyday life is orientational bias. Did you ever notice that whenever you go to a movie or lecture without assigned seats you tend to sit on one side (left or right) of the room rather than the other; did you ever notice that when you are standing or sitting your range of vision is greater on one side than the other? The reason is that one's body frequently has an orientational bias; many people feel more comfortable turning toward one side rather than another, and this bias is also reflected in posture, as a tendency (when standing or sitting) to have one's body or head not perfectly straight but slightly turned toward one direction. Perhaps you sit on the right side of the movie theatre because your left eye is stronger and thus sitting on the right puts the left eye more toward the center especially when tilting your gaze leftwards (which sitting on the right enables you more comfortably to do). Or perhaps your right-side seating habit is because you implicitly feel (for a variety of possible reasons relating to your somatic history) more comfortable with your body slightly turned or shifted toward your left.

There is nothing wrong with this sort of postural bias in itself, but if we fail to recognize it and compensate for its effects, it can lead to problems. For instance, a teacher or lecturer who has a left orientational bias will often unintentionally turn his side or even back to those people in the audience who are seated to his right, without even knowing that he is excluding them from eye contact. If he is aware of this bias, he can correct for it by readjusting his posture so that he is facing more of his audience (either by centering his orientation or by stepping further back to minimize the effects of the bias). A much more dangerous result of such orientational bias is reduced ability to notice oncoming traffic from the side somewhat blinded by the bias; experience shows that many individuals tend to suffer accidents significantly more on one side than another. If orientational bias seems a likely cause for such accidents, then improved awareness of such bias through heightened somaesthetic perception is a likely remedy.

As orientational bias relates to issues of how we situate ourselves *in* space, so there are everyday somaesthetic pathologies of navigating our trajectories *through* space. Too many times my muscle memory directs my walking and driving through habitual paths toward familiar locations that are, however, not the ones I meant to choose; so I am forced to backtrack and consciously remind myself of the right destination and path. Muscle memory likewise induces everyday somaesthetic pathologies of inhabiting place, one of which was already introduced in discussing my implicit "chair's office" memory. It was pathological to be suddenly thrust into a state of breathless tension (and without even explicitly recognizing it) just by entering that place, even if I had nothing more urgent to do there that day than chat with an old friend who found it the most convenient place to meet. After somatic training improved my somaesthetic awareness, I was able to identify my pathological reaction and then treat it by explicitly applying various strategies of breathing and muscle relaxation.

3. In my discussion of implicit interpersonal muscle memory, I argued that racial and ethnic prejudice – an all-too common everyday pathology – has roots in visceral feeling, and its incorporation in implicit memory makes it very difficult for the person with the prejudice to properly recognize it, let alone extinguish it by a mere conscious judgment that such prejudice is unreasonable. Sharpening a person's awareness of her bodily feelings so that she can recognize the mild discomfort that certain races or ethnicities or other groups provoke in her can help her identify the prejudice and its roots, so that she may try to contain it or even overcome it – if she wishes to – perhaps by trying to reeducate her somatic feelings. As we know from acquired tastes in food and drink, visceral reactions or dispositions can, to some extent, be refined or transformed through sensory reeducation. Of course, if the person with prejudice has no such meliorative desire for reform, then heightening the awareness of visceral discomfort and its relation to the prejudice may not result in efforts to control or eliminate the prejudice. Indeed, heightened awareness might even strengthen the feelings of discomfort, and in that way reinforce the prejudice in rendering it more conscious. Knowledge, including self-knowledge, is not always beneficial; it depends on how it is used. One could argue that knowing one is prejudiced is a cognitive improvement on not knowing it, even if positive ethical results of such knowledge are not forthcoming.

Muscle memory can generate another minor pathology of interpersonal interaction. Some persons have characteristic postures that others find disturbing, even if the disturbing feelings remain rather mild and implicit. For example, some individuals have a way of engaging their interlocutors in conversation by coming very close to them and then tilting or leaning toward them with a rather tensely contracted soma. The motivation for this posture is typically friendly, but it often conveys a disturbingly aggressive stance to the interlocutor, who feels somehow threatened by this intrusion in her personal space, especially if the overly proximate body leaning toward her is considerably larger than her own. Her implicit reaction is to withdraw both posturally and psychologically from the friendly speaker with the aggressive stance, which tends to evoke in him a further implicit adjustment of looming still closer, perhaps with the feeling that his interlocutor is not a friendly person, even if she did harbor friendly inclinations to him – at least initially – before this unfortunate dance of approach and withdrawal resulting from his somaesthetic insensitivity to posture.

Such interpersonal problems are magnified when culturally different senses of appropriate distance come into play. Recall the joke about the international conference cocktail party where one can identify the Finns by the fact that they're the ones gradually withdrawing toward the walls of the room, retreating while conversing with the Brazilians, who are recognized by their constant forward-pressing, hands-on approach in the same conversations. Consulting intercultural guidebooks about the appropriate posture to adopt in various cultures will not solve the problem if one remains insufficiently aware of the posture one is actually assuming as well as the postural reaction of the soma with whom one is interacting. Somaesthetic awareness is necessary for both; and while many individuals spontaneously display such awareness, many others require an effort of conscious attention to cultivate and deploy this awareness.

4. Muscle memory's incorporation of social roles can create its own somaesthetic pathologies of everyday life. Take the drill sergeant from my days as an officer in Israeli military intelligence. So fully had he absorbed his professional persona – with his body always held rigidly erect in hyperextension and his habitual stiff, jerky gait and sharp, mechanical hand movements – that he seemed incapable of shedding this attitude. We laughingly imagined how he returned home to make love to his wife in the same barking cadence, mechanical gestures, and jerky rhythms that defined his somatic behavior, without him even realizing that he was behaving like a drill sergeant rather than a lover, thus missing out on love's more tender and fluid communicative pleasures. Although we never followed him home to see (or ask his wife) whether he indeed suffered from this somaesthetic pathology, I did indeed witness during my years in Israel a different form of incorporated role fixation that was implicit, unintentional, and unnoticed by the role player.

My former father-in-law, a Tel Aviv judge who dearly loved his family, did not realize that he daily brought his courtroom habitus back to the dinner table, augustly bellowing orders to family members as if they were bailiffs or accused criminals. He did not realize that his tone and body language were inappropriate, until his daughter and wife called them to his attention, and he apologized with genuine embarrassment. Fortunately, after his postprandial siesta, he awoke largely freed from his courtroom soma that had earlier been primed by a stressful morning at his job. Because it often takes time, distraction, and relaxing substances to free oneself from a deeply embodied and labor-intensified social role and prepare a differently embodied persona, I understand why bars are so important on evening commuter trains and on the pedestrian's and motorist's way home from work.

5. Implicit performative or procedural memory is indispensable for getting us efficiently through countless everyday activities. By enabling us to perform so many familiar tasks with no explicit attention, it allows us to direct our limited resources of attentive consciousness to more difficult problems. As noted earlier, a writer can focus on how to express his philosophical ideas instead of how to position his hands to perform the necessary actions for pressing the right keys to generate the letters of the words he wishes. A violinist can likewise concentrate on the expressive qualities she wants to produce rather than on the way she is gripping her instrument and positioning or moving her shoulders, torso, and arms when performing. In the same way, a DJ can concentrate on the songs or tracks he is sampling rather than on the posture of his ribcage and hips when he is spinning those records. In these and similar cases, their muscle memory performs the necessary sequential acts of muscular contraction, positioning, and movement without explicit consciousness. Unfortunately, however, as I learned from clinical practice, the habits of muscle memory formed to perform such spontaneous body adjustments often do so in ways that are not somatically advantageous and lead to unnecessary fatigue, pain, or injury. The writer develops carpal tunnel syndrome from holding his wrists too rigidly; the violinist suffers pain in the back, neck, and arms because she holds her shoulders and ribcage too tight, thus forcing her bow strokes to be more effortful. The DJ (who happened to be a grad student at the New School) fell victim to a very sore elbow, because his habit of freezing his hips and ribcage in mental concentration (a habit quite common in academic readers who daily spend many hours in focused seated study) put extra pressure on the elbow joint in his efforts of spinning records. However, when he learned how to relax the hips and torso so they could rotate with the record-spinning arm, his elbow problem disappeared.

Let me conclude by noting some pathologies relating to a much more basic activity typically governed by performative muscle memory: eating. For all its natural or instinctive aspects, eating is a sequential activity that we learn how to perform, both through implicit and explicit forms of learning. We learn the sequence of cutting and chewing a large slice of meat before we swallow it; or the sequence of first lifting and then tilting the cup to one's mouth to drink our water rather than lowering the mouth and extending the tongue to lap it up. We develop distinctive habits in the way we eat, and these go beyond the obvious examples of formal table manners and the handling of various eating utensils (knives, forks, spoons, chopsticks, cups, glasses, bowls, pitchers, salt shakers, etc.). There are different habits of how one deploys one's lips and tongue; what part of the mouth one uses in chewing; how fast, how long, and how vigorously one chews; how fast, how often, and how hard one swallows; how often one pauses in eating to drink, to speak to one's dining companion, or to reflect on the food's taste, aroma, or texture or on one's diverse feelings in eating, including the feeling of becoming satiated. The performative muscle memory of eating is very deeply entrenched because it is a procedural skill we use daily. The result is that we typically eat without thinking explicitly about it.

This is surely convenient because attention instead can be wholly absorbed on something more interesting or useful, such as reviewing the lecture notes for an ensuing lecture. Such muscle-memory automatism of eating can prove problematic, however, if one's dining habits are faulty, and they can be flawed in a variety of everyday ways. For example, there are people with habits of ugly, sloppy, or excessively noisy ways of eating that pose somaesthetic problems for dining companions who have to witness them. Besides the visual or auditory displeasure they experience, observing such unaesthetic eating styles may rob them of their own appetite and enjoyment of food. Other somaesthetic pathologies resulting from habits of muscle memory can affect the problematic eater himself. One touted feature of habit is that its muscle memory increases speed of performance because no time is taken (or needed) to deliberate in action. So relying purely on muscle memory without attentive deliberation about how we eat enables us to eat more quickly. But those who habitually eat very quickly often suffer from poor digestion and a variety of related somatic discomforts (whose portrayal and medicinal remedies fill countless hours of television advertising). Many who suffer in this way know that part of their problem is eating too fast, but one reason they continue to eat too fast is that they do not notice how fast they are eating because muscle memory sets the rhythm and style of their eating. They thus pay no attention to how they perform this sequential, temporal activity; and without such attention they cannot monitor it to slow it down. Recent studies show, moreover, that eating fast also promotes obesity. Once again, if we are unaware of our speed of eating, we cannot know how to slow it down to avoid its negative consequences.[17]

---

[17] There are studies linking fast eating with obese adults and adolescents, but also experimental studies that show that "increase in the speed of eating in normal weight volunteers caused overeating... replicating the pattern of eating in a group of obese patients." One study showed that the use of Mandometer (a machine that tells eaters while they are

Another somaesthetic pathology of inattentive habit contributes to overeating. When food or drink is consumed rapidly and inattentively, we are less able to appreciate its taste. As our eating enjoyment is diminished by this inability to properly savor our food, so we tend to compensate by eating more. Unsatisfied by the flavors and textures of what we've already eaten (because they have gone largely unnoticed through our habitual hurried or inattentive eating), our quest for the satisfaction which we know *should* come from food drives us to continue eating in the hope that such satisfaction *will* eventually come. This unfulfilled hope often keeps us eating even after we've already had our fill. Such frustrations of satisfaction through inattentive eating habits that rely entirely on the swift efficiency of muscle memory may be one cause for the common pathology of overeating in America and other fast-food, rapid consumption societies. In any case, its failure of gustatory and hedonic appreciation constitutes in itself a regrettable somaesthetic pathology of everyday life.

These are not the only somaesthetic pathologies that contribute to the overeating and consequent obesity from which so many suffer in contemporary consumerist culture. Driven to consume through persistent and ever increasing stimulation that continuously strains and blunts our discriminatory sensitivities (in ways described by the Weber-Fechner law), many people are unable to perceive that they have eaten enough until they have considerably overeaten.[18] They have lost the somaesthetic discrimination of the proprioceptive feelings of having their hunger satiated or being comfortably full. They can only discriminate the stronger, discomforting overstimulation of feeling "stuffed," so they identify that unpleasant feeling with having reached satiety or eating satisfaction, and thus continue to eat until they feel such discomfort. Thus, we have a

---

eating that they are consuming food more rapidly than their eating therapist designates) led to loss of weight. See S. Shechner and J. Ronin, *Obese Humans and Rats* (New York: Wiley, 1974), 6–9; M. Zandian, I. Ioakimidis, C. Bergh, and P. Södersten, "Decelerated and Linear Eaters: Effect of Eating Rate on Food Intake and Satiety," *Physiological Behavior* 96 (2009): 270–275; I. Ioakimidis, M. Zandian, C. Bergh, and P. Södersten, "A Method for the Control of Eating Rate: A Potential Intervention in Eating Disorders," *Behavioral Research Methods* 41 (2009): 755–760; and A. Ford, C. Bergh, P. Södersten et al., "Treatment of Childhood Obesity by Retraining Eating Behaviour: Randomized Controlled Trial," *British Medical Journal* 340b (2010): 5388. In this article, the authors note that earlier efforts to reduce obesity through therapy lifestyle interventions were more effective in younger children than in adolescents; there may be many reasons for this, but one reason might be that the eating habits of adolescents are more deeply entrenched, hence more resistant to change.

[18] For more discussion of the relation of the Weber-Fechner law to issues in somaesthetics, see *Body Consciousness*, 38–39.

vicious cycle of eating more but enjoying it less because one is not properly aware of when to stop eating; and such awareness is a matter of somaesthetic discrimination.

These arguments regarding eating and obesity have a particular relevance to the ramified project of somaesthetics, an interdisciplinary field of theory and practice broadly defined as the critical study and meliorative cultivation of the soma as a site both of sensory appreciation (aesthesis) and creative self-fashioning. As creative self-fashioning suggests the aesthetic stylizing of the soma as an external object of attractive representations, so the focus on aesthesis concerns the soma's perceptual acuity and inner experience, where cultivation of improved aesthesis means "feeling better" both in the sense of enjoying better feelings but also in the sense of perceiving what we experience more accurately and clearly. It is sometimes useful to emphasize the distinction between the perceptual or inner dimension of somaesthetics and the dimension of external body representations that so dominates our culture's concerns with embodiment. But if deficient somaesthetic perception of our eating can be casually linked to problems in maintaining one's external somaesthetic form, then there exists an important connection between somaesthetics' perceptual and representational dimensions. It is a commonplace to say that how we feel affects how we look; happiness can give us a winning smile while depression, pains of illness, or fatigue can make us look unattractively dull and diminished. Our brief, closing arguments for deploying somaesthetic perception to overcome obesity from eating habits of inattentive muscle memory provides, however, a new meaning to this familiar saying.

5

Somaesthetics in the Philosophy Classroom

A Practical Approach

I

"Please take off your shoes and lie down on your back. Keep your legs long, lengthened, if that is not uncomfortable. But if it is, just put something under the backs of your knees or lie with your knees bent and your soles on the floor. Close your eyes so that you can concentrate on feeling your body, and notice that you don't really need to see your legs (or to remember what they looked like) in order to know that your legs are long or instead bent sharply at the knee. We can sense this directly through proprioception (our inner bodily sense) and our tactile sense of the body's contact with the floor. What we're going to do in this lesson is to come to know ourselves better somatically by examining how our body feels through such proprioception and bodily tactile feeling. We're going to do it in an organized way that will take about ten minutes, proceeding systematically from one body area to another, comparing and contrasting felt positions, angles, weights, volumes, etc.

"In following my instructions *and* my questions – for example, about which side, arm, leg, shoulder (left or right) feels heavier or lighter – you should not worry about the responses of others; just answer on the basis of your own experience and to yourself – do not answer aloud, so as not to interfere with the experience and replies of others. Different people have different bodies and different habits of bodily posture and use, and those differences will be reflected in their experience of self-examination in this supine position. Always make sure you're breathing comfortably, lying comfortably, and are not straining. If you feel you are getting sore or stiff, find a more comfortable position. The purpose of this lesson is not to embarrass, shock, provoke, or give you the giggles, but to instruct you in a method that can contribute to the realization of one of philosophy's central goals – that of self-knowledge; here, somatic self-knowledge. Philosophy has traditionally linked its central goal of self-knowledge with the goal of self-cultivation or self-care, on the grounds that we can care for something better if we know more about it; that to effectively cultivate or improve the self and its behavior we need to know those aspects of the self and behavior we wish to improve or cultivate; here, our somatic selves. So please relax with your eyes closed (eyes probably tired from too much reading or video viewing), and follow my instructions...."

II

I won't continue here with this body-scan protocol, but that is how I would like to begin a lesson in practical somaesthetics, a field whose name I first proposed in 1996 but whose content and agenda can be traced back to the beginnings of philosophy. Construed as the critical study of one's experience and meliorative cultivation of the body in perception, performance, and creative self-fashioning, somaesthetics is a field of both theory and practice; it aims to improve our somatic understanding, experience, performance, and self-stylizing, not just examine it in the abstract. Its concerns go beyond the soma's external forms and norms and the ways it can be beautified and employed to express our personal and social values; somaesthetics, in its experiential mode, also focuses on the powers, feelings, and pleasures of inner somatic perception and on ways of enhancing the quality and acuity of such perception. The lesson that I began to sketch in opening this chapter is a practical lesson of experiential somaesthetics aimed at heightening somatic awareness; but the value of such lessons is not confined to the field of somaesthetics. They can be useful more generally in teaching philosophy because they relate to the central issue of self-knowledge that has so powerfully shaped philosophy, as Chapter 3 has shown.

Although convinced of the philosophical relevance of such lessons in somatic self-awareness, I have never really dared to use them systematically to teach philosophy in the standard undergraduate academic philosophy course for two kinds of reasons.[1] First, because of the implicit norms and concrete physical conditions of academic philosophy instruction: philosophical thinking in the classroom is expected to be done by

---

[1] I have, however, used them frequently in special practical workshops and advanced seminars in somaesthetics. Video clips from one of those workshops can be found at https://sites.google.com/site/somaesthetics/.

the students in a sitting position with their eyes open; such instruction is to be essentially conceptual rather than experiential; and the floors of philosophy classrooms are totally unsuited for lying down – they are typically hard, cold, and dirty with no available mats to make lying down a comfortable possibility for learning. All these reasons could be designated as practical or external reasons against such somatic teaching of philosophy. There are, however, other reasons that discourage the use of such somatic study of philosophy, reasons that are internal to the dominant philosophical tradition. These include the dogma that attentive, perceptive consciousness of one's body cannot really provide self-knowledge because the body is not truly the self, as the Platonic-Cartesian tradition argues.[2] There is also the frequently voiced worry that enhanced somatic consciousness would provide only an inferior, dangerous form of self-knowledge that, rather than contributing positively to self-cultivation, tends to promote self-damaging morbidity, passivity, and weakness.

II

Having already dealt in earlier chapters with these theoretical arguments against cultivating enhanced body consciousness, I now address the practical task of showing how exercises for improving somatic awareness can indeed be taught in an academic philosophical classroom. The most useful way to do this (within the print format limits of this book) is by giving the reader a textual example or script of one such exercise – the body scan – whose preparatory instructions opened this chapter. In this example, I will show how the body scan can be adapted to conditions more acceptable to the standard classroom, conditions that do not require lying on the floor but instead permit a seated position for performance. The chapter then concludes by analyzing the logical principles of consciousness that underlie the body scan. By combining such analysis with the experiential learning process of doing the scan itself, one can offer a

---

[2] As noted earlier, Plato's *Alcibiades* insists that "the command that we should know ourselves means that we should know our souls" and make them the object of our self-cultivation. Hence, a man's knowing or caring for his body is merely knowing or "caring for something that belongs to him, and not [knowing or caring] for himself." Despite affirming the value of bodily training in some other dialogues (such as *Timaeus* and *The Laws*), in *Phaedo* Plato most influentially argues that the philosopher should not concern himself at all "with the body," but rather turn attention away from it "as much as possible ... because the body confuses the soul," distorts perception, and distracts from the pursuit of truth. See *Alcibiades* and *Phaedo*, in John Cooper (ed.), *Plato: The Complete Works* (Indianapolis: Hackett, 1997), 56–58, 589, 590.

distinctive, fruitful way of integrating somaesthetic theory and practice in the classroom. Because it is not specifically associated with any religious tradition, the body scan might be easier to introduce into academic contexts of philosophical instruction, which are most often secular (and sometimes even ferociously so). Deployed by numerous body-mind disciplines (including the Feldenkrais Method developed by a twentieth-century scientist trained in Israel and France), the body scan involves systematically scanning or surveying one's own body, not by regarding or touching it from the outside but instead by introspectively, proprioceptively feeling ourselves as we rest motionless, typically on our backs with our eyes closed.

The supine position is particularly advantageous for developing acute body awareness because it not only relieves the habitually more intense stress of gravity that we feel in holding ourselves erect in standing or sitting, but by being a non-habitual position for awareness, it enables one's awareness to be freer from – hence, less distracted by – the habitual associations of action we have in our more habitual and active postures. Similarly, the closing of the eyes is advantageous for avoiding visual stimuli that would distract from our proprioceptive attention and awareness. However, the self-examining discipline of the body scan can be adapted to other postures. If lying down is very embarrassing or uncomfortable, then it will not be a good position to do the body scan because attention will focus on one's embarrassment or discomfort rather than on the more subtle dimensions of one's bodily state and feelings. Because this chapter aims to offer a practical orientation to teaching somatic philosophy, I will now provide a very brief textual demonstration of the body scan that I have adapted to the sitting position, which is the position that could most easily be used in a philosophy classroom, where students typically feel most comfortable sitting. I have condensed the scan to its most basic elements to make it easier to follow, and have deleted the sort of introductory remarks about breathing, comfort, and so on with which this chapter opened. Those remarks are worth adding in giving this lesson in the classroom.

III

Seated Body Scan

> Remove your shoes. Sit toward the front edge of the chair, with your feet flat on the floor. Place your hands on your thighs where they feel comfortable. If you wish, close your eyes, as it may help you do the following.

Starting with your left foot, notice how your heel makes contact with the floor. Does most of the weight go to the center of the heel or to the right or left of the heel? We do not want to change anything or to judge how it should be; we simply want to feel where the heel contacts the floor.

Does your left foot carry most of its weight on the heel or on the ball of the foot? Is there more weight on the inside of the foot or the outside? Do all your toes make contact with the floor? Which of the toes make clear contact with the floor and which do not? Notice how your left foot is turned in or out, or does it point straight ahead?

Now move your attention from your left foot, up your lower leg, to your left knee. Where is your left knee in relation to your heel? Is it in front of it, behind it, or right above your heel?

As you continue to move your attention up your left leg, notice the angle at which your left leg turns out or in. If you drew a line from your belly button straight out in front of you, how far would your knee be from this center line?

Now notice your right foot. How does your right heel make contact with the floor; at what point on the heel, at the center of the heel, to the right, or to the left? How does it compare with the left heel? Which heel seems to make more contact with the floor?

Where does the right foot carry most of its weight, on the heel or on the ball of the foot? Does the foot make more contact with the floor on the inside of the foot or the outside? Which toes are making contact with the floor and which are not? How does the right foot, in these matters, compare with the left foot? How much does the right foot turn in or turn out? How does it compare with the left foot in terms of this positioning?

Move your attention up your right lower leg, and find the relationship between your right knee and right heel. Is the knee over the heel or is one in front of or behind the other?

As you bring your attention higher up your right leg, notice the angle at which your leg turns out. How far is your right knee from the center line that you drew straight out from your belly button? Which knee, the right or the left, is further away from this center line?

Now notice your pelvis and how it rests on the chair. Does the right side or the left side feel heavier? Which side feels that it makes more contact with the chair? Do you feel your entire buttocks on the chair? Is there more pressure felt on the left or right cheek? Do you find the contact also on your upper thighs? Which has more? Do you feel any changes of pressure as your awareness is directed to the left or right buttock, left or right thigh?

Move your attention to your lower back. Which side, the right side or the left side, feels longer? Which side feels wider?

As you move your attention to your middle back, do you feel it as clearly as you do your lower back? Which side feels longer, the right side or the left side? Which side feels wider?

Now feel the width of your upper back. Which side feels as if it takes up more space? Which side feels longer? Which side feels wider?

Move your attention to your neck. Does the right side or the left side feel longer? Does your head feel that it is sitting on top of your neck, or is it to the front or to the back of it? Is there any tension in your neck from holding your head above it? Notice whether your head feels as if it is tilting right or left. Notice the space between your chin and your throat.

Check in with your mouth. Is it open or shut? How wide or how tight?

Sense your shoulders. Which shoulder seems higher, the left or the right? If you were to draw a line between your right shoulder and your ear, and another line between your left shoulder and your left ear, which line would be longer?

Now move your attention to your arms. Which feels longer? Which feels heavier? Notice how far your right arm is from your body. Then notice how far your left arm is from your body. Are your hands resting palms up on your legs or do they face down?

Sense how you feel overall. Do you feel that one side of you is lighter than the other? Is one side of you wider than the other? Taller? Stand up for a minute or two to give yourself a feeling of how you feel standing. Do you still feel any difference in the two sides? Do you feel different from what you remember you felt when you were standing earlier in the day? If so, how?

IV

Having performed a body scan, we can now inquire more deeply into the logic of its method. What strategies help us, in practical terms, to make our somaesthetic introspection more effective? One crucial way is to make it more attentive, and certain techniques for heightening attentiveness emerge from considering two key principles of attention: change and interest. As human consciousness evolved to help us survive in an ever-changing world, our attention has become habituated to and requires change. One cannot attend continuously for very long to an object that does not change, which suggests the paradoxical argument that in order to keep attention unchangingly fixed on the very same object of thought, one must somehow ensure that some kind of change is introduced in it, even if it is only a difference of the perspective from which it is examined as an object of thought. Similarly, because consciousness evolved to serve our interests, continued interest is required to sustain attention. We cannot focus for long on things that do not interest us, and even our interest in the thought of something we care about (say, our right hand) can soon be exhausted unless we find some way of reviving that interest and introducing some change of consciousness. From these basic features of change and interest, six distinct introspective strategies of the body scan (and of somaesthetic reflection more generally) can be elaborated.

1. *Questions*: We can better sustain attention to a given topic of thought, including a somatic object or perception, by considering different aspects and relations of it in turn to avoid monotony that destroys attention. One useful technique of doing this is by asking a variety of questions about the object on which we want to fix continued attention. Such questions provoke renewed interest in the object by prompting us to reconsider the object in order to answer the questions. Moreover, the very effort of considering the questions effectively changes the way or aspect in which the object is perceived. It is hard, for example, to keep our attention focused on the feeling of our breathing. But if we ask ourselves a series of questions about it – is our breath deep or shallow, rapid or slow? Is it felt more in the chest or in the diaphragm? What does it feel like in the mouth or in the nose? Does the inhalation or exhalation feel longer? – then we will be able to sustain attention much longer and introspect our feelings more carefully.

2. *Division into parts*: As William James notes, if we try to examine our "corporeal sensations . . . as we lie or sit motionless, we find it very difficult to feel distinctly the length of our back or the direction of our feet from our shoulders." Even if we succeed "by a strong effort" to feel our whole self at once, such perception is remarkably "vague and ambiguous," and only "a few parts are strongly emphasized to consciousness."[3] The key to a more precise bodily introspection is therefore to systematically scan the body by subdividing it in our awareness, directing our focused attention first to one part then to another, so that each part can be given proper attention and a clearer sense of the relations of parts to whole can be obtained. The transition of focus not only provides the sense of change that continued attention requires; it also provides renewed interest with each newly examined part presenting a new challenge.

---

[3] William James, *The Principles of Psychology* (Cambridge, MA: Harvard University Press, 1983), 788; hereafter PP.

3. Moreover, this transition of introspective probing from one body part to another helps in providing successive *contrasts of feeling*, and such contrasts help sharpen the discrimination of what we feel. Enhancing discrimination is another crucial strategy for more effective introspection, and we readily see how questions and divisions into parts also encourage discrimination by discriminating foci of interest. However, let me now focus on how this works through contrast of feelings. If asked to assess the felt heaviness of one of our shoulders as we lie on the floor, we are not likely to get a clear impression of this feeling. But if we first focus on one shoulder and then on the other, we can more easily get a clearer impression of each by noticing which feels heavier and rests firmer on the floor. Contrast makes feelings easier to discriminate, and we can distinguish different kinds of contrast.

First, we can distinguish between "existential" and "differential" contrasts. The first is the simple contrast between whether the feeling in question is actually there or is absent, without considering the specific nature or quality of that feeling. For example, a person can more clearly perceive her body's contact with the floor by noticing which parts of the body make contact with the floor and which do not. Differential contrast is a matter of comparing the nature or quality of existing feelings. We could, for example, compare the contact feeling of our two shoulders with the floor, and ask which shoulder feels it rests heavier on the floor or feels more fully or firmly on the floor. Both kinds of contrast can be helpful in somaesthetic introspection. One can, for example, learn to discriminate a previously unnoticed feeling of chronic muscular contraction in one's antigravity back extensors by suddenly feeling what it is like to have those muscles relaxed and thus to have a momentary absence of the contraction. (To initiate this feeling of relaxation, the somatic therapist might have the patient recline and then support the patient's back by holding it in his hands until the patient feels herself fully supported and releases her contractions.) But we can also learn to discriminate the degree of felt tension in, say, a clenched fist by the differential contrast of intensifying the fist's muscular contraction through one's own greater effort of flexion or through the therapist's squeezing of that fist (or indeed, the other fist).

With respect to both existential and differential contrasts, we can further distinguish between simultaneous contrasts (when we compare perceptions at the very same time) and successive contrasts (when we first attend to one perception and then compare it to another immediately thereafter). The comparative efficacy or acuity of simultaneous and successive contrasts seems to differ somewhat in terms of the contexts, tasks, and sense modalities. In many visual comparisons (such as which color is darker), simultaneous contrasts are more accurate; in certain tasks of spatial perception, however, it seems that successive presentations are more effective.[4] In any case, the body scan is not about visual perception but about proprioceptive perception; its perceived contrasts (whether existential or differential and whether simultaneous or successive) are about feelings of different body parts or areas.

Here it is best to leave each person to experience or experiment for herself whether simultaneous or successive contrasting works best in the sense of being clearer and more accurate. For example, in your seated position, please compare for a moment the different feelings of pressure of your left buttock on your chair and of your right buttock on your chair. Which buttock feels as if it rests more heavily or firmly on the chair? Is it clearer to compare these feelings in one simultaneous perception or is your discrimination of a difference more effective by focusing first on one buttock then the other? If you lie on your back and try to discriminate which vertebrae make contact with the floor and which do not, is it not easier to go successively, vertebra by vertebra, rather than trying to grasp their felt (or absent) contact with the floor in one simultaneous act of attention? In that same lying position, if we wish to compare which shoulder feels higher or closer to our head, is it also easier to focus on one side and then the other or instead to try to capture the two sides in a simultaneous perception? Clearly, when it comes to large areas of the body and more global discriminations of body experience – as when trying to feel which parts of the body feel the heaviest or densest or tensest – we cannot rely on a simultaneous comparative grasp of the feelings of all our body parts, but must instead proceed by successive examination and comparison of parts. That, indeed, is what a body scan is all about.

4. *Associative interest*: Besides the use of focusing questions and the transitions, subdivisions, and contrasts of the body scan, there are other principles to sustain the interest necessary for effective somaesthetic introspection. One is associative interest. Just as the faint knock of an expected lover at one's door will be heard over louder sounds simultaneously made in the same environment simply because the listener is

---

[4] Liqiang Huang and Harold Pashler, "Attention Capacity and Task Difficulty in Visual Search," *Cognition* 94 (2005): B101–B111.

eagerly interested in hearing that sign of arrival, so we can stimulate attention to a bodily feeling by making its recognition a key to something we care about. For example, the recognition of a certain feeling of muscle relaxation or rhythm of breathing whose presence and perception can sustain a feeling of calm that leads into desired sleep; or the associated interest of recognizing that attention to a particular body part or feeling in a body scan has had the capacity to induce a muscular readjustment associated with feelings of somatic ease and cognitive empowerment.

5. *Avoiding distracting interests*: Another strategy for enhancing introspective attention to bodily feelings is by taking steps to ward off competing interests, since any form of attention constitutes a focalization of consciousness that implies ignoring other things in order to concentrate on the object in focus. That is why introspective body scans and other forms of meditation are performed with the eyes closed (or half-closed), so that our minds will not be stimulated by perceptions from the external world of sight that would distract our interest. Internal perception is thus indirectly improved by blunting external perception.

6. Still another technique for sharpening our attention to a feeling we are trying to discriminate is by preparing for or anticipating its perception because, as James remarks, "*preperception*... is half of the perception of the looked-for thing" (PP, 419). With respect to the body scan or other forms of somaesthetic introspection, such preparation (which in itself heightens interest) can take different forms. One can prepare oneself to discriminate a feeling by conceptualizing where in one's felt body to look for it or by imagining how it will be induced and felt there. Such conceptualization and imagining clearly involves linguistic thought, which means that language can be an aid to somaesthetic insight, though it can also be a distracting obstacle when the range of language is assumed to exhaust the entire range of experience. While emphasizing the limits of language and the importance of nameless feelings, we must also recognize that language can improve our perception of what we feel.

For such reasons, the use of language to guide and sharpen somaesthetic introspection – through preparatory instructions, focusing questions, anticipatory imaginative descriptions of what will be experienced and how it will feel, and contrasting descriptions or names of feelings – is crucial even to those disciplines of body consciousness that regard the range and meaning of our feelings as going well beyond the limits of language. Body and language, so often posed as oppositional forces competing for primacy or all-subsuming privilege, are both essential for somaesthetics. The key is not to side with one against the other, nor to rank them in importance, but rather (just as we argued with respect to the duo of spontaneous versus self-conscious action) to coordinate them more effectively so that they can work best together. The body scan I gave you in this chapter required linguistic instructions, but, if you really followed its instructions in experiential practice, it also required from you more than mere conceptual understanding. Philosophy, especially if practiced as a way of life, is a complex enterprise that demands a multiplicity of tools; and so, I think, does the teaching of philosophy.

PART II

SOMAESTHETICS, AESTHETICS, AND CULTURE

6

Somaesthetics and the Limits of Aesthetics

I

What is the origin of somaesthetics? Like most cultural products and research projects, somaesthetics has multiple roots and generative influences. It was engendered not only from a vast variety of philosophical ideas but through the inspiration of somatic therapies and other body disciplines, as well as more general influences in contemporary culture. The full genealogy of somaesthetics would thus present a complex task of historical analysis, too complex to undertake here. However, as the individual who initially conceived and coined the project of somaesthetics, I should provide an account of how I came to propose this field of inquiry. In tracing how somaesthetics emerged from my struggle with the limits of philosophical aesthetics, this chapter also seeks to demonstrate how the struggle with limits is not a purely idiosyncratic matter, but rather a struggle that somehow pervades and structures the field of aesthetics. My personal philosophical trajectory from analytic philosophy of art to somaesthetics can thus help illuminate more generally the structure and limits of the aesthetic field.

Reviewing my almost thirty-year career in philosophical aesthetics, I realize that much of it has been a struggle with the limits that define this field, although I did not always see it in those terms. When I was still a student at Oxford specializing in analytic aesthetics, my first publications were papers protesting the limits of prevailing monistic doctrines in the philosophy of literature: theories claiming that poetry (and by extension, literature in general) is essentially an oral-based performative art without real visual import; and theories arguing that beneath the varying interpretations and evaluations of works of art there was nonetheless only one basic logic of interpretation and one basic logic of evaluation (though philosophers differed as to what that basic logic was and whether it was the same for both interpretation and evaluation). When I proposed contrastingly pluralistic accounts of interpretive and evaluative logic, while suggesting that literature could be appreciated in terms of sight as well as sound, I was not consciously aiming at transgressing the prevailing limits. I was more interested in being right than in being different or original, and I saw myself as working fully within the limits of analytic aesthetics.[1]

My initial decision to focus on philosophy of literature was motivated by the analytic critique of essentialism – too much bad aesthetic theory had resulted from taking what was obviously true in one art and then generalizing it for all arts. This key tenet of Wittgensteinian and Austinian analytic philosophy of art, which I first learned in Jerusalem, was reinforced in my doctoral studies at Oxford. I nonetheless realized that to understand literature properly (indeed, to understand its special features or singularity) I had to relate it to the other arts and thus go beyond the limits of working merely in literary theory. So while *The Object of Literary Criticism* (based on my Oxford dissertation) formulated its analysis of work-identity and ontological status and the logics of interpretation and evaluation in terms of literary works, I also indicated how some dimensions of this analysis could be applied to other arts.

In my second book, *T.S. Eliot and the Philosophy of Criticism* (1988), I also sought to focus on issues in philosophy of literature by selecting a paradigmatic literary figure as the prism for my inquiries into such issues as objectivity, subjectivity, pleasure, history, and tradition in critical judgment and reasoning, while deepening my study of interpretation. But once again, I found that my investigation inevitably took me beyond the limits of literature because Eliot himself came increasingly to realize that literature and its criticism were significantly shaped by sociohistorical factors and broader cultural ideologies. My philosophical analyses thus followed his lead by going into more than literary matters, such as the analysis of tradition and the interpretation of culture and its historical changes.

In examining Eliot's turn from his early objectivism to a more historicist, hermeneutic stance, I was also impelled to read more deeply into hermeneutic theory and other schools of continental philosophy

---

[1] See Richard Shusterman, "The Anomalous Nature of Literature," *British Journal of Aesthetics* 18 (1978): 317–329; "The Logic of Interpretation," *Philosophy Quarterly* 28 (1978): 310–324; "The Logic of Evaluation," *Philosophy Quarterly* 30 (1980): 327–341.

that emphasized the sociohistorical shaping of art and criticism. Thus, although the book's declared philosophical approach remained analytic philosophy, its topics led me to explore other philosophical perspectives. If its first chapter, "Eliot and Analytic Philosophy," explored how that philosophy's new ideas and ideals shaped Eliot's early objectivist literary and critical doctrines, the book's final chapter, "Pragmatism and Practical Wisdom," highlighted the pragmatic dimension of Eliot's critical theory while relating it both to classical and contemporary versions of pragmatist philosophy. This made me increasingly appreciative of the rich variety, powers, and resources of philosophical pragmatism.

When, in the late 1980s, I expanded my horizons to embrace pragmatism more explicitly, I became conscious of pushing at the limits of analytic aesthetics, though I still considered my work to be continuous with the basic topics and modes of reasoning of analytic philosophy – much in the way that Nelson Goodman, Richard Rorty, Hilary Putnam, and Joseph Margolis were combining pragmatist insights with analytic styles of argument.[2] And although I summoned some continental philosophy for inspirational insight (from Nietzsche and Adorno to Foucault and Bourdieu), I could assure myself that the most respected analytic philosopher of art, Arthur Danto, had constructed much of his art theory on Hegelian ideas.

Of course, when *Pragmatist Aesthetics* (1992) devoted its largest chapter to an advocatory exposition of hip hop,[3] I could no longer pretend to myself that I was essentially working within the traditional framework of analytic philosophizing. Formerly friendly colleagues began to see me as a sensationalist transgressor, reminding me through painful words or even more painfully silent shunning that I had passed beyond limits that defined acceptable work in analytic philosophy. Though my new work continued to command respect (and was even appreciated by some analytic colleagues as a useful tool to save them the time of studying pragmatist and continental authors for themselves), I could no longer fully be trusted. My subsequent turn to somaesthetics, crowned by my professional training as a somatic educator in the Feldenkrais Method, confirmed my image as what the Germans call a Grenzgänger, a border-crosser, a transgressor of boundaries. The French, for their part,

---

[2] In my "Introduction" to *Analytic Aesthetics* (Oxford: Blackwell, 1989), 1–19, I explore how some pragmatist perspectives can be seen as convergent with important approaches in analytic aesthetics.

[3] See Richard Shusterman, *Pragmatist Aesthetics: Living Beauty, Rethinking Art* (Oxford: Blackwell, 1992), ch. 8.

have also characterized me as a "nomad philosopher" and *passeur culturel* (a term hard to translate into English because "cultural smuggler" sounds too narrowly criminal, while "cultural mediator" too bureaucratically bland). Whatever its translation, the term was used to suggest that my philosophical explorations crossed the standard disciplinary borders that divide philosophies from each other and from other domains of thought and life. Like it or not (and initially I greatly disliked it), my image had evolved from a mainstream, Oxford-trained analytic aesthetician into a limit-defying provocateur, who had to be kept at some distance from the inner circles of power within the mainstream aesthetics establishment however much it still accorded my work a respectful hearing.

Pierre Bourdieu once suggested to me, in conversation, a sociological explanation of my philosophical trajectory: My binational, transcultural background tends to make boundary crossing (and pluralistic vision) a necessity of life, and this would promote a habitus of cultural pluralism and transgressing limits that would likely be mirrored in philosophical work. Although I had seemed to achieve insider status in Anglo-American analytic aesthetics (as editor of an important Blackwell collection on that topic and as a tenured professor in Temple University's philosophy department that was famous for analytic aesthetics), this insider persona could not really fit with my entrenched habitus as a displaced intellectual, a wandering Jew who had left America for Israel at age sixteen and then experienced outsider status there, and again at Oxford, before returning – in my mid-thirties – as an academic stranger to the United States, though frequently departing again for long periods of research and teaching in France, Germany, and Japan. Perhaps Bourdieu's explanation was right. But rather than going further into this line of social self-analysis (which I elsewhere explore in an overtly autobiographical essay[4]), this chapter is devoted to a much broader hypothesis: that the play of limit transgression is a central feature of the field of aesthetics in the West, a key aspect of its history and structure. If this is right, then my trajectory reflects not simply the idiosyncratic passions of an unsettled mind but also a deep current in the history of aesthetics.

---

[4] Richard Shusterman, "Regarding Oneself and Seeing Double: Fragments of Autobiography," in George Yancy (ed.), *The Philosophical I: Personal Reflections on Life in Philosophy* (New York: Rowman and Littlefield, 2002), 1–21.

II

Modern Western aesthetics defined itself from the beginning as transgressing boundaries and exceeding limits. Alexander Baumgarten introduced aesthetics precisely to extend philosophy beyond the limits of conceptual knowledge and into the sphere of sensory perceptions and what he calls "the lower cognitive faculties." As he insists in paragraph three of *Aesthetica*'s "Prolegomena," one of aesthetics' goals is "improving knowledge also beyond the borders of the distinctly knowable" (*"Die Verbesserung der Erkenntnis auch über die Grenzen des deutlich Erkennbaren hinaus vorantreibt"*). There is a basic logic at play here: To justify a new philosophical discipline or science like aesthetics, Baumgarten must argue that the new field is needed to go beyond the limits of the studies we already have, that it occupies a place beyond the boundaries defined by other fields. Hence, Baumgarten likewise defends the need for aesthetics by saying it goes beyond the limits of *Rhetorik* and *Poetik* by comprehending a larger field (*"Sie umfaßt ein weiteres Gebiet"*) by including objects of other arts. Nor can aesthetics be simply equated with criticism or with art, Baumgarten argues, because criticism in general includes critique of logic, while aesthetics is said to deal specifically with matters of sensibility, and because aesthetics is claimed to be a science (*Wissenschaft*) rather than just an art.[5]

Beyond Baumgarten, the modern field of aesthetics can be seen as an attempt to go beyond the limits of older philosophies of beauty, sublimity, and taste to engage a much wider domain of qualities and judgments relating to our pleasurable and meaningful experience of art and nature. Moreover, we can see the essential move of Hegelian aesthetics (and other aesthetic idealisms) as moving the essence of aesthetics beyond the limits of sensuous and nonconceptual experience and instead toward the idea of art as purveying the very highest spiritual truths, albeit in a somewhat sensuous form. Moreover, we can certainly see modernity's progressive revolutions of artistic forms and styles in the same Hegelian spirit of dynamic movement that progresses by encountering and overcoming boundaries.[6]

---

[5] My citations from Baumgarten are from the bilingual (Latin-German) abridged edition of this work: Alexander Baumgarten, *Theoretische Ästhetik: Die grundlengenden Abschnitte aus der "Aesthetica"* (1750/58), trans. H.R. Schweizer (Hamburg: Felix Meiner, 1988), 3, 5.

[6] I raised these same points in "Somaesthetics at the Limits," *Nordic Journal of Aesthetics* 35 (2008): 7–23, and redeploy its arguments here.

We may have forgotten the limit-defying trend in aesthetics because the dominant Anglo-American aesthetic school of the last half century, analytic aesthetics, has been keen to insist on defining limits and policing them. Initially, it had the best of reasons to stress the need for more recognition of limits and distinctions in order to remedy the limit-defying confusions of the dominant aesthetic idealism of the early twentieth century, perhaps most powerfully exemplified in Benedetto Croce. As I have argued elsewhere, analytic aesthetics emerged from dissatisfaction with the wooly vagueness of idealist, Hegelian-inspired aesthetic theories such as Croce's that affirm a more unbounded aesthetics whose project is limit defiance.[7]

Croce's project was shaped by a struggle to defend the transcendent power of aesthetic insight from the limitations of encroaching positivisms with respect to art's meaning: whether such positivism was expressed by subordinating artistic creation and evaluation to the strict rules of genre criticism or to historical and sociological causal explanations, such as Hippolyte Taine's famous formula that art could be defined and explained simply in terms of "race, milieu, and moment."[8] For Croce, who defines the aesthetic in terms of a basic formative power of intuition that pervades all meaningful perception, aesthetics cannot be confined to a narrow domain of poetics and fine arts nor to questions of natural beauty. The aesthetic instead is a fundamental principle of intuitive perception that pervades the experienced world as a whole. All the world, Croce argues, is essentially a matter of aesthetics, since "all this world is intuition," "it is nothing but intuition or aesthetic fact."[9]

Identifying intuition with expression and language, and insisting that the nature of intuitions and language is "perpetual creation" and change, Croce argues that any attempt to limit aesthetic intuition into fixed boundaries, categories, or meanings is as useless and perverse as "to seek the immobility of motion." Traditional limits of aesthetic genres and rhetorical categories are thus completely swept away: "Expression is an indivisible whole," Croce claims; hence, "a philosophical classification of expressions is impossible," for there is no essential distinguishing

---

[7] See Richard Shusterman, "Analytic Aesthetics, Literary Theory, and Deconstruction," *The Monist* 69 (1986): 22–38. For an account of Croce's relationship to pragmatist philosophy, see "Croce on Interpretation: Deconstruction and Pragmatism," *New Literary History* 20 (1988): 199–216.

[8] See Hippolyte Taine, *History of English Literature*, trans. H. van Laun (New York: Henry Hold and Company, 1886), 18.

[9] For these and ensuing Croce quotations, see Benedetto Croce, *Aesthetic*, trans. Douglas Ainslie (London: Macmillan, 1922), 22–23, 26, 30, 110–113, 146, 197–198, 234, 247.

principles or fixed "formal differences" to justify such categorical limits, only differences of degree and context and changing convention. The same goes for the alleged limits between artist, critic, and audience, and even between art and non-art: "The limits of the expressions and intuitions that are called art, as opposed to those that are vulgarly called non-art, are empirical and impossible to define. If an epigram be art, why not a single word?" Challenging not only the limits but even the standard distinctions between disciplines, Croce declares that "philosophy of language and philosophy of art are the same thing." By asserting that traditional aesthetic distinctions cannot rely on fixed essential principles – as aesthetic perception is always a matter of the changing play of language and experience – yet failing to equally insist that pragmatic distinctions can nonetheless be usefully made, Croce's theory falls into a much wider essentialism, a monism of the world as intuition-expression or language. (Deconstruction, I have argued, in pursuing a very similar argument against the foundations and fixity of genre and disciplinary distinctions, also tends to fall into the trap of linguistic essentialism where all the world is nothing but text.[10])

Analytic aesthetics emerged as a power in the mid-twentieth century by attacking the influential Crocean view for the dreary, vague, and apparently useless monotony of its distinction-demolishing essentialism. By that time, art no longer needed to be defended against positivist, reductionist explanatory models, whether of traditional rhetoric or of sociological determinism. This was because more autonomously aesthetic varieties of art criticism and literary criticism had by then been firmly established, for example that advocated by the New Criticism. Croce's early analytic critics did not generally maintain that the genre distinctions Croce dismissed could be justified by appeal to real metaphysical essences or to tradition. On the contrary, they themselves offered critical revisions of traditional essentialisms about art and its genres. But they did maintain that in order to talk illuminatingly about art one must draw some distinctions and respect some limits of signification of one's theoretical terms; and that to define these boundaries more clearly and maintain them more consistently could promote better ways of talking about art.

Monroe Beardsley, for example, in distinguishing the perceptual object from its physical base and authorial intention, explicitly argued that since

---

[10] See Richard Shusterman, "Analytic Aesthetics, Literary Theory, and Deconstruction," and "Deconstruction and Analysis: Confrontation and Convergence," *British Journal of Aesthetics* 26 (1986): 311–327.

there is no essence of the aesthetic object to be discovered, we have "to propose a way of making the distinction," which itself can only be justified pragmatically. "One can only point to the conveniences of adopting it and to the inconveniences of rejecting it, . . . [and] its own inconveniences."[11] Similarly, John Passmore, in complaining of "the dreariness of aesthetics," prescribed the remedy of a "ruthlessness in making distinctions," in drawing limits that may "seem arbitrary" but can be justified pragmatically by the fact that certain distinctions or limits can structure the aesthetic field in a way that "gives rise to interesting generalizations."[12] He even suggested "that the dullness of aesthetics arises from the attempt to construct a subject where there isn't one", "that there is no aesthetics and yet there are principles of literary criticism, musical criticism, etc.," and that general aesthetics should be abandoned "for an intensive special study of the separate arts," whose specific differences should be respected.

But most analysts in aesthetics still pursued projects of finding general limits to distinguish aesthetics from other fields. J.O. Urmson, my supervisor at Oxford, for example, argued that, "We should expect to find a criterion which allows us to distinguish the aesthetic, the moral, the economic, the intellectual and other evaluations by a single *fundamentum divisionis*," and that "to call an appreciation aesthetic has as part of its point the effect of ruling out the moral as irrelevant."[13] Stuart Hampshire devoted an entire article, "Ethics and Appreciation," to arguing likewise that ethical and aesthetic judgments were entirely different in logical form, and that aesthetics should confine itself to the limits of its own subjective and particularist logic.[14]

III

The history of analytic philosophy's attempts to draw firm and convincing distinctions can instructively illustrate how aesthetics tends to resist clear and strict limits. Analysts such as Beardsley and Urmson tried to distinguish the aesthetic from the nonaesthetic in terms of the former's being narrowly concerned with the perceptual appearance or surface "look of

---

[11] See Monroe C. Beardsley, *Aesthetics: Problems in the Philosophy of Criticism* (New York: Harcourt, Brace, 1958), 53.

[12] See John Passmore, "The Dreariness of Aesthetics," in W. Elton (ed.), *Aesthetics and Language*, (Oxford: Blackwell, 1954), 45–50, 55.

[13] See J.O. Urmson, "What Makes a Situation Aesthetic?" in F. J. Coleman (ed.), *Aesthetics: Contemporary Studies in Aesthetics* (New York: McGraw-Hill, 1968), 360, 368.

[14] See Stuart Hampshire, "Logic and Appreciation," in Elton (ed.), *Aesthetics and Language*, 169.

things."¹⁵ Yet this appearance-based limit was shown to break down once we realize that what we know about an artwork's material properties and purpose will in fact affect, and should affect, how that work appears to us, thus reversing the primacy of appearance over non-perceptual knowledge in aesthetic appreciation.

Other analysts, such as Frank Sibley, tried to draw a sharp aesthetic/nonaesthetic limit in terms of the alleged logically anomalous and independent status of aesthetic terms. The claim was that such terms were neither rule-governed nor conditioned by and inferable from any set of nonaesthetic features of the artwork, but instead rely on aesthetic taste alone for their application.¹⁶ Yet closer analysis showed that this alleged independence from nonaesthetic properties could not be maintained, since aesthetic properties must be at least causally and ontologically dependent on the work's other properties, and since it was also clear that the prominent presence of some nonaesthetic properties (such as great size, mass, weight, bulky shape) could entail that certain aesthetic properties (such as delicate fragility) would not be appropriate for describing the work.¹⁷ Moreover, predicates such as unity and balance seemed to straddle the alleged distinction because they could be conceived in both aesthetic and nonaesthetic (computational) terms.

Similarly, the attempt to limit aesthetics to a realm devoid of all ethical considerations met the insurmountable difficulty that ethical content so often deeply pervaded the artwork's meaning that the work could not be properly understood without attending to its ethical dimensions. Attempts to distinguish a special aesthetic attitude or experience that is limited to artworks and natural beauty (and arises always and only in their presence) have likewise proven very problematic; indeed, so problematic that analysts have persistently questioned whether the notions of aesthetic attitude and aesthetic experience are at all useful for defining the field.

Increasingly aware of the problem of determining the limits of the aesthetic, analytic philosophers have devoted increasingly greater attention to defining the limits of art instead. Two different limit-defining projects can be noted here: first, drawing the boundaries of the realm of art as a

---

¹⁵ See Monroe C. Beardsley, *Aesthetics*, 29–52; J.O. Urmson, "What Makes a Situation Aesthetic?" *Proceedings of the Aristotelian Society*, supp. 131 (1957): 72–92.
¹⁶ See Frank Sibley, "Aesthetic Concepts," *Philosophical Review* 68 (1959): 421–50.
¹⁷ For these and other criticisms of Sibley's theory, see Ted Cohen, "Aesthetic/Non-aesthetic and the Concept of Taste: A Critique of Sibley's Position," *Theoria* 39 (1979): 113–152; Peter Kivy, *Speaking of Art* (The Hague: Martinus Nijhoff, 1973), ch. 2, 3; Gary Stahl, "Sibley's Aesthetic Concepts: An Ontological Mistake," *Journal of Aesthetics and Art Criticism* 29 (1971): 385–389.

whole to distinguish it precisely from the rest of life and what Danto calls "mere real things"; and second, defining the specific borders of individual artworks, that is, the borders that mark off a true instance of a given work (say a genuine text or performance of *Hamlet* or an authentic copy of an etching) from objects that are inauthentic presentations, copies, or forgeries of the artworks they claim to be. Both these projects aim at perfectly covering the extension of the concepts they define (whether art as a whole or a particular artwork) by providing a verbal formula that would fit all and only the right objects for the concept in question; namely, with respect to the general concept of art, those objects that are accepted as works of art; or, with respect to a particular artwork, those objects or events that are accepted as authentic instances of the particular work in question (in painting, this is most often a single object).

Any proposed definition of this sort can be challenged by bringing counterexamples that its verbal formula would either wrongly cover or fail to cover and so would either wrongly include or exclude from art's domain or from the particular artwork's authentic instances. The proposed definition is thus shown to be either too wide or too narrow; its motivating ideal is perfect coverage, and I have therefore called this definitional style "the wrapper model of theory." For like the better food wraps, such theories of art transparently present, contain, and conserve their object – our conventional view of art. They aim to preserve rather than transform art's practice and experience. Like the condom, another form of elastic transparent wrapper (which the French aptly designate *preservatif*), such definitions aim to preserve the conventional limits of art (and thus art itself) from contamination by art's exciting yet impure enveloping environment, while at the same time preserving that environment from art's potential to create new life by its penetration beyond the limits that seek to compartmentalize it within the established art world and within the established criteria of legitimately authentic performances or instances of a particular artwork.

Let us first consider the issue of defining the limits of the particular artwork's identity. This was of crucial importance to analytic aesthetics as part of its preoccupation with art's objects that in turn arose from academic criticism's preoccupation with objective critical truth, which seemed to demand a clearly defined object to serve as the standard of truth. Thus Beardsley claimed, "The first thing to make criticism possible is an object... with its own properties against which interpretations can be checked," and artworks therefore must be such "self-sufficient entities" whose properties and meaning are independent of their contexts of genesis and reception.[18] The object of art becomes a fetishized "icon" whose limits of identity and authenticity must be strictly defined and protected from fakes and corruptions.[19] In Nelson Goodman's influential theory of work-identity, we see, however, how the drive to precisely define the work's identity leads to the paradoxical result of defining it independently of its aesthetically important properties, since such properties are too vague and variable for providing clear definitions. For Goodman, the identity of a musical work must be defined only by the notes of the score because only the notes are clearly definable and defining. This means admitting that the most miserable performance without mistaken notes counts as a fully authentic instance of the musical artwork, "while the most brilliant performance with a single wrong note does not."[20] But what is the real point of defining an artwork to preserve it if the aesthetically important properties of that work are not meant to be preserved? Is it not more fruitful to concentrate on preserving or enriching the aesthetic values of aesthetic experience, even if this involves admitting some wrong notes or letters or reproductions? Such analytic perversities helped push me toward pragmatism, as did the analytic attempts to define art in general.

The most influential of these attempts to define art have likewise tried to do so without appealing to the notion of the aesthetic (whose limits and essence analysis had earlier failed to effectively define). Instead, these theories define art in terms of something beyond aesthetic perception but alleged as necessary for shaping such perception in appreciating art; namely, the art world, a notion that Arthur Danto introduced to analytic aesthetics through his beloved example of Warhol's *Brillo Boxes*, and that George Dickie then interpreted in terms of the institutional theory of art. That institutional theory, which defines an artwork as simply any "artifact upon which some person or persons acting on behalf of a certain social institution (the art world) has conferred the status of candidate for appreciation,"[21] is purely procedural and formal. It leaves all substantive decisions and principles to the art world. By stressing this social

---

[18] See Monroe C. Beardsley, *The Possibility of Criticism* (Detroit: Wayne State University Press, 1970), 16.

[19] See W.K. Wimsatt (with Monroe Beardsley), *The Verbal Icon: Studies in the Meaning of Poetry* (Lexington: University of Kentucky Press, 1967), 3–39.

[20] See Nelson Goodman, *Languages of Art* (Oxford: Oxford University Press, 1969), 120, 186, 209–210.

[21] See George Dickie, *Aesthetics* (Indianapolis: Bobbs-Merrill, 1971), 101; and *Art and the Aesthetic: An Institutional Analysis* (Ithaca: Cornell University Press, 1974), 19–52. I provide a more detailed critique of his theory in *Pragmatist Aesthetics*, 38–40.

context through which art is generated and provided with properties not directly exhibited to the senses (properties that distinguish between Warhol's *Brillo Boxes* and their visually identical counterparts), the institutional theory can explain how art can have a definitional essence without its objects sharing a core of exhibited aesthetic properties. The theory's success in covering all and only authorized artworks is matched by its explanatory poverty. It provides no explanation of the reasons or constraints for proposing art-world membership, no explanation of the art world's history and structure or of the art world's relationship to the wider sociocultural and politico-economic world in which the art world is embedded and by which the art world is significantly shaped.

Danto rejects the institutional theory of art as lacking explanatory value because of its historical emptiness. Ignoring Wölfflin's insight that not everything is possible at every time, the institutional theory fails to consider the historical conditions that structure the art world and that therefore shape and limit its participants' actions in creating and interpreting art. It cannot explain why Warhol's work would not have been accepted had he produced it in fin-de-siècle Paris or quattrocento Florence, but could be art in Manhattan in the 1960s. The explanation, Danto argues, depends on the history of art and art theory because objects are artworks only if they can be interpreted as such by the art world. Thus, the *Brillo Boxes* as a work of art required an interpretation to that effect, both creatively by Warhol and responsively by his audience; and the art world "required a certain historical development" to make that interpretation possible.[22] And since the art world is but an abstraction from the artistic, critical, historiographical, and theoretical practices that constitute art's history, art is essentially a complex historical practice that must be defined and understood historically.

So far so good; but Danto also insists on viewing the structure and history of the art world simply in terms of "its own internal development," in essential isolation from history's wider social and cultural contexts, economic factors, and political struggles. This compartmentalization from the rest of life is part and parcel of Danto's insistence that the distinction between art and reality is absolute. However, as Danto surely knows, conditions and powers of the wider life-world are significantly formative of directions in the art world. Why was it Warhol's *Brillo Boxes* rather than Duchamp's much earlier *objets trouvés* (or readymades) that so strongly

---

[22] Arthur C. Danto, *The Transfiguration of the Commonplace* (Cambridge, MA: Harvard University Press, 1981), 208.

captured Danto and the wider public's interest and thus more decisively transformed our notion of contemporary art? Is not the wider social and cultural revolution of the 1960s part of the explanation, along with the ever-increasing power of consumerist culture and popular media culture to which Warhol himself was so attached? How can we explain the emergence of graffiti art and the work of Keith Haring and Jean-Michel Basquiat without looking to social and cultural movements such as hip hop that were initially beyond the established limits of the art world?

By faithfully representing our established concept of art and insisting on its objects' radical distinction from "mere real things," Danto's theory best realizes the dual goals of wrapper definitions: accurate reflection and compartmental differentiation that set art apart from the rest of life.[23] My dissatisfaction with the value of these goals helped push me toward the path of pragmatism. If all substantive decisions as to what counts as art are left to the internal decisions of the art world as recorded by art history, then what useful purpose does simply reflecting those decisions in a philosophical formula serve, apart from appeasing the old philosophical urge for theory as mirroring reflection of the real?

Accurate reflection seems an eminently valuable philosophical ideal when reality is conceived in terms of fixed, necessary essences lying beyond ordinary empirical understanding. This is because an adequate representation of this reality would always remain valid and effective as a criterion for assessing ordinary understanding and practice. But if art's realities are the empirical and changing contingencies of art's historical career, then the reflective model seems pointless. For here, theory's representation neither penetrates beyond changing phenomena nor can sustain their changes. Instead, it must run a hopeless race of perpetual narrative revision, holding the mirror of reflective theory up to art's changing nature by representing its history.[24]

---

[23] See Danto, *The Transfiguration of the Commonplace*, ch. 1.

[24] Danto tries to avoid this worry by insisting that despite art's changing history it has a defining and unchanging "transhistorical essence" that "is always the same." His claim is that there is "a fixed and universal artistic identity" or "unchangeable" essence of art, even an "extrahistorical concept of art," but that this essence merely "discloses itself through history." See Arthur Danto, *After the End of Art* (Princeton: Princeton University Press, 1997), 28, 187, 193. Likewise, although this defining essence determines the limits of art (by marking art off from what is not art), it does not in any way limit how art can appear because aesthetic properties are excluded from this essence. So in that sense, for Danto, anything could be a work of art, despite the fact that many things are not

But art's mutable history need not be merely represented; pragmatism urges that it can also be made through theoretical interventions; so pragmatism also rethinks the roles and limits of aesthetic theory and philosophy. No longer content with simply analyzing realities and concepts, it seeks to improve them and thereby promote better experience. Such theoretical activism does not entail abandoning philosophy altogether by forsaking its traditional project and self-image as the wholly disinterested pursuit of truth. For philosophy's most powerful achievements were not always, if ever, really governed by this goal. Certainly, Plato's aesthetic theory cannot be seen as disinterestedly representing the nature of art. It was clearly a politically motivated response to the pressing problem of whose intellectual leadership (art's ancient wisdom or philosophy's new rationality) should guide Athenian society at a time of troubled change, political dissension, and military defeat. The influential political theories of Thomas Hobbes and John Locke were also responses to political crisis and shaped by political motives. Moreover, the very ideal of pure, neutral reflection typically disguises an impure bias. Fixation on the facts often reflects the interest of a conservatism that is happy to reinforce the status quo by representing it in definition or is simply too timid to take part in the messy struggle over the shaping of culture. The fetishism of disinterested knowledge obscures the truth that philosophy's ultimate aim is to benefit human life rather than serving pure truth for truth's sake. If art and aesthetic experience are crucial forms of human flourishing, then philosophy betrays its role if it merely looks on with neutrality without joining the struggle to extend their breadth and power.

> works of art. The problem with this essentialist strategy is that the definition it provides is not at all helpful in telling us how to recognize a work of art, which is one of the reasons why essential definitions were sought. Nor does Danto's notion of essence make stylistic suggestions for creating art or provide effective criteria for evaluating art, which are the other important practical motives for seeking an essential definition of art. Both good and bad artworks, Danto realizes, must have the same essence because both are works of art by virtue of that essence, and that essence is not at all a matter of aesthetic or artistic quality. See *After the End of Art*, 197; and Arthur Danto, *The Madonna of the Future* (New York: Farrar, Straus, and Giroux, 2000), 427. Danto's essentialist strategy also fails to define art's essence in a narrow enough way. His two criteria for the essence of an artwork (which he admits are too "meager" to "be the entire story") are to "have a content or meaning" and "to embody its meaning" (*The Madonna of the Future*, xix). Yet iconic signs and all sorts of cultural objects also do that, and so do most intentional actions. A real-life kiss has meaning and embodies it, but that does not make it a work of art. Of course, one could stage a kiss as an artwork or represent one, as Klimt and Rodin did so sensually.

IV

For such reasons, I turned from analytic philosophy to pragmatism, while also enlisting insights from hermeneutics, critical theory, and poststructuralism that challenge in different ways some of the problematic assumptions and limits of analytic aesthetics. These problems include its fetishized concern with precisely defining art's objects (presumed to have a fixed identity, unity, and ontology); its exaggerated sense of art's demarcation from the rest of life and its autonomy from wider social and political forces that, in fact, penetrate even into the very forms of artistic expression; and its essentially descriptivist conceptual approach that typically eschews revisionary projects and sociopolitical engagement so as to represent and reinforce the established cultural status quo.[25]

If analytic theory is essentially demarcational – seeking to define by delimiting the concepts it analyzes in terms of wrapper definitions of extension, then the pragmatism I practice tries to be more transformational in style. Although beginning with a recognition of the established meanings and limits of the concepts it treats, the pragmatist examines whether a concept's range can be usefully extended (or narrowed) in places where its borders seem vague or flexible enough to allow such extension (or restriction) without destroying the concept's principal meaning and value, but instead making it more meaningful and useful in improving our aesthetic understanding and experience. Recognizing that Dewey's definition of art as experience was hopelessly inadequate as an extensional or wrapper theory, I argued (in *Pragmatist Aesthetics*) that it was nonetheless useful as a transformational theory. Its emphasizing aesthetic experience could not only help break the hold of object fetishism in contemporary art, aesthetics, and culture; it could also be used to help acquire artistic legitimacy for popular arts (such as rap music) that provided powerful aesthetic experience but were not yet granted genuine aesthetic or artistic status.

My own subsequent proposal to define art as dramatization was not aimed at perfect wrapper coverage of the extension of art, but instead sought to highlight two crucial aspects of art – intensity of presence and formal framing – that have generated conflicting theories that divide contemporary aesthetics.[26] The concept of dramatization connotes both

---

[25] For more on these themes, see Shusterman, *Pragmatist Aesthetics*, ch. 1, 2, and 6.
[26] See Richard Shusterman, *Surface and Depth* (Ithaca: Cornell University Press, 2002), ch. 13.

intensity of meaningful appearance, action, or experience (which generates theories that define art in terms of immediate, captivating presence or experience). But it also connotes the formal framing of an action, appearance, or experience through a historically established conventional framework that differentiates what is framed from the ordinary flow of life. This second feature lies at the core of contemporary theories that define art in terms of its historically constructed social differentiation from other realms, theories such as Pierre Bourdieu's, Danto's, and Dickie's. In proposing the idea of art as dramatization, my aims were also transformational in that the definition will take us beyond the conventional limits of established art by applying also to forms of ritual and athletics that display significant artistry and aesthetic experience but do not fall under the concept of art. It can also apply (as I argue in Chapter 12) to practices of lovemaking, the so-called erotic arts, whose status as art and potential to provide intense and artistically dramatized aesthetic experience has been neglected in the West. These arts certainly merit somaesthetic analysis and cultivation.

V

Somaesthetics, of course, is a natural extension of my work in pragmatist aesthetics. Bringing aesthetics closer to the realm of life and practice, I realized, entails bringing the body more centrally into aesthetic focus, as all life and practice – all perception, cognition, and action – is crucially performed through the body. Somaesthetics was thus conceived to complement the basic project of pragmatist aesthetics by elaborating the ways that a disciplined, ramified, and interdisciplinary attention to bodily experience, methods, discourses, and performances could enrich our aesthetic experience and practice, not only in the fine arts but in the diverse arts of living. It originated as an attempt to go beyond the limits not only of Baumgarten's neglect of somatic cultivation in his original project of aesthetic cultivation but also beyond the rejection of body and desire that is so prominent in the Western tradition of philosophical aesthetics (from Shaftesbury and Kant through Schopenhauer and into the present), despite the fact that body and desire are so important in Western art and literature, even in its religious forms.

Beyond its roots in pragmatist aesthetics, the somaesthetic project was equally inspired by the ancient idea of philosophy as a way of life, and my efforts to apply the pragmatist tradition to revive this idea in order to overcome the limits of philosophy's institutionalized confinement as a purely academic practice of teaching, reading, and writing texts. Thus, it is in my book *Practicing Philosophy: Pragmatism and the Philosophical Life* (1997) that I first discussed the idea of somaesthetics in a substantive way, explicitly using this term.[27] For me, the notion of philosophy as an art of living (rather than an "art of dying," as Plato's *Phaedo* described it) entails that embodiment should be a meaningful aspect of philosophical practice because it is an essential aspect of life. Philosophers in the ancient world were assessed not simply by the words they wrote or spoke but by the virtue of their actions and the quality of their comportment. Confucius thus could propose to his disciples that he simply give up lecturing and teach (as nature does) by exemplary wordless behavior; and Mencius indeed praised this style of teaching: "His every limb bears wordless testimony."[28] *Practicing Philosophy* thus introduced somaesthetics as a way of reminding contemporary readers that philosophy could and should be practiced with one's body rather than being confined to "the life of the mind." It likewise highlighted the role of embodiment in political issues of justice, freedom, and liberal democracy that the book also treated.

Somaesthetics further transcends the conventional limits of philosophical aesthetics as a field of mere theory, for it insists on a practical dimension of actually cultivating somatic disciplines. Although Baumgarten originally conceived aesthetics as a discipline involving both theoretical study and practical aesthetic exercises, he rejected somatic exercises from the field because he associated the body with mere flesh devoid of capacity for perception (aesthesis). My concept of soma as a living, purposive, sentient, perceptive body or bodily subjectivity provides an altogether different direction. We can, as I have tried to demonstrate, improve our perceptual faculties through better use of the soma. Because the most convincing demonstrations of this truth are not in verbal arguments but in lived perceptual experience, there is great importance to the actual experience of somaesthetic exercises that heighten perception. I have therefore felt obliged not only to lecture on somaesthetics but also to give practical workshops that convey and underline its practical dimension.[29] These workshops exhaust a great amount of time and energy that I would

---

[27] Richard Shusterman, *Practicing Philosophy: Pragmatism and the Philosophical Life* (New York: Routledge, 1997), 128–29, 176–77. As I note in the Preface, my first published reference to the somaesthetic project was in my German book *Vor der Interpretation* (Vienna: Passagen Verlag, 1996).

[28] For more on these points, see Shusterman, "Pragmatist Aesthetics and East-Asian Thought," in *The Range of Pragmatism and the Limits of Philosophy* (Oxford: Blackwell, 2004), 13–42.

[29] For some clips of one such workshop, see https://sites.google.com/site/somaesthetics/home/video-clips.

otherwise be happy to devote to reading and writing, but they are necessary for insuring that somaesthetics goes beyond the limits of a merely theoretical discursive pursuit and for showing how it fruitfully expands the menu of methods for transmitting philosophical ideas.

Finally, somaesthetics, even in its more theoretical pursuits, goes beyond the typical disciplinary limits of philosophy. Although I initially conceived it as entirely nested within philosophy – most likely as a subdiscipline of aesthetics – I soon realized that it would be more fruitfully pursued as an interdisciplinary field, enlisting a variety of disciplines (such as history, sociology, cosmetics, anatomy, meditative and martial arts, physiology, nutrition, kinesiology, psychology, and neuroscience) that enrich our understanding of how we experience and use the body in appreciative perception, aesthetic performance, and creative self-fashioning, and for examining the methods of improving such experience and use.

If some critics worry that this breaking out of philosophy's disciplinary limits risks making somaesthetics an incoherent and unstructured field with no center relating to aesthetics, my response (already made in Chapter 1) is that aesthetic research should be properly informed by the best relevant scientific knowledge, as Renaissance art and art theory clearly show with their use of anatomy, mathematics, and the optics of perspective. In any case, the sciences that explain somatic functioning are surely relevant to somaesthetics' core mission of improving our understanding of the body's use in perception, performance, and self-fashioning, while also enhancing the quality of our somatic experience in these matters. If this forms the field's structuring focus, then there are certainly many things that fall outside its limits. Issues in formal logic and income tax hardly pertain to somaesthetics, but what would be the point of outlawing their possible relevance a priori from the outset? If some aspect of knowledge can be convincingly shown to relate importantly and productively to somaesthetics' central concerns, then somaesthetics can reinterpret or extend its borders at that precise place to take it in, recognizing that limits (just like concepts) can still function when they are flexible and vague. Somaesthetics, moreover, contains some structuring distinctions that provide some flexible and somewhat overlapping borders within the field. The different branches of analytic somaesthetics (essentially descriptive theory), pragmatic somaesthetics (comparative evaluation of methodologies of practice), and practical somaesthetics (actual performance of somatic disciplines) have been explained in Chapter 1 and need no further elaboration here.

Instead, I wish to close by briefly considering another kind of limit with which somaesthetics is concerned and that has been especially emphasized by some important contemporary French philosophers of the body, such as Georges Bataille and Michel Foucault. It is not so much a conceptual limit or disciplinary boundary but an experiential one, which they sometimes call "limit-experience" (*expérience-limite*) and which they describe as an experience of violent intensity typically involving some violent form of somatic transgression that is also typically a transgression of moral as well as somatic norms.[30] The value of these limit-experiences lies not simply in their experiential intensity that seems related to the intense sublimities of aesthetic experience but in their power to transform us by showing us the limits of our conventional experience and subjectivity and by introducing us to something fascinatingly powerful beyond those limits, an *au delà* of what we are and know. Is somaesthetics committed to such limit-experiences? And what would such commitment imply about its general viability and value – in pragmatic, ethical, social, and health-related terms?

Certainly, somaesthetics is committed to studying the use of such forms of limit-experiences, but that does not imply a commitment to advocating them as the best way to enlarge our somaesthetic capacities and to achieve wider transformational improvements of ourselves and our self-knowledge. In fact, there is growing evidence from recent studies in psychology and neurophysiology that indicate the dangers of such sensory violence for our powers and pleasures of perception. These studies reinforce perspectives of the old Weber-Fechner law of psychophysics, which explains how increased intensity of stimulus reduces the power to perceive and appreciate smaller sensory differences – thus tending to generate a spiral effect where ever-stronger stimulation is demanded to meet the rising sensory thresholds, habits, and needs. Somaesthetics can therefore involve also a critique of the limits (cognitive and aesthetic, as well as practical, moral, and social) of these violent limit experiences, while exploring other limit-experiences that deploy more gentle, subtle means to probe a wide range of somaesthetic limits (of sensory attention, somatic flexibility, habitual breathing rhythms, and muscular tensions) that can equally achieve powerful experiences of transformative exultation that expand the self.

[30] See Michel Foucault, "How an 'Experience-Book' is Born," in *Remarks on Marx: Conversations with Duccio Trombadori*, trans. R.J. Goldstein and J. Cascaito (New York, 1991), 25–42; and Georges Bataille, *Inner Experience*, trans. Leslie Boldt (Albany: SUNY, 1988), 1–61 for discussion of this idea.

Moreover, somaesthetics should not limit itself to the realm of ecstatic limit-experiences. There is a range of different somaesthetic limits that we fail to appreciate in everyday life, and a better experiential knowledge of them could significantly improve the ways we live. Lacking the sensitivity to sense these limits – such as the border between satiating our hunger and being full, between engaging perceptual interest and overstimulation, between proper tonus for postural poise and excessive muscular contraction – has led all too much of our population to problems of obesity, insomnia, and chronic back pain. We often do not perceive these borders because our somaesthetic awareness has not been sufficiently sharpened and sensitized to grasp them. The problems arising from failure to recognize such limits belong to what I call the somaesthetic pathologies of everyday life, whose frequent etiology in implicit muscle memory formed the focus of Chapter 4.

7

Somaesthetics and Burke's Sublime

I

Targeting his influential predecessors Immanuel Kant and Arthur Schopenhauer, Friedrich Nietzsche mordantly mocks the dogma of aesthetic disinterestedness, which defines beauty in terms of a purely disinterested pleasure that is inconsistent with will and desire. He denigrates this attitude as an expression of the prudish innocence of philosophers, whose second-hand, spectator's view of art compares unfavorably to the creative, hands-on, passionately desiring experience of the artist. The power of art and beauty, Nietzsche argues, derives not from disinterest but rather from "the excitement of the will, of 'interest'" ("die Erregung des Willes, 'des Interesses'"). "When our estheticians tirelessly rehearse, in support of Kant's view, that the spell of beauty enables us to view even *nude* female statues 'disinterestedly' we may be allowed to laugh a little at their expense. The experiences of artists in this delicate matter are rather more 'interesting'; certainly Pygmalion was not entirely devoid of esthetic feeling."[1]

Such failure to appreciate the role of will and sensuality in aesthetic experience, Nietzsche suggests, is linked to a much more general philosophical bias toward ignoring the somatic dimension of the aesthetic. This neglect derives not only from an idealist-rationalist repugnance for

---

[1] See Friedrich Nietzsche, *Zur Genealogie der Moral*, in G. Colli and M. Montinari (eds.), *Friedrich Nietzsche: Sämtliche Werke*, vol. 5, (Berlin: de Gruyter, 1999), 347. For the English translation, see *The Birth of Tragedy and The Genealogy of Morals*, trans. Francis Golffing (New York: Doubleday, 1956), 239, 240.

the body but also from a corresponding ignorance of the "Physiologie der Ästhetik" whose issues and import, he complains, "have scarcely been touched to this day."[2] Edmund Burke's aesthetics provides an important exception to Nietzsche's claim. Not only does Burke recognize that interest and even sexual desire are compatible with the appreciation of beauty, his theory of the sublime similarly implies the notion of interest while also offering a physiological explanation of our feelings of sublimity that explicitly defines certain conditions of our nerves as the "efficient cause" of such feelings.[3]

Although Burke's general account of the sublime is widely appreciated, its somatic dimension has been dismissed as hopelessly misguided. In W.J. Hipple's damning verdict, "This physiological theory was reckoned an absurdity even in the eighteenth century," so that Burke's most vigorous supporters, such as Uvedale Price, tended to downplay or displace it. Hipple's influential study of eighteenth-century aesthetics has no doubt contributed to the continuing neglect of the somatic dimension of Burke's thought. Thus, an admirably inclusive anthology of British eighteenth-century theories of the sublime completely omits Burke's somatic approach, although it is a major aspect of his theory and constitutes the entire fourth part of his *Philosophical Enquiry*.[4]

This chapter explores the somatic aspect of Burke's aesthetics, paying special attention to his treatment of the sublime, and connecting his ideas with more contemporary theoretical perspectives, particularly that of somaesthetics. Though Burke's somatic arguments and conclusions can surely be criticized as overly simplistic, one-sidedly mechanistic, and unnecessarily reductionistic, his recognition of the

---

[2] Nietzsche, *Zur Genealogie*, 356; my translation; cf., *The Genealogy of Morals*, 247.
[3] Edmund Burke, *A Philosophical Enquiry into the Origin of our Ideas of the Sublime and Beautiful* (London: Penguin, 1998), 159; hereafter PE.
[4] Walter J. Hipple, Jr., *The Beautiful, the Sublime, and the Picturesque in Eighteenth-Century British Aesthetic Theory* (Carbondale: Southern Illinois University Press, 1957), 92. With respect to Burke's central thesis that the sublime acts by tensing the nerves and muscles while beauty acts by relaxing them, Price is unwilling to affirm that "they are really stretched or relaxed," but merely remarks that "this account ... presents a lively image of the sensations often produced by love and astonishment," which Burke associates respectively with beauty and the sublime. See Uvedale Price, *An Essay on the Picturesque, as Compared with the Sublime and Beautiful*, in Andrew Ashfield and Peter de Bolla (eds.), *The Sublime: A Reader in British Eighteenth-century Aesthetic Theory* (Cambridge: Cambridge University Press, 1996), 274. Although this fine anthology selects large chunks of Burke's *Enquiry* on the sublime and the beautiful, it does not include any of Part IV of that treatise, in which his physiological theory is presented and defended.

crucial bodily dimensions of aesthetic experience needs to be taken more seriously. As somaesthetics seeks to refine and extend Burke's insight that bodily factors can help explain our aesthetic reactions, it further urges that improved somatic understanding and performance can also provide valuable means for enhancing our aesthetic response, not just explaining it.

Recognizing the physiological dimension of aesthetics is crucial in at least three ways. First and most basic is that the structure, conditions, and functioning of our bodily apparatus are essential conditions for the sensory perceptions that shape aesthetic experience and constitute the processes of creating and appreciating art. Our sense of rhythm is grounded on bodily rhythms; our sense of balance and our perception of movement involve, in an essential way, bodily proprioception; our very ability to direct and sustain our attention depends on the exercise of muscular capacities. Second, heightened qualities of affect or emotion are often an important and valued feature of aesthetic experience (both of art and nature), but such heightened feeling or emotion essentially involves bodily reactions along with cognitive content. Third, the somatic dimension of aesthetic experience helps explain art's claim to distinctive cognitive value. There has long been considerable debate about whether art provides a special source of truth and whether such truth is central to art's value. Art's propositional character can surely be questioned, and thus also art's ability to supply special or especially valuable propositional truth. But the strong emotional content or quality of much art, through the bodily roots and effects of such emotion, suggests a way of understanding art's special cognitive contribution. Even if art does not provide new truths, its emotive power gives the beliefs it creates and the truths it purveys an especially strong appeal and sticking power, since such belief is embodied in heightened flesh-and-blood feelings rather than simply understood as an intellectual abstraction. Such belief leaves deeper traces in our mental attitudes and habits of thought because of their reverberations through the body. More generally, as we already argued, knowledge anchored in embodied practice is more firmly secure than if merely fastened to abstract thought; so "we must not attach learning [merely] to the mind, we must incorporate it; we must not sprinkle, but dye."[5]

---

[5] Michel de Montaigne, *The Complete Essays of Montaigne*, trans. Donald Frame (Stanford: Stanford University Press, 1958), 103.

II

If such arguments quell the impulse to dismiss the very idea of Burke's somatic approach as altogether outré, then what remains for somaesthetics is to examine Burke's important theoretical precedent, profit from its insights, and critically address its limitations with the aim of providing a sounder somatic theory of aesthetic experience.

1. We can begin by noting how bravely distinctive Burke's somaticism is, how sharply it departs from the orientation of his most important philosophical predecessors in eighteenth-century aesthetics: Alexander Baumgarten and the Earl of Shaftesbury. Coining the term "aesthetics," Baumgarten defined this field as a theoretical but also practical "science of sensory cognition" aimed at "the perfection of sensory cognition, this implying beauty" (§§ 1, 14). Though the quality of sensory perception surely depends on the acuity and proper functioning of our bodily sense receptors, Baumgarten excludes somatic study and exercise from his aesthetic enterprise, probably because of the religious pressures of his sociohistorical context and the rationalist philosophical tradition in which he worked.[6] Shaftesbury, who helped introduce the influential ideas of disinterestedness and the sublime (which he classified as a kind of beauty), staunchly rejects (as part of his pervasive Platonism) the body's role in aesthetics in order to affirm mind as the sole formative power: "there is no principle of beauty in body.... body can no way be the cause of beauty... *the beautiful, the fair, the comely, were never in the matter but in the art and design, never in body itself but in the form or forming power*.... It is mind alone which forms."[7]

In stark contrast, Burke's aesthetics is distinctively embodied, relying on an implicit naturalistic, empiricist ontology that affirms the intimate union of mind and body while claiming that mental contents are ultimately the product of sensations involving bodily effects. Aesthetic taste is based on natural "sensibility" to "the primary pleasures of sense," as further developed by the powers of imagination and honed by judgment and understanding (PE, 74–75). As our mental life is nourished by the

---

[6] I quote from the bilingual (Latin-German) abridged edition of Alexander Baumgarten's *Aesthetica*, entitled *Theoretische Ästhetik: die grundlegenden Abschnitte aus der "Aesthetica" (1750/58)*, trans. H.R. Schweizer (Hamburg: Meiner, 1988), 3, 11. English translations are mine. For more details on Baumgarten's neglect of the somatic, see Richard Shusterman, *Pragmatist Aesthetics: Living Beauty, Rethinking Art*, 2nd ed. (New York: Rowman and Littlefield, 2000), ch. 10.

[7] Anthony, Earl of Shaftesbury, *Characteristics of Men, Manners, Opinions, Times*, ed. Lawrence Klein (Cambridge: Cambridge University Press, 1999), 322.

bodily senses, so our mental activities rely on corporeal forces: "it is probable, that not only the inferior parts of the soul, as the passions are called, but the understanding itself makes use of some fine corporeal instruments in its operation... [as] appears from hence; that a long exercise of the mental powers induces a remarkable lassitude of the whole body; and, on the other hand, that great bodily labour, or pain, weakens, and sometimes, actually destroys the mental faculties" (PE, 164–165).

Even when we do not perceive a particular bodily reaction as mediating our mental reaction to a state of affairs (such as our disappointment at bad weather), Burke suggests that "the bodily organs suffer first, and the mind through these organs" (PE, 175). Far from a passive epiphenomenon, the mind's perceptions and passions reciprocally influence our bodily states and behavior: "things that cause terror generally affect the bodily organs by the operation of the mind suggesting the danger" (PE, 162). Burke argues that the interactive character of the mind-body unity enables somatic interventions to modify our mental states, much as William James's somatic theory of emotion did two centuries later. Noting the ability of "the celebrated physiognomist Campanella" to "enter into the dispositions and thoughts of people" by imitating their "face," "gesture," and "whole body," Burke claims that he himself "involuntarily found [his own] mind turned to that passion whose appearance [he] endeavoured to imitate" (PE, 162–163).

He thus concludes: "Our minds and bodies are so closely and intimately connected, that one is incapable of pain or pleasure without the other." Here again, Burke invokes Campanella, who "could so abstract his attention from any sufferings of his body, that he was able to endure the rack itself without much pain; and in lesser pains, every body must have observed that when we can employ our attention on any thing else, the pain has been for a time suspended." Similarly, Burke argues, "if by any means the body is indisposed to perform such gestures, or to be stimulated in to such emotions as any passion usually produces in it, that passion itself never can arise; though it should be merely mental, and immediately affecting none of the senses." For example, "an opiate... shall suspend the operation of grief, or fear, or anger, in spite of all our efforts to the contrary; and this by inducing in the body a disposition contrary to that which it receives from these passions" (PE, 163).

Without contesting the general thrust of Burke's arguments for the essential interactive unity of the mind-body nexus, we should critically note that his formulation of these examples paradoxically suggests that mental and somatic life can in fact be made to go their separate ways;

for example, by mentally abstracting attention from the pain of physical injury or, conversely, by physically blocking with drugs the somatic expression of emotion, even in a passion that "should be merely mental." A more accurate and rigorous recognition of body-mind integrity would realize that any Campanella-like effort to mentally abstract or distract attention always engages also bodily means, since muscular contractions, particularly in the area of the head and eyes, are habitually involved in all efforts of mental concentration and attentive thought. We should also note that the notion of a merely mental passion is a problematic residue of dualist thinking.

2. A point already implied in our discussion of somatic interventions but worth highlighting explicitly is the underlying meliorism that Burke's project shares with somaesthetics. Urging that "elevation of the mind ought to be the principal end of our studies," Burke also insists that understanding our passions (their variety, rationale, and generative mechanisms) has indispensable practical value for regulating them, such knowledge being "very necessary for all who would affect them upon solid and sure principles" (PE, 98). If our passions cannot be regulated, our efforts at elevating the mind will be hampered. Moreover, Burke insists, our understanding of the passions must be specific and practical: "It is not enough to know them in general; to affect them . . . we should pursue them through all their variety of operations, and pierce into the inmost, and what might appear inaccessible parts of our nature" (PE, 98). Given the somatic roots and dimensions of our passions, Burke's project invites somaesthetic research of various forms: phenomenological inquiries of introspection into the diverse ways we experience these feelings; physiological studies of the mechanisms of such feeling; sociological and psychological research on the social, behavioral, and cognitive conditions that structure and habituate our modes of feeling; pragmatic somatic studies of how we can better know, regulate, deploy, and refine these feelings in our conduct of life or arts of living.

3. In exploring the ways we use our bodies to improve our experience, somaesthetics insists on the variety of pleasures. Failure to appreciate this variety has led to assimilating pleasure to mere pleasant sensations or fun, which, in turn, has resulted in a philosophical tendency to deprecate the value of pleasure in aesthetic experience and more generally in life.[8] Burke's theory of the sublime is an important precedent for

---

[8] For more on the important plurality of aesthetic pleasures, see my papers "Entertainment: A Question for Aesthetics," *British Journal of Aesthetics* 43 (2003): 289–307; and

asserting the plurality of pleasure.[9] He famously distinguishes between the "positive pleasure" of beauty (among other positive pleasures) and what he calls "the relative pleasure" produced by the sublime, which he dubs "Delight" (PE, 81–84). In contrast to positive pleasure, which is entirely independent of pain, delight is only a relative pleasure because it is essentially related to pain or to danger (which he understands as the threat of pain). Burke defines delight as "the sensation which accompanies the removal of pain or danger" or as "the feeling which results from the ceasing or diminution of pain" or from "the removal or moderation of pain." Although not a positive pleasure in the sense of being entirely independent of pain, delight is certainly experienced as a genuine "pleasure" or "satisfaction"; it is a "feeling" or "affection" that (despite being generated by some sort of "Privation") is felt "undoubtedly positive" "in the mind of him who feels it" (PE, 83–84).

Burke distinguishes delight from pleasure not only in terms of its generating cause and relational dependence but also, quite significantly, in terms of its different bodily expression. Describing the delight of the sublime as "a sort of tranquility shadowed with horror," which we would experience, for example, "upon escaping some imminent danger, or on being released from the severity of some cruel pain," Burke remarks that "the countenance and the gesture of the body on such occasions" of this enjoyable affect is such "that any person . . . would rather judge [the subject experiencing the sublime as being] under some consternation, than in the enjoyment of any thing like positive pleasure" (PE, 82). This should not surprise us, since Burke defines the sublime in terms of terror, pain, and danger; and he describes its signature "passions" of

---

"Interpretation, Pleasure, and Value in Aesthetic Experience," *Journal of Aesthetics and Art Criticism* 56 (1998): 51–53. The latter is a response to the critique of Alexander Nehamas, "Richard Shusterman on Pleasure and Aesthetic Experience," *Journal of Aesthetics and Art Criticism* 56 (1998): 49–51.

[9] Burke's aesthetics is also important for affirming the plurality or independent existence of "positive" pains and "positive" pleasures rather than simply regarding pain and pleasure as "mere relations, which can only exist as they are contrasted" to each other (PE, 81). This implies that pleasure cannot simply be defined in terms of absence of pain, nor can pain be defined as mere absence of pleasure. Burke's view that pain and pleasure are bivalent rather than bipolar is confirmed by contemporary psychological and neurological research. Pain and pleasure involve different electromyographic changes in facial muscles, differences in cortical activation patterns and neural pathways, just as approach and avoidance behavior (behavioral correlates of pleasure and pain) are associated with different neurotransmitters and can occur virtually simultaneously (thus generating conflict). See Daniel Kahneman "Objective Happiness," in Daniel Kahneman, Ed Diener, and Norbert Schwarz (eds.), *Well-being: the Foundations of Hedonic Psychology* (New York: Russell Sage, 1999), 3–25.

awe and astonishment (as well as its lesser manifestations of admiration, reverence, and respect) as feelings that tense up the body in contrast to the passion of love, which is caused by beauty and is claimed to melt, relax, or soften the body.

4. Burke's somatic approach links the sublime's feelings of delight to biological instincts of "self-preservation," which are now very familiar to us from evolutionary theory. Feelings of pain and danger provide us with crucial warnings that help us to adjust and to survive. "The passions which concern self-preservation," Burke argues, "turn mostly on *pain* or *danger*... and they are the most powerful of all the passions." Thus the same relationship to pain and danger that qualifies the sublime as only a relative pleasure paradoxically renders it "more powerful" than simple positive pleasures because it is engaged with what "is productive of the strongest emotion which the mind is capable of feeling" (PE, 86). Since the "delightful horror" of the sublime "belongs to self-preservation," not only is it "one of the strongest of all passions" (PE, 165); it is also not purely disinterested, because it is clearly rooted in our powerful interest to survive and avoid pain.

Beauty is contrastingly defined as a positive pleasure and linked to "the passions... of society," one principal form of which is the "society of sex," whose passion of love contains "a mixture of lust" and whose object is "the *beauty* of the *sex*," which he later tends to describe in more narrowly sexist fashion as "the beauty of women" (PE, 87, 89, 97).[10] As appreciation of bodily beauty can be sexually interested and appetitive or lustful (thus serving the ends of procreation), so Burke conversely stresses that one may love (in a social but nonsexual sense) the beauty of people and animals without any admixture of lust. By highlighting the sublime's passions of self-preservation and beauty's link to "*generation*" (PE, 87), Burke provides an aesthetic presciently based on two naturalistic pillars of evolutionary thought. Just as we need to recognize and avoid pain and danger, so are we spurred to enjoy the positive pleasure of love and beauty, whose most powerful expression is *sexual* – a pleasure he describes as "rapturous and violent, and confessedly the highest pleasure of sense" (87).[11]

---

[10] See also Burke's sexist remarks that, "An air of robustness and strength is very prejudicial to beauty. An appearance of *delicacy*, and even of fragility, is almost essential to it.... The beauty of women is considerably owing to their weakness, or delicacy, and is even enhanced by their timidity, a quality of mind analogous to it" (PE, 150).

[11] For a contemporary philosophical defense of the aesthetic potential of erotic experience, see Richard Shusterman, "Aesthetic Experience: From Analysis to Eros," *Journal of Aesthetics and Art Criticism* 64 (2006): 217–229; and Chapter 9 in this book.

5. Burke, however, affirms an intriguing power asymmetry of pain over pleasure: "the ideas of pain are much more powerful than those which enter on the part of pleasure. Without all doubt, the torments which we may be made to suffer are much greater in their effect on the body and mind than any pleasures which the most learned voluptuary could suggest, or than the liveliest imagination and the most sound and exquisitely sensible body could enjoy" (PE, 86). This more powerfully positive negativity of pain and danger can be transmuted into very strong positive affect when it is relieved, distanced, or diminished. On the other hand, the privation of sexual pleasure, Burke argues, does not cause real pain or significant discomfort, and only on occasion "affects at all" (PE, 87). Of course, "when danger and pain press too nearly, they are incapable of giving any delight, and are simply terrible; but at certain distances, and with certain modifications, they may be, and they are delightful, as we every day experience" (PE, 86–87). Particularly delightful is the passage from intense pain to the relief of its removal, which Montaigne, two centuries earlier, so ardently celebrated: "But is there anything so sweet as that sudden change, when from extreme pain, by the voiding of my stone, I come to recover as if by lightning the beautiful light of my health, so free and so full, as happens in our sudden and sharpest attacks of colic? Is there anything in this pain we suffer that can be said to counterbalance the pleasure of such sudden improvement?" It seems "that nature has lent us pain for the honor and service of pleasure and painlessness."[12]

Burke's advocacy of the power asymmetry of pain and pleasure finds remarkable support in contemporary psychological studies concerning choice and hedonics. We are keener to avoid pain than gain positive pleasure, more concerned about loss than gain. Findings with respect to "loss aversion" show that "losing $100 produces a feeling of negativity that is more intense than the feelings of elation produced by a gain. Some studies have estimated that losses have twice the psychological impact as equivalent gains."[13] Recent experiments also support the notion that the removal or diminution of suffering has a particularly positive affect. Daniel Kahneman and his associates have shown that our judgment of the pleasurable quality of past experiences is almost entirely determined by the twin factors of their qualitative peak (best or worst) and their concluding tone. In one experimental study, people listened to a pair of

---

[12] Montaigne, *Complete Essays*, 838.
[13] Barry Schwartz, *The Paradox of Choice* (New York: HarperCollins, 2004), 70.

unpleasant loud noises and subsequently had to choose which one they would prefer to hear repeated. One noise lasted ten seconds, the other fourteen. The initial ten seconds of each noise were identical, but the continuation of the longer noise, though still loud and unpleasant, was not as loud as in the beginning. Objectively, the second noise should seem much worse because its peak unpleasantness is identical and just as long, and its overall unpleasantness is 40 percent longer. Yet the overwhelming majority of people preferred it as their choice for repetition. The reason for this logically puzzling preference clearly seems to be that the end of the preferred noise involved a significant diminution of earlier pain, producing such a positive feeling of relief that the whole experience was more favorably colored and remembered.[14]

6. Another way in which Burke links the sublime to self-preservation focuses not on the horrors of danger and pain but on the health benefits of their neurological analogues. From the premise that pain and terror share a physiological essence of intensified muscular "contraction" or "unnatural tension of the nerves" (which he identifies as the "mechanical cause" or "efficient cause" of the sublime), Burke first argues "it easily follows... that whatever is fitted to produce such a tension must be productive of a passion similar to terror, and consequently must be a source of the sublime, though it should have no idea of danger connected with it" or indeed real pain (PE, 107, 159, 161, 163, 164).

Though Burke's reasoning here is highly contestable, he tries to show how the various formal qualities he earlier claimed to be productive of the sublime (e.g., magnitude, uniformity of vastness, the artificial infinite, visual succession, darkness, and blackness) do in fact generate such heightened contraction; for example, when very large, vast, or dark objects strain the eyes. He then argues that this "unnatural [level of] tension" is in fact essential for the natural health of our bodily and mental being in order to remedy the dangers of rest. Besides its tendency to "flatter our indolence," it is "the nature of rest to suffer all the parts of our bodies to fall into a relaxation, that not only disables the members from performing their functions, but takes away the vigorous tone of fibre which is requisite for carrying on the natural and necessary secretions." The noxious result of "this relaxed state of body," claims Burke, is "melancholy, dejection, despair, and often self-murder," and "the best remedy for all these evils is exercise or... an exertion of the contracting power of the muscles," which "resembles pain [since pain "consists in

[14] See, for example, Daniel Kahneman, "Objective Happiness," in *Well-being*, 3–25.

tension or contraction"] ... in every thing but degree." As "due exercise is essential to the coarse muscular parts of the constitution and that without this rousing they would become languid, and diseased, the very same rule holds with regard to those finer [corporeal] parts [of the mind]; to have them in proper order, they must be shaken and worked to a proper degree" (PE, 164–165). Such arguments, of course, provide a wonderful physiological and psychological justification for the ascending Protestant work ethic of Burke's time.

In short, the sublime (either through ideas of real pain and terror or merely through physiological contractions resembling those of pain and terror) promotes self-preservation by stimulating a tonicity that prevents us from falling into a morbid lassitude of relaxation. And this same stimulating bracing of the nerves, he argues (in an explanation that recalls Aristotelian catharsis), is what creates the feeling of sublime delight: "if the pain is not carried to violence, and the terror is not conversant about the present destruction of the person, as these [sublime, contraction-based] emotions clear the parts, whether fine, or gross, of a dangerous and troublesome encumbrance, they are capable of producing delight; not pleasure, but a sort of delightful horror, a sort of tranquility tinged with terror, which as it belongs to self-preservation, is one of the strongest of all the passions" (PE, 165).

Though ingenious, Burke's argument is deeply flawed. First, to ensure our survival and well-being, rest is just as necessary as strenuous contraction and heightened tension; so why should the allegedly relaxing (hence restful) feelings of love not be likewise related to self-preservation? Yet Burke defines love's relaxing pleasures as pertaining only to the "passions of society" rather than self-preservation. Though Burke concedes "that great bodily labour, or pain, weakens, and sometimes actually destroys the mental faculties" and that "long exercise of the mental powers induces a remarkable lassitude of the whole body" (PE, 164–165), he fails to appreciate the value of beauty's relaxation for sustaining the self.

Second, Burke seems to waffle between defining the pain- and terror-related nervous tensions of the sublime as "unnatural" and "violent" in their intensity and regarding them instead as merely contractions "to a proper degree" and "not carried to violence." He similarly vacillates between explaining sublime delight in terms of "the removal or moderation of [real] pain" and describing it as merely approaching "the verge of pain" without really incurring it (PE, 83, 163, 165, 169). Of course, these different descriptions could be the result of real diversity in the experience of sublimity. But this cannot be Burke's response. For rather than affirming the irreducible variety of different sublime feelings, he displays an essentialist tendency to understand the sublime (as well as all terror and pain) in terms of a single mechanism of contraction that simply varies in degree. What he first identifies as diverse causes or sources of the sublime (such as feelings of terror or perceptions of danger, power, darkness, vastness, bodily pain, magnitude, etc.), Burke later portrays as merely instrumental conditions for producing the physiological mechanism of contraction or tension, which he identifies as the essential cause of our feeling of sublimity. They are simply "fitted by nature to produce this sort of tension, either by the primary operation of the mind or the body" (PE, 163).

III

This mechanistic essentialism is the most problematic aspect of Burke's somatic theory of the sublime. Arguing from an allegedly identical physiognomic expression of pain and fear ("teeth set,... eyebrows... violently contracted, forehead... wrinkled, eyes... dragged inwards... and rolled with great vehemence," "short shrieks and groans" and a body that "totters"), Burke is far too quick to "conclude that pain, and fear, act upon the same parts of the body, and in the same manner, though somewhat differing in degree. That pain and fear consist in an unnatural tension of the nerves" (PE, 161). Apart from such difference of degree (that Burke leaves unspecified), "the only difference between pain and terror" Burke acknowledges is that pain affects the mind through the intervention of the body, while terror affects the body by the intervention of mind. Both feelings agree "in producing a tension, contraction, or violent emotion of the nerves, they agree likewise in every thing else" (PE, 162).

This is a grossly erroneous simplification whose enormity has helped render Burke's whole somatic orientation suspect. First, contractions cannot be narrowly identified with pain and terror; nor can they be confined to the delight of sublime passions in contrast to the positive pleasures of beauty and love. Smiles of pleasure involve contractions of facial muscles. Orgasm, which Burke affirms as a positive pleasure of love, consists of a violent wave of contractions, and it is no less pleasurable for that. Moreover, all pains and fears are not identical in their somatic expression or bodily behavior. We may suffer in cries or in silence, tense up rigidly or collapse into tears; and fear can make us fight or flee.

By ultimately making the mechanism of contraction the sole efficient cause for the sublime, Burke's physiological reductionism neglects the crucial role that diverse intentional objects and cognitive contents have in generating our feelings of sublimity, which render such feelings far from identical.

Burke also fails to do justice to the complex variety of physiological conditions involved in the feelings we identify as feelings of the sublime. The experienced sublimity of a raging forest fire or furious hurricane is different from that of a tranquil, endless ocean view at dusk; and these differences, which we feel in terms of the different objects experienced (and from which the experiences cannot logically be separated) are also expressed in physiological differences. These are not simply differences in the degree of contraction (as Burke would have it), but in the whole coordinated pattern of response throughout our bodies: contractions, relaxations, directional orientations, gestures, breathing, heartbeat, and so on.

It would be wrong to condemn Burke's aesthetic theory for being confined to physiology, because the earlier parts of his *Enquiry* are largely devoted to discussing the sources of sublimity and beauty in terms of their experienced objects or qualities rather than in terms of physiological mechanisms of contraction and relaxation. Thus, among what he calls "the causes of the sublime," he first lists terror ("in all cases whatsoever... the ruling principle of the sublime"), and then obscurity, power, privation, vastness, infinity, the "succession and uniformity" that "constitute the artificial infinite," magnitude, difficulty, magnificence, excessive light, loudness, suddenness, intermitting sound, "excessive bitters" of taste, intolerable stenches, and bodily pain (PE, 102, 107, 113, 114, 115, 116, 118, 119, 121, 123, 124, 125, 127). Burke even suggests at one point that our elevated feeling of the sublime is inherently bound up with its impressive or awe-inspiring "terrible objects, [because] the mind [is] always claiming to itself some part of the dignity and importance of the things which it contemplates" (PE, 96).

However, when he comes to formulating his theory of the efficient cause of the sublime, these diverse objects and properties are totally eclipsed by his one-sided advocacy of heightened tension as the necessary but physiologically mechanical "efficient cause." The mind's recognition of such features as terror, power, obscurity, magnitude, and the rest seems only to serve as an optional means "to produce this sort of tension" in our muscular and nerve fibers, which Burke thinks can be equally produced by mere mechanisms of the body alone (PE, 163). A converse but equally mechanical explanation is given for the pleasure of beauty, which is simply generated by a "relaxation" of "the fibres" (PE, 178).

This purely physiological sufficiency seems not only false; it is inconsistent with Burke's earlier insistence that pleasure itself requires the mind's actual awareness or perception. Opposing the idea that pleasure could be "of so low of a degree as to be perceived only by [its] removal," he claims, "if… I do not feel any actual pleasure, I have no reason to judge that any such thing exists; since pleasure is only pleasure as it is felt. The same may be said of pain, and with equal reason" (PE, 81). But if pleasure and pain require intentional awareness, the same should follow for sublime delight. To feel it requires more than a mere physical tensing of nerves. It needs a sentient consciousness, an intentional (even if wordless and ineffable) awareness of feeling that prompts us to recognize such experience as sublime or delightful or extraordinary in some way (even if such recognition comes only after a moment of self-interrogational reflection). Delight that we do not consciously feel is not really delight.

Why advocate an essentialism of mechanistic cause after so carefully outlining a diversity of things that generate sublime feelings, including such clearly mental things as having "an idea of pain and danger, without being actually in such circumstances" (PE, 97)? Burke's likely motive is an understandable reluctance to attribute too much of our aesthetic feelings to the faculty of reason. As self-appointed champions of rationality, philosophers tend to stress its overriding primacy in every valuable aspect of life, including our feelings and tastes. This rationalist essentialism, Burke suggests, is unreasonable, because it ignores the role of non-reasoning, nondiscursive, somatic factors in our mental life, and especially in our passions: "I am afraid it is a practice much too common in inquiries of this nature, to attribute the cause of feelings which merely arise from the mechanical structure of our bodies, or from the natural frame and constitution of our minds, to certain conclusions of the reasoning faculty on the objects presented to us; for I should imagine, that the influence of reason in producing our passions is nothing near so extensive as it is commonly believed (PE, 91).[15]

---

[15] As with the sublime, Burke argues that beauty cannot have reason as its cause, since it strikes us so unreasonably "without any reference to use." Instead, it is caused by certain "sensible qualities" of things "acting mechanically upon the human mind by the intervention of the senses" to produce a relaxation of the nerves that gives the positive pleasure of beauty. Such mechanically relaxing properties include smallness,

To compensate for the excesses of aesthetic rationalism, Burke advocates an excessively one-sided somatic mechanism, which is different but, unfortunately, no better. He therefore seeks to minimize the role of mental associations in generating sublime feelings. Burke cannot help but recognize that acquired associations of ideas often do play a role in determining the objects that inspire our feelings of terror and hence of sublimity. A non-terrifying object that becomes associated with something terrible can then itself come to inspire terror. Though mental associations do not in themselves necessarily constitute reasoning and could even be partly described in terms of unconscious psychic mechanisms, they can indeed figure in reasoning, and always do entail cognitive processing that is more than physiological. So associationist accounts of the sublime, Burke seems to fear, will lead us away from the somatic and back to the philosophical errors of overly rationalizing all affect. Moreover, associations are often very contingent and contextual, varying greatly not only from culture to culture but also from person to person within a culture because of what an individual happens to experience and how it is experienced. Such variability admirably accounts for the diversity of taste, but Burke is more interested in affirming that, similar to reason, "Taste is the same in all human creatures" and we differ merely in "the degree" in which we have and exercise it (PE, 63, 74).

If reason offers a universal norm that is overused in explaining taste and feelings, then, Burke argues, our natural bodily reactions – undistorted by the idiosyncrasies of individual experience, personal associations, and the vagaries of cultural custom – could provide a more promising natural normativity to ground and compel a certain uniformity for our sentiments and judgments (aesthetic or otherwise), which Burke (as David Hume and Immanuel Kant after him) held necessary for sustaining a coherent society "to maintain the ordinary correspondence of life" (PE, 63).[16] Associated ideas or feelings, Burke further claims, must rely on more basic natural reactions; otherwise, we face an infinite regress or circularity of association. It is "absurd... to say that all things affect us by association only; since some things must have been originally and naturally agreeable or disagreeable, from which the others derive their

---

smoothness, gradual variation, lack of angularity, delicacy, and clear but not overly glaring or undiversified colors (PE, 146–151).

[16] For a comparative analysis of the implicit social agenda in the aesthetics of Hume and Kant, see my essay "Of the Scandal of Taste: Social Privilege as Nature in the Aesthetics of Hume and Kant," in Richard Shusterman, *Surface and Depth: Dialectics of Criticism and Culture* (Ithaca: Cornell University Press, 2002), 91–107.

associated powers." Hence, there is "little purpose to look for the cause of our passions in association, until we fail of it in the natural properties of things" (PE, 160).

Burke's drive to displace associational accounts of the sublime with what he regards as deeper, more natural, somatic explanations is most evident in his treatment of darkness. Contesting John Locke's view that fear of the dark is not naturally generated but instead caused by our early associations of darkness with frightening stories of ghosts, Burke argues that this fear is more naturally rooted in the fact that darkness puts our bodily safety in question by preventing us from seeing "some dangerous obstruction" or "precipice" or "enemy" (PE, 172). If this explanation still involves the association of ideas of danger and harm, Burke goes on to offer an account that claims to show how darkness can be "painful" or "terrible in its own nature," irrespective of any such mental associations and relying only on its physiological characteristic of heightened tension: "contraction of the radial fibres of the iris is proportionately greater [in the dark]...so...as to strain the nerves that compose it beyond their natural tone...and [thus]...produce a painful sensation....I believe that any one will find if he opens his eyes and makes an effort to see in a dark place, that a very perceivable pain ensues" (PE, 173, 174). In short, Burke claims, darkness evokes the sublime because it makes us strain our eyes and therefore tense our eye muscles beyond their natural state.

The matter, however, is not so simple. First, anatomically, the iris is in fact regulated by two different groups of smooth muscles: the pupillary dilator muscles, whose contraction enlarges the pupils in reaction to darkness or dim light; and the pupillary constrictor muscles, which contract the pupil when light is bright. So light as well as darkness involves muscular contractions of the iris. Moreover, the muscles involved are smooth muscles governed by the autonomic system rather than voluntary striated muscles, so effort is not the cause of contraction. If we feel muscle strain in looking in the dark, it is due to our occipital muscles, not our pupils. More importantly, what if we do not open our eyes and thus avoid the ocular tension? Is the darkness, then, no longer terrible? Can we not experience the sublime with our eyes closed? Certainly we could still fear the anxiety of not seeing what could harm us.

Burke's mechanistic theory, moreover, ignores the fact that our very will to look – to open, direct, and focus our eyes – is not a merely mechanical physiological reaction but the dynamic response of a somatic intentionality, a bodily subjectivity of active, engaged openness to the world, even if such sentient response is mute and devoid of explicit, reflective consciousness. Sentient bodies are not simply machines, so even automatic, unthinking somatic responses are deeply informed by our habits, desires, and projects. Breathing may be an instinctive reflex, but how we breathe depends on our habits and (often implicit) perceptions of our current circumstances and aims. Somaesthetics, by relying on more advanced physiological findings while also treating the body as sentient, active subjectivity, can critically engage Burke's analysis while respecting his basic insight into the body's indispensably formative role in aesthetic experience.

Burke's theory is further troubled by relying on the problematic notion of "unnatural tension," which is claimed to cause the sublime. It is not at all clear what the limits of natural tension are that would render a particular degree of tension unnatural. It cannot be a matter of the degree of contraction of a muscle fiber because contraction is an all-or-nothing affair on the level of individual fibers. So it must mean an unnatural number of fibers being contracted or perhaps an unnatural duration of time in which they are contracted or perhaps even an unnatural number of different muscles groups whose fibers are being contracted. But what exactly would constitute such an unnatural number of fibers or groups or an unnatural duration of contractions? And would it be the same for every person in every situation?

Contemporary physiology recognizes the concept of background muscle tone. Our muscles are always tensed to some extent, which is how (through our antigravity muscles) we are able to sit or stand erect. Heightened tension must thus be defined in terms of departure from background muscle tone. Yet background muscle tone is not fixed or universal; it varies among individuals and can be significantly raised – for any individual – through exercise training. Does this mean that a person with higher background muscle tone is less likely to experience the sublime because her contractions then need to be much stronger for them to stand out from the background tone as painful or unnatural? Or does it instead suggest that people whose muscles are in a chronic state of hypertension (and are thus always close to pain and stiffness) are compensated for their discomfort by being more easily able to experience the sublime because they are always already closer to "unnatural tension"? Should one aspire to keep one's "natural tension" or should one improve one's background muscle tone toward the condition that is more optimal for efficient functioning or health or aesthetic experience? Are the optima for these aims always consistent? Is natural tension to be equated with optimal tension, so that any transformation of background muscle tone or any other change of tendencies of contraction should be rejected? As partly the products of culturally shaping, can we ever find our muscles in a totally natural state of tension? Or is natural tension to be understood as what feels natural to culturally groomed individuals (though this hardly would seem uniform)? Burke's theory offers no real help with such questions because its notion of natural tension is extremely unclear and problematic.

Burke is committed to working with a notion of nature that is altogether free of culture and habit. Although he recognizes that habit or "use" is "justly... called... a second nature" and that it can establish regularities of feeling and expectation whose violation creates the unnatural tension of "convulsive" shock (PE, 139, 175), Burke still clings to the idea of totally pure natural reactions, of primordial behavior entirely unshaped by the second nature of culture and "custom," because such a pure nature – uncorrupted by the variance of different habits, cultures, and individual experience – could best guarantee consensus of aesthetic judgment. Just as the same objects "present similar images to the whole species," Burke argues, so "the pleasures and the pains which every object excites in one man, it must raise in all mankind, whilst it operates naturally, simply, and by its proper powers only" (PE, 65–66).

Unfortunately, this pristinely natural, simple, and independent condition of taste never really exists. Even in the womb, one's tastes are already being culturally shaped by the foods, odors, sounds, and movement rhythms of one's cultural environment, which of course includes the physical culture of the mother's body. It is part of our human nature to have, and to require for our survival, an acquired cultural second nature. Thus, as Helmuth Plessner strikingly puts it, "man is 'by nature' artificial."[17] Of course, we may be evolutionary programmed to like fatty, salty, and sweet foods, but these basic preferences are very differently inflected or expressed through different eating habits, and these biological predilections themselves must have also been partly shaped by the physical culture and ways of living of our evolutionary ancestors rather than by pure body mechanics. Similarly, *pace* Burke, the same objects often present very different images or aspects to people of different cultures or simply different orientations. The woodsman perceives a different forest than

---

[17] Helmuth Plessner, *Macht und menschliche Natur: Ein Versuch zur Anthropologie der geschichtlichen Weltansicht* (1931), in vol. 5 of *Gesammelte Schriften* (Frankfurt: Suhrkamp, 1982), 199. For a detailed study of Plessner's thought and its contemporary relevance, see Hans-Peter Krüger, *Zwischen Lachen und Weinen*, 2 vols. (Berlin: Akademie Verlag, 1999, 2001).

the unschooled urbanite; the physician sees a different body than the pornographer; the casual tourist contemplates a different totem than the devout totem worshipper.

IV

Burke's physiological account of the sublime is clearly flawed, but what should we conclude from its errors?[18] One lesson is to avoid narrowly mechanistic theories of somaesthetic reactions that ignore the sentient or cognitive aspects of our body's intentionality and physiological response. A somatic approach to aesthetic experience, or any meaningful human experience, must not be reductively mechanistic and causal. Blushing relies on physiological mechanisms, but we cannot understand its full meaning in purely mechanistic, physical terms. Second, we need a clearer recognition that our physiological response in aesthetic experience is always somehow culturally conditioned, so that our natural reactions in this area always involve the second nature of habit or custom. Like so many thinkers, Burke fails to realize that between the poles of blind, physical mechanism and conscious, deliberative reason there exists in human behavior a wide realm of habit that is automatic and unreflective but nonetheless purposively intelligent and often skilled. Similarly, between discursive consciousness and mechanical physical reactions there is immediate somatic perception – bodily but intentional and perceptive, though not necessarily self-reflective. Third, somatic approaches to aesthetic experience should deploy more accurate physiology than Burke's eighteenth-century knowledge. It is plausible that sublime feelings (through their links to terror, power, darkness, and more generally concerns of survival) involve more severe tension and contraction, while feelings of beauty are more relaxing. But a physiological account of these feelings must be more nuanced to the complexity of patterns of tension and relaxation and the way they are affected by training and contextual conditions, and such theoretical accounts must be submitted to empirical testing.

Philosophers suspicious of the somatic are likely to draw more extreme conclusions from Burke's unsuccessful physiological theory. Reviewing

---

[18] We should remember that Burke offers his theory not as infallible fact, but in the experimental spirit of furthering inquiry toward the eventual finding of truth: "A man who works beneath the surface of things, though he may be wrong himself, yet he clears the way for others, and may chance to make even his errors subservient to the cause of truth" (PE, 100).

the sharp criticism historically heaped upon it, Hipple suggests that Burke should have forsaken his physiological approach altogether and instead employed the familiar empiricist notion of mental association. It is best, he concludes, "to leave unbridged the chasm between mind and body."[19] This is a rash and wrong inference. The failures of Burke's mechanistic theory do not entail that we must resign ourselves to metaphysical dualism and reject any aesthetic theory that is grounded in recognition of the somatic roots and physiological dimensions of aesthetic experience. As I argued earlier, if aesthetics is concerned with our sensory perception of art, beauty, and sublimity and with our experiential response to what we perceive, then the sentient body – as the locus of our senses and experience – surely cannot be irrelevant to theories that aim to understand aesthetic reactions or to improve them by cultivating the somatic medium of aesthetic experience.

Appreciating the body's role in aesthetic experience can also help explain why art (long criticized as falsehood and fiction) has so much potency in conveying its visions and making them seem compellingly real or true. Feelings, as William James long ago argued and as neuroscience confirms today, tend to direct our thinking, and strong emotions tend to compel attention and often also belief; such emotions, in turn, are deeply grounded in the body and cannot be adequately understood without it.[20] By involving the body and leaving traces in our muscles, flesh, and bones, the emotionally charged visions of art have an abiding and motivating power that they would not have as mere intellectual content.

Moreover, if there is some truth to Burke's theory that the sublime more than the beautiful engages our instincts of self-preservation, heightens tension, and thus provides stronger experiences than those of beauty, then this could help explain why contemporary art has tended to prefer sublimity to beauty. Walter Benjamin, T.W. Adorno, and others have argued that our capacities for deeply meaningful and moving experience have been increasingly eroded by modern life. If the sublime – because of its arousal of heightened tension – provides more intense

---

[19] Hipple, *The Beautiful*, 205.
[20] See, for example, William James, *The Principles of Psychology* (Cambridge, MA: Harvard University Press, 1983), chs. 21, 25; Antonio Demasio, *Descartes' Error: Emotion, Reason, and the Human Brain* (New York: Avon, 1994), chs. 5–6 and my discussion of their theories on these points in *Body Consciousness: A Philosophy of Mindfulness and Somaesthetics* (Cambridge: Cambridge University Press, 2008), ch. 5. For a detailed study of the power of affect on belief in the realm of popular art, my essay "Affect and Authenticity in Country Musicals," in *Performing Live: Aesthetic Alternatives for the Ends of Art* (Ithaca: Cornell University Press, 2000), ch. 4.

feelings that can combat what Fredric Jameson calls our postmodern "waning of affect," then it would be logical for art to prefer sublimity to beauty in its attempt to provide powerful aesthetic experience. If Adorno and Marcuse have criticized beauty for being too affirmative, then a parallel critique based on Burke could argue that beauty is too easy, too unchallenging, too relaxing, and thus not sufficiently stimulating – in today's opulent societies of facile comfort – for deeply engaging aesthetic encounters.[21]

Finally, somaesthetics can help not only explain but also improve aesthetic experience. Better mastery of our somatic selves obviously allows performing artists to perform with greater grace and with less pain, which is why they not only engage in forms of somatic training but often seek help from somatic therapists. Somaesthetic mastery can also improve the appreciative powers of the audience, whose heightened fitness and skills of awareness can help intensify attention and avoid distractions of pain and fatigue that result from poor somatic self-use.

If the somatic route to improving aesthetic experience still seems too vague, let me conclude by suggesting one brief example related to Burke's theory of the sublime. If sublime feelings are provoked by danger but cannot be realized when we experience danger in a panicked or frantic state, then our somaesthetic ability to recognize when we are in such a frenzied state and to transform it toward greater tranquility – for example, by regulating our breathing and relaxing some spasmodic muscular contractions – can better enable us to achieve the sublime. For Burke, this requires tranquility and is indeed defined as "tranquility shadowed with horror" or "tranquility tinged with terror" (PE, 82,165). To rescue sublime delight from the maw of plain terror is a skill that aesthetics should want to cultivate.

---

[21] On these points, see, for example, Walter Benjamin, *Illuminations*, trans. Harry Zohn (New York: Schocken, 1968), 83–110, 155–200; T.W. Adorno, *Aesthetic Theory*, trans. C. Lenhardt (London: Routledge, 1984) 46; Fredric Jameson, *Postmodernism, or the Cultural Logic of Late Capitalism* (Durham: Duke University Press, 1991) 1–54, quotation p. 10; Herbert Marcuse, "The Affirmative Character of Culture," in *Negations*, trans. Jeremy Shapiro (Boston: Beacon Press, 1968), 88–133. For an analysis of the erosion of aesthetic experience in twentieth-century theory, see my essay "The End of Aesthetic Experience," in *Performing Live*, ch. 1. For a richly detailed study of Adorno's and Benjamin's concerns about the general crisis of experience, see Martin Jay, *Songs of Experience* (Berkeley: University of California Press, 2005), ch. 8.

8

Pragmatism and Cultural Politics

From Textualism to Somaesthetics

I

Despite a name suggesting philistinism, pragmatism is fundamentally a philosophy of culture. If most philosophies readily recognize that culture is both an essential value and the ineliminable matrix of human life, pragmatism goes further by insisting that philosophy itself is essentially the historical product of culture, and therefore should (and does) change through more general cultural change. Philosophy's problems, values, terms, aims, and styles reflect those of the culture that shapes it. Even the most basic concepts of truth, knowledge, reality, meaning, and identity can derive their concrete significance only from the roles they play in the diverse practices of a culture. So pragmatism finds no helpful sense in the idea of an absolute, unmediated view of reality, a vision wholly independent of cultural shaping.[1]

Pragmatism, therefore, is also an essentially pluralistic philosophy. Insisting on the plurality of values and beliefs expressed in the language games of different cultures and even in what we call a single culture, pragmatism affirms its pluralistic open-mindedness (which is more than mere tolerance) toward individuals who adopt these different perspectives. Culture can be made richer through the interchange of different views on life, which can stimulate productive new ways of thinking while also conserving valuable aspects of tradition. Deriving from the Latin for cultivation, the concept of culture carries a sense of value and improvement.

---

[1] Though Hegel also recognized that philosophy expressed the spirit of its age in thought, he argued that the vagaries of its historical paths reflected a logically compelling master narrative pointing to a universal, encompassing vision of absolute knowledge that his system succeeded in formulating. This narrative included a Eurocentric disrespect for the philosophy of other cultures and an overriding emphasis on the unified whole, in which differences were overcome.

As it shapes and unites the people who share it, so its value and its rich plurality of expression also make culture an essentially contested concept, with different factions debating over the precise meaning of culture, just as individuals and institutions compete for cultural prestige (whether in terms of prizes, market share, or government funding). Because it is both a publicly shared and contested good, culture is inevitably also a political arena, even if it claims to eschew the political for purer, higher values. If pragmatism is a philosophy of culture, then cultural politics should be a key pragmatist concern. This is especially true because pragmatism shares with culture an essential melioristic impulse: the desire to improve not only our theoretical understanding of culture but also the quality of our cultural products and the lived experience of culture itself. Moreover, like culture, pragmatist philosophy is a diverse and contested field, presenting no monolithic school but a variety of related approaches, a collection of different philosophical voices that, while sharing many of the same songs, often interpret them in contrasting ways.

This chapter examines somaesthetics as an expression of pragmatist cultural politics by situating somaesthetics in the broader, contestatory field of contemporary pragmatism. Having shown in earlier chapters how somaesthetics emerged from the transformative cultural agenda of pragmatist aesthetics, I here concentrate on the challenges it faces from a powerful rival pragmatist philosophy of culture that denies the value, and indeed the philosophical sense, of somaesthetics. That philosophy is Richard Rorty's, to which I remain profoundly indebted in ways this chapter will also clarify in exploring the agonistics of our theories.

Before turning to Rorty, however, I should begin by roughly distinguishing three varieties of cultural politics. The first concerns the politics that a government pursues with respect to culture in the social field over which it exercises political or institutional control. When a government decides to establish new museums, concert halls, or provide subventions and educational programs to support the arts, it is engaging in cultural politics. The government is using its political power to advance certain cultural goals and objectives that it feels are worth pursuing. These goals may be altruistically aimed at directly benefitting its citizens, but perhaps are more often aimed at strengthening the state's own authority by encouraging those cultural values that are central to the state's governing ideology, or by commanding greater appreciation and respect for the government through the admiration of the cultural goods or enterprises that the government's cultural politics promotes. These two types of goals are not in principle contradictory – a state may reinforce its power by providing its citizens with the sort of cultural products they want. This notion of cultural politics, with its principle of governing by significantly utilizing the arts and culture, lies at the heart of Confucian philosophy, whose two prime ethical pillars of government (including self-government) are arts and ritual. By such aesthetic means, an excellent ruler can govern his citizens by also providing them, through his own exemplary behavior, a model of the harmonious order he seeks to establish in the state.

John Dewey explored this notion of cultural politics in 1939, when confronted with the totalitarian regimes in Germany and Russia. Insisting that "works of art... are the most compelling of the means of communication by which emotions are stirred and opinions formed," Dewey notes that the arts and culture, "the theater, the movie and music hall, even the picture gallery, eloquence, popular parades, common sports and recreative agencies, have all been brought under regulation as part of the propaganda agencies by which dictatorship is kept in power without being regarded by the masses as oppressive." Realizing "that emotions and imagination are more potent in shaping public sentiment and opinion than information and reason," Dewey reminds us of the old saying "that if one could control the songs of a nation one need not care who made its laws."[2] In France, discussions of cultural politics (both in the academy and in the wider public realm) generally focus on this first notion of cultural politics. This is partly because the French have long taken pride in being a "cultural state," a nation whose greatness is both expressed and reinforced through its cultural grandeur. Its magnificent cultural heritage continues to enrich the state's coffers and more broadly strengthen the French economy through cultural tourism that helps make France (and more particularly Paris) the world's top tourist destination. In 2009, France proudly celebrated fifty years of establishing what they regard as the first ministry of culture in Europe (founded by Andre Malraux), although they should perhaps be reminded of Nazi Germany's ministry of Volksaufklarung und Propaganda, which effectively controlled and deployed all of the arts and culture to glorify that state and promote its ideology and fierce loyalty to it.

A rather different notion of cultural politics dominates American discussions of this concept (especially since the 1990s), where such terms as "identity politics," "multiculturalism," and the "culture wars" have played

---

[2] John Dewey, *Freedom and Culture* (Carbondale: Southern Illinois University Press, 1988), 70.

a significant role. Here, specific (most frequently subordinate) cultural groups engage in political activities of a distinctly cultural form in order to advance not only their cultural aims but also their political and social status. Greater cultural recognition is sought as an effective means to achieve higher social standing or increased political power. Thus, university professors have worked hard to change the canon of "great works" and "great thinkers" studied in different academic fields of literature, philosophy, history, and the arts in order to include figures from minority cultural groups or to give greater cultural recognition to what are perceived as subordinated cultural identities (whether they be racial, ethnic, or gender identities). Such activities of academic cultural politics are not simply expressed in the explicit political activism of petitioning or campaigning for such curricular or canon reform. They are persistently and effectively pursued through the cultural work of showing the aesthetic, social, and cultural importance of the topics and authors that had been excluded.

A third form of cultural politics may be distinguished that is not a matter of official government policy, nor is it narrowly focused on issues of identity politics and the advancement of specific, identifiable groups within society. Instead, it aims more generally to improve humankind's ongoing conversation about how to improve our lives and practices. It does this by criticizing and reconstructing established ways of living, talking, acting, and thinking, but also by proposing new ways of life; new practices and disciplines for improved experience or performance; new ideas of social life and community; new vocabularies, techniques, and roles for self-realization and ethical practice.

I now turn to Richard Rorty (1931–2007), who essentially ignores the first notion, while criticizing the second and advocating the third. I focus on Rorty for two important reasons. First, Rorty was pragmatism's most prominent voice in the late twentieth century. Not only did he revive the pragmatist tradition by extending it and giving it increased visibility and credibility in mainstream academic philosophy, but also – by especially emphasizing aesthetic and literary values – Rorty made pragmatism a serious player in humanistic culture at large, transforming its older image as a dull, overly rationalistic instrumentalism that cared little for the arts and the yearnings of imagination. My other reason for focusing on Rorty is personal; he converted me to pragmatism and delivered the harshest denunciatory verdict on somaesthetics. So, in defending that project, this chapter is both homage and critique.

II

When I first met Rorty in the early-eighties in the Negev desert, I was an ardently analytic, Oxford-trained Israeli philosopher who knew virtually nothing about pragmatism except that I shared my analytic mentors' disdain for its mushy way of thinking. Rorty soon convinced me, through conversation, correspondence, and his exemplary new writings, that the American pragmatist tradition (and especially John Dewey) had a great deal to offer a philosopher like me, who was particularly interested in aesthetics, the arts, and culture. I was surprised that a famous American philosopher like Rorty would pay so much attention to an unknown young lecturer in peripheral Israel. However, as I eventually learned, I was not at all exceptional in receiving such kindness. It was characteristic of Rorty's open-minded largesse to notice and help people in the margins.

Within a few years, through his inspiration and encouragement, I moved to the United States and devoted myself to pragmatist philosophy. As my work was deeply indebted to Rorty, so much of it was polemically engaged with articulating my differences from his views. With characteristic generosity, Rorty remained supportive of my work despite my frequently sharp criticism. He had a familiar way, at once endearing and frustrating, of casually shrugging off and defusing such criticism by humbly acknowledging in personal conversation or correspondence that perhaps I had a point or that he should have formulated his position more carefully. I gradually lost my taste for criticizing Rorty, as such critique increasingly left an aftertaste of ingratitude toward someone whom I gratefully acknowledge as having made my career in pragmatism possible. So I preferred to move on to other targets of analysis and critique. Even when I knew our positions were at odds, I decided simply to present mine and make no effort to criticize his. There is thus no mention of Rorty in my *Body Consciousness*, even if its topic – somaesthetics – is the target of his most animated critique of my views.[3]

Rorty's compelling example taught me to pursue the basic orientations of Deweyan pragmatism without eschewing the crisper, more linear style of argument characteristic of the ordinary-language analytic

---

[3] See Richard Shusterman, *Body Consciousness: A Philosophy of Mindfulness and Somaesthetics* (Cambridge: Cambridge University Press, 2008). For Rorty's critique of what he calls my "somatic aesthetics," see Richard Rorty, "Response to Richard Shusterman," in Matthew Festenstein and Simon Thompson (eds.), *Richard Rorty: Critical Dialogues* (Cambridge: Polity Press, 2001), 153–157; hereafter RRS.

philosophy in which I was trained at Jerusalem and Oxford. I also followed Rorty in highlighting the aesthetic dimension of Deweyan pragmatism and emphasizing genealogical and cultural critique rather than trying to articulate a systematic pragmatist metaphysics, as some other contemporary pragmatists have been keen to do. Although advocating Dewey and the aesthetic, Rorty devotes almost no discussion to Dewey's aesthetic masterpiece, *Art as Experience*, probably because its key concept of experience is an anathema to him. Rorty's celebration of the aesthetic, I believe, derives primarily from his great love of literature.

Nonetheless, by championing both Dewey and the aesthetic, Rorty led me to undertake a more serious and sympathetic rereading of *Art as Experience*, which my analytically trained eyes had initially rejected as a thick blob of rebarbative mush. And through its rich resources I tried to reconstruct a pragmatist aesthetic theory that, while Deweyan in spirit, is more suitable to our contemporary arts and postmodern times; for example, in being more appreciative than Dewey was to the aesthetic value of rupture, incompleteness, and discordant difference, but without, of course, gainsaying the wonderful values of harmony and unity of consummation to which Dewey's aesthetic was wholeheartedly – and I think one-sidedly – committed.

Although Rorty repudiated Dewey's use of the notion of experience, I defended it as an astute and essential strategy in his very effective attack on the compartmentalized, elitist isolation of fine art and his corresponding attempt to bring art and aesthetics more fully into the practices of democratic living. I was, in fact, critical of Dewey's idea that aesthetic experience could provide an adequate definition of art in standard philosophical terms, arguing (after Wittgenstein) that such definitions were inevitably inadequate or so general and vague as to be culturally useless. Nonetheless, I insisted that Dewey's reorienting emphasis on aesthetic experience was worthwhile because it usefully directs us toward appreciating what is especially valuable in art and life, and thus could promote their flourishing. Moreover, I tried to extend Dewey's experiential strategy and democratic impulse toward a revaluation of the popular arts and the distinctively embodied styles of the art of living that are so central to contemporary culture. Though Rorty has shown no sympathy for these aesthetic projects, I would like to suggest that his final work on philosophy as cultural politics might have brought him closer to accepting them.

Because many philosophers and literary theorists have read my philosophy of culture as essentially Rortian, it seems useful to define more generally what differentiates our styles of pragmatism.[4] So before going further into our conflicting views on aesthetics, somaesthetics, and cultural politics, I should begin by articulating important differences on other philosophical topics. Let me group them into the two general areas into which Germans traditionally divide the philosophical field: theoretical philosophy (epistemology and metaphysics) and practical philosophy (ethics and political theory).

III

Rorty regards all thought and understanding as essentially interpretation, a view that has its roots in Nietzsche but is shared by much more moderate, traditional thinkers such as Gadamer. Rorty embraces this "hermeneutic universalism" for a number of reasons. First and foremost is his opposition to epistemological foundationalism. For this doctrine typically appeals to apodictically unmediated perceptions and understandings that can infallibly justify truth claims because they simply grasp things the way they are (or are experienced), with no linguistic or interpretive gloss that would render their evidence fallible or prejudiced. Interpretation, in contrast, is traditionally associated with fallible and contested claims to knowledge, and thus is congenial to pragmatism's essential stance of open-minded fallibilism, the idea that any belief now held to be true could prove false and require correction in the future. Perspectival pluralism is another good pragmatist motive for arguing that everything we understand and talk about is interpretation. For the very notion of an interpretation implies that other interpretations are,

---

[4] Joseph Margolis, for example, accuses me of having "fallen too far under Rorty's spell" and "its illogic." Joseph Margolis, "Replies in Search of Self-Discovery," in Michael Krausz and Richard Shusterman (eds.), *Interpretation, Relativism, and the Metaphysics of Culture* (Amherst, NY: Humanity Books, 1999), 342. Paul Taylor similarly claims that "Shusterman subscribes to a way of reading Dewey that we might trace to Richard Rorty, an approach that posits two Dewey's, one good, one less so. On the good side, there is an edifying, therapeutic thinker who looks past, or seeks to expand, the limits of professional philosophy. But on the bad side, there is a systematic philosopher, a metaphysician-epistemologist-philosophical anthropologist." See Paul Taylor, "The Two-Dewey Thesis, Continued: Shusterman's *Pragmatist Aesthetics*," *Journal of Speculative Philosophy* 16 (2002): 17–25. In Europe, I have often been asked to distinguish my views from Rorty's, as for example in the interview-article by Gunther Leypoldt, "The Pragmatist Aesthetics of Richard Shusterman: A Conversation." *Zeitschrift für Anglistik und Amerikanistik: A Quarterly of Language, Literature, and Culture* 48 (2000): 57–71. Leypoldt has more recently defended Rorty against my critique (and that of others) while underlining Rorty's rejection of somaesthetics. See Gunther Leypoldt, "Uses of Metaphor: Richard Rorty's Literary Criticism and the Poetics of World-Making," *New Literary History* 39 (2008): 145–163.

in principle, possible (and may be even reasonable or somehow valid); even if one of the interpretations seems right or best, its rightness does not entail that all the others are wrong. Works of art and literature are notoriously open to multiple interpretations (and they are wonderfully fascinating for that reason). But contracts, treaties, and religious texts are likewise open to interpretive ambiguity, although rival interpreters of the latter are far less tolerant of such plurality than they usually are in the arts.

If Rorty's aestheticism and pragmatist pluralism reinforce each other in highlighting interpretation as the basic mode of all cognition, so do the ideas that perception, understanding, and inquiry are always contextual and active and motivated in terms of purposes. Different contexts involve different aims of understanding, and those aims shape what we interpret the objects of understanding to be, by selecting what realist parlance would call those aspects of the object (or situation) that are pertinent to our aims. Rather than regarding our objects as having fixed essences on which we base our interpretations of significance, interpretation instead goes "all the way down" into the very constitution of our objects: "*all* inquiry is interpretation," Rorty claims, just as "*all* thought consists in recontextualization." The notion of interpretation is thus stretched to such all-encompassing breadth that it loses the "contrastive and polemical force" it has when opposed to more immediate understanding, which is traditionally taken to be foundational, objective, unbiased, and indifferent to perspectival context. But that is a worthy – because necessary – price to pay for freeing ourselves from foundationalism and essentialism.[5]

Although I embrace Rorty's antiessentialist, anti-foundationalist stance and his respect for the pervasive importance of interpretation in our experience, I think a useful distinction between understanding and interpretation can be made by decoupling understanding from its foundational associations (which, though familiar, are not at all essential for the concept's meaning). Understanding, in my view, can itself be non-foundationally construed as perspectival, fallible, partial, plural, selective, and goal directed. Moreover (and more importantly), it is typically deployed that way in ordinary language usage. In such usage, it is also often functionally contrasted with interpretation in terms of being immediate, unreflective, or direct, whereas interpretations imply some

---

[5] See Richard Rorty, "Inquiry as Recontextualization: An Anti-Dualist Account of Interpretation," in David Hiley, James Bohman, and Richard Shusterman (eds.), *The Interpretive Turn: Philosophy, Science, Culture* (Ithaca: Cornell University Press, 1991), 70–71.

reflective awareness of alternatives or problems. Understanding, though not foundational or apodictic, is thus functionally more basic or prior than interpretation; it is what interpretation relies or builds on, even if such basic understandings were at some point shaped by earlier interpretations, which relied on still earlier understandings. The most basic unreflective understandings that underlie and guide our interpretations are, moreover, nonetheless corrigible through interpretation.

This functional distinction between understanding and interpretation, which is endorsed by ordinary usage, provides interpretation not only with a contrast-class that helps give interpretation a clearer meaning but also with a grounding background of material on which to work and through which to guide its activity. Moreover, by recognizing a form of understanding that is immediate or spontaneous (despite being culturally mediated), we can do justice to the important unreflective dimension of our cognitive life. Most of the time, when we intelligently understand and react to situations through appropriate behavior we are not engaging in reflection, thinking, or interpretation; we respond through intelligent, unreflective habit without having to interpret or consciously decide what should be done. Interpretive thought instead suggests reflective construing or conscious deliberation about possible alternatives.

The idea that all understanding is interpretation is usually linked to the idea that all understanding is linguistic. In this view, language always somehow pre-shapes or preselects what we perceive or consider, and thus already essentially interprets it for us. For Rorty, the very idea of any sort of understanding beneath interpretation implies the misguided epistemological "dream" of foundationalism, "the philosopher's attempt to acquire non-linguistic access to the really real" that would provide absolute, infallible knowledge.[6] The distinction between understanding and interpretation should not, however, be simply conflated with the distinction between linguistic and nonlinguistic comprehension. As I've often explained, they are different because there are linguistic understandings that are not interpretations. In most normal, everyday situations, we understand unproblematic linguistic statements (oral or written) immediately and unreflectively without interpreting them.[7] When someone

---

[6] Richard Rorty, "The Fire of Life," *Poetry* 191, November 2007: 129.

[7] Philosophers sometimes mistakenly conflate my notion of uninterpreted understanding with nonlinguistic experience, although I have always insisted on distinguishing between them. See, for example, David Granger, "Review Essay of *Pragmatist Aesthetics*, 2nd edition," *Studies in Philosophy of Education* 22 (2003): 381–402. In my invited response to his essay, I refer to the passages in my work where I insist on this distinction and illustrate

at my hotel answers my question about what time breakfast is served by saying, "Seven to ten," I don't need to interpret this linguistic response; I understand it immediately. Interpretation is needed only when there is something puzzling or especially interesting in an utterance or text so that we need or want to look deeper into its meaning.

I do, however, go further in affirming that immediate understanding can also be nonlinguistic. Our behavior sometimes includes nondiscursive responses that are directed to nonlinguistic actions or situations and that demonstrate without words (or conscious representations of them in one's mind) that one has understood. The intentional gestures or movements of a dancer, lover, or ballplayer can be understood and appropriately responded to (by a partner, teammate, or audience) without ever being articulated into words (real or imagined). Such recognition of the nonlinguistic, however, does not make me a foundationalist in the epistemological or metaphysical sense that Rorty repudiates as regressive. For the important nonlinguistic intelligence and understanding that we demonstrate in gestures, sports, and various arts of movement are not, in my account, invoked as being in touch with anything more "really real" than language is. These nonlinguistic understandings are not metaphysically primordial, purely physical "raw feels" that exist beyond the world of culture and thus inform us of the absolute nature of reality. Instead (like the rest of our experience), they are deeply shaped by culture and history, as are even the size and shape of our bodies (which obviously vary in terms of the diet and exercise we take). Rorty is therefore wrong to conclude that rejecting foundationalism entails rejecting the notion of nonlinguistic understanding.

If Rorty's rejection of the nonlinguistic is motivated by fears of foundationalism and essentialism, he himself advocates what could be described as an essentialist view of human nature as essentially linguistic.[8] We are "nothing more than sentential attitudes – nothing more than the presence or absence of dispositions toward the use of sentences phrased

---

it. See Richard Shusterman, "Pragmatist Aesthetics: Between Aesthetic Experience and Aesthetic Education," *Studies in Philosophy and Education* 22 (2003): 403–412.

[8] Rorty concedes this: "There is a sense in which Shusterman is right that I hold 'an essentialist view of human nature as essentially linguistic'" (RSS, 155), where he continues that this essentialism isn't so baneful because it is not intended as a "metaphysical suggestion" that claims to "divide nature at the joints" (something like the point I've made about understanding). My opposition to Rorty's linguistic essentialism (as I explain later in this chapter) is not a mere critique of his textualist metaphysics but a pragmatic argument that we need to recognize that there is something valuable in life besides language so that we can cultivate that nonlinguistic realm to improve our lives.

in some historically conditioned vocabulary." "To create one's mind is to create one's own language," since it is only "words which... made us what we are."⁹ Though language may provide the most pervasive matrix of our lives, there is an important nonpropositional, nondiscursive dimension of experience that, I will argue, is important for philosophy to recognize and that can be discerned and cultivated by more attention to somatic experience through the field I call somaesthetics. Yet discourse is a crucial tool in cultivating this attention, so somaesthetics involves both discursive and nondiscursive dimensions of somatic experience.

Rorty, however, radically rejects the whole concept of experience as philosophically worse than useless, because he thinks it misleads us into the epistemological "myth of the given," the idea of experiences that are so immediately present that they could not be false and thus can serve as indisputable foundations in justifying knowledge claims.[10] But philosophy, I believe, can effectively deploy the concept of experience without falling into the myth of the given, by using it in various ways that lie outside the framework of foundational justifications. For example, by emphasizing aesthetic experience in the philosophy of art, Dewey is not claiming (as Schopenhauer did) that art provides the path for reaching "the really real" (of Platonic ideas). Rather, he is usefully reminding us that art is not primarily an affair of autonomous and highly valued objects, but is more essentially a matter of how those objects function in and for experience, such experiential enrichment being art's most important source of value. Talking about aesthetic experience rather than art likewise helps highlight that there are aesthetic dimensions beyond the official realm of art that are worth noticing and cultivating, just as it reminds us that the appreciation of art does not require the discursive complexity of a critical essay. Art can be relished in wordless

---

[9] Richard Rorty, *Contingency, Irony, and Solidarity* (Cambridge: Cambridge University Press, 1989), 27, 88, 117; hereafter CIS.

[10] Rorty repeatedly argues that "Dewey should have dropped the term 'experience'" instead of making it central to his philosophy. See Richard Rorty, "Dewey Between Darwin and Hegel," reprinted in *Truth and Progress: Philosophical Papers*, vol. 3 (Cambridge: Cambridge University Press, 1998), 297; also his "Dewey's Metaphysics," reprinted in *Consequences of Pragmatism* (Minneapolis: University of Minnesota Press, 1984), 72–89; and his "Afterword: Intellectual Historians and Pragmatism," in John Pettegrew (ed.), *A Pragmatist's Progress?* (Lanham, MD: Rowman & Littlefield, 2000), 209, where he states: "Cutting out the intermediary – experience – between the causal impact of the environment and our linguistic response to the environment is an idea whose time has come." For a more detailed pragmatist defense of the concept of experience against Rorty's critique, see Richard Shusterman, *Practicing Philosophy: Pragmatism and the Philosophical Life* (New York: Routledge, 1997), ch. 6.

wonder. Experience, moreover, can likewise be usefully deployed as a general term to designate the consequences and fruits of action and ideas in ways that may not be articulated (or even articulable) in language.[11]

In his polemics against the idea of experience as inevitably a form of foundational metaphysics, Rorty often sounds like he is rejecting metaphysics of any kind. Yet his repeated insistence that reality is thoroughly and essentially contingent might itself be construed as a metaphysical view, the familiar pragmatist metaphysics of an open, changing world of continued and contingent flux. Whether or not we take Rorty's position as metaphysical, I think he exaggerates and thus confuses the basic pragmatist idea of contingency by giving it a more radical sense of idiosyncratic arbitrariness or random accident rather than simply the sense of not being logically or ontologically necessary. He argues, for example, that if there is no ahistorical essence of human nature or "permanent ahistorical context of human life" that dictates what the self must be, then it is entirely a "random" product, "a matter of chance, a mere contingency." Thus, even our ethical attitudes and sense of duty are merely the result of "a host of idiosyncratic, accidental episodes."[12] By failing to distinguish between contingencies that are merely capricious, random, or idiosyncratic and those that are so deeply pervasive and socially or functionally entrenched that they are practically indispensable ("contingent necessities" or "historicized essences," so to speak), Rorty manifests a cavalier disregard with respect to stubbornly persistent realities that are often expressed in powerful social norms and reinforced by social institutions. He further displays a shocking (and very un-Deweyan) contempt for the social sciences that empirically study those realities, norms, and institutions. Following his favorite literary critic, Harold Bloom, Rorty condemns such sciences as "dismal."[13]

---

[11] As Dewey puts it, "we need a cautionary and directive word, like experience, to remind us that the world which is lived, suffered and enjoyed, as well as logically thought of, has the last word in all human inquiries and surmises." See John Dewey, *Experience and Nature* 1925, rev. 1929 (Carbondale: Southern Illinois University Press, 1981), 372. For further discussion of the value of deploying the concept of aesthetic experience, see Richard Shusterman, *Pragmatist Aesthetics: Living Beauty, Rethinking Art* (Oxford: Blackwell, 1992), ch. 2; *Performing Live: Aesthetic Alternatives for the Ends of Art* (Ithaca: Cornell University Press, 2000), ch. 1; and "Aesthetic Experience: From Analysis to Eros," *Journal of Aesthetics and Art Criticism* 64 (2006): 217–229.

[12] See Rorty, CIS, 26, 37; and *Essays on Heidegger and Others: Philosophical Papers*, vol. 2 (Cambridge: Cambridge University Press, 1991), 157.

[13] Richard Rorty, "The Inspirational Value of Great Literature," in *Achieving Our Country* (Cambridge, MA: Harvard University Press, 1999), 127; hereafter AC.

Combining his global textualism and hermeneutics with his notion of contingency, Rorty makes an intriguing argument for treating philosophy as primarily a private pursuit for perfection.[14] If our world and selves are contingent and linguistic, we can then reshape them to our tastes by virtuoso linguistic reinterpretation through new vocabularies. He therefore declares his allegiance to the path of inspirational, revisionary literary theory, illustrated by Bloom and Jacques Derrida, rather than looking at literature and other artistic practices through Foucault's method of genealogical critique of cultural institutions. He completely ignores the aesthetic theory of critical social theorists like Pierre Bourdieu, who combines philosophical theory with empirical social research to advance a progressive social agenda very much in the spirit of engaged Deweyan pragmatism. Rather than looking to the social sciences for resources to diagnose problems and formulate and test remedies to solve them, Rorty one-sidedly insists on "the hope for a religion of literature" to improve our world by giving us inspirational visions and teaching us to be kinder to others by helping us to imagine more clearly their needs, aims, and problems (AC, 136).

Despite such advocacy of the literary imagination over empirical social science as the way to cope with and improve our realities, Rorty's political philosophy has repeatedly drawn a very sharp distinction between what he calls "real politics" and what he denigrated as the "cultural politics" practiced by many progressive literary scholars in the academy whose political activism he saw as principally engaged in feminist, gay, racial, and ethnic issues of what is often called identity politics. This activism, he complained, was focused on dealing with these issues as expressed in academic life (from affirmative action and courses on marginalized identities to efforts to revise the literary and artistic canon to be more reflective of minority diversities). In "distinguishing cultural politics" from real politics, Rorty defined "real" not as "a metaphysical status" but as "electoral politics" or "*real* actions and events in the political sphere" that are "likely to redress the balance of power between the rich and

---

[14] Rorty affirms that some forms of philosophy serve a more public function of critically examining procedures of justice and democracy. However, this function receives far less attention from him than that of developing visions of private perfection and self-creation, which he celebrates but cautions against importing into the public sphere as a program that all selves must realize. In Rorty's account of the value of literature, there is a somewhat parallel pair of functions, where literature is praised for teaching us to be kind to others, but seems to get more praise (or at least more attention) for providing vocabularies for self-enrichment and self-fashioning. See, especially, Rorty, CIS, ch. 2-8; and my critical discussion in *Pragmatist Aesthetics*, ch. 9 and *Practicing Philosophy*, ch. 2.

the poor."[15] Elsewhere, he explains that "emphasizing the difference between real and cultural politics [means] alleviating suffering and equalizing opportunities on the one hand and redirecting the uses of learning and leisure on the other."[16]

In contrast, I have argued that there exist substantial continuities and useful overlaps between the arenas that Rorty divides as real and cultural politics. This is because of the political, social, and economic power of cultural imagery and production. Race, gender, and minority identities constitute cultural issues that go far beyond the academy and clearly connect with what Rorty calls real politics, not simply with respect to issues of discrimination in employment and the judicial system but also because race, gender, and ethnicity play an important role in electoral politics – as the 2008 presidential primaries and national election made strikingly evident. Similarly, cultural issues regarding the acceptability of homosexuality and same-sex partnerships have clearly moved from academic explorations on the campus to judicial and legislative activity and even to electoral referendums. It seems to me dangerously simplistic (though typically neoliberal) for Rorty to portray political suffering and injustice in narrowly economic terms of rich and poor. Identity politics has an unhappy history of mattering in the most painful ways; wealthy German Jews could not buy an Aryan manumission to escape the horribly real politics of Nazi persecution.

As I resist Rorty's sharp distinction between cultural and real politics, so (like many others) I have criticized his claimed "firm distinction between the private and the public" (CIS, 83). Though we can often, in particular cases, clearly distinguish between public matters and private ones, the distinction is more porous than Rorty suggests. We cannot limit public issues to those concerning the rules and procedures of the official public institutions that structure our democracy while regarding the private as relating to purely personal visions of the good life or self-realization, a question of "what should I do with my aloneness?"[17] Perhaps through his neglect of the social sciences, Rorty fails to appreciate how pervasively the public, social, and economic fields (through our shared public language, social norms, and advertised ideals of fulfillment) shape what he advocates as the individual's original, private visions of self-perfection.

---

[15] See Richard Rorty, "Intellectuals in Politics: Too Far In? Too Far Out?," *Dissent* (1991): 488, 489; hereafter IPP.
[16] Richard Rorty, "The Intellectuals at the End of Socialism," *Yale Review* 80 (1992): 7.
[17] Richard Rorty, *Objectivity, Relativism, and Truth: Philosophical Papers*, vol. 1 (Cambridge: Cambridge University Press, 1991), 13.

His own ethical ideal of the liberal ironist in constant search for new vocabularies, I have argued, seems an obvious echo of the consumer's quest for new commodities, and both are obviously shaped by the public framework that supports neoliberal capitalism. Likewise, Rorty's definition of autonomy as original, distinctly individualist self-creation seems a clear echo of neoliberalist self-seeking and self-absorption. This philosophy perhaps aptly reflects Rorty's Hegelian view of what philosophy must be: "its time held in thought" (PCP, ix). But his standard of successful self-cultivation is so ambitiously demanding and elitist that we must question whether many people could really live that way, and whether we should morally expect (or even want) them to.[18]

When forced to concede that the so-called private self and the language it builds upon for self-creation are always already socially constituted and structured by a public field, Rorty responds by redefining "the private-public distinction I want [as] that between responsibilities to ourselves and responsibilities to others" (RSS, 155). But for most people (even in neoliberal society) these different responsibilities are too deeply intertwined to split them sharply. It is hard to envisage acceptable projects of self-realization that swing free of what we feel (and cherish) as our bonds to those significant others who are so crucial to making us who we are and what we want to be. Pragmatists like Dewey and Mead thus emphasized that an individual's sense of self is essentially shaped by his relationship to others and his sense of how they view him. Rorty ignores this point in his advocacy of American neoliberalism and pursuit of original self-creation. His intriguing reconstruction of Deweyan thought in these directions has been wonderfully fruitful in reviving international interest in pragmatism, but it has also raised a backlash of suspicion that sees pragmatism as a sinister ideological tool and cultural expression of American global domination.

IV

Because Rorty's writings in the early nineties were so sharply critical of the notion of cultural politics, I was surprised that his final collection of papers, *Philosophy as Cultural Politics*, contrastingly embraces this notion as the core project he recommends for philosophy.[19] Though

---

[18] For my more detailed discussion of these points, see *Pragmatist Aesthetics*, 255–257.

[19] Richard Rorty, *Philosophy as Cultural Politics: Philosophical Papers*, vol. 4 (Cambridge: Cambridge University Press, 2007); hereafter PCP.

Rorty claims that "readers of his previous books" will find "no novel ideas or arguments" in the new volume, his revaluation of cultural politics is a noteworthy development (PCP, x). Even if we construe this development as more a change in the meaning Rorty gives to the term cultural politics than a new attitude to the things he previously designated by that term, the transformation is still important.[20] His new account of cultural politics especially intrigues me as offering a way through which I could bring him to appreciate my central project of somaesthetics, which he previously quite vehemently dismissed. To place this issue in proper context, I should briefly note some of our other conflicting views in the cultural field of aesthetics, beyond the difference already discussed about aesthetic experience.

With respect to interpretation in the specifically literary (rather than the deeper, more general philosophical sense), I have argued that Rorty is too one-sided in embracing Harold Bloom's advocacy of interpretation as "strong misreading." While Rorty asserts that the good critic "simply beats the text into a shape which will serve his own purpose," I maintain that such a policy is destructive of the very alterity that makes reading a dialogical hermeneutic project from which we can learn something new.[21] The aggressively domineering approach of strong misreading, moreover, hardly seems a helpful attitude for Rorty's project of realizing the "inspirational value of great works of literature" (AC, 125). Instead, we need a hermeneutics of greater balance and pluralism by appreciating the value of a more receptive stance in reading, where we let the text lead us rather than forcing it to mean what we want. The Bloomian masculinist strategy of bullying the text into fitting one's purpose, Rorty argues, helps promote the critical and cultural demand for new interpretations. But if we practice interpretive *yin* as well as overassertive *yang*, by letting the text lead us to places where we never dreamt of going rather than imposing our will on its possible meanings, we are likely to find still more unexpected and richer novelties.

In any case, I do not regard interpretive novelty as the only valuable form of literary understanding. More ordinary, traditional understandings of texts offer their own communicative, emotional, and edifying satisfactions, besides their crucial role as the necessary background or

---

[20] Rorty's transformation could be described as a move from the second to the third conception of cultural politics in terms of the three conceptions I outlined in the first section of this chapter.

[21] Richard Rorty, *Consequences of Pragmatism*, 151. For my critique, see *Pragmatist Aesthetics*, ch. 4.

base for radically innovative interpretations.[22] Rorty's praise of literature sometimes strikes me as too narrowly focused on its use for generating new vocabularies to enhance moral reflection, while failing to give enough attention to the aesthetics of pleasure, beauty, and entertainment. Pleasure, I argue, must be emphasized along with literature's functions of meliorism (cognitive, ethical, and social), and not simply because it is in fact productively related to them.

Pleasure helped bring me to an aesthetic appreciation and philosophical analysis of popular art that Rorty thought were deeply misguided. He refrained from examining in what ways popular art might positively contribute to a culture's aesthetics or an individual's vocabulary and self-fashioning; instead, he blasted it with a global, undifferentiated condemnation, denouncing it as "schlock" that "is sexist, racist, and militarist" in contrast to the wonderful "'high culture' that Trotsky shared with Dewey and Dubois" (IPP, 488). Here again, I argue that pragmatism should maintain a more productive pluralist position that celebrates high culture yet also recognizes the merits of many works of popular art, while nonetheless urging in meliorist fashion that popular art still leaves much room for improvement. Because works of popular art are understood by more people, they can be especially effective in sensitizing our society to moral and political injustice. Thus, popular novels like *Uncle Tom's Cabin* can dwarf the likes of Henry James's *Portrait of a Lady* with respect to ethical and political impact. To defend popular art's aesthetic legitimacy and explore its cultural contribution while engaging in constructive critique aimed at making it better, therefore, seems a useful direction for pragmatist cultural politics. This position of meliorism (between global condemnation and uncritical celebration) has always guided my writings on rap, country music, and other styles of popular culture.[23]

V

The same meliorist orientation shapes my project of somaesthetics, which, to recall, can be briefly defined as the critical meliorative study of the experience and use of one's body as a locus of sensory-aesthetic

---

[22] For similar pluralist reasons, I resist Rorty's one-sided identification of the aesthetic life with singular genius and originality – not because I have something against original genius, but again, only because this unwisely excludes other rewarding modes of aesthetic living that are less demanding and more accessible. See Shusterman, *Pragmatist Aesthetics*, ch. 9; and *Practicing Philosophy*, ch. 1.

[23] See Shusterman, *Pragmatist Aesthetics*, ch. 7-8; and *Performing Live*, ch. 3-4.

appreciation (aesthesis) and creative self-fashioning. In examining the forms of knowledge and disciplines of practice that structure such somatic care or can improve it, somaesthetics involves the critical study of society's somatic values and comportment, so as to redirect our body consciousness and practice away from the oppressively narrow and injurious stereotypes of somatic success that pervade our advertising culture and to focus instead on exploring more rewarding visions of somatic value and fulfillment and better methods for attaining them. Despite the fact that Rorty sharply attacks my project of somaesthetics, it constitutes precisely the kind of project that his final account of philosophy as cultural politics could embrace.

Rorty describes his account as emerging from Hegel's and Dewey's historicist views "that philosophy is its time held in thought," rather than an eternal, God's-eye vision of the world, and that the philosopher's job should therefore be "to contribute to humanity's ongoing conversation" about how to improve our time and practices. "The progress of this conversation has engendered new social practices, and changes in the vocabularies deployed in moral and political deliberation. To suggest further novelties is to intervene in cultural politics," Rorty concludes, affirming Dewey's hope "that philosophy professors would see such intervention as their principal assignment," and endorsing "the pragmatist maxim that what makes no difference to practice should make no difference to philosophy." He also cites Dewey's radically visionary claim that "philosophy is not in any sense whatever a form of knowledge," but rather "a social hope reduced to a working program of action, a prophecy of the future" (PCP, ix).

Rorty's citation perfectly captures Dewey's vision, and we can bring other quotes from Dewey to reinforce it. Chiding his philosophical contemporaries in the academy for "lack of imagination in generating leading ideas," Dewey claims philosophy can prove its value only "with the formation of directive hypotheses instead of with a sweeping pretension to knowledge of universal Being."[24] In proposing concrete means and ends, philosophy should be "thinking which is operative – which frames and defines ideas in terms of what may be done, and which uses the conclusions of science as instrumentalities." In earlier writings, Rorty seems more skeptical about philosophy's sociopolitical utility. Claiming

---

[24] John Dewey, *Philosophy and Civilization* (New York: Capricorn, 1963), 11; and *The Quest for Certainty* (Carbondale: Southern Illinois University Press, 1988), 248. The quotation following is from the same volume, 227.

he "cannot find much use for philosophy in formulating means to the ends which we social democrats share," Rorty affirms philosophy's "main use" as helping us think through our personal utopian visions by supplying vocabularies that we can appropriate, transform, and transcend in our quest for self-realization; so "philosophy has become more important for the pursuit of private perfection rather than for any social task."[25] But if we affirm the continuity of the private and the public, then the individual's use of new vocabularies for projects of enriched self-realization are always already shaped by the social environment and, conversely, feed back into enriching that environment's resources.

When philosophy is construed as cultural politics rather than the pursuit of absolute, eternal truth, then its history, says Rorty, "is best seen as a series of efforts to modify people's sense of who they are, what matters to them," and this leads to new images or ideals of self and society. "Interventions in cultural politics," Rorty continues, "have sometimes taken the form of proposals for new roles that men and women might play: the ascetic, the prophet, the dispassionate seeker after truth, the good citizen, the aesthete, the revolutionary." But cultural politics, he adds, has also taken different forms, such as "sketches of an ideal community – the perfected Greek polis, the Christian Church, the republic of letters, the cooperative commonwealth" or "suggestions about how to reconcile seemingly incompatible outlooks – to resolve Greek rationalism and Christian faith, or between natural science and the common moral consciousness." What Rorty asserts as common and crucial to these and other forms of philosophical interventions in cultural politics is that they aim to make "a difference to the way human beings live," not just to address specialist "technical debates" in the academic field (PCP, ix–x).

Philosophy as cultural politics, Rorty further insists, should have an interdisciplinary orientation, for by engaging with other fields that deal with our multidimensional existence, philosophy can augment its resources for productively affecting our lives: "The more philosophy interacts with other human activities – not just natural science, but art, literature, religion, and politics as well – the more relevant to cultural politics it becomes, and thus the more useful. The more it strives for autonomy, the less attention it deserves" (PCP, x). Note, however, how Rorty strikingly omits the social sciences in his list of disciplines. Why don't they belong there; why shouldn't the social sciences help philosophy "make a difference to the ways human beings live," especially since human life

---

[25] Richard Rorty, "Thugs and Theorists," *Political Theory* 15 (1987): 569; and CIS, 94.

is so thoroughly shaped by its essentially social character? Rorty provides no arguments for rejecting the social sciences, apart from the fact that his aesthetic taste finds them grimmer and less imaginatively inspiring than literature. That, however, hardly seems reason enough, especially because natural science also has its dull and dismal dimensions, while classics of social science can be inspiringly and imaginatively insightful. Think of the works of Weber, Simmel, Mauss, and Bourdieu.

In recommending interaction with other activities as essential to philosophy's cultural politics, Rorty is not at all explicit about the nature or style of this interaction. How does philosophy engage with these activities? Does it intervene only on the theoretical level by proposing critiques of theories of natural science, art, religion, and so on? Or does philosophy more closely engage the actual concrete practice of these activities by detailed critical analysis of the particular forms they take, and by proposing new methods to improve practice (say, new scientific or artistic methods, new techniques for religious meditation or political engagement)? Could philosophy as cultural politics connect itself still more intimately with the various practices that give our lives meaning by providing in itself a philosophical form of those practices? For example, could philosophy as cultural politics intervene in literary practice by making itself a self-conscious form of literary composition – say, philosophy as literature in the essay style of Montaigne or Emerson; the fictional style of Sartre, Camus, Beauvoir, or Musil; the dramatic dialogical style of Plato; the poetic style of Lucretius or Dante; or in the form of literary criticism that Rorty at times has practiced with great skill?

If philosophy aims to make a difference in our lives, then why not practice it as an art of living, as most ancient philosophers recommended and several modern greats (such as Wittgenstein, James, Dewey, and Foucault) have likewise affirmed? Here philosophy's cultural politics could take the eminently pragmatic form of seeking to benefit life not merely by writing texts but by other forms of concrete praxis in the world; by more robustly embodied forms of action and cultivation, including somatic disciplines that can make a positive difference to the perception, performance, and attitudes of the practitioner and to her capacities to understand and productively engage with the people and environments that surround her.

Rorty, however, seems unwilling to go this far. The evidence of his career shows that he sees philosophy's cultural politics as essentially confined to *textual* politics or writing, especially in composing "arguments about what words to use" (PCP, 3). In the many conversations we shared over the years, I often urged him to do more. If he thought that analytic philosophy had essentially deconstructed itself and outlived its usefulness, while Deweyan pragmatism should be reclaimed as a more promising philosophical direction, then why, I asked, did he not try to use his symbolic power as America's most important philosopher to try to engage in institution building that could help the pragmatic turn he initiated? He could have organized a corps of new pragmatist philosophers inspired by his work, perhaps creating an interdisciplinary center for pragmatism when he held an endowed chair at the University of Virginia or initiating some new pragmatist journals or book series. Such acts of cultural politics that transcend mere philosophical writing to include institutional praxis could help reorient philosophy and make pragmatism more influential in the American and international philosophical scene. When his fame surged beyond academic philosophical circles and won him international cultural celebrity as America's most excitingly original intellectual, I repeatedly pressed him about his neglect of more concrete praxis to redirect philosophy and culture more generally in the pragmatist directions he advocated.[26] After all, I argued, his famous European counterparts typically engaged in institution development and robust cultural-political praxis to promote the theoretical orientations or social changes they thought were needed; and Rorty's great hero, John Dewey, was famous for his vigorous engagement in political activism and institution building (including his famous Laboratory School, various labor unions, the National Association for the Advancement of Colored People, and the New School for Social Research).[27]

---

[26] These concerns were also expressed in the *New York Times Magazine* article on Rorty, where I am quoted as criticizing Rorty's reluctance to deploy his intellectual influence for cultural politics and social causes by taking "an active public role." See Larry Klepp, "Every Man a Philosopher King," *New York Times Magazine* (December 2, 1990): 124. I am happy to admit that Rorty later did take a more active public role at least in textual politics, writing more social criticism in nonphilosophical venues that enjoy wider circulation and public impact.

[27] Consider, for example, Foucault's organizational activism on matters of prison reform and gay rights; and Derrida and Lyotard's founding of the Collège International de Philosophie to challenge the academic conservatism of French university philosophy; Bourdieu's Centre de Sociologie Européenne, the journal he founded (*Actes de Recherche en Sciences Sociales*), and his different book series with Minuit, Seuil, and Raisons d'agir. For a German example, consider Habermas's role of leadership in preserving the continuity and deepening the institutional influence of the Frankfurt School, his role as codirector in the publisher Suhrkamp's "Theorie" collection, and his role as codirector of the Max-Planck-Institut zur Erforschung der Lebensbedingungen der wissenschaftlich-technischen Welt in Starnberg.

Rorty replied that such institution building would be a time-wasting distraction from his research and writing; that attempts to build up a corps of pragmatist philosophers through organizational means would most likely attract the most mediocre of minds. I remember him saying that smart people will get the pragmatist message by reading his books (*if* they want to), and they will spread it by writing their own good books. That argument never entirely convinced me. It struck me, however, as a compelling rationalization for what I suspect was Rorty's strongest reason for eschewing such cultural-political praxis: His personality – much more shy, bookish, and individualistic than group oriented and socially suave – made a leading, active role in organizational, social, and public praxis too unappealing for him to embrace. I accept and respect that, and am grateful to Rorty for all the great things he was in fact able to do for philosophy and culture.

VI

I am, however, unwilling to accept his rejection of somaesthetics. So let me conclude by first considering his critique and then showing how somaesthetics effectively serves the key functions that Rorty demands of philosophy as cultural politics. Despite his continued insistence that "all awareness is a linguistic affair," Rorty concedes to me and somaesthetics that we can experience and create things that allow us to "revel, however briefly, in nondiscursive sensual joy."[28] However, he questions the idea of somaesthetics as a project or "programme" that, by thinking through the body and working on it, could bring more of this nondiscursive joy and more understanding of how it is achieved, experienced, and deployed in our lives. More precisely, he challenges somaesthetics by assimilating it into traditional aesthetic theory of the Kantian variety that aims to isolate a pure aesthetic essence that defines all things aesthetic and differentiates them from everything else. Rorty doubts we "need 'a somatic aesthetics,'" because we do not "need an aesthetic theory, or an aesthetic programme, at all." And he immediately supplies the anti-essentialist reason for his skepticism: "I doubt there is much to be said about what unites painting, literature, music, sex, and birdwatching while distinguishing all these from science, morals, politics, philosophy and religion" (RRS, 156).

---

[28] Rorty affirms the exclusively linguistic character of consciousness to the very end of his life, as this quote (PCP, 12) makes clear. The concession is made in RRS, 155–156.

I share Rorty's resistance to the essentialism of traditional aesthetics, and I even criticize our hero Dewey for courting it too closely.[29] However, "scepticism about 'aesthetics' as a field of inquiry" in its traditional essentialist sense, which Rorty calls "another of Kant's bad ideas" (RRS, 156), has no relevance to the somaesthetic project, which could not be farther from an attempt to define and compartmentalize a pure aesthetic domain. Somaesthetics is instead a distinctively interdisciplinary enterprise, radiating out of the concept of soma – the living, feeling, sentient, purposive body that implies the essential union of body-mind. The somaesthetic program – of studying the ways we use our soma in perception, performance, and self-fashioning; the ways that physiology and society shape and constrain those uses; and the methods we have developed or can invent to enhance those uses and provide newer and better forms of somatic awareness and functioning – implies engaging with science, morals, politics, art, and religion as well as with history and other disciplines.

In somaesthetics, the aim is not to provide essentialist philosophical definitions, but to bring together and deploy the various things we know (or can learn) about embodied perception (aesthesis) and action and about socially entrenched body norms and practical somatic disciplines, so that this knowledge can be used in practice to enrich our lives and extend the frontiers of human experience as we now know and imagine it. Somaesthetics, as I repeatedly insist, is a field of practice as well as theory, a field admittedly far too large for any one researcher to explore or master on her own, and too complex in structure for me to summarize here. It may be useful, however, to recall here that this field includes three major branches: The first (analytic somaesthetics) involves philosophical, empirical, and critical study of the principles of somatic functioning in perception and of our culture's body norms, practices, and values, along with the ideologies and institutions that shape them. The second (pragmatic somaesthetics) deals with the comparative study and critique of practical methods aimed at improving somatic awareness, performance, and care. The third branch (practical somaesthetics) involves the actual practice of body disciplines aimed at such improvements.

If, in Rorty's conception, philosophy as cultural politics seeks "to contribute to humanity's ongoing conversation about what to do with itself,"

---

[29] See Shusterman, *Pragmatist Aesthetics*, ch. 2; *Performing Live*, ch. 1; and "Aesthetic Experience: From Analysis to Eros," *Journal of Aesthetics and Art Criticism* 64 (2006): 217–229.

to make "efforts to modify people's sense of who they are, what matters to them" by initiating new practices or "changes in the vocabularies" that we use to think about ourselves and our society, and "to reconcile seemingly incompatible outlooks," if Rorty indeed recommends philosophy as "a social hope" expressed in working "programs of action" that make a "difference to practice," then he should endorse somaesthetics as providing just such an intervention (PCP, ix, x). By critically examining our culture's oppressively narrow ideals of good looks and somatic satisfaction, while exploring alternative notions of bodily beauty and sources of somatic pleasures, somaesthetics can surely help improve "people's sense of who they are" and "what matters to them," and can promote new ways of talking about our embodied selves that are more liberating and rewarding. Through its comparative critique and exploration of various somatic disciplines and how they can be productively introduced into the project of philosophy as an art of living, and still further through the actual practice of such disciplines in one's life, somaesthetics not only offers suggestions for personal cultivation but also resources for "social hope" and "working programs of action." Moreover, if a key goal of cultural politics is "to reconcile seemingly incompatible outlooks" whose apparent conflict tortures both individual and society, then somaesthetics can help remedy the pervasive body/mind and materialist/spiritual schisms in our culture through its recognition and cultivation of the soma as integrating material, mental, and spiritual dimensions of human life.

Heightened body awareness is usually thought to be a necessarily private, selfish affair. But, in fact, as the somatic self is always essentially situated in an environment, somatic awareness cannot really ever be of the self alone. To feel itself means always feeling its environment in some way, at the very least sensing the surface we are sitting, standing, or lying on; feeling the air that envelops us; and the gravitational force that weighs on us. But the soma's environment is generally social as well as physical; thus, heightened somatic awareness can help sensitize us to social relations so that we can improve them.

Recall, for example, the problems of racism and ethnic enmity that I noted in earlier chapters. Such hostility does not stem from rational thought but from deep prejudices that are somatically marked in terms of vague uncomfortable feelings aroused by alien bodies, feelings experienced implicitly and thus engrained beneath the level of explicit consciousness. As such, these feelings and the negative attitudes they engender cannot be properly controlled without bringing them into clear consciousness by cultivating heightened somatic awareness.[30] Likewise, as ancient Greek and Asian philosophers have repeatedly asserted, taking care of one's own somatic efficacy is a necessary means for effectively taking care of others. Diogenes the Cynic was not alone in employing it to advocate rigorous body training as "that whereby, with constant exercise, perceptions are formed such as secure freedom of movement for virtuous deeds."[31] When air-safety policy instructs parents to take care of their own oxygen supply before worrying about their children's, it is not a lesson in selfishness but the basic insight that to care effectively for others requires a certain level of somatic care for the self. As Mencius urged from the Confucian standpoint, we cannot meet our duties to our parents or society unless we first take care of keeping our bodies in effective health, for only through our bodies can we act to help others.[32]

Moreover, given Rorty's own ardent arguments for affect as the true ground of morality and human solidarity, he should recognize that somaesthetics has significant ethical and social potential. Rorty repeatedly insists that our commitment to human rights and other central moral principles cannot be effectively justified by appeals to universal rationality but instead depend on common sentiments about how people should be treated. Noting that cultures who do not share our moral beliefs are perfectly able to perform all sorts of difficult rational tasks, Rorty argues that their immoral treatment of subordinate groups they oppress cannot be the product of irrationality, but is rather because they do not feel that the creatures they oppress are "people like ourselves"

---

[30] Here somaesthetic efforts could go further than the remedy of diagnosis and isolation by actually transforming the undesirable, "intolerant" bodily feelings. Somatic feelings can be transformed through training because they are already the product of training. One's normal feelings and tastes are largely the result of learning rather than innate instinct; as habits derived from our experience and sociocultural formation, they are malleable to efforts of reformation. Disciplines of somaesthetic training can therefore reconstruct our attitudes or habits of feeling and also give us greater flexibility and tolerance to different kinds of somatic feeling and behavior. This is a commonplace of gastronomy, athletics, and somatic therapies; but modern philosophical ethics and political theory have not given it enough attention.

[31] See Diogenes Laertius, *Lives of Eminent Philosophers*, trans. R.D. Hicks (Cambridge, MA: Harvard University Press, 1991), vol. 2, 71. For more discussion of ancient Greek and Asian philosophers on the essential value of one's somatic care and training for the practice of virtue, see Shusterman, *Body Consciousness*, ch. 1 and Chapter 9 of this book.

[32] *Mencius: A New Translation*, trans. W.A.C.H. Dobson (Toronto: Toronto University Press, 1969), 138–139.

(PCP, 53) and merit "full personhood."[33] What makes us more moral than other animals, Rorty claims, is that, "We can feel *for each other* to a much greater extent than they can," and we progress in morality (both as individuals and as societies) the more we can feel for more kinds of people (RR, 358). Moral progress is therefore "a progress of sentiments" (RR, 362). Thus, rather than focusing on the search for universal rational principles to ground our own moral beliefs and convince others of their absolute validity, we should "put foundationalism behind us" and instead "concentrate our energies on manipulating sentiments, on sentimental education," so that we can empathize with more kinds of people, imaginatively feel ourselves "in the shoes of the despised and oppressed" (RR, 358, 360). "That sort of education sufficiently acquaints people of different kinds with one another so that they are less tempted to think of those different from themselves as only quasi-human. The goal of this manipulation of sentiment is to expand the reference" class of those we treat as humans like ourselves, of "people like us" (RR, 358). Moral persuasion is thus more essentially a matter of "rhetorical manipulation" of feeling than "genuine validity-seeking argument" (PCP, 53).

Rorty celebrates literature as the best means of "manipulating sentiments," but feelings can be effectively manipulated through somatic as well as literary means. We can bring strangers (and even enemies) to feel more comfortable with each other by having them share the pleasures of eating and drinking together. As William James famously argues, we can also to some extent transform our own moods and feelings by taking on the postures and bodily behaviors of those feelings and moods we wish to feel.[34] Furthermore, to imagine empathetically what it feels like to be oppressed or despised (or even simply insulted or offended) is an act of somatic consciousness that can be done more powerfully when we have a more developed somatic imagination, when our somatic sensibility and awareness has been cultivated to be more keenly perceptive and subtle. There is thus a deep connection between somaesthetics and the cultivation of sentiment that Rorty seeks as a means to moral progress, although he totally neglects it.

Rorty is perhaps blind to the value of somaesthetics as a resource for social hope because he tends to identify it (and perhaps all somatically

---

[33] See also Richard Rorty, "Human Rights, Rationality, and Sentimentality," in Christopher Voparil and Richard Bernstein (eds.), *The Rorty Reader* (Oxford: Blackwell, 2010), 358; hereafter RR; and, "Feminism and Pragmatism," in that same volume, 348.

[34] William James, *The Principles of Psychology* (Cambridge, MA: Harvard University Press, 1983), ch. 4.

oriented philosophy) with the views of the most famous body philosophers of the late twentieth century, who controversially emphasized the body's use in radical, violent "limit-experiences" and social transgression largely centered on sex and drugs. "Foucault's, Bataille's and Deleuze's discussions of the body leave me cold," Rorty writes, in contesting somaesthetics' claim that the body is a place where we can go beyond the limits of discursive reason (RSS, 156). For some mysterious reason, he completely ignores that I explicitly critique their somatic extremism for confusing the need to transcend the limits of discursive rationality with the need to engage in violently irrational, transgressively "rabid Dionysiac excess." "The conflation of these two senses, in thinkers like Bataille, Deleuze, and Foucault, comes only by coupling the idea of somatic aesthetics with the avant-garde ideology of radical transgression and shocking extremes," I objected, urging that somaesthetics instead give more attention to the kind of nondiscursive experience and action that, although not ruled by "discursive rationality, is not devoid of intelligent direction."[35]

"But," Rorty continues, "even if they [Foucault, Bataille, and Deleuze] turned me on, I would still resist talk about where discursive reason meets its limits. I do not see a difference between 'discursive reason' and talking about things, and I cannot see that talking about things has either 'limits' or an 'other'" (RRS, 156). Such statements seem foreign to the pragmatist spirit of philosophy as a working program of action, and to the classical pragmatist insight that there are important dimensions of human life beyond the limits of discursive rationality, and that philosophy should attend to those dimensions. Hence, William James and Dewey emphasize the nondiscursively affective and the somatic, recognizing the importance of intelligent embodied habit that cannot be reduced to a verbal formula of discursive reason.

Even if we rightly acknowledge that discourse itself always involves some dimension of action (whether actions of writing or reading or speech), we should not deny the very useful common sense distinction between mere words and real action, between talking about doing something and really doing it. Such a distinction between merely saying something and actually doing it is crucial to our entire network of ethical, artistic, commercial, athletic, and juridical practices. Playing a Beethoven sonata or running a four-minute mile goes beyond the limits of merely talking about those things. "Talking about things is one of the things we do," Rorty persists, "Experiencing moments of sensual joy is another," and there is absolutely

---

[35] These quotations are from Shusterman, *Practicing Philosophy*, 128.

no meaningful relationship between discourse and nondiscursive experience that warrants any theoretical attention or systematic intervention. "The two do not stand in any dialectical relationship, get in each others' way, or need synthesis in a programme or theory" (RRS, 156). Would performing an embodied nonverbal action to generate an experience of sensual joy constitute, for Rorty, still another thing we do, or would it be assimilated into the joyful experience it generates?

It hardly matters because, in any case, it is clear that many fields do essentially rely on significantly relating the discursive and nondiscursive. In music, for example, there is a purposeful, effective linkage between discourse and nondiscursive experience – for example, between interpretive critical discussions of a musical piece, comments on relevant aspects of musical and performance theory, and specific discursive performance instructions on the one hand, and nondiscursive movements and experiences of nondiscursive musical joy experienced by the performers or audience on the other. The same might be said about how wordless sexual pleasures rely not only nondiscursive actions but on helpful erotic discourse about what precise actions to perform and how or when to perform them as well as verbal expressions that contribute to the mood. (Of course, in lovemaking, no more than in music, does skillful discourse entail skillful performance, which is another reason why the common sense distinction between words and actions is often useful.) Somatic disciplines are essentially constituted through systematic programs, methods, and theories that relate discourse to the nondiscursive, and in various texts I have tried to show how somaesthetics combines the discursive and the nondiscursive in the process of reforming habits and acquiring skills.[36] Rorty's refusal to acknowledge fruitfully significant relations between discursive understanding and nondiscursive enjoyment seems an unnecessarily rigid, unproductive dualism that is not only alien to pragmatism's emphasis on the continuity of theory and practice but also at odds with its meliorist impulse to use discursive theory – as cultural politics – to intervene in actual practice to improve our lives.

When Rorty claims "we can agree with Gadamer that 'being that can be understood is language' while remaining aware that there is more to life than understanding," he denies the existence of nonlinguistic understanding (RRS, 156–157). However, nonlinguistic understanding seems not only quite evident in nonverbal arts like music, painting, dance, and (if you will) erotic artistry, but also in a variety of everyday somatic

---

[36] See for example, Shusterman, *Practicing Philosophy*, ch. 6; and *Body Consciousness*, chs. 2–6.

interactions that rely on a host of implicit understandings, most of which never reach the level of explicit thematized awareness. Moreover, by Rorty's own principles of cultural politics, we cannot reject somaesthetics by a mere appeal to ontological claims like the alleged inexistence of nonlinguistic awareness or understanding. For according to Rorty's ultimate view, as articulated in *Philosophy as Cultural Politics*, such politics should always trump or "replace ontology" (PCP, 5). In other words, the essential question is not whether nondiscursive understanding and awareness exist or not, but whether it is useful or not to believe they exist because of the benefits that are generated by such beliefs (which include the benefits of the diverse practices and actions emerging from those beliefs).

Somaesthetics articulates, explores, and seeks to develop those benefits. In contrast, by denying the existence of nondiscursive understanding and awareness, Rorty tries to block the path of inquiry by ridiculing as meaningless fantasy the pursuit of disciplines that treat the nondiscursive aspects of life and offer helpful methods for improving how we experience them. We can surely find some mumbo jumbo and superstition within the enormously vast array of body disciplines that human history has produced, but there are also many somatic disciplines whose methods have won substantial empirical confirmation through centuries of successful traditions of practice and through contemporary clinical studies.[37]

"Inventing others to reason and then purporting to provide a better discursive understanding of these nondiscursive others," Rorty concludes, "seems to me a beautiful example of kicking up dust and then complaining that we cannot see" (RRS, 157). To justify this critique of my project, he simply (without argument) assimilates somaesthetics into a long epistemological tradition, "a project that stretches from British empiricism through Bergson to existential phenomenology" (ibid.) and that aims to put us in discursive touch with the really real, an immediate primordial pristine perception of reality upon which all other knowledge must somehow be constructed. Presumably, he is again assuming that any philosophical concern with the body must have foundationalist epistemology as its agenda.

In response to this final objection of Rorty's, I should first say that somaesthetics did not invent something other than reason; it simply

---

[37] For some of this evidence, see Shusterman, *Body Consciousness*, ch. 5–6, and Chapter 3 of this book.

responded to problems and pleasures of life that discursive reason cannot adequately address on its own because those problematic and pleasurable things have an important nondiscursive dimension.[38] Second, somaesthetics has nothing in common with the traditional foundationalist project that Rorty evokes. The goal is not to discursively describe (or even nondiscursively capture) a putative originary vision of the world – elemental, pristine, and universally shared; the sort of primordial perception celebrated by Merleau-Ponty, which allegedly reveals the "things themselves" as they "are first given to us" in our most basic spontaneous level of perception, a primordial level that remains forever unchanging although obscured by conventional vision.[39] As a nonfoundationalist pragmatist, I see little point in trying to capture such an elemental perception. This is not simply because it would seem too primitive (in its absolutely primordial essence) to be very useful or interesting, but because I doubt whether there is such an underlying primordial perception that remains unchanging and universally shared. Even our most basic nondiscursive experiences are significantly shaped by the cultures and environments we inhabit, and these are neither uniform nor unchanging. We are already shaped by culture in the womb.

Besides, as I have repeatedly emphasized, the central goal of somaesthetics is not a discursive theory that defines the true, originary essence of nondiscursive experience. Somaesthetics' discursive aims are instead focused on articulating frameworks and improving methods that themselves serve as means for the improvement of our nondiscursive experience and of the multitude of discursive practices that structure the ways we regard and use our bodies and the ways that other people regard and treat them. Of course, a good bit of the discourse of somaesthetics must also be directed to the cultural politics of arguing against theorists like Rorty who refuse to admit that talking about the body and its nondiscursive experience is a useful thing to do.

I'd like to believe that if Rorty had reviewed my vision of somaesthetics in the light of his evolving views on philosophy as cultural politics, he would have been more sympathetic toward what the somaesthetic project

---

[38] In the same way, James's and Dewey's talk about nondiscursive experience – nameless feelings, nonlinguistic qualities, nonverbal understandings, and nondiscursively coordinated interaction – was not about inventing something to idly spin their theoretical wheels about, but was necessary for explaining and promoting their exploration of interventions to improve such nonlinguistic experience.

[39] Merleau-Ponty, *The Phenomenology of Perception*, trans. Colin Smith (London: Routledge, 1962), ix, 57; and *In Praise of Philosophy and Other Essays*, trans. John Wild, James Edie, and John O'Neill (Evanston, IL: Northwestern University Press, 1970), 63.

could pragmatically offer to individuals and to society as a whole. On a couple of occasions when we met in the last few years of his life, well after he wrote his critical rebuke of my somaesthetic project, he suggested that he might be growing more receptive to it, although it was a project very remote from his personal style and professional skills in doing philosophy as cultural politics.[40] His apparent change of attitude greatly pleased but did not much surprise me, because Rorty was exemplary not only in his kindness but in his open-minded tolerance and curiosity to learn new things. His untimely death ended a life of bold and wide-ranging philosophical inquiry, but leaves us with a legacy to pursue the conversations he shaped in ever more adventurous and experimental ways.

---

[40] On one occasion, when we were walking in Paris, he asked me (in a modestly self-deprecating but genuinely interested tone) what somaesthetic disciplines I could recommend to an overweight philosopher in advancing middle age. Before I could launch much of an answer, we suddenly came across something in the street that took our conversation in an altogether different direction.

9

Body Consciousness and Performance

Somaesthetics East and West

I

Embodiment is a universal feature of human life, and so is body consciousness. Body consciousness, as I understand it, is not merely the consciousness that a mind may have of the body as an object, but includes the embodied consciousness that a living sentient body directs at the world and also experiences in itself (and through which it indeed can experience itself as both subject and object). Enhancing one's body consciousness to achieve better self-awareness and self-use is central to the project of somaesthetics and helpful in promoting philosophy's traditional goals of knowledge, self-knowledge, virtue, happiness, and justice.

Consciousness has different levels. At its most basic form of primitive body intentionality, we can even describe a level of what could paradoxically be called unconscious consciousness. This is the sort of limited, obscure awareness we exhibit in our sleep, when, for example, we intentionally (though unconsciously) move a pillow that is disturbing our breathing.[1] Beyond this level is the stage when we are awake and clearly

---

[1] We should also note that there are apparently different levels of consciousness during sleep. In non-REM sleep, "especially early in the night when EEG slow waves are prevalent," there seems to be a much lower level of consciousness or sense of experience than during "REM sleep late in the night, when dreams become long and vivid and consciousness returns to levels close to those of wakefulness." See Giulio Tononi and Christof Koch, "The Neural Correlates of Consciousness: An Update," *Annals of the New York Academy of Science* 1124 (2008): 239–261. The range of levels of consciousness is further complicated by the fact that different levels can be produced through different degrees of induced anesthesia. These different levels include milder anesthetic states that are more conscious than normal sleep but also extend to deeply anesthetic states of extreme unresponsiveness, even to painful stimuli. See ibid., 243–244. Different degrees of consciousness could also be distinguished in the levels of wakeful (and non-anesthetized)

conscious of the object we perceive, say the cup of coffee we are holding and drinking from, but are not explicitly aware of it as a distinct object of consciousness, as when we are drinking the coffee absentmindedly or simply noticing the coffee's taste and not the cup. Yet, even without explicit awareness, we can handle the cup with efficiency and ease. This level of unreflective, unthematized perception is what Merleau-Ponty hails as "primary consciousness" and the fundamental, unappreciated key to the mystery of our successful perception and action.[2] We reach a higher level of consciousness when we have explicit awareness of the cup, when we attend to it as a distinct object of consciousness; and we can distinguish a fourth, more reflective, level when we are not only explicitly conscious of the object but also conscious of how (and that) we are conscious of it. Here we consciously monitor our awareness of the object as an explicit datum of consciousness; noticing, for example, how our attention to the cup makes it look bigger or feel heavier.

These different levels of consciousness that we noted with respect to objects like pillows or cups can also be found in the sense we have of our embodied selves. When asleep, the soma feels its positionality and breathing well enough to move the pillow or to reposition itself when it feels it is getting too close to the edge of the bed. We often pay no attention to our feet nor have an explicit awareness of them when we are walking. Sometimes, however we do make our feet an explicit object of consciousness – when we are crossing difficult terrain, when we have problems of balance, or when our feet are hurting. Similarly, we sometimes move from inexplicit consciousness of breathing to situations where our breathing becomes an explicit object of our somatic consciousness, as when we notice we are short of breath. Finally, there are cases of more reflective somatic consciousness, such as when we are not only explicitly aware that we are breathing but also clearly conscious of our conscious awareness of breathing and of how that reflexive consciousness affects our breathing and other dimensions of somatic experience. These explicit and reflective levels of consciousness, which can blend or overlap

consciousness I describe here, so my classification of levels here is not meant to be entirely exhaustive but rather to suggest the complexity that tends to get flattened in discussions of consciousness.

[2] See Maurice Merleau-Ponty, *The Phenomenology of Perception*, trans. Colin Smith (London: Routledge, 1962), xv–xvi, who affirms phenomenology's essential aim as recapturing that unreflective vision. It is "a philosophy for which the world is always 'already there' before reflection begins – as an inalienable presence; and all its efforts are concentrated upon re-achieving a direct and primitive contact with the world, and endowing that contact with a philosophical status" (ibid. vii).

into each other, I describe respectively as somaesthetic perception and somaesthetic reflection.³

Although they undoubtedly contribute to self-knowledge, to what extent and in what ways are somaesthetic perception and reflection really useful in improving the use of ourselves in performance? That our actions require bodily means and control for their successful execution does not entail that such control or skillful guidance requires heightened, reflective somatic awareness. On the contrary, the skillful performance of bodily action can usually rely on unreflective sensorimotor schemata established through training and habit. Moreover, as many theorists have noted, such skilled, smoothly flowing spontaneous performance can be hindered by reflection. I, too, have long advocated the positive and necessary role of unreflective somatic understanding and spontaneous performance.⁴ However, we need a double-barreled approach that also highlights the uses of explicit, critical somatic awareness or somaesthetic reflection and that explains how unreflective and reflective body consciousness can best be integrated for improving the quality of our experience and the efficacy of our self-use. The wide-ranging value of unreflective habits in our perception and action does not entail that these habits are fully adequate and do not need correction through a process involving critically reflective awareness of what those habits are. We acquire bad habits as easily as good ones.⁵ To correct our bad habits we cannot simply rely on spontaneity, which, as the product of habit, is precisely part of the problem.⁶ Improved, reflective body

---

³ For more details on these levels of consciousness, see Richard Shusterman, *Body Consciousness: A Philosophy of Mindfulness and Somaesthetics* (Cambridge: Cambridge University Press, 2008), 53–56.

⁴ See especially Richard Shusterman, "Beneath Interpretation," in *Pragmatist Aesthetics: Living Beauty, Rethinking Art* (Oxford: Blackwell, 1992); and "Somatic Experience," in *Practicing Philosophy: Pragmatism and the Philosophical Life* (New York: Routledge, 1997).

⁵ One reason for this is that habits incorporate aspects of the environment in which the habits are conditioned, and many of those environments are far from optimal or unproblematic. Moreover, as Michel Foucault and Pierre Bourdieu have argued, oppressive regimes and institutions often seek to preserve their power by instilling in us bodily habits of blind docility and automatic compliance that can be bad for us in a different sense than that we ordinarily ascribe to bad habits. Such habits of compliance (which tend to be socially endorsed as good habits) can nonetheless be bad because they weaken our powers of critique and resistance and thus reinforce our hopeless subservience to powers that dominate us in unfortunate ways, preventing the emergence of better social orders.

⁶ Nor can we rely on mere trial and error to form new habits because the sedimentation process would likely be too slow and most likely be inclined to repeat the bad habit unless that habit was critically thematized in explicit consciousness for correction.

consciousness is therefore necessary for correcting such bad habits and achieving better control of the use of ourselves. This is why various disciplines of body training typically invoke representations and self-conscious somatic focusing in order to correct our faulty self-perception and self-use. These disciplines do not aim to erase the crucial level of unreflective behavior by the (impossible) effort of making us explicitly conscious of all our perception and action. They simply seek to improve unreflective behavior that hinders our experience and performance. But in order to effect this improvement, the unreflective action or habit must be brought into conscious critical reflection (though only for a limited time), so that it can be grasped and worked on more precisely.

II

In making my case for the value of somaesthetic reflection, I have thus far concentrated on Western philosophy and its critique of such reflection. I now wish to focus on Asian thought. Although it is common to contrast Western and Asian philosophies of embodiment, both traditions manifest a similar divergence between philosophies advocating reflective analysis and conscious control of the embodied self and those that instead advocate spontaneity. In the Confucian tradition, the founding *Analects* affirm a daily self-examination of behavior (where the term for self or person is the same as that for body, i.e., 身 *shen*).[7] Later, Mencius advocates cultivating the "flood-like *qi* [*ch'i*]" that "fills the body" by giving it the controlling attention of will and mind, while Xunzi argues that the exemplary person should master "the method of controlling the vital breath" and be "absorbed in the examination of his inner self" and "scorn mere external things."[8]

In contrast, although the Daoist tradition very strongly emphasizes somatic attentiveness in terms of caring for the body,[9] it is also famous

---

[7] Roger Ames and Henry Rosemont, Jr. (trans.), *The Analects of Confucius: A Philosophical Translation* (New York: Ballantine, 1998), Book 1: 4, 72.

[8] D.C. Lau (trans.), *Mencius* (London: Penguin, 1970), 77. J. Knoblock, *Xunzi: A Translation and Study of the Complete Works*, 3 vols. (Stanford: Stanford University Press, 1988–1994), vol. 1, 154; hereafter X.

[9] Its legendary founder Laozi claims, for instance, "He who loves his body more than dominion over the empire can be given the custody of the empire." D.C. Lau (trans.), *Lao Tzu* (London: Penguin, 1963), 17. I use the more contemporary *pinyin* transliteration for Chinese names and terms (e.g., Laozi), except when citing translated works that use the older Wade-Giles transliteration system (e.g., Lao-Tzu). In quotations from such works in the body of the text, I convert Chinese terms and names to pinyin, while placing

for championing unreflective spontaneity of action and the release from willful self-consciousness. In the *Zhuangzi* (the most influential Daoist classic after the *Daodejing*), one is urged to be "a forgetter of self" because "the man who has forgotten self may be said to have entered heaven."[10] "When a man does not dwell in self, then things will of themselves reveal their forms to him" (Z, 372). The message is apparently more than a mere rejection of selfishness, but rather a repudiation of examining the self at all, and with it a critical, reflective examination of the outside world. Blind spontaneity seems to be the secret to successful living and action. Hence, "When the eye does not see, the ear does not hear, and the mind does not know, then your spirit will protect the body, and the body will enjoy long life. Be cautious of what is within you; block off what is outside you, for much knowledge will do you harm" (Z, 119). In one striking passage of the *Zhuangzi*, this rejection of reflection is associated with mere sitting – a remarkable foreshadowing of Zen's practice of sitting meditation (*zazen*) which the Japanese Zen master Dōgen later describes as "sitting fixedly, think of no thinking."[11] As the *Zhuangzi* more dramatically puts it: "I smash up my limbs and body, drive out perception and intellect, cast off form, do away with understanding, and make myself identical with the Great Thoroughfare. This is what I mean by sitting down and forgetting everything" (Z, 90).

A similar sort of unreflective spontaneity is affirmed in skillful action: "Artisan Chui [Ch'ui] could draw as true as a compass or a T square because his fingers changed along with things and he didn't let his mind get in the way" (Z, 206). The *Liezi*, the third most influential Daoist classic, seems to express the same advocacy of unreflective, spontaneous action,

---

the Wade-Giles transliteration in brackets. Daoist somatic cultivation included special breathing exercises, dietetics, gymnastics, and sexual disciplines. For more details on this subject, see Joseph Needham, *Science and Civilisation in China*, vol. 2 (Cambridge: Cambridge University Press, 1956); and R.H. van Gulik, *Sexual Life in Ancient China* (Leiden: Brill, 2003).

[10] Zhuangzi apparently lived in the latter half of the fourth century B.C., and the book bearing his name is usually thought to be at least partly written by him and to date from around that time, though some date it slightly later. The founding text of Daoism, the *Laozi* or (as it later became more commonly known) the *Daodejing*, is attributed to Laozi of the sixth century B.C., allegedly an older contemporary of Confucius but now thought by most experts to be an entirely legendary figure. There is considerable controversy about the dating of *Daodejing*, some putting it in the sixth century, most in the fourth century B.C. For Zhuangzi, I use the translation of Burton Watson, *The Complete Works of Chuang Tzu* (New York: Columbia University Press, 1968), 133; hereafter Z.

[11] Carl Bielefeldt (trans.), *Dōgen's Manuals of Zen Meditation* (Berkeley: University of California Press, 1988), 181.

which its translator, the distinguished scholar A.C. Graham, formulates as "thinking does [one] harm instead of good," and that "it is especially dangerous to be conscious of oneself."[12] Arguing that a drunken man, by being largely unconscious, is likely to be less injured in falling from a cart than a conscious man who stiffens and tries to brace his fall, the *Liezi* likewise notes that the good swimmer says, "I do it without knowing how I do it" (L, 44). The book also remarks how a Daoist disciple of Laozi claims to be so unified in himself and with nature that he confesses that although aware of whatever affects him, "I do not know whether I perceived it with the seven holes in my head and my four limbs, or knew it through my heart and belly and internal organs. It is simply self-knowledge" (L, 78). Likewise, "I did not notice what my body leaned against and my feet trod, I drifted with the wind East or West like a leaf... and never knew whether it was the wind that rode me or I that rode the wind" (L, 37).

But alongside this advocacy of unreflective spontaneity, one also finds a deep respect for self-examination in these classic Daoist texts. Thus, the *Zhuangzi* insists: "When I speak of good hearing, I do not mean listening to others; I mean simply listening to yourself. When I speak of good eyesight, I do not mean looking at others; I mean simply looking at yourself. He who does not look at himself but looks at others, who does not get hold of himself but gets hold of others, is getting what other men have got and failing to get what he himself has got. He finds joy in what brings joy to other men, but finds no joy in what would bring joy to himself" (Z, 103). In contrast, the sage "returns to himself and finds the inexhaustible" (Z, 273); "he who practices the cultivation of what is within him will not be ashamed because he holds no position in society" (Z, 317). "He who concentrates upon the internal does deeds that bring no fame... [but] is forever the possessor of light" (Z, 255). Hence, for sagely wisdom, "I examine what is within me and am never blocked off from the Way" (Z, 319). At one point, even bodily action or movement is said to be improved by looking inward to establish a stable sense of self from which action can more effectively emerge. "If you do not perceive the sincerity within yourself and yet try to move forth, each movement

---

[12] A.C. Graham (trans.), *The Book of Lieh-tzu* (New York: Columbia University Press, 1990), 32; hereafter L. As Graham notes, the book bears the name of a famous Daoist sage mentioned by Zhuangzi but whose "historicity is doubtful" and whose alleged dates of existence are also very unclear, "some indications pointing to 600, others to 400 B.C. Graham (L, xiii) dates the book "not much earlier than its commentary by Chang Chan (*c.* A.D. 370)."

will miss the mark. If outside concerns enter and are not expelled, each movement will only add failure to failure" (Z, 245).

The *Liezi* likewise affirms the value of self-examination: "You busy yourself with outward travel and do not know how to busy yourself with inward contemplation. By outward travel we seek what we lack in things outside us, while by inward contemplation we find sufficiency in ourselves. The latter is the perfect, the former an imperfect kind of traveling" (L, 82). With respect to skilled action, the *Liezi* similarly suggests that underlying masterful performance is a mastery of self, achieved through attention to oneself, because underlying the self is the unfathomable, empowering Way that guides us best. Thus, the musician insists on first finding the harmony in himself before venturing to play: "What I have in mind is not in the strings, what I am aiming at is not in the notes. Unless I grasp it inwardly in my heart, it will not answer from the instrument outside me" (L, 107).

We should likewise note that Daoism's founding *Daodejing* clearly affirms the importance of self-knowledge ("He who knows himself has discernment"; "the sage knows himself"[13]), while also suggesting that critical self-monitoring is important for attaining its cherished goals of stillness, suppleness, and mental clarity.[14] This idea of self-monitoring is extensively developed in another classic text associated with Daoism, the "Neiye" chapter of the *Guanzi*. This text, which seems to date from the middle of the fourth century B.C., focuses on the use of "inner cultivation" as a method to grasp the Dao and thereby achieve the most effective perception and most successful manner of action that is so effortless as to be described as non-action or *wuwei*.[15] Such inner cultivation requires a careful attention to regulating body and mind toward tranquility so that the Way can be found within the individual's own mind. I quote

---

[13] Lau (trans.) *Lao Tzu*, 38, 79.
[14] See, for example, the self-monitoring implied in the following questions of Chapter 10: "In carrying about your more spiritual and more physical aspects and embracing their oneness,/Are you able to keep them from separating?/In concentrating your *qi* and making it pliant,/Are you able to become the newborn babe?/In scrubbing and cleansing your profound mirror [i.e., the mind],/Are you able to rid it of all imperfections?" I here use the translation from Roger Ames and David Hall, *Daodejing: "Making This Life Significant": A Philosophical Translation* (New York: Ballantine Books, 2003), 90.
[15] The concept of *wuwei* does not imply mere passive quiescence or inaction but a mode of action that is not forced, willful, or burdened with effortful striving. I use the translation by Harold Roth, in *Original Tao: Inward Training (Nei-yeh) and the Foundations of Taoist Mysticism* (New York: Columbia University Press, 1999), 7. The translated passages I cite are from pages 54 and 82.

briefly from two sections of the "Neiye," and other sections reinforce these points.

> V
>
> The Way has no fixed position;
> It abides within the excellent mind.
> When the mind is tranquil and the vital breath is regular,
> The Way can thereby be halted.
> That Way is not distant from us;
> When people attain it they are sustained.
> That Way is not separated from us;
> When people accord with it they are harmonious.
> Therefore....
> Cultivate your mind, make your thoughts tranquil,
> And the Way can thereby be attained.
>
> XIX
>
> By concentrating your vital breath as if numinous,
> The myriad things will all be contained within you.
> Can you concentrate? Can you unite with them?
> ...
> When the four limbs are aligned
> And the blood and vital breath are tranquil,
> Unify your awareness, concentrate your mind,
> Then your eyes and ears will not be overstimulated.
> And even the far-off will seem close at hand.

I should note that the term "mind" here is a translation of the Chinese term *xin* (心), whose primary meaning is "heart" and is often translated as such or as "heart-and-mind" to emphasize that in Chinese thought one's mental life is essentially also somatic. Thus, attending to the mind (*xin*) by cultivating it and making it tranquil would automatically imply attention to one's somatic self.

III

How, then, can we reconcile these conflicting views between attending to self and unreflective forgetting of self in spontaneous action as keys to effective self-use, not only within Daoism and Chinese philosophy but also within the Western philosophical tradition and even within the narrower scope of pragmatist philosophy (as exemplified in the contrasting views of William James and John Dewey)? One strategy that I outlined in past writings is that of interchanging phases or stages. Although spontaneous unreflective action is generally the most effective way to perform, even strong proponents of spontaneity tend to acknowledge that in the early stages of learning a sensorimotor skill (like riding a bicycle or playing an instrument), we must direct careful, critical attention to the body parts engaged in that action. But critics of reflection insist that once this learning stage is over, so is the need for explicit attention to what our bodies are doing.

My position, however (which I share with body theorists like Alexander and Feldenkrais and philosophers like Dewey), is that there is also need for critical self-attention after the learning process is considered finished. This is because the learning process is never entirely complete. As Xunzi long ago put it, "Learning must never be concluded" (X, 135). Learning is never over because there is not only room for further refinements and extensions of the acquired skill, but also because we often lapse into bad habits of performance or face new conditions of the self (such as injury or aging) and new environments that require relearning to revise or adjust our habits of spontaneous performance. Not that all our actions must always be given explicit attention; that would be both impossible and undesirable. We need to focus attention on what needs it the most – usually the world in which we act (though we should never forget that careful explicit attention to one's body in action always involves attention to its environment; one cannot feel one's body alone).[16]

However, on many occasions, in order to deal more effectively with things in the world of action, we need either to acquire new habits or refine or reconstruct our habitual modes of action, and this process requires redirecting explicit attention to our somatic behavior. Once the new or reconstructed habits are acquired, we can forego special attention to one's body in action and instead move into the more uncritical, unreflective spontaneous mode with our attention focused on the targets or ends of action, not the somatic means for attaining them.

In the *Liezi*, we find the same advocacy of careful attending to self to establish the harmony needed for successful spontaneous action. The great archer succeeds with even a poor bow not simply "because his

---

[16] More generally, a pure feeling of one's body alone is an abstraction. One always feels something of the external world, though one may not notice it explicitly until one attends to it. Even if I lie down and close my eyes and focus on feeling my body only in itself, I will feel the surface on which I am lying; even if I try focusing on my internal organs, I cannot escape feeling the force of gravity on them (or, for example, the air that I take into my lungs).

attention was concentrated" on the target but because he had already trained his body so that "the movement of his hand equalised the give and pull" of the bow (L, 105).[17] For archery, moreover, "you must learn not to blink" and "how to look" (L, 112), which also requires critically examining our somatic behavior in looking and blinking. Similar points are made with the skills of fishing and charioteering, where spontaneity and focused response to the target rely on having acquired somatic control of the bodily means to attend and respond with calm and perceptive hands. And the only sure way to establish the necessary calmness in oneself is by looking attentively within to know one's nature and develop its virtues: "He will cling to his degree and not exceed it... he will unify his nature, tend his energies, maintain the virtues inside him, until he penetrates to the place where things are created. If you can be like this, the Heaven inside you will keep its integrity, the spirit inside you will have no flaws" (L, 37–38). And this is immediately asserted as superior to the drunken man whose fearlessness in falling comes only through the unknowingness provoked by the foreign substance of wine, rather than from knowing the heaven within the self.

Moreover, the *Liezi* shows how our already acquired skills of spontaneous performance require reconstruction when they face new conditions. The accomplished archer totally loses his skill of unthinking habit and his masterful posture of stillness "like a statue" when he is asked to perform on a mountain cliff, where he trembles and falls on his face in fear, because he had not learned to master himself so that "his spirit and breathing do not change" in new conditions that provoke anxiety (L, 39). One's skill in other actions is likewise overwhelmed when one thinks of failure or reward: "you give weight to something outside you; and whoever does that is inwardly clumsy" (L, 44).

Similarly, in the *Zhuangzi*, the great carver Qing who creates marvelous works with apparently effortless spontaneity explains that his skill depends on the somatic self-preparation of fasting: "I always fast in order to still my mind. When I have fasted for three days, I no longer have any thought of congratulations or rewards, of titles or stipends. When I have fasted for five days, I no longer have any thought of praise or blame, of skill or clumsiness. And when I have fasted for seven days, I am so still that I forget I have four limbs and a form and body. By that time, the ruler and

---

[17] In the same way, the catcher of cicadas must not only have his attention solely on them but must also already have learned how to "hold [his] body... and hold [his] hand as steady as a branch on a withered tree" (L, 45).

his court no longer exist for me. My skill is concentrated and all outside distractions fade away" (Z, 206). In order to forget body and mind, the carver first cultivates their stillness and focus through the somatic means of fasting. Thus, he can focus on the work with no distracting ideas of bodily rewards and punishments or mental blame and praise.

These colorful fables suggest a critical point. Many of the cases that William James and other advocates of spontaneity allude to, where reflection on our somatic means of performance seems to make us stumble, stutter, and fail, could well be cases in which it is not really the somatic focus (on our feet or tongue) that makes us stumble and stutter. Rather, it is the anxiety of falling or failing in some way that causes such lapses and that intimately accompanies our attention to our body parts in our concern to help them do the job we fear they will not properly accomplish. In other words, such instances where attention to bodily movements in action seems to interfere in successful performance are really cases where one's actual attention to the bodily parts is obscured by emotions and thoughts of failure, success, or one's image in the eyes of others. For example, am I really focusing carefully on my finger and hand movements in my problematic lifting of a slippery pea with my chopsticks, or is my mental focus, when looking at my hand, equally suffused or even dominated by the thoughts and attendant emotions of whether I will manage to do it successfully and how I am regarded (or judged) by others who see my efforts? Is my consciousness calmly observant or anxiously flustered? There is also the question of whether I have skill and accuracy in somaesthetic self-observation, or whether my somaesthetic sense of self is not very clear, so that I am not even aware that I have become anxious and that the quality or precision of my attention to my fingers has been thereby distracted, even if my eyes remain fixed on them.

Some people have better skills of perception and performance than others, and training is one way they have acquired them. Maurice Merleau-Ponty's essentialist phenomenology may presume that all normal people enjoy the same primordial level of spontaneous perception and action that functions with marvelous efficiency (and only proves dysfunctional in clearly abnormal individuals with pathological cases of brain lesions or other forms of trauma). However, the situation is more complex. Many (if not most) of us manage to get by with habits of sensorimotor spontaneity that have various minor defects that do not disqualify us from being normal in the sense of having more or less average functioning but that do result in unneeded pain, discomfort, inefficiency, more rapid fatigue, and a tendency to certain kinds of errors or accidents. These more subtle pathologies prevent one's action from being normal in the sense of defining the norm for exemplary, healthy functioning.

Keen to insist on the efficacy of a universal and unchanging primordial body consciousness, Merleau-Ponty describes our spontaneous performance as being marvelously effective.[18] While sharing Merleau-Ponty's appreciation of our inexplicit, unreflective somatic perception, we should also recognize that such perception (along with the action it guides) is often painfully inaccurate and dysfunctional. I may think I am keeping my head down when swinging a golf club although an observer will easily see I do not, and therefore why I miss the ball. To correct the habit of raising one's head and taking one's eyes off the ball, one must bring one's bodily performance into clearer critical consciousness. Besides its value for correcting bad habits or unlearning problematic patterns of behavior, such heightened reflective consciousness can stimulate new ways of thinking that increase the mind's flexibility and creativity, even in terms of enhancing the plasticity and efficiency of the brain's neural networks.[19]

Recent studies suggest the value of explicit, critical, and even reflective somatic awareness both for the stages of learning skills and for continuing efforts of extending and refining them.[20] Even China's famous advocates

---

[18] See, Maurice Merleau-Ponty, *Signs*, trans. Richard McCleary (Evanston, IL: Northwestern University Press, 1964), 65–66, and my more detailed account of his view in *Body Consciousness*, ch. 2. Contemporary phenomenologists such as Shaun Gallagher continue to defend Merleau-Ponty's view of the "*performative forgetfulness of the body*," claiming that spontaneous, somatically inattentive action works best and "that heightened body consciousness gets in the way of performance." See Shaun Gallagher, "Somaesthetics and the Care of the Body," *Metaphilosophy*, 42 (2011): 305–313, quotation p. 305; and my reply, "Soma, Self, and Society," *Metaphilosophy*, 42 (2011): 314–327.

[19] On such matters of learning-based brain plasticity, which is now widely recognized to occur in the fully adult brain (rather than only in earlier stages of development), see B. Draganski and A. May, "Training-induced Structural Changes in the Adult Human Brain," *Behavioural Brain Research* 192 (2008): 137–142; and Norman Doidge, *The Brain That Changes Itself* (New York: Viking, 2007), 27–92.

[20] Numerous studies have demonstrated that mental practice through explicitly imagining, visualizing, or mentally rehearsing the activity or steps of performing an action has a significant positive effect on performance and improves the learning process. See, for example, Stefan Vogt, "On Relations between Perceiving, Imagining, and Performing in the Learning of Cyclical Movement Sequences," *British Journal of Psychology* 86 (1995): 191–216; A. Pascual-Leone et al. "Modulation of Muscle Responses Evoked by Transcranial Magnetic Stimulation during the Acquisition of New Fine Motor Skills," *Journal of Neurophysiology* 74 (1995): 1037–1045; and J. Driskell et al. "Does Mental Practice Enhance Performance?" *Journal of Applied Psychology*, 79 (1974): 481–489. Explicit mental representation of motor activity can even lead to an increase in muscle strength for

of spontaneity recognize the continuing importance of self-monitoring, affirming its use even in the efforts to transcend the self to concentrate on harmonizing one's actions with the world or the Way. These convincing points of learning, unlearning, and relearning of improved habits would seem sufficient for establishing the importance of explicit somaesthetic awareness and reflection. But could we go further? Can explicit or even reflective somaesthetic attention be usefully directed to action beyond these diverse stages of learning to phases of full mastery where the focus is on successful performance rather than learning?

There is certainly a presumption, apparently founded on real-life experience and some experimental studies, that explicit attention to the bodily means of movement will somehow distract us from the ends of action and thus diminish performance. Perhaps, however, this is because our powers of attention and coordination are insufficiently trained to simultaneously encompass multiple targets or inputs, such as would be involved in monitoring both our bodily movements and the targets of our action. Yet we seem able to listen attentively to the narration of news while also watching attentively the visual news images on the television screen, just as we can carefully listen to the news while we are driving a car and attending to traffic. Perhaps those more experienced and skilled in attending to bodily behavior can combine such explicit or reflective attention with smooth effective performance that equally attends to the targets of action. Perhaps many of us can already do so with familiar tasks. In buttoning my shirt, for example, I do not find that noticing my finger movements and positions interferes in my monitoring the buttons to be fastened; rather, it improves my performance of buttoning.

IV

The great master of Nō theatre, Zeami Motokiyo, provides some encouragement for thinking that attention can be trained to encompass simultaneously very different and even opposing directions. In one of his most important texts, *Kakyō* ("A Mirror Held to the Flower"), while explaining the training of performance skills in Nō, Zeami delineates "the Five Skills of dancing." The first is "the Skill of Self-Conscious Movement," which involves an explicitly conscious attention to the body in technique,

---

performing the action. See G. Yue and K. Cole. "Strength Increases from the Motor Program. Comparison of Training with Maximal Voluntary and Imagined Muscle Contractions," *Journal of Neurophysiology* 67 (1992): 1114–1123.

"placing the various elements of the body into motion, moving the hands in appropriate gestures, controlling the performance so that it will fall into the proper structure of *jo, ha,* and *kyū*" (rhythms of movement).[21] The second skill is described as "the Skill of Movement beyond Consciousness," which is not a matter of the particular movements the actor makes but rather "the creation of an atmosphere" that goes beyond explicit matters of technique (Ze, 80). This second skill is not meant to supersede the former in the way that spontaneous skilled action is thought to supersede explicit or reflective attention to bodily position or movement in the learning of a skill.

The continued need for self-monitoring in action is made clear by Zeami's emphasis that such self-reflection "is a crucial element in the creation of ... the Movement beyond Consciousness," wherein "the eyes look ahead and the spirit looks behind" (Ze, 81). Here, while not concentrating especially on where he is placing his hands and feet, "the actor looks in front of him with his physical eyes" so that he can see the other actors and the audience and thereby harmonize his performance with the full theatrical environment; "but his inner concentration must be directed to the appearance of his movements from behind" (ibid.). In other words, the actor is performing with an explicit, reflective image of himself, not only his internal image of his somatic bearing (his proprioceptive sense of balance, position, muscle tension, expressiveness, grace, etc.), but also the image of how he senses he appears to the audience.

Zeami explains this complicated consciousness as follows: "The appearance of the actor, seen from the spectator in the seating area, produces a different image than the actor can have of himself. What the spectator sees is the outer image of the actor. What an actor himself sees, on the other hand, forms his own internal image of himself." The actor therefore "must make still another effort in order to grasp his own internalized outer image, a step possible only through assiduous training. Once he obtains this, the actor and the spectator can share the same image. Only then can it actually be said that an actor has truly grasped the nature of his appearance." In other words, "For an actor to grasp his true appearance implies that he has under his control the space to the left and to the right of him, and to the front and to the rear of him." Although most actors only succeed in looking to the front and side, "if the actor cannot somehow come to a sense of how he looks from behind, he will

---

[21] See J.T. Rimer and Y. Masakazu (trans.), *On the Art of the Nō Drama: The Major Treatises of Zeami* (Princeton: Princeton University Press, 1983), 79; hereafter Ze.

not be able to become conscious of any possible vulgarities in his performance. Therefore, an actor must look at himself using his internalized outer image, come to share the same view as the audience, examine his appearance with his spiritual eyes and so maintain a graceful appearance with his entire body" (Ze, 81).[22]

From such descriptions, we see that even when Zeami is not talking about the "self-conscious movement" of the body's limbs but instead about the so-called movement beyond consciousness, he still insists that acting excellence requires the focus of sustained self-consciousness, whose acquisition is not a native or easily learned skill but instead requires "assiduous training." Indeed, even when the actor is not moving at all, Zeami claims it is the actor's focus on his own expressive "inner tension" or "inner state of control" in performance that gives life to the performance (Ze, 97). The actor's ability to "keep his consciousness of that inner tension" even when he is not saying or doing anything, is what makes such moments "when nothing happens" nonetheless full of theatrical power and meaning.[23] In fact, self-consciousness for Zeami is essential to fine performance in a more general way, as artistic mastery is primarily a mastery of self through self-understanding: "if an actor really wants to become a master, he cannot simply depend on his skill in dance and gesture. Rather, mastery seems to depend on the actor's own state of self-understanding and the sense of style with which he has been blessed" (Ze, 90).

If the actor thus needs enhanced critical self-consciousness and self-monitoring to achieve true excellence, how does he achieve it? How does one acquire the extraordinary skill to be attentively conscious of the bodily action one performs, one's inner feeling or image as one performs it, the reaction of the audience, and also the image one's audience has of one performing that includes the appearance of how one looks from the back and other dimensions of one's appearance that one cannot logically see (say, the expression of one's eyes)? Zeami answers, of

---

[22] "To repeat again, an actor must come to have an ability to see himself as the spectators do, grasp the logic of the fact that the eyes cannot see themselves, and find the skill to grasp the whole – left and right, ahead and behind. If an actor can achieve this, his peerless appearance will be as elegant as that of a flower or a jewel and will serve as a living proof of his understanding" (Ze, 81).

[23] Zeami at one point affirms that the actor must also direct his concentration to what in the artwork precedes and follows the actor's inner tension of doing nothing in a way "that transcends his own consciousness," but this concentration still involves the artist's mental mastery of consciousness, which is described as "connecting all the arts through one intensity of mind" (Ze, 97).

course, that this requires assiduous training. But what precisely constitutes the nature, basis, or direction of such training? Zeami does not reveal the secret; he was an esoteric thinker, whose texts were not even meant to be circulated beyond his acting troop.[24] Ancient meditative traditions have developed a number of techniques for developing skill in self-monitoring and heightened, perspicacious, self-consciousness, some of which should have been known to Zeami from his close relationship to Zen Buddhism. Yet none of those seem designed to address the most mysterious feat of self-consciousness that Zeami demands of the actor: seeing one's appearance from behind as one's audience sees it. I conclude this chapter by briefly considering three possible ways to help explain this mysterious secret, relying not on special textual or other evidence from Zeami's time or from the inner circle of continuing Nō tradition but instead on our own philosophical imaginations, together with some recent discoveries in neuroscience.

V

At least three different strategies might explain how the actor can share his audience's vision of himself and grasp his visual appearance from behind despite the fact he cannot really see it with his physical eyes. The first might involve a program of training with mirrors. By looking through a properly configured set of mirrors, an actor could see how his back looks in various postures. Then by noting the proprioceptive sensations he has in the different postures, he could consequently associate or correlate the different visual looks with different proprioceptive feelings.[25] Through a rigorous program of such associative training, the actor then should be able to infer from his proprioceptive feelings what his posture from the back would look like in actual performance (without using any mirrors), although he does not strictly see himself from the back. This transmodal training through vision and proprioception would be significantly aided by the presence of underlying neurological links between these sense modalities. Proprioception and vision are linked,

---

[24] Zeami and his son-in-law, Kamparu Zenchiku (1405–1468), to whom he entrusted his Nō writings, describe them as "a secret" that "must not be shown carelessly to others" and particularly "should not be shown to actors from other troupes" (Ze, 110).

[25] For insightful discussion of the aesthetic and affective dimensions of proprioception, see Barbara Montero, "Proprioception as an Aesthetic Sense," *Journal of Aesthetics and Art Criticism* 64 (2006): 230–242; and Jonathan Cole and Barbara Montero, "Affective Proprioception," *Janus Head*, 9 (2007), 299–317.

for example, through the vestibular system, which, in governing balance, integrates information about head position and oculumotor information about eye-movements and proprioceptive information about the rest of the body.[26] Proprioception and vision are also linked through the visuomotor mirror neuron system. These mirror neurons discharge both when an individual performs a particular action of motor movement and when the individual simply sees such actions done by others. Such neurons can help explain our natural abilities to imitate and understand others and to communicate with them. They also provide a way to explain our basic powers of integrating visual and motor-proprioceptive perceptions.[27]

A second strategy would be more other-oriented or transpersonal. It would require someone else assuming the actor's postures and movements while the actor (taking the audience's role) would observe them from behind, and would empathetically appreciate them and simulate them in his mind. Notions of empathetic perception and simulation are no longer merely appeals to vague romantic notions of imagination but are solidly grounded in experimental studies and neurological research. Mental rehearsal or representation of a movement has been shown to activate not only similar areas of the brain to those involved in the movement itself but also to activate muscular and other physiological responses related to such a movement or action.[28] Moreover, just as recent research in the mirror-neuron system has shown that one's watching an action leads to activation of brain areas involved in actually performing that movement, so experimental studies in learning have demonstrated that simply observing others repeatedly performing a task of movement can significantly improve the learning observer's subsequent performance of

---

[26] Moreover, as vision is affected by vestibular stimulation (for example, through rotation or shaking of the head), so vestibular neurons respond to proprioceptive and optokinetic stimuli. People with problems of the vestibular organs of the inner ear can use visual information to help maintain their balance; conversely, in conditions where normal visual information and vestibular information are denied, other proprioceptive or tactile input can help determine one's sense of posture. For more on the intermodal linkage of the visual and proprioceptive system, see J.R. Lackner and P. Zio, "Aspects of Body Self-Calibration," *Trends in Cognitive Science* 4 (2000): 279–282; "Vestibular, Proprioceptive, and Haptic Contributions to Spatial Organization," *Annual Review of Psychology* 56 (2005): 115–147; and Shaun Gallagher, *How the Body Shapes the Mind* (Oxford: Oxford University Press, 2005), 45–47, 73–77.

[27] See, for example, G. Rizzolati and L. Craighero, "The Mirror Neuron System," *Annual Review of Neuroscience* 27 (2004): 169–192; and V. Gallese et al., "Action Recognition in the Premotor Cortex," *Brain* 119 (1996): 593–609.

[28] See Alain Berthoz, *The Brain's Sense of Movement* (Cambridge: Harvard University Press, 2000), 31–32; also Yue et al., "Strength increases."

the task.[29] This means that looking at another actor's assuming of a posture could stimulate in the observing actor a proprioceptive feel of that action, a felt understanding that the actor could confirm perhaps by then imitating the posture and seeing whether his taking this postural attitude indeed produces that kind of proprioceptive feelings. Through extensive training in associative linking of his visual and proprioceptive images of graceful posture in others and of his proprioceptive feelings in imitating such posture, a skilled actor might be able to intuitively or immediately infer from the proprioceptive feel of his own body what it would look like to spectators observing him, even when they are observing him from the rear.

These two strategies could not be implemented simultaneously by the same actor but could be combined in a sequenced program of training, and both rely on associative training that grounds an inference about one's postural appearance. Can we speak of such an inference – no matter how immediate – as really seeing? Zeami may be speaking metaphorically about one's mentally seeing what one's physical eyes cannot see. But the idea of mirror neurons suggests a third possible strategy, which though highly speculative and improbable, is worth noting because it would involve a more direct way for realizing Zeami's idea of the actor's mind seeing his body even where his eyes cannot see it. If proprioceptive feelings of posture could generate, through mirror neuron systems, a corresponding visual input of that posture, then, in principle, someone very skilled in vivid proprioceptive awareness might be able to generate a visual image in his mind of how his posture would look not from a physical mirror or the empathetic mirror of looking at others but from his own proprioceptive self-observation of his posture or movement. So rigorous training in acute proprioceptive self-awareness might, ideally, enable Zeami's actor to immediately grasp and represent to consciousness the visual effect of his body, even from behind.

This strategy may seem particularly farfetched because mirror-neuron research connecting the brain's visual and motor areas has focused on how visual inputs stimulate corresponding motor area brain activation, rather than the other direction. There seem to be no experimental studies of how blind movements with their attendant proprioceptive sensations stimulate visual brain areas, as Vittorio Gallese, a leader in mirror-neuron research, has confirmed. One recent study he coauthored, however, shows "activation of motion-sensitive visual areas during

---

[29] See Vogt, "On Relations," 209–213.

tactile stimulation of participants, who nevertheless kept their eyes closed," and he thinks that in principle, "one should be able to see activation in visual areas after a proprioceptive stimulus like tendon vibration" because "multimodal integration is...a pervasive functional feature of our brain."[30] Of course, such visual activation does not imply the generation of clear, accurate, and aesthetically discerning visual perceptions of what external spectators in the theatre would see. So this strategy, like the others, remains a mere hypothesis, and Zeami's secret remains safely kept. His teaching, nonetheless, strengthens the case for the value of paying explicitly conscious attention to the body in action.[31]

---

[30] E-mail message from V. Gallese, May 29, 2008. The article is S.J.H. Ebisch et al., "The Sense of Touch: Embodied Simulation in a Visuotactile Mirroring Mechanism for Observed Animate or Inanimate Touch," *Journal of Cognitive Neuroscience* 20 (2008):1–13.

[31] I thank Professor Aoki Takao of Hiroshima University (where I was Visiting Professor in 2002–2003) for first introducing me to Nō theater and for improving my understanding of Zeami's writings and terminology.

PART III

THE ARTS AND THE ART OF LIVING

10

Somaesthetics and Architecture

A Critical Option

I

Criticality is a much discussed and contested issue in recent architectural theory. It is also clearly a topic that architecture shares with philosophy, as philosophy has long defined itself in terms of its fundamentally critical stance and methodology. The critique of dogma has been crucial to the philosophical project at least since Socrates, and perhaps constitutes the signature style of philosophical argumentation. In any case, such critique has been forcefully deployed throughout the field of philosophy, from logic, epistemology, and metaphysics to ethics, political theory, and aesthetics. In modernity, this essential critical function has even been thematized in the titles of some of modern philosophy's most influential books, not only the three famous critiques of Kant but also some of Marx's seminal works (*Critique of Hegel's Philosophy of Right, Contribution to a Critique of Political Economy, Capital: The Critique of Political Economy, Critique of the Gotha Programme*). While critique pervades the entire modern project of philosophy, the twentieth century has also witnessed the emergence of a school or movement of thought distinctively titled "Critical Theory."

With respect to architecture, it is not simply modernity but more distinctively the twentieth-century's movement of modernism in which the notion of criticality emerged as increasingly central. Architecture was seen to have an important critical function in remaking the lived environment in the direction of progress, rationality, and democracy. Its new forms were to be an expression of a new critical and liberating spirit that by offering new forms of dwelling would introduce new ways of living as an alternative to the reigning social injustice, hardship, and exploitation. Consider a few brief examples.

Some early twentieth-century advocates of glass architecture argued that one could help free people by freeing rooms of their closed heavy atmosphere through the use of glass and its light: "In order to raise our culture to a higher level, we are forced, whether we like it or not, to change our architecture."[1] The Bauhaus school was established through the same sort of critical utopian approach to architecture. As one of its important members, Oskar Schlemmer recalls:

> Originally the Bauhaus was founded with visions of erecting the cathedral of socialism and the workshops were established in the manner of the cathedral building lodges [*Dombauhütten*]. The idea of the cathedral has for the time being receded into the background and with it certain definite ideas of an artistic nature. Today we must think at best in terms of the house, perhaps even only *think* so.... In the face of the economic plight, it is our task to become pioneers of simplicity, that is, to find a simple form for all life's necessities, which is at the same time respectable and genuine.[2]

Mies van der Rohe, the school's final director, likewise viewed architecture as a way to "set up new values" of critical rationality and freedom through "rationalized building methods" involving "skeletal construction" and a flexible partitioning of space through "movable walls."[3]

Le Corbusier was another extremely influential figure of modernist architecture who similarly advocated its critical meliorative thrust: "The machinery of society... [is] profoundly out of gear.... The various classes of workers in society today no longer have dwellings adapted to their needs; neither the artisan nor the intellectual. It is a question of building which is at the root of the social unrest of today; architecture or revolution."[4] As one recent commentator summarizes modernism's critical utopian program: "The new architecture with its bare interiors, its open plan and its rational kitchens would teach people that material belongings are less important than a social spirit, they would liberate women from the burden of too heavy domestic duties and they would act as perfect accommodations for a life that would be much more mobile and flexible."[5]

---

[1] Paul Scheerbart, *Glasarchitektur*, 1914; cited in Kenneth Frampton, *Modern Architecture: A Critical History*, 4th ed. (London: Thames and Hudson, 2007), 116.

[2] From a 1922 letter of Oskar Schlemmer, cited in Frampton, *Modern Architecture*, 124.

[3] Ludwig Mies van der Rohe, "The New Era" (1930), cited in Frampton, *Modern Architecture*, 164, 166.

[4] Le Corbusier (Charles-Édouard Jeanneret-Gris), *Vers une architecture*, 1923; cited in Frampton, *Modern Architecture*, 178.

[5] Hilde Heynen, "A Critical Position for Architecture?" in Jane Rendell and Jonathan Hill (eds.), *Critical Architecture* (London: Routledge, 2007), 48–56, citation, 49.

With the waning of modernism's dominion (not only through varieties of so-called postmodern ideas but also through its own immanent critique and loss of confidence, coupled with the new social, economic, and political realities of the postcolonial world), the critical role of architecture has been increasingly put in question.[6] In today's complex political and economic realities, the most spectacular and progressive architecture is often commissioned from repressive autocratic regimes who need not democratically consult the affected populations or adhere to established planning or building codes. And architects seem generally very willing to accept these commissions without raising ideological issues of critical resistance to these regimes. Many have come to speak of contemporary architecture (and, with it, architectural theory) as being in a post-critical stage, a stage where ideological critique and resistance retreat before the dominating desire for performative success, pragmatic efficiency, and creative freedom.

In some post-critical theorists, the very idea of resistance is explicitly abandoned as a futile "negativity," along with the utopian critical impulse that inspires it. Thus, Michael Speaks cheerfully reports that "visionary ideas have given way to the 'chatter' of intelligence," so that progressive architecture should now be inspired not by utopian ideals but by "design intelligence" that deploys and manipulates the prosaic (if not also tendentiously distorted) "little truths" spun on the web, the sort of "open source intelligence" sources used by the CIA and big business, all in the pragmatic quest for greater efficiency of performance or effect. As one architectural theorist recently remarked, "Today, 'criticality' is under attack, being seen by its critics as obsolete, as irrelevant, and/or

---

[6] To avoid a wrongly one-sided equation of modernist architecture and critical resistance, we should recall that key modernist figures also advocated a realistic, pragmatic policy of reconciling architectural ambitions with the realities of the socioeconomic world. For instance, Bauhaus visionaries such as Walter Gropius and Ludwig Mies van der Rohe justified their departure from the earlier, romantically utopian, expressionist architecture by emphasizing the need for a pragmatic acceptance of the new realities of technological production, new materials, and living conditions. If Gropius urged a "resolute affirmation of the lived environment of machines and automotive vehicles" without "romantic beautification," then Mies insisted that "we take the changed economic and social conditions as a fact," because "these things go their own destined way, blind to values," and the designer can only accept these realities in order to bring out from them something of value. See Walter Gropius, "Grundsätze der Bauhausproduktion" (Dessau), 1926. In Ulrich Conrad (ed.), *Programme und Manifeste zur Architektur des 20. Jahrhunderts* (Bauwelt Fundamente: Braunschweig, 1975), 90; Ludwig Mies van der Rohe, "Die neue Zeit," 1930, in Conrad, 114; my translations.

as an inhibitor of design creativity."[7] Although much post-critical theory seems largely inspired by strains of French poststructuralist or postmodernist philosophy, philosophical pragmatism has also been identified as a post-critical influence.[8]

If criticality is still staunchly defended by many architectural theorists, then it has also been interpreted in very different ways; and this ambiguity makes the notion of critical architecture even more complexly contested. Some theorists still see architectural criticality primarily in terms of advancing the project of social critique by offering new alternatives to the established structures of dwelling and working and furthering the aims of progress to a more just society by providing better social and living conditions for all. Others, like the architect Peter Eisenman, see the critical moment in architecture not in serving social aims that oppose and seek to transform the sociopolitical status quo but in architecture's assertion of autonomy from any given social or political agenda. Such autonomy is thought to provide architecture with a critical distance from the established social norms and institutional forces, a distance that somehow enables it to break not only with such norms but also with architectural tradition (that in Eisenman's view still pervades modernism) and to instead create something really new. This breaking with architectural tradition is especially difficult because that tradition is precisely what shapes the fundamental architectural attitudes of even the most critical, questioning, exploratory architect. Thus, Eisenman's critical project involves an effort to decenter or displace the architectural subject from that subject's deeply entrenched and formative presumptions.

Michael Hays offers a somewhat similar form of architectural criticality based on the notion of architecture's relative autonomy both from the various social, economic, political, and personal forces that

---

[7] George Baird, "Criticality and its Discontents," in A. Graafland, L. Kavanaugh, G. Baird (eds.), *Crossover: Architecture, urbanism, technology* (Rotterdam: 010 Publishers, 2006), 648–659, citation on 649.

[8] See Baird, *Crossover*, 651, n. 4; K. Michael Hays, "Wider den Pragmatismus," *ARCH+* 156 (2001): 50–51; Hans-Joachim Dahms, Joachim Krausse, Nikolaus Kuhnert, and Angelika Schnell, "Editorial: Neuer Pragmatismus in der Architektur," *ARCH+* 156 (2001): 26–29. The pragmatist convergence discussed here focuses largely on a conference at the MOMA and a book publication, both devoted to pragmatism and architecture and both organized by Joan Ockman of Columbia University. The book, *The Pragmatist Imagination* (New York: Princeton Architectural Press, 2000), includes a short essay by me, "On Pragmatist Aesthetics," 116–120, which concluded by evoking the field of somaesthetics but did not yet apply it to architecture.

influence architecture and from the notion of a purely aesthetic architectural form. Hays's exemplar is Mies van der Rohe, some of whose works are described not only as critical but as resistant and oppositional, displaying "an architecture that cannot be reduced either to a conciliatory representation of external forces or to a dogmatic, reproducible formal system." To articulate this autonomy of in between more clearly, Hays elaborates:

> Distinguishing architecture from the forces that influence architecture – the conditions established by the market and by taste, the personal aspirations of its author, its technical origins, even its purpose defined by its own tradition – became the objective of Mies. To achieve this, he placed his architecture in a critical position between culture as a massive body of self-perpetuating ideas and form supposedly free of circumstance.[9]

If contemporary architectural theory is currently caught up in a debate about criticality, the terms and positions of this debate are often insufficiently articulated. For just as criticality is differently interpreted, so is the notion of post-criticality. It remains far from clear what exactly this post-critical stage is or means, and to what extent it has really jettisoned architecture's critical orientation or merely reformulated and redirected it. This chapter explores how somaesthetics could be useful in clarifying and treating two central issues in today's debate about criticality: the problems of autonomy and atmosphere. Before going into the particularities of those problems, however, I should indicate how somaesthetics more generally relates to architecture.

II

Somaesthetics should be pertinent for architecture if the soma is, and although this pertinence should be obvious, let me briefly highlight some features of the soma's architectural centrality. First, we should note that the body – as a composite structure through which we live – is itself symbolically understood through tectonic notions. This symbolic connection extends from ancient Greek philosophers like Plato, Roman architects like Vitruvius, and early Christian thinkers like St. Paul through Renaissance writers like Henry Wotton, and all the way into modern

---

[9] K. Michael Hays, "Critical Architecture between Form and Culture," *Perspecta: The Yale Architectural Journal* 21 (1984): 15–29; quotations, 17, 22.

scientific critics of religion such as Freud.[10] As Plato analogized the body's architectural structure to a prison, so Vitruvius and Paul highlighted the body-temple analogy: Vitruvius in terms of their attractively symmetrical proportions of parts to whole, while Paul emphasizing "that your body is the temple of the Holy Ghost that is in you" (1 *Corinthians* 6:19). This analogy is later secularized by Freud, whose interpretation of dreams identifies the house as the dream-work's symbol for the body, the place where one's far from immaculate psyche is housed.

Besides this symbolic linkage, the soma fundamentally shapes some of the most basic concepts of architectural design. Consider the following features.

1. If architecture is the articulation of space for the purposes of enhancing our living, dwelling, and experience, then the soma provides the most basic tool for all spatial articulation by constituting the point from which space can be experienced and articulated. As I argued in Chapter 1, to see the world at all, we must see it from some point of view that structures our directional planes of observation, defining what is left and right, up and down, forward and backward, inside and outside. The soma provides that primordial point of view through its location both in physical and social space.

2. Our lived experience of space essentially involves distance, and it is through the soma's powers of locomotion that we get our sense of distance and space. The soma is thus what enables us to appreciate not only the visual effects and structural design features that rely on perceiving distance and depth, but also the multisensorial feelings of moving through space (with their kinesthetic, tactile, proprioceptive qualities) that are crucial to the experience of living with, in, and through architecture. The concrete living space that the soma architecturally defines is not an abstract, fully homogeneous space but rather a space shaped

---

[10] Plato's famous image is most influentially evoked in the *Phaedo* (82d); See Vitruvius, *The Ten Books on Architecture*, trans. M.H. Morgan (Cambridge, MA: Harvard University Press, 1914), book III, i. Henry Wotton, in *The Elements of Architecture* (London, 1624), a book based on Vitruvius, advised his architectural viewers "to pass a running examination over the whole edifice, according to the properties of a well shaped man." For a discussion of Wotton, which contains this citation, see Vaughan Hart, "On Inigo Jones and the Stuart Legal Body: 'Justice and Equity...and Proportions Appertaining,'" in George Dodds, Robert Tavernor, and Joseph Rykwert (eds.), *Body and Building* (Cambridge, MA: MIT Press, 2002), 137–149; quotation, 138. Freud explains the body-house analogy in his *Introductory Lectures on Psycho-analysis*, trans. James Strachey (New York: Norton, 1966), 153, 159; see also Freud's *The Interpretation of Dreams*, trans. James Strachey (New York: Avon, 1965), 117, 258–259, 381–382.

by the body's directionality – with its front, sides, and back. The essential architectural feature of façade expresses this notion of directional facing.

3. If architecture involves mass as well as space, then the soma likewise provides our most immediate sense of mass and volume. We feel the solid mass and thickness of our body; we also feel the liquids and gases that move through its volume. If verticality is basic to architecture, then the body is our basic experiential model of verticality and of the need to both deploy and resist gravitational forces to achieve it. The soma's vertical posture and ability to maintain it in locomotion not only enables the particular perspective we have in seeing but also is what frees our hands so that we can use them to handle objects more effectively in order to draw, design, and build skillfully. Moreover, the architecture of the body (the fact that we are essentially top-heavy – our heavier head, shoulders, and torso resting on our significantly less massive legs) is part of what impels the soma to move because its vertical equilibrium is more easily sustained in motion than in standing still. It is hard to stand motionless in place for more than a few minutes, but we can enjoy walking for much longer periods without any strain.

4. Key principles of architectural form, as Vitruvius long ago remarked, seem derived from the soma. "Without symmetry and proportion there can be no principles in the design of any temple," he argues, defining these formal features in terms of the "relation" between the building's "different parts to the general magnitude of the whole," "as in the case of a well shaped man," and justifying this relational principle on the grounds that "nature has designed the human body so that its members are duly proportioned to the frame as a whole."[11] He likewise claims the basic forms of circle and square can be derived from the body, as can the basic notions of measurement needed in design. A case for the soma's role in determining architectural scale could similarly be made, just as one could argue that the body centrally informs the architectural feature of pillars, which Vitruvius saw as imitating male or female forms.

5. Despite its nondiscursive materialityity (which suggests mute dumbness), architecture, as artistic design, is expressive. The soma's nondiscursive expressivity through gesture provides a central model for architecture's expressive power. So much so, that Wittgenstein deploys it to define architecture and distinguish it from mere building: "Architecture is a *gesture*. Not every purposive movement of the human body is a gesture. And no more is every building designed for a purpose architecture."[12]

[11] Vitruvius, *The Ten Books on Architecture*, 72–73.
[12] Ludwig Wittgenstein, *Culture and Value* (Oxford: Blackwell, 1980), 42.

6. The soma further provides a basic model for the relationship of architectural design to the environment. An architecturally successful building must both fit in and stand out as a distinctive achievement, just as a soma must do in order to survive and flourish, performing a balancing act of absorbing and relying on the wider natural and social resources of its environment but at the same time asserting its distinctive individuality. Just as we always experience a building in terms of its background environmental framing, so we cannot feel the body alone independent of its wider *Umwelt*. Recall the example from Chapter 9 (note 16). If we lie down, close our eyes, and simply try to feel ourselves alone and motionless, what we will feel, if we are attentive, is the environmental surface on which we are lying and the environing air we are breathing and feeling on our exposed body surfaces.

7. Such non-visual feelings of the body remind us that if architectural design is based on the soma and aims to enhance somatic experience, it should be critically attentive to the soma's multiplicity of senses. These senses, as neurophysiologists now realize, go beyond the traditional five and include some that are identified as distinctively somaesthetic senses in the narrow sense of dealing with sensory perception through the body per se rather than through its particular sense organs (eyes, ears, nose, tongue, etc.). One of the most prominent of those senses is proprioception, which concerns the orientation of the body's parts relative to each other and the orientation of the body in space, and which therefore includes both our sense of balance and our kinesthetic sense or sense of our bodily movement in space. Proprioception and particularly kinesthesia seem important for the appreciation of architecture as an environment through which we move and orient our bodies, maintaining a dynamic equilibrium as we navigate entrances, corridors, and staircases. I will return to these senses later in this chapter in discussing atmosphere, but here let me briefly acknowledge Goethe's early insight in appreciating this point. Though one might "think that architecture as fine art functions merely for the eyes," he insists that it "functions especially for what one least attends to, for the sense of the human body's mechanical movement. We feel a pleasant sensation by moving in dance according to certain rules; we could arouse a similar feeling in someone by leading him with blindfolded eyes through a well-built house."[13]

---

[13] Goethe, Johann Wolfgang, "Baukunst," in Friedmar Apel (ed.), *Ästhetische Schriften 1771–1805*, in *Sämtliche Werke*, vol. 8 (Frankfurt: Deutscher Klassiker Verlag, 1998), 368.

If the soma is the crucial medium through which architecture is experienced and created, then developing its discriminatory powers could enrich architecture's critical and creative arsenal, as critical perception is always part of the creative process. The Japanese architect Ando Tadao seems to be working in this direction, expressly deploying the Japanese term *shintai* rather than body (its standard English translation) in order to distinguish and underline what I emphasize in deploying the term soma rather than body. The soma is a living, perceptive, sentient, dynamic, intelligent corporeality that involves intentionality, mind, and the spiritual rather than being a brute material counterpart from which mind and spirit must be distinguished and opposed. Ando explicitly states that he uses the term *shintai* rather than body so as not "to make a clear distinction between mind and body," but instead to denote "a union of spirit and the flesh" that is in a "dynamic relationship with the world." He insists: "It is only the *shintai* in this sense that builds or understands architecture. The *shintai* is a sentient being that responds to the world.... Architecture must also be understood through the senses of the *shintai*."[14]

In affirming Ando's theoretical position (which is also reflected in his architectural practice), I would reformulate and expand it in terms of somaesthetics' pragmatic, disciplined cultivation of the senses and of their critical reflective discrimination. It is not surprising that Ando's use of *shintai* anticipates my somaesthetic approach to architecture, since East-Asian somatic theory and practice were influential in shaping my vision of somaesthetics. The Japanese term *shintai* derives from the earlier Chinese term *shenti* 身体, which also denotes the living soma and is formed from the two characters *shen* and *ti*. The character shen 身 was used in classical Chinese to denote the whole person (including the moral and spiritual self that should be cultivated, rather than the mere material, animal body), and the character is derived from an image of a standing pregnant woman, a charged symbol of the living, creative, dynamic body that is directionally asymmetrical and also top-heavy.[15]

---

[14] Ando Tadao, "Shintai and Space," in Francesco Dal Co (ed.), *Tadao Ando:Complete Works* (London: Phaidon, 1995), 453.

[15] The two parts of the modern character *ti* relate to the 本 (*běn*) foundation or main part of a person (人 *ren*), thus suggesting how crucial the somatic dimension is to our personhood, while the original ancient form of ti was written as 體, whose two parts respectively designate bone and vessel. In classical Chinese, the terms *shen* and *ti* were used separately to designate the body, with *shen* focused more on embodied personhood while *ti* emphasized life and generative growth and was also widely applied to nonhuman bodies. For more details on this ancient usage, see Deborah Sommer, "Boundaries of the *Ti* Body," *Asia Major* 21 (2008): 293–324.

III

Let us turn from Asian etymology back to the critical issues of architecture in its contemporary Western theoretical contexts. In surveying the recent literature on architectural criticality, one finds a diversity of competing ideas about what such criticality means and aims at. Sometimes the target of critique is portrayed as the dominant, oppressive forces of social reality or more generally as the problems of social life. At other times, the critical target seems to be the traditional, mainstream institutional practices of architecture (or more generally building) itself. These targeted practices can be interpreted as the architectural reflection, expression, or incarnation of those undesirable social realities, but they can also be understood as problems more inherent in architecture as an institutional, relatively autonomous, discipline. Thus, for example, the critical character of some so-called post-critical architectural theory involves criticizing architecture's claims to *autonomous* disciplinarity, if not also to distinctive disciplinarity *tout court*. Architectural theory also identifies and recommends a variety of different ways, acts, or attitudes of being critical. For the continuing modernist tradition, the most influential of these critical modes seem to focus on negation and resistance, often through some notion of architectural autonomy; other modes highlight more explicit social interventions and militancy while rejecting the very idea of autonomy as an outmoded modernist ideology steeped in sinister, elitist complicity. Given the diversity of ways of being critical (and I have only noted a few), I would urge the logical point that rejection of one target or mode of criticality does not entail that one has abandoned criticality altogether and thus has necessarily degenerated into post-critical frivolity or uncritical pragmatism.[16] Although

---

[16] Nor does adopting one critical mode imply rejecting all others. One can be critical of society (and of architecture's role in it) and yet also be critical of architectural autonomy. Faced with the diversity of critical perspectives, the basic pragmatist stance, as I have elsewhere explained, is one of inclusive disjunction. Rather than assuming an exclusive either/or that forces us to adopt only one critical mode and reject all the others, pragmatic pluralism construes the either/or disjunction in the way it often functions in everyday life – as when one can have wine or water but also both. If our goal is to maximize our goods, including the goods that criticism offers, our approach should be to assume that we can embrace and deploy different modes and methods until we are shown that they are not only different but incompatible. I should underline that this basic orientation of pragmatist pluralism is expressed by the indefinite article in this chapter's subtitle. I am proposing somaesthetics as merely one possible critical option or perspective for architecture, not the only useful critical perspective or the best one. Architectural issues (and the world in which architecture is necessarily enmeshed) are too complex and multifaceted to rely on a single, one-size-fits-all method of criticism.

pragmatism is emphatically pluralistic, it is also, in its non-vulgar philosophical sense and as part of its meliorist stance, a distinctly critical posture, so much so that John Dewey defined philosophy as "a criticism of criticisms."[17] For this reason (and others), it is wrongly simplistic to see philosophical pragmatism as encouraging an acritical or post-critical attitude.

Dewey saw criticism in the arts as embracing social, political, and philosophical factors, but also as fundamentally perceptual. The principal value of critical judgment is not in discursive verdicts of praise, blame, or ranking but rather in improving discrimination for "the reeducation of perception," and, through it, the reformation of life as well as art. It is often said that our term "criticism" comes from the Greek word for a judge, *krites* (κριτής), but it ultimately comes from the Greek verb *krinō* (κρίνω), which means to distinguish, discriminate, separate; hence the adjective (κριτικὸς), the counterpart of our term "critical," means "able to discern" or discriminate.[18] Recalling this core sense of discrimination can help us address, with the help of somaesthetics, two of the greatest challenges to criticality in architecture: the problem of autonomy and the problem of atmosphere.

1. Autonomy connotes independence, and one prominent (spatially derived) notion of independence implies a separation from that of which one is independent. That separation is reflected in the notion of critical distance, where the critic sustains her objective judgment by having a point of view somehow external to the object or situation she is judging rather than being essentially involved or implicated in it. The idea of the judge as disinterested observer conveys the same sense of critical distance. But contemporary theory has shown that a purely external viewpoint for judging our natural, social, and cultural world is logically untenable; such a view would be a view from nowhere and from which we would see nothing meaningfully. We simply cannot stand outside the world to assess it altogether apart from the interests we have and seek in it. Today's thoroughly globalized political, economic, and media networks reinforce in concrete sociocultural terms this message of our essential, inextricable implication in the world and world order.

---

[17] John Dewey, *Experience and Nature* (Carbondale: Southern Illinois University Press, 1981), 298.

[18] Dewey accordingly describes criticism as "discriminating judgment" (ibid.). Interestingly, design – a core concept of architecture has a rather similar etymology of distinguishing or marking off, deriving from the Latin *de* + *signare*, to "mark off" or "separate" – as in the articulation of space through making signs or marks.

Architects have not been slow to draw the conclusion by questioning the notion of autonomy on which several versions of critical architecture rely. In proposing a "post-critical" architectural approach, Somol and Whiting define the critical position (exemplified in different ways by Michael Hays and Peter Eisenman) as presuming "that autonomy is a precondition for engagement" and that such autonomy implies some sort of separation or distance from other things, sometimes described as being "between" other disciplines or discursive formations.[19] But in order to create a real and significant building in today's pervasively complex and administratively regulated world, one cannot stand outside of all entanglements with that world. In using the energies, institutions, permissions, monies, and other affordances of establishment society, the architect cannot avoid being entangled and complicit with it. Recognizing that the architect is in some way "a surfer on the waves of societal forces" seems to be part of Rem Koolhaas's questioning of architecture's critical posture, a suspicion that "there is in the deepest motivations of architecture something that cannot be critical" and that leads him (in the architecturally related but far broader and less manageable field of urbanism) to urge a radically uncritical outlook: "we have to dare to be utterly uncritical...we have to become irresponsible," embracing a "Nietzschean frivolity."[20]

Such post-critical arguments may seem compelling if the critical attitude is presumed to require an external, autonomous standpoint – altogether detached and disinterested. But that basic presumption can be challenged by recalling the soma. We can critically examine aspects of our somatic experience without going outside our bodies to some putative detached, disembodied mind. We use a finger to probe a small bump on our face; we use our tongue to discover and remove the traces of food on our upper lip or on our teeth. We discriminate or assess our pain *within* the painful experience, not only after it has passed and we are, in that sense, outside it. Beyond these ordinary practices of

---

[19] Robert Somol and Sarah Whiting, "Notes Around the Doppler Effect and Other Moods of Modernism," in *Perspecta* 33 (2002): 73.

[20] Rem Koolhaas, "What Ever Happened to Urbanism," in Rem Koolhaas and Bruce Mau, *S, M, L, XL* (New York: Monacelli Press, 1995), 971, for the quotes on uncritical Nietzschean frivolity. The others are taken from Hilde Heynen, "A Critical Posture for Architecture?" in Jane Rendell and Jonathan Hill (eds.), *Critical Architecture* (London: Routledge, 2007), 51; and George Baird, "Criticality and its Discontents," *Harvard Design Magazine*, 21 (2003–2004): 649, who takes this Koolhaas quote about architecture's deepest (and uncritical) motivations from an oral remark, quoted by Beth Kapusta, in *The Canadian Architect Magazine* 39 (August 1994): 10.

somatic consciousness, a variety of meditative disciplines are structured on heightening the soma's conscious critical self-examination. Moreover, even beneath explicit conscious awareness, the soma critically monitors and corrects itself unreflectively through entrenched motor schemas. Indeed, even in the unconsciousness of sleep, the soma will recognize that it is too close to the edge of the bed and will readjust itself accordingly.

In short, somatic self-examination provides a model of immanent critique where one's critical perspective does not require being entirely outside the situation critically examined but merely requires a reflective perspective on it that is not wholly absorbed in the immediacy of what is experienced; a perspective better described as positionally eccentric (or decentered) rather than as external. Such perspectives can be achieved by efforts of disciplined willful attention, but also often arise spontaneously through experiences of somatic dissonance where unreflective coordination is disrupted, which thus stimulates a decentered, reflective critical attention to what is going on. Critical somatic consciousness involves some aspects of the soma's complex array of systems examining other aspects of that complexity. In the same way, we can explain how individuals pervasively shaped by societal forces can develop critical social consciousness through internal tensions or coordination breakdowns between diverse ideals embedded in the society's traditions and actual practices. Since ancient times, the body has served as a model not only for architectural structures but also for the structure of society – conceived as a comprehensive, cohesive, relatively stable system that integrates smaller systems (which cohere but can also function somewhat independently), such that its different functionings can sometimes fail to integrate harmoniously, and this experienced dissonance can stimulate critical consciousness.

There are many things worth exploring about the relations between unreflective immediacy and reflection in somatic consciousness, and how these different modes of consciousness need to be integrated to maximize the quality of our experience and performance. But retaining the crucial point already made, that criticality requires no position of complete independence or externality, I now turn to a second major challenge to architectural criticality: the problem of atmosphere.

2. Deriving from the Greek words for vapor and sphere, atmosphere's primary meaning is air, thus suggesting lightness, intangibility, a certain formlessness and elusiveness that can readily evoke a sense of frivolity or lack of gravitas, structure, or substance. In modernist architectural discourse, the notion of atmosphere had a typically negative nuance, suggesting a vaguely subjective quality without clear structural form or function but also something gratuitous, frivolous, contrived, and artificial or impure.[21]

With the decline of architecture's modernist paradigm (and its positivist, rationalist, objectivist, and minimalist ideologies), there has been increasing recognition of atmosphere's important architectural role. Architectural meaning and value cannot be reduced to tectonics and definable visual or structural forms. A crucial dimension of architecture is what its articulated spaces mean and contribute to the lived experience of those who dwell in those spaces and pass through them. A significant part of that lived experience of meaning and value is what architectural theorists now generally denote as atmosphere. This notion, which deserves extended analysis, seems to encompass the vast array of perceptual qualities, dominant feelings or moods, and ambient effects that emerge not only from the complexity of forms, relations, and materials of the articulated space but also from the complexity of practices, environmental factors, and experienced qualities that pervade the lived space of a building or other architectural structure.

The increasing attention given to atmosphere can be traced to new directions in aesthetic theory, but also to broader cultural trends that challenge the traditional emphasis on the weighty, the substantive, the resistant, as defining what is truly real. Our new media and technologies (with their corresponding new economies and ethos) are dematerializing the traditional heaviness of the life-world, so that the previously invisible atmospheric dimension of our environments (through which our ever more electronically and nano-technically shaped experience is conducted) now emerges as powerfully real and essential. As one popular thinker puts it (with characteristic errant faith in our unlimited resources): "It is through the occurrence of abundance in the modern

---

[21] Despite atmosphere's primary sense of air and hence lightness, modernism's critique of atmosphere focused on the sort of artificially intensified atmosphere that was thickly laid on as an ornamental effect to heighten mood or intoxicate perception. Although air is essentially light, we can speak of a heavy or stale atmosphere. The contrast can be seen in Walt Whitman's poetry, where perfumed air (artificially contrived) is contrasted to true atmosphere, which is pure and odorless yet all the more attractive: "Houses and rooms are full of perfumes.... The distillation would intoxicate me also, but I shall not let it. The atmosphere is not a perfume, it has no taste of the distillation, it is odorless.... I am in love with it... I am mad for it to be in contact with me." Walt Whitman, "Song of Myself," in *Whitman: Poetry and Prose* (New York: Library of America, 1996): canto 2, 188–189.

that the heavy has turned into appearance – and the 'essential' now dwells in lightness, in the air, in the atmosphere."[22] We should also remember, however, that airiness has, in our cultural history, very strong associations with spirituality.[23] This extends even to architecture, where, as Peter Eisenman notes, "the airy" is associated with "the sublime" in contrast to the materiality of the grotesque.[24] Aura, which is also frequently used to convey the notion of atmosphere (and derives from the Greek for air or breath), is often applied with lofty or spiritual connotations. Walter Benjamin's famous theory of art's aura, for example, clearly links it to the elevated, religious atmosphere of ritual or cultic use.[25]

In recent architectural theory, the turn to atmosphere has been closely linked to the so-called post-critical project. But post-critical should not be confused with *acritical*. The post-critical turn to atmosphere is also a serious critical response to the perceived limits of earlier views of architecture that denigrated or neglected the atmospheric as irrelevant to architecture's disciplinary practice and mission, and that defined architecture's disciplinarity (and criticality) in terms of autonomy. Thus, Somol and Whiting affirm the post-critical trend as a move "that shifts the understanding of disciplinarity as autonomy to disciplinarity as performance or practice," and that regards the defining core of architectural practice in a broad notion of design that includes the atmospheric: "Design encompasses object qualities (form, proportion, materiality, composition, etc.) but it also includes qualities of sensibility, such as effect, ambiance, and atmosphere."[26]

If traditional criticality is perceived heroically in terms of serious resistance to powerful, substantial forces, then it seems harder to maintain its importance and gravitas when directing it at a target as apparently light and insubstantial as atmosphere. Atmosphere's challenge to criticality does not disappear, however, even if we take a more comprehensive and more sensible view of criticism as involving not only negations,

---

[22] Peter Sloterdijk, "Against Gravity," an interview with Bettina Funcke, *Bookforum* (February/March, 2005), cited from http://www.bookforum.com/archive/feb_05/funcke.html

[23] There are etymological roots for this spirituality, as the Greek root is related to the Sanskrit word for breath or soul (*atman*).

[24] Peter Eisenman, "En Terror Firma: In Trails of Grotexts," *Architectural Design* 1–2 (1989): 41.

[25] Walter Benjamin, "The Work of Art in the Age of Mechanical Reproduction," in *Illuminations*, trans. Harry Zohn (New York: Schocken, 1969), 221–227; hereafter IL.

[26] Robert E Somol and Sarah Whiting, "Notes around the Doppler Effect and other Moods of Modernism," *Perspecta* 33 (2002): 75.

resistances, and oppositional attitudes but also constructive assessments, interpretations, and positive appreciations. Atmosphere remains problematic for criticality because any mode of criticism that claims to be reasonable, principled, and in some sense objective rather than arbitrary seems to logically require some object against which critical propositions can be measured for accuracy and insight. But atmosphere does not provide such an object because it is precisely something that is defined by its contrast to conventional objecthood. It distinctively lacks the clear contours, firm and enduring substance, and discrete individuality of ordinary objects in space. Nor is atmosphere something that can be reduced to a mere matter of purely private inner space, a merely personal, idiosyncratic reaction, because different individuals often clearly share common perceptions of atmosphere. Theorists of atmosphere have noticed that it hovers in an intermediate realm between the objective and subjective.[27]

Atmosphere is, I think, best understood as an experienced quality of a situation, and such qualities are notoriously resistant to conceptual definition and discursive analysis. If it defies clear categorization as objective or subjective, this is because atmosphere is a qualitative feature of a situation that is typically grasped before that situation is divided into its objective and subjective elements. Atmosphere is experienced by the subject as a perceptual feeling that emerges from and pervades a situation; like other perceptual feelings, atmosphere is experienced in large part as a bodily feeling. Walter Benjamin likewise describes the aura as something that we perceive bodily by "breathing" in the atmosphere of its situation – "a peculiar web of space and time."[28]

Such somatic experienced qualities are typically very difficult to analyze because they are not fixed in stable objects, and they tend to be felt in terms of nameless, elusive, and often transient feelings. This elusive namelessness is partly a product of their not being objects (which are easier to identify, individuate, and thus name), but rather qualities. Further difficulties in critically analyzing these somatically perceived atmospheric qualities derive from the fact that we are unaccustomed to pay explicit attention to the bodily feelings involved in our perception because the habitual focus of our attention and interest is the external world of

---

[27] See Gernot Böhme, "Atmosphere as the Fundamental Concept of a New Aesthetics," *Thesis Eleven* 36 (1993): 113–126.
[28] I here quote from the first German version of Benjamin's essay, reprinted in Walter Benjamin, *Gesammelte Schriften* (Frankfurt: Suhrkamp, 1991), vol. 1, 440.

objects. Perceptual feelings are experienced somatically with different levels of awareness, and most of these feelings function beneath full consciousness. As was noted earlier, even when asleep, we can notice that a pillow inhibits our breathing and then purposively move it without regaining consciousness. Likewise, our waking states are full of somatic feelings that do not reach explicit consciousness because our attention is directed elsewhere. In descending a staircase, we are rarely aware of our kinesthetic feelings of movement, our proprioceptive feelings of balance and extension in space, and the tactile qualities of contact that our feet make with the steps. But we must at least implicitly feel these qualities for the soma to react properly in coordinating our movement. Such implicitly grasped qualities exert a significant influence on our behavior, attitudes, and moods. They constitute the core of atmosphere, which also often affects us without our even being aware of it as an explicit dimension of our experience. Just as a vague feeling of discomfort may long go unnoticed until its intensity reaches the threshold of consciousness through pain, an atmosphere may go largely unnoticed unless its intensity demands our attention, even though its pervasive quality may significantly affect our mood and behavior.

Many of the qualities that constitute atmosphere are perceived through senses that are distinctively bodily – namely, our proprioceptive, kinesthetic, vestibular, tactile, senses. Our sensory experience of architecture is far more than the changing visual input as we survey and traverse its spaces. There are feelings of light and shade that are felt on our flesh and not just through vision. We feel the different temperatures and movements of air on our skin as we move through architectural space (along with the smells that the air brings us that stimulate the senses in our nostrils and mouth). There are also all the tactile and muscular sensations of walking through the space – the feel of the surface material beneath our feet; the rhythm of our footsteps; the kinesthetic feel, proprioceptive balance, and muscular effort of traversing a courtyard or ascending or descending a staircase or adjusting one's gait and posture to negotiate a narrow corridor or low door. As the soma is trained or habituated to adjust to different kinds of spaces (at once physical and social), so it implicitly reacts proprioceptively to the changing kinesphere without one usually noticing it; and such reactions often have an affective dimension with real aesthetic significance and sociopolitical import. A huge kinesphere that dwarfs the visitor entering the space of an authoritative power, a demanding staircase to approach the elevated throne of authority, provide familiar examples of how architecture can instill an atmosphere of majesty that is at once potently aesthetic and political.

The tactile and proprioceptive senses, associated with what neurologists call the somaesthetic system, are commonly distinguished from our more distant senses of sight and hearing, which have long been philosophically privileged for their cognitive precision and clarity. Vision is especially privileged in this regard, and architecture provides no exception. Our most conscious and therefore most acutely critical grasp of architecture is in terms of its visual appearance; and this emphasis on the visual is only heightened by the cultural dominance of visual telecommunications and the increasing use of digital images in the design process.

If architectural theory recognizes that the more tactile, somaesthetic senses are crucial to architecture's experienced atmosphere, the presumption remains that these dimensions of atmosphere are in principle too elusive for the exercise of criticality, except indirectly in terms of its pernicious political and mercenary uses. The locus classicus of this influential presumption is Walter Benjamin's famous account of architectural experience that contrasts tactile and optical perception while also comparing architectural experience to that of film. Toward the end of his essay "The Work of Art in the Age of Mechanical Reproduction," in which Benjamin earlier expounds his theory of aura, he claims that unlike painting (with its traditional aura of uniqueness), film and architecture both enable a "simultaneous, collective experience" for aesthetic reception "by the mass audience" (IL, 234). Benjamin, however, then contrasts film and architecture in terms of the former's greater possibilities for critical consciousness through its objectifying, representational, photographic technologies and optic focus as opposed to architecture's problematic resistance to critical consciousness through its predominant reliance on habits of tactile reception.

"Buildings," writes Benjamin, "are appropriated [the German is the less dynamic *rezipiert*] in a twofold manner: by use and by perception – or rather, by touch and sight. Such appropriation [*Rezeption*] cannot be understood in terms of the attentive concentration of a tourist before a famous building. On the tactile side there is no counterpart to contemplation on the optical side. Tactile appropriation is accomplished not so much by attention as by habit" (IL, 240). We should note how Benjamin's terminology does not even give tactile experience the full status of perception (*Wahrnemung*), which connotes cognition and active consciousness, but rather suggests blind absorption (*Rezeption*) through the mechanism of habit. Benjamin goes on to argue that this unthinking, uncritical tactile absorption through habit also "determines to a large extent even optical reception" in architecture (ibid).

Moreover, through its persistent deployment in the ubiquitous realm of architecture, this uncritical mode of habitual, somatic reception "acquires canonical value" or pervasive power that extends to other domains of culture and of life, where, in times of great historical change, the challenges that face human perception and adjustment "cannot be solved by optical means, that is, by contemplation [or focused attentive consciousness], alone" (ibid.). Benjamin can then return to film experience and argue that there, too, reception by the masses, although optical, is still essentially a reception governed by habit and characterized by distraction that "requires no attention" (IL, 241). Thus, the mechanical reproduction of art is matched by an unfocussed, absentminded, uncritical reception through the mechanism of habit. "The public," he concludes "is an examiner, but an absent-minded [or distracted, *zerstreuter*] one" (ibid.)

Benjamin, however, provides no evidence that the tactile feelings we experience in architecture *must* remain in the realm of inattentive, absentminded, mechanical habit that precludes explicit awareness for critical assessment. There is nothing in tactile and other distinctively somatic feelings that prohibits our perceiving them with conscious, focused attention, and in many conditions we do. In everyday experience, we often notice and even try to describe varieties of pain, itches, tickles, caresses, sensual pleasures, feelings of dizziness, speed, hot, cold, and the feel of different surfaces and fabrics on our skin. Benjamin, of course, is right that our habitual way of experiencing architecture is in terms of blind inattentive habit. But habits, as learned behavior (even if implicitly learned behavior), can be changed; and not all habits are blind and inattentive. Although Benjamin understandably contrasts habit with attention, there are indeed habits of attention, and developing such habits is an essential key for success in education and life.

It is certainly true that most of us are far better at focusing critical attention on visual representations than on tactile or somaesthetic feelings, and there may be reasons for this beyond the effects of mere habit (for example, evolutionary reasons and factors concerning the way that distance and visual spatial array can facilitate individuation and objectification). However, we should not erect a dualism between optical and tactile perception because the former in fact intrinsically involves the latter, as the very act of vision necessarily deploys the muscular movement of our eyes and thus the tactility of proprioception – or feeling of muscular movement. Moreover, as recent research in the visuomotor neuron system has shown, perception is significantly transmodal, such that seeing an action will also activate neurons involved in the motor or muscular performance of that action, and apparently vice versa.

If Benjamin argues that our habitual and absent-minded tactile reception of architecture has rendered its optical reception likewise inattentively absentminded, then why not take the visual-tactile linkage in a more positive direction? Why not turn the tables and argue that, by heightening our attention to the tactile or somaesthetic feelings of architectural perception, we could render such perception not only more acute, penetrating, and critical but also sharpen our attentiveness and penetration of architecture's optical experience? It is an anatomical fact that one's rotational range and ease of vision can be increased by improving, through proprioceptive sensitivity, the rotational range of one's spine. Likewise, by training and exercising somaesthetic attention, we can improve our consciousness of the vague but influential somatic feelings that constitute our experience of architectural atmosphere and thus gain a more focused, more discerning awareness for its critical analysis.

Such training is valuable for improving the critical sensibilities not only of designing architects but also of the various populations who inhabit architectural spaces and whose informed input on architectural design would be useful, if such design is truly meant to serve them best. There are a variety of methods for training such somaesthetic sensibility. Some of them are discussed in my books *Body Consciousness* and *Performing Live*. Such methods, however, are best demonstrated in practical, experiential workshop settings; not from the podium of a large plenary lecture for which this text was originally written, or in the merely printed textual form the reader encounters here.

11

Photography as Performative Process

I

Photography pervades our lives. Its multiple and wide-ranging roles make it not only ubiquitous but also immensely diverse. There are photo IDs; all sorts and styles of advertising images; documentary shots of news and sports events; criminal "wanted" posters; scientific photographs to serve either as heuristics in the process of discovery or as evidentiary tools for proof and teaching; portrait shots of individuals, families, or other groups (including school or conference pictures); candidly intimate photos reserved for someone special; personal travel photos (now typically in digital form and shared with friends through some internet network); and then there is art photography, which is what concerns me here and which constitutes a diversely mixed genre in itself.

A distinctively modern art (one not to be found in Hegel's famous nineteenth-century classificatory rankings), photography's association with newness is not merely temporal but indeed reflects a tendency toward continuing innovation. Its original photochemical film technique engendered new forms such as movies and videos, but it also led to the new varieties of digital photography that dispense with the photochemistry of film and instead use sensors that convert light into electrical charges that are then digitally analyzed and converted back into images. Photography's artistic uses display continuing innovation, such as the distinctive trend that began in the late 1970s of creating very large-scale photographs expressly meant for posting on the gallery wall and typically "summoning a confrontational experience on the part of the spectator that sharply contrasts with the habitual processes of appropriation and projection whereby photographic images are normally received and consumed."[1]

Heterogeneity and novelty are familiar themes in theorizing photography. Faced with its intractable diversity (that he described as an "unclassifiable" "disorder"), Roland Barthes wondered whether photography had an essence, but then argued that its "essence... can only be (if it exists at all) the New of which it has been the advent."[2] Walter Benjamin even more influentially characterized photography in terms of its transformational novelty. Besides generating the further novelty of cinema, photography's powers of mechanical reproduction "transformed the entire nature of art" by shifting art from its original essentially ritualistic use (with its auratic cult value of the authentic original) to an "absolute emphasis on its exhibition value" instead. Moreover, its automatic mechanism of capturing attractive, accurate images likewise removed the traditional need for skilled artistic hands to create them. "For the first time in the process of pictorial reproduction, photography freed the hand of the most important artistic functions which henceforth devolved only upon the eye looking into a lens."[3]

Given such heterogeneous and innovative tendencies, I dare not presume that there must be a distinct and permanent essence of photography whose identity it is my duty as theorist to define. If there is such an essence, I hope this essay will shed light on it, but my purpose here is rather to highlight a dimension of photographic art that has been

---

[1] Jean-Francois Chevrier, "The Adventures of the Picture Form in the History of Photography," Michael Gilson (trans.), in *The Last Picture Show: Artists Using Photography, 1960–1982*; exhibition catalogue curated by Douglas Fogle. Michael Fried cites and develops Chevrier's insight in his *Why Photography Matters as Art as Never Before* (New Haven: Yale University Press, 2008). Susan Sontag claims that earlier "the book has been the most influential way of arranging (and usually miniaturizing) photographs," in her influential *On Photography* (New York: Farrar, Straus and Giroux, 1977), 4; hereafter S.

[2] Roland Barthes, *Camera Lucida: Reflections on Photography*, trans. Richard Howard (New York: Hill and Wang, 1981), 4; hereafter Ba. Later, however, when Barthes focuses his discussion of photography on the photograph, he describes its "very essence" in terms of reference to the past: "What I intentionalize in a photograph is neither Art nor Communication, it is Reference.... The name of Photography's *noeme* would therefore be 'That-has-been'" (Ba, 76–77). As an "emanation of *past reality*," he continues, "the Photograph... is *without future* (this is its pathos, its melancholy)" (Ba, 88, 90). Barthes' paradoxical identification of photography's essence with both future and past might be mitigated by insisting on a distinction between photography and the photograph. I argue in this chapter for the capital importance of this distinction, but primarily for other reasons than this paradox of Barthes.

[3] Walter Benjamin, "The Work of Art in the Age of Mechanical Reproduction," in *Illuminations*, trans. Harry Zohn (New York: Schocken, 1969), 227, 225, 219; hereafter IL.

largely neglected but that can constitute the locus of real aesthetic experience and value. This dimension concerns the performative process of making a photograph of a human subject, and the sorts of artistic performances and aesthetic experiences that this process involves.[4] These performances and experiences have a clearly somatic aspect, which I initially failed to recognize despite my interest in developing a somaesthetic perspective on art. There is likewise a salient dramatic dimension to the photographic performative process that also escaped me, despite my having advanced a general theory of art as dramatization.[5] The import of these somatic and dramatic aspects of photography only recently became evident to me through collaborations with photographic artists and curators interested in somaesthetics. I then realized that photography's dimension of somatic, dramatic, performative process (and its potential for enhanced artistic use and aesthetic experience) is occluded by our one-sided concentration on the photograph itself (a static object), with which we tend to identify photographic art.

I argue, however, that an important distinction can be made between photography and the photograph. Although the photograph (whether in hard-copy print or in digital display) is surely the standard end product of photography and conventionally recognized as the goal and work of photographic art, there is more to photography than the

---

[4] David Davies, in *Art as Performance* (Oxford: Blackwell, 2004), has argued for the far more extreme claim that artworks in general (not just in photography) are not the physical objects with which they are commonly identified but rather the actual performances of artists that create such objects, and that appreciating those objects properly requires relating them to the actual performance that (according to this theory) is the work. I do not subscribe to this radically revisionist ontological and aesthetic theory, which departs too much from our established conceptual scheme to be convincing. In arguing for the artistic dimension and aesthetic value of the (dramatic, somatic) performative process of photography, I am not urging that this process deprive the photograph of its artwork status by usurping its role as the standard end product of photography. Nor am I arguing that the photograph must be evaluated in terms of the performance that engenders it; process and product can be judged separately and with different evaluative verdicts. My claim is rather that photography is a complex art that offers various objects for aesthetic appreciation (such as photographs and photographic performance processes or events), and that these objects are differently individuated for our purposes of aesthetic appreciation. Our individuation of the performative process of a photo session would diverge sharply from the way we identify a particular photographic image or a photographic print that results from a particular moment or part of that performative process.

[5] See Richard Shusterman, "Art as Dramatization," *Journal of Aesthetics and Art Criticism* 59 (2001): 361–372, revised and reprinted in my *Surface and Depth: Dialectics of Criticism and Culture* (Ithaca: Cornell University Press, 2002), ch. 13.

photograph.⁶ To appreciate this distinction and see that the photograph and its aesthetic perception are only part of a larger complex of elements that constitutes photography as an activity and as an art, we first need to examine these other elements, which include the photographer, the target that he photographs, the photographic equipment, and the spatiotemporal context or scene in which the target is posed and photographed. In reducing photography to the photograph, we diminish its aesthetic scope and power, by limiting the elements that can manifest artistic value and provide aesthetic experience. Moreover, as the essential meaning of the photograph (at least in philosophical discussions) often gets reduced to the object photographed, so reducing the aesthetics of photography to the photograph risks reducing it to the aesthetics of an object (i.e., the real-world referent) actually outside the photograph, hence allegedly beyond photography; and this would leave the aesthetic value of photography gravely in question.⁷

Given the diversity of photographic art, I will limit my analysis to photographic art that takes a knowing, voluntary individual human subject as its photographic target, by which I mean a human subject who is both aware that she is being photographed and is also willing to be. In

---

⁶ In his historically instructive book, Patrick Maynard similarly claims that photography is something different and more than the photograph. But he uses this distinction to argue his central thesis that "photography is a kind of technology" or, more precisely, "a branching family of technologies" or "set of technological procedures" rather than to argue, as I do here, for the *aesthetic* dimensions of the performative and experiential process of photographic art. See Patrick Maynard, *The Engine of Visualization: Thinking Through Photography* (Ithaca: Cornell University Press, 1997), x, 3, 9.

⁷ Both continental theorists and analytic philosophers often insist on the photograph's direct and transparent presentation of the object it renders (rather than being a mediated representation of it) because it results from a mechanical, causal process. Barthes describes the photograph as "pure deictic language . . . a photograph is always invisible: it is not it that we see," but "its referent," the object photographed (Ba, 5, 6). Sontag speaks of such transparency in terms of the photograph's "identity of image and object," its presenting "a piece of the world" through "mechanical genesis"; hence, in appreciating photography, the object or "what the photograph is *of* is always of primary importance" (S, 98, 158). Roger Scruton, from the perspective of analytic aesthetics, claims "the photograph is transparent to its subject, and if it holds our interest, it does so because it acts as a surrogate for the thing which it shows." This is because the relationship of the photograph to its generating process is "causal not intentional," hence, "photography is not a representational art." See Roger Scrution, "Photography and Representation," in *The Aesthetic Understanding* (London: Methuen, 1983), 103, 114. Kendall Walton also speaks of the photograph's transparency in "Transparent Pictures: On the Nature of Photographic Realism," *Noûs* 18:1 (1984): 67–72. For a useful analytic reconstruction and response to Scruton's argument, see D.M. Lopes, "The Aesthetics of Photographic Transparency," *Mind*, 36:1 (2003): 335–348.

articulating key elements of the artistic photographic process, I will suggest how some of them can display significant aspects of artistic creativity and aesthetic experience. These can be manifested not only in the photographer's mise-en-scène of himself, his camera, and his subject within the photographic context and process, but also in the photographed subject's posing, self-presentation, or self-styling before the camera within the mise-en-scène of the photographic situation and in critical communication with the photographer. Indeed, if communicative expression in artistic creation contributes significantly to the value of aesthetic experience, then the communicative interaction between photographer and subject in the process of setting up and taking the shot could provide a rich source for such experiential value.

Why have these aesthetic aspects of photography as process been neglected? It is not enough to posit our one-sided preoccupation with the photograph as the sole explanation of this neglect because that preoccupation may itself be partly the result of other reasons that discourage attention to photography as performative process. I will therefore devote a brief section to discussing those other reasons. Finally, to bring out more clearly the range and interplay of these artistic and aesthetic features of photography as performative process, I discuss my experience of this process in collaborating with the Parisan artist Yann Toma, whose photographic work in the genre he calls Radiant Flux usefully recalls photography's etymological roots while intriguingly problematizing the conventional idea that photography transparently gives us the object photographed. I recognize that first-person testimony is not the standard way of making an argument in contemporary philosophical aesthetics; yet, despite its limitations, first-hand personal testimony has some evidentiary value, particularly when it comes to talking about the experiential dimensions of making and appreciating art.

II

In its simplest form, the photographic situation treated here involves a photographer, a human subject who knowingly and willingly serves as the photographic target, the camera (with its necessary accessory photographic equipment), and the scene or context in which the photography session takes place.[8] What I wish to highlight as the photographic process

---

[8] The photographer and the subject photographed can, in principle, be the same person, although performing the different functions.

of performance is essentially what goes on in the process of setting up, preparing, and taking the photographic shots in a photography session. Although the technique of film photography involves the further process of developing the film to produce a negative (or positive) image, this procedure does not involve the artistic process and interaction between photographer and subject whose neglected aesthetic potential I wish to explore in this chapter.[9] For the same reason, although art photography also includes the subsequent critical process of selecting which shots are worth exhibiting and the best ways to mount or show them, I will not discuss that process here but will instead focus on the aesthetic experience of photography before the existence of the photograph that is its product.

1. Taking a photographic shot, like any action we perform, always involves some bodily action. At the bare minimum, one must use a body part to activate the camera's shutter release, usually by an action involving one's fingers. But there are obviously further somatic skills, such as properly steadying the camera in one's hands to ensure a clear shot and being able to effectively maneuver one's photographic equipment along with one's own bodily position, posture, and balance so that one can best aim the camera to get the desired optical image. Taking a picture is a bodily act that requires a certain effort and competence of somatic self-use, despite the advertising myth that photographic technology is so magically simple that even a child or dumb brute can produce an excellent photo. This need for somatic skill despite photography's mechanical magic is comically thematized in Buster Keaton's *The Cameraman*, where the hero clumsily struggles with his photographic equipment, knocking out windows and doors with his tripod, while his pet monkey manages to load and aim the camera with considerably less clumsiness and more success, producing some excellent footage of fighting in New York's Chinatown.

In real life, I have witnessed many comic instances of the photographer's need for somatic control and awareness, such as friends losing their balance and falling off a curb or into a pool as they backed up to get a better shot, eyes locked on the optical image in the camera, hands tightly grasping the camera itself. Some people like photography but dislike taking pictures because of its somatic constraints; they prefer having their hands unencumbered and their gaze free to survey the horizon

---

[9] Digital photography, which immediately provides a photographic image, does not require the process of developing and fixing the image but does allow further creative processes such as enlarging and cropping the photographic image.

rather than narrowly fixed on a small aperture or screen held in their hands. There are good evolutionary reasons why one would instinctively want to have one's hands free for action and one's gaze free to survey the horizon and thus more readily able to identify friends, prey, and predators at a distance. Although many people, on the contrary, love to use cameras and feel empowered by wielding them, it is obvious that handling and looking through a camera involve sensorimotor skills that need to be learned.

Besides the somatic skill of controlling camera, posture, and balance, there is also the photographer's skill in winning the confidence of the person photographed. This is important for making the subject feel more comfortable and cooperative rather than guarded and ill at ease, thus rendering her more suitable for photography's dominant dual aims of not only portraying the real but also producing aesthetic objects and experiences, even from people who in real life are painfully unattractive. Susan Sontag thus praises Diane Arbus's frontal photographs of "freaks and pariahs," for capturing "subjects ... one would not expect to surrender themselves so amiably and ingenuously to the camera.... To get these people to pose, the photographer has had to gain their confidence" (S, 35, 38), and this requires social skills that also have a somatic dimension. The photographer's body language must not be threatening; it must be friendly, even intimate in a way, but not intrusive. It needs to show a quality of real attentiveness and interest regarding the person photographed (even if that attention and interest is temporary and professional), and this quality of attention and interest will be expressed somatically in posture, gesture, and facial expression.

The photographer's expression of sympathetic attentive interest is not simply necessary for putting a subject at ease but further aids as a stimulus in engaging the subject's own attentive interest and heightened focus on the photographic situation or event. It is as if the photographer's quality of attention and presence infects the photographed subject as well, thus raising her quality of presence that can then be captured in the resulting photograph, a presence that transfigures even ordinary faces into beautifully expressive ones. The masterful Richard Avedon describes this process of contagion where the subjects come to him "to be photographed as they would go to a doctor or a fortune teller – to find out how they are," and in the hope of feeling better through the transfigurative experience of self-exposure before a charismatic observer: "I have to engage them. Otherwise there's nothing to photograph. The concentration has to come from me and involve them. Sometimes the force of it grows so strong that sounds in the studio go unheard. Time stops. We share a brief, intense intimacy. But... when the sitting is over... there's nothing left except the photograph... the photograph and a kind of embarrassment."[10] This experience of deeply felt and focused communicative expression structured through the mise-en-scène of the photographic process is a form of aesthetic experience whose transfiguring intensity leaves its participants embarrassed once the drama of the shooting is over and they return to their everyday routine.

Of course, photography that seeks veracity and drama by catching its subject up close yet totally unaware involves an altogether sort of photographic skill. Its secrecy generally includes a dimension of somatic virtuosity in order to keep the camera (or at least its use) concealed. Think, for example, of how Walker Evans secretly took his close-up, frontal shots of New York subway passengers, "with the lens of his camera peering between two buttons of his topcoat," so that he could catch them unaware that they were being considered as photographic objects, and thus capture a look free from any posing, posturing, or self-consciousness. If some prefer such candid shots, others find them ethically suspect. Nonetheless, there is little doubt that people display a different demeanor when they know they are being photographed; and often there is something awkward and false about it.[11]

2. Overcoming the awkwardness of posing also requires from the photographic subject a certain talent or effort, no matter how skillful the

[10] This quote from Avedon is taken from Sontag (S, 187).

[11] See Sontag (S, 37) for these points. Important ethical issues can also arise when subjects know they are posing for the camera. For example, the photographer may abuse the confidence and trust that the posing subject grants him and exploit the subject's openness and cooperation by creating a photograph that presents the subject in a way she does not want to be presented, in a permanent, infinitely reproducible and displayable image that violates the subject's own self-image. Arthur Danto notes how Richard Avedon cruelly violates the trust of a transvestite subject – the psychologically delicate and physically "willowy" Candy Darling – by photographing "her" "in makeup and garter belt, and with her long hair" but in frontal nudity with the penis displayed, making her look not like the delicate feminine personality she identified herself with but rather as "a sexual freak." Danto rightly describes this as an "exceedingly cruel image" that is ethically suspect, and he goes on to argue more generally (using the further example of Avedon's portrait of Isaiah Berlin) that Avedon "has no interest in the sitter's wishes" but selfishly "asserts his autonomy over the subject." See Arthur Danto, "The Naked Truth," in Jerrold Levinson (ed.), *Aesthetics and Ethics: Essays at the Intersection* (Cambridge: Cambridge University Press, 2001), 270, 274, 275. Danto's analysis suggests that the intense engagement and intimacy Avedon describes as having with his subjects is essentially exploitative or even feigned rather than ethically honest. This predatory, manipulative, falseness may well explain Avedon's feeling of "embarrassment" once "the sitting is over" and he has the photograph that he (rather than the sitter) wanted.

photographer is at making his subject feel natural and uninhibited in exposing herself to the camera. Roland Barthes poignantly confesses his own complex problems as a posing subject. On the one hand, as soon as he knows he is "observed by the lens," Barthes feels the need to reconstitute himself "in the process of posing... I instantaneously make another body for myself, I transform myself in advance into an image" (Ba, 10). On the other hand, Barthes knows his image will ultimately be controlled by the photographer and the photographic equipment, so there is the added anxiety of having no real control of the self that will emerge from his creative posing, "the anguish" of not knowing whether one will be reborn as an "antipathetic individual" or "a good sort" (Ba 11); and this anxiety exacerbates the discomfort or awkwardness of posing.

A further difficulty is how to organize oneself somatically in the pose to achieve the look one wants to convey. It is not easy to control one's facial and postural expression, especially when one cannot use a mirror but must rely only on proprioception. Barthes provides a wonderful description of this effort to strike the right pose: "I don't know how to work on my skin from within. I decide to 'let drift' over my lips and in my eyes a faint smile which I mean to be 'indefinable,' in which I might suggest, along with the qualities of my nature, my amused consciousness of the whole photographic ritual" (Ba, 11). For Barthes there are two essential and discomforting paradoxes in the act of photographic posing or self-presentation. First, is the desire for the photographic image to "coincide with my (profound) 'self,'" while knowing that "'myself' never coincides with my image... For the Photograph is the advent of myself as other" (Ba, 12). Second, the posing subject is made into an object, not only in the actual photographic print but in the very process of objectifying oneself before the camera, by representing or reshaping oneself through one's pose. Such a process, Barthes confesses, makes him "invariably suffer from a sensation of inauthenticity, sometimes of imposture" (Ba, 13). "I am neither subject nor object but a subject who feels he is becoming an object" (Ba, 14). Such feelings make it difficult to achieve an attractive pose.

The subject who poses for a photograph therefore has an important aesthetic role to perform: to escape these feelings of inauthenticity and render her pose less awkward, forced, and false or, to put it positively, to render herself more photographically attractive by being more vitally or authentically present. Though Barthes himself lacked this skill, he recognized it in his mother – a skill in posing through which "she 'let' herself be photographed" in a free and natural way that would suggest her "essential identity" even when the different photographs did not fully capture it; "she triumphed over this ideal of placing herself in front of the lens (an inevitable action) *with discretion* (but without a touch of the tense theatricalism of humility or sulkiness) . . . She did not struggle with her image, as I do with mine: she did not *suppose* herself" (Ba, 66–67).

3. The camera is the essential element in the photographic situation that turns the encounter between photographer and the voluntary subject into a scene of posing that so often renders the subject ill at ease despite her willingness to be photographed. There is not merely the feeling of wanting to project a certain look to the public, to be seen by others in a specific way that may not be precisely the way one actually is or feels at that moment. Such a desire is present in many kinds of social situations where we perform the role playing of self-presentation in everyday life without feeling especially self-consciousness. But the camera thematizes this self-presentation, making it explicit by focusing on framing a particular moment of such self-presentation and fixing it in a permanent image that objectifies and defines the self in terms of that experiential moment, an image that can be indefinitely reproduced and circulated as a representation of what the self really is.

The camera thus creates a particular pressure of posing not only because it typically requires the subject to arrest her movement (or at least control it) to ensure that her image is captured clearly but also because it raises the stakes of one's self presentation by harboring the threat of permanently representing the self as an object in ways that the self as subject may not want to be represented or defined. Although experience itself is elusively evanescent and significantly subjective, the photograph has the powers of durability, fixity, and objectivity that belong to real physical things. These powers constitute one reason why the experiential process of photography is obscured by the photograph as object. In thus framing a real moment and giving it permanence, public representation, and wide-ranging reproducibility and circulation, the camera intensifies or magnifies that moment; it dramatizes it in precisely the way in which I argue that all art dramatizes things by putting them in an intensifying frame, thus giving them a sense of heightened reality or vividness.[12]

---

[12] See my "Art as Dramatization," 234–238. In his influential work on photography, Laszlo Moholy-Nagy (of the Bauhaus) speaks of how this art can produce a "heightened reality of an everyday object." See his book, *Painting, Photography, Film*, trans. Janet Seligman (Cambridge, MA: MIT Press, 1987), 62.

4. The performative process of having a subject pose for the camera always involves posing that subject in some setting – a situational or environmental background that, if successful, can enhance the interest and quality of the photographic act and resulting photograph. Important situations (such as a wedding or a funeral) can give special meaning and gravitas to a work of photography and provide a characteristic background with relevant props imbued with situational meaning. If the posing subject can be likened to an actor, then determining the background can be likened to stage setting. If the photography studio offers only a limited range of situations and backgrounds, then it compensates by providing better control of the settings it does provide (for example, by regulating conditions of light and temperature and preventing excessive noise, crowds, or other factors that would interfere in producing a desired image of the subject). Here again, in the choice and regulation of situations or backgrounds, there is considerable room for aesthetic mise-en-scène – an artistic dramatization that intensifies experience through formal framing or stage setting, well before the photographer decides to release the mechanism that produces the photograph.

III

Besides our preoccupation with the photograph as object, other factors contribute to obscuring the aesthetic significance of photography as performative process. First, the automatic mechanism involved in making a photograph – the fact that pressing the release of the camera shutter requires no special skill or thought and that the camera mechanism automatically does all the rest to produce a realistic photograph – diminishes the sense of photography as a performance achievement.[13] Thus, Susan Sontag speaks of "the effortlessness of picture-taking, which must be the sole activity resulting in accredited works of art in which a single movement, a touch of the finger, produces a complete work" (S, 164). The instantaneous act of shutter release likewise suggests that there is no sustained duration of effort involved, as one would expect in a performative process.[14] These reasons, however, neglect the complex performative

---

[13] Sontag writes, "The sales pitch for the first Kodak, in 1888, was: 'You press the button, we do the rest.' The purchaser was guaranteed that the picture would be 'without any mistake'" (S, 53).

[14] It is interesting that in contrast to the art of painting, whose noun has a gerund form suggesting action over time, photography does not. Although we do use the verb "to photograph," we more often speak of "taking/making a photograph" or "taking a picture."

process that occurs *before* the shutter release and the camera's ensuing mechanism of producing the photographic image. But that prior process – involving the mise-en-scène performative activity of the photographer and the posing subject – is necessary for achieving the desired optical image in the camera lens that one then seeks to fix in the photographic image.

The fact that this performative process is ontologically complex and difficult to demarcate in its experiential dimensions provides further reasons for its neglect. The process is complex in that it involves the action and thought of both the photographer and the subject. It is difficult to define not only because it involves the elusive experiential flow of these two subjectivities but also because its physical actions of positioning and posing are typically performed without a formal script or scenario that defines the mise-en-scène, clearly demarcating its essential components and structure.[15] Moreover, as an experiential event, the performance is transient and cannot, strictly speaking, be perfectly repeated, if we admit that the subject's expression and state of consciousness (if not also the photographer's posture and feelings) will always change in some way, even if only through the recognition that one is repeating the mise-en-scène of a prior shooting. Although the photograph documents in some way the performative process through which it is engendered, it only documents a particular moment in that process and does so from a particular angle and in terms of its visual qualities. But the performative process itself includes also other sensory, semantic, and affective qualities that have aesthetic import and whose resources for aesthetic experience in photography should not be ignored.

Still another likely reason for such neglect is that the photographer and the subject – who are the best (and often the only) candidates for observing and appreciating the performative process – may be too absorbed in performing the process to pay proper attention to its aesthetic qualities and potential. Because our powers of consciousness are limited, the efficacy of actions is often harmed if we also pay distinct reflexive attention to the precise feelings we have or qualities we experience in performing

---

[15] One structural issue of demarcation is when the performative process begins. Clearly, the photographer can plan the background setting, the camera equipment, and the desired poses or outfit of the subject well before he meets with the subject at the chosen photographic scene. This means that the performative process can begin without the photographic target or subject being present, even though some such subject will always be implied.

those actions. So, it is understandable for photographer and subject to execute the performative process without thematizing its actions and qualities in explicit, reflective consciousness, even if they implicitly feel them and use them to guide and inspire their performance.

If such "parsimony of consciousness" is a psychological commonplace, it has an analogue or corollary in the familiar notion of aesthetic distance; namely, that a certain psychological distance or detachment from an object or event aids the appreciation of its aesthetic features. When one is in the performative moment, one is by definition very close to it; when one is looking at a photograph, one is by definition distanced from the real moment taken by the photograph, a moment that has already passed or died. "Aesthetic distance seems built into the very experience of looking at photographs," writes Sontag (S, 21). For such reasons, she and Roland Barthes link photography very closely with death. "All photographs are *momento mori*," Sontag claims. "To take a photograph is to participate in another person's (or thing's) mortality... Precisely by slicing out this moment and freezing it, all photographs testify to time's relentless melt"(S, 15). For Barthes, because the photograph presents "the absolute past of the pose," it constitutes an "image which produces Death while trying to preserve life" (Ba, 96, 92).

The history of photography's theoretical reception provides two other reasons for neglect of its art of performative process. From the outset, photography was seen as an analogue and rival to the art of painting. If Baudelaire described "the photographic industry [as] the refuge of every would-be painter, every painter too ill-endowed or too lazy to complete his studies," and thus "art's most mortal enemy," others defended photography for liberating painting from the duty of mimetic exactness that the photograph could more easily and better provide instead.[16] As painting is grouped with the nontemporal, nonperformative arts, whose end product is a flat object portraying a two-dimensional image and is immediately grasped without unfolding in time, so photography (through association with painting) came to be identified entirely with its two-dimensional

[16] See Charles Baudelaire, "The Salon of 1859," in *Art in Paris, 1845–1862*, trans. Jonathan Mayne (London: Phaidon, 1965), 153–154. Delacroix offered early praise of photography for its benefits to painting in providing a far clearer vision of real objects than drawing could, while Weston in the following century argued that photography was a great gift to painting by relieving it of "public demands" for "representation," by making "realistic painting superfluous," so painting could focus on other goals than exact representation. See Edward Weston, "Photography – Not Pictorial," *Camera Craft*, 37 (1930), 313–320.

end product or photograph as object, while its performative, temporal dimension was neglected.

We should recall, however, that photography's early history had strong links to theatre as well as to painting. Daguerre, an influential photography pioneer in Paris, "was running a panorama theater animated by light shows and movements in the Place du Château" when he began his photographic work (Ba, 31), while Baudelaire condemned photography for "committing a double sacrilege and insulting at one and the same time the divine art of painting and the noble art of the actor."[17] To dismiss photography's performative, dramatizing process as not really belonging to photography per se but instead pertaining merely to theater is not only wrong historically; it errs conceptually in presuming that photographic art exists in a pure form, unmarked by other arts that helped engender it.

Walter Benjamin's influential views on photography further contribute to theory's ignoring the aesthetics of its performative process while focusing on the photograph as the sole site for photography's aesthetic experience. Benjamin (whom Sontag describes as "photography's most original and important critic," S, 76) argued that photography's epoch-making transformation of art through mechanical reproduction involved changing art's essential nature from cult value to exhibition value. If art originally emerged from "magic" and religious ritual, "with ceremonial objects destined to serve in a cult," whose transcendent quality imbued artworks with an elevated sense of "aura" and "unique existence," then photography (as "the first truly revolutionary means of reproduction") "emancipates the work of art from its parasitical dependence on ritual" and "the unique value of the 'authentic' work" that has its role in ritual or cultic use; for "to ask for the [one] 'authentic' print makes no sense" (IL, 220, 221, 224, 225).

Art's essential nature, Benjamin argues, was therefore transformed from emphasizing "cult value" (where the work could serve effectively even when hidden from view but recognized as being kept in its hallowed place) to instead emphasizing the "exhibition value of the work," because the work's "fitness for exhibition increased" through photography's new

---

[17] See Baudelaire, *Art in Paris*, 154. Barthes links photography to theatre not in terms of the aesthetics of experiential process, but through "the singular intermediary... of Death." Just as "the first actors separated themselves from the community by playing the role of the Dead" (a theme he sees continued in the make-up and masks of traditional theatre), so "the Photograph... is a figuration of the motionless and made-up face beneath which we see the dead" (Ba, 31–32).

powers of "mechanical reproduction" (IL, 225). What gets widely exhibited through such mechanical reproduction is the photographic print (or now, ever increasingly, the digital image); so if art has essentially lost its function as ritual (which is a performative process) and is instead constituted by an "absolute emphasis on its exhibition value" (ibid.), then photography should be identified with the photograph and thus its performative process should be neglected as irrelevant or anachronistic.

Despite the obvious force of this argument, there remains a distinctive ritualistic element in photography. Many ritual events (weddings, graduations, baptisms, conference meetings, award ceremonies, and so on) include the taking of posed pictures that serve not simply to recall the event in future times but to mark out and heighten the current moment as one worth savoring in present experience, by putting that moment in a formal frame or mise-en-scène that dramatizes its qualitative presence and meaning. Though serving as the relentless motor of exhibition value, photography still displays a ritual dimension of performative, dramatizing process. Is it mere coincidence that contemporary cultures still strongly shaped by rich aesthetic traditions of ritual (such as Japan's) display an especially strong tendency to perform the process of taking photographs with a dedication and style suggestive of ritual performance?

Moreover, a closer look at Benjamin's views on photography reveals that he indeed recognized the photograph's power to maintain art's auratic "cult value," for instance in "the cult of remembrance of loved ones, absent or dead" (IL, 226). In an earlier, less familiar, essay explicitly devoted to photography, he insists on this "magical value" and "auratic appearance," affirming that the portrait subjects of "early photography" indeed "had an aura about them." But this was destroyed when photography was "invaded on all sides by businessmen" who, "more concerned with eventual saleability than with understanding," pandered to "changing lights of fashion" and reduced the experienced time and absorption of posing toward the momentary "snapshot." Benjamin also praises early photography for the way it required its subjects "to live inside rather than outside the moment" of the photographic shoot. "During the long duration of these shots they grew as it were into the picture and in this way presented an extreme opposite to the figures on a snapshot." And this absorption of the subject, Benjamin further suggests, had a counterpart in the photographer's absorption and his ability to make his subjects feel comfortably "at home," for example by deploying the camera with "discreet reserve."[18] One gets the impression that such photography provided a profound, sustained experience of performative process, and that such an experience could still be available today if one only took the time, care, and effort to develop this dimension of photographic art.

IV

I had ignored the aesthetics of photography as a somatically performative and dramatic process until a Parisian artist, Yann Toma, asked me to pose for his work in the photographic genre he calls Radiant Flux. In this genre, Toma tries to capture and visually represent the invisible aura of the person posing for him, an aura he conceives and perceives as a temporally changing energetic force emanating from the person's body. To perform this photographic work, Toma has the person pose in a totally dark setting, typically indoors for better control but sometimes outside at night. After positioning his camera on a tripod, adjusting it to a special setting for the long exposure, and aiming it at the photographic subject, Toma – who is dressed in black so as to make himself less visible and holding a hand lamp (or sometimes two different hand lamps, one in each hand) – releases the shutter and approaches the posed subject, seeking to sense the subject's aura and trace it with the light of his lamps.[19] To do so, he hovers very close to the subject's body, dancing rapidly and nimbly around it, with his lamps energetically whirling about

---

[18] Walter Benjamin, "A Short History of Photography," trans. Stanley Mitchell, *Screen* 13 (1972): 7, 8, 17, 18, 19, 24. It is important to remember that Benjamin also advocated photography's crucial transformative value in areas beyond the reproduction and creation of artworks for aesthetic enjoyment. In particular, he celebrated its cognitive power to reveal things that are concealed in our ordinary (non-technologically aided) consciousness; for example, through photography's use of special lenses, methods of enlargement, or simply its freezing of a visual moment whose details can never be observed in the rapid flow of ordinary visual experience. The camera can "capture transitory and secret pictures" that the unaided eye cannot see and that can be used both for scientific and ethical-political purposes; for instance, "to uncover guilt and name the guilty in [its] pictures," Benjamin insists. "Photography makes aware for the first time the optical unconscious, just as psychoanalysis discloses the instinctual unconscious" (ibid., 7, 25). Similar statements about photography (including film) can be found in "The Work of Art in the Age of Mechanical Reproduction," such as the photograph's use in "establishing evidence," and thus its "hidden political significance" (IL, 220). In contrast to both cult value and exhibition value, we could name this its "cognitive, revelatory value." Such cognitive value can, of course, also have aesthetic and artistic significance.

[19] Although he sometimes uses a digital camera, Toma prefers film photography, his camera of choice being a Zeiss Pentacon 6, deploying the "B setting" of manual shutter control that allows one manually to control the time the shutter is open and the film is exposed.

the body's contours in their attempt to track the auratic energy that the artist senses.

Toma needs to move swiftly, not only to catch the moving, changing flow of the person's auratic energy but also to ensure that only the stationary posing subject and the tracing of the lights (but not the artist's body or the lamps tracing them) will be captured on film. He relies on his background in dance to perform this act of rapid and proximate twirling, with both aesthetic grace and attentive care, so as not to frighten, distract, or accidentally strike his subject. After a burst of such energetic swirling (whose duration depends on what he feels, but, in my experience, usually lasted less than a minute), Toma returns to the tripod and closes the shot. He then catches his breath for another sortie. The photograph that emerges portrays the posing subject surrounded by the lines of light created by the trajectory of Toma's hand-held, moving lamps.

In thus tracing the subject's aura, Toma is drawing or painting with light; and this indeed is the root meaning of photography, for etymologically "photo" derives from the Greek word for light, while the Greek verb γράφειν (*graphein*) means to draw, paint, or write. Man Ray was the first known photographer to use this technique of light drawing in his series called "Space Writing" from 1935. Pablo Picasso gave the technique worldwide fame in 1949, when *Life Magazine* photographer Gjon Mili published some pictures of him making images in the air with a small flashlight in a dark room.[20] Toma's work distinctively deploys this technique to probe and portray the elusive quality of personal aura or energy, thus enlisting his art to render vividly visible what is normally invisible.

Occasionally, Toma has his subjects pose in a gold body stocking rather than ordinary clothes. This unitard, he believes, renders the aura more perceptible not only by magnifying both its own energy and the effect of Toma's tracing light but also by revealing the soma's lines and subtle energetic qualities more directly and transparently.[21] With its radical departure from ordinary apparel, the gold body stocking, moreover, effectively marks the photographic situation as genuinely special, dramatizing and defamiliarizing it to create for the photographic subject a new look and feel that can create new energies and a new sense of identity. Although at first extremely reluctant to put that unitard on, I later realized it was an

---

[20] Some of these images, originally published in *Life* (January 1949) are available on the Web at http://www.life.com/image/50695728/in-gallery/24871#index/0.

[21] For such reasons, Toma has also worked with nude subjects.

essential part of the performative process and mise-en-scène that made our photography collaboration such a memorable aesthetic experience. I conclude now by noting the significant aesthetic dimensions and qualities of that experience in terms of key elements of the photographic situation articulated above.

1. The setting for our photography session was carefully chosen to heighten its aesthetic quality and meaning. The Abbey of Royaumont – founded in 1228 by Saint Louis, King of France, and used by the Cistercian monks until the French Revolution – is situated in the beautiful countryside of the Val d'Oise, about 30 kilometers north of Paris. Surrounded by streams, forests, and glorious wheat fields, its public section is now primarily devoted to prominent programs in the arts. It is philosophically famous for having hosted, in 1958, an important first conference between the leading representatives of analytic philosophy (such as Austin, Ryle, Quine, Strawson, and Ayer) and major French philosophers, including Maurice Merleau-Ponty. The conference papers were subsequently published by Minuit as *La philosophie analytique*, the book that first introduced analytic philosophy to French readers (and whose first essay was by my Oxford supervisor, J.O. Urmson). As an analytically trained philosopher striving to blend analytic and French thinking to develop a new style of cosmopolitan pragmatism (and as an author with Minuit), I had long been interested in visiting the Abbey. My first visit there (in August 2009) was, however, not to lecture in philosophy but to teach a three-day workshop in practical somaesthetics to a group of professional choreographers and dancers.[22] It was my very first invitation to teach somaesthetics to dancers (who have been a major inspiration for my aesthetic thinking), and this gave the Abbey a special personal meaning for me. But Yann Toma's connections to Royaumont were much deeper. A close friend of the owner of the Abbey's private quarters, he was also the designer of a geyser art installation for its central cloister between the Abbey's private and public wings. Having met there by chance during my dance workshop visit, Toma and I enthusiastically agreed that the Abbey's rooms and gardens would provide a wonderful setting for our photographic encounter between Radiant Flux and somaesthetics, and we settled on a weekend in mid-June (2010), when the Abbey's fragrant beauty and magical atmosphere would be especially energizing.

---

[22] For video clips of that workshop, see https://sites.google.com/site/somaesthetics/home/video-clips/.

The delicious outdoor scents of pine and roses lingered in my sensorium and imagination, intensifying the dramatic contrast between the glorious June sunshine and the blackened, musty, shuttered Abbey chamber into which Toma led me, then enclosed me for the photographic shoot. This experiential passage from bright beauty to dark sublimity evoked a transition into an excitingly magical world of artistic creation, one that demanded the askesis of confinement and deprivation of light, but also the attentive sharpening of my other senses as my vision struggled in the blackness to see how Toma was setting up his camera to capture my inner somatic radiance in this cell of obscurity. This preparation for the first afternoon shoot was thus already an experience rich in aesthetic qualities and meanings, especially those emerging from the dramatic contrasts of darkness and light, inside and outside. The aesthetics of setting involves not only space but also time. Crossing the medieval cloister for our post-midnight séance in the same Abbey chamber provided its own special aesthetic feelings of eeriness and sublimity, as did the intoxicating blend of fatigue with creative excitement in working through the night.

2. What turns a mere setting into a photographic mise-en-scène or situation is the presence of a camera intended and aimed for use. It is also the camera that likewise transfigures an ordinary person into a photographic subject. Knowing the camera's power to make a permanent and widely reproducible image, the person at whom the camera is directed instinctively recomposes her image, transforms her expression or posture, and typically arrests her movement in order to strike an effective pose. She stylizes herself, even if only minimally and barely self-consciously, for the camera. Barthes laments this posing effect as a betrayal of personal identity, as the objectifying of a subject, as the transformation of an indefinable essence of lived, inner identity into a frozen external image that traps and stifles his felt flow of subjectivity. But the problem here (as Barthes almost seems to recognize) may be that he takes himself or his identity too seriously and essentialistically. With a more creative, fluid attitude, one can see the camera's invitation to pose as an opportunity to create a new look, a new posture, a new element in the construction of the self whose identity is not a fixed essence but an ongoing project whose continuous construction can either reinforce habitual modes of being or creatively seek new ones.

Though I suffer something like Barthes' unease in posing for the standard headshots desired by most institutions and news media, Toma's project of art photography to manifest a new dimension of self – an energetic aura never before revealed – proved instead extremely liberating. To find this new self, I should open myself to creative self-fashioning, to experiment with different poses, expressions, attitudes; and the special situation of art photography provides a circumscribed, protected stage to try out such experiments and then resume one's habitual modes of being and self-presentation, if one prefers them (or requires them) for dealing with the needs of everyday life. The setting up of the camera on the tripod was part of the ritual of creating that special transformative space of photographic art, just as the click of the shutter release ritually signaled the beginning of each aura-probing sortie and then its conclusion. I could enjoy the rhythmic punctuation of those clicks as an important musical element that also helped shape an essentially silent aesthetic experience, for they indicated when I should keep my posture firmly fixed in the pose and when I could release it to assume another. Our agreed protocol was to refrain from conversation during the shootings (so as to reduce the "noise" that could interfere with nonverbal somatic communication) and instead allow the posings and probing sorties to be guided freely by the quality and direction of the experience that we shared and improvised together.

3. If the camera was an essential ritual prop for liberating my sense of self to assume new expressive forms and attitudes, transfiguring me from an ordinary person to an artistically stylized subject, then so indeed was the gold-colored body stocking. Although wearing it posed a multiple challenge, it ultimately made me into a much more versatile and liberated poser, paving the path to forging new looks, new feelings, and new identities partly by making it extremely hard to feel my familiar everyday self.[23] The golden unitard empowered me to enjoy the aesthetic experience of imaginative role playing through costumes, the kind of aesthetic play of make-believe that children enjoy but that I had long ago forgotten. This playful creative energy also empowered me artistically to take a more active role in the photographic mise-en-scène. So (on the second day of shooting) having grown painfully tired of posing

---

[23] Besides the psychological barrier of displaying my sixty-year-old philosopher's figure in a revealing skin-tight garment designed for lithe young dancers, there was also the physical challenge of squeezing into its extremely snug dimensions. If alchemists since the Middle Ages have sought the legendary philosopher's stone that could transmute base metal into gold, then the medieval Royaumont Abbey became a crucible of artistic alchemy with an ordinary philosopher transmuted into a golden work of art, although surely not one to be admired for its beauty.

motionless in the blackened closed cell, I suddenly skipped out of the room and down the long corridor and staircase to burst blithely into the sunny courtyard, while Yann hurried after me, grabbing his camera to capture me in movement and in different light. When residents of the Abbey discovered me in the body stocking, they affectionately dubbed me the Man in Gold (*L'homme en or*), a fictional aesthetic identity I have happily adopted in my ongoing work with Toma, which has evolved into a special series of SOMAFLUX photographs and some films with the Man in Gold.

4. If my aesthetic experience as photographic subject was rich in the pleasures of creative participation (not only of self-stylizing through posing but of reshaping the precise setting or scenario of the photographic shoot), it was further enriched by the aesthetic appreciation of Toma's art of movement; the agile, smooth control of his swiftly twirling body and waving hand-held lamps as they circled my soma in tracing its aura in graceful, supple lines. The aesthetic appreciation of this movement was remarkably transmodal: While his black-clad body was still somewhat visible at close quarters and illuminated by his lamps, I could also feel it in its energetic movement around me, just as I could feel the waving light as well as see it. I could hear his bodily efforts through his heavy breathing and the sound of his hurried steps; I could sense his movement through the smell and touch of his breath and clothes as he moved so closely to the contours of my body that he occasionally made unintentional contact with it. There was also the proprioceptive feeling of my changes of muscular tension and adjustments of posture as Toma moved about my somatic kinesphere. From my own sensory experience, I could also imaginatively project Toma's somatic sensations of kinesthesis and proprioception. Once I gained confidence in his skill and method, I would sometimes close my eyes to heighten my aesthetic focus on the non-visual appreciation of Toma's dance, in which my body felt as if it were being massaged and not just drawn by light and movement. I know that Toma, too, intensely enjoys his own aesthetic experience of his drawing dance of light.

But in the performative photographic process that we shared, it is wrong to think that the photographer's aesthetic experience and the posing subject's can be neatly separated. Among the most powerful and inspiring aesthetic dimensions of our performative process was the nonverbal, somatic communication between us; the way we reciprocally sensed and responded to each other's energy. As the work progressed, I learned to understand not only the movements Toma made with his lamps and body but also the artistic intentions and sensibility these movements expressed, while he was obviously fully absorbed in understanding me, in feeling and responding to my energy, which in turn inspired my trust to give myself more fully to the experience of his understanding and to seek to understand him more. This shared experience of common exploration and dialogical experimentation had its own auratic quality of aesthetic co-creation that transformed us both. Thus, as Toma probed and traced my energy he also reshaped it with his own, while conversely reshaping his own energy by probing and processing mine. It was therefore fitting that on the last sortie of each session, he would finally stop to pose next to me, moving only his arms to manipulate the lights and to trace the aura he felt of his own body next to mine, intentionally making himself part of the photographic target whose energy he was making manifest, his body appearing like mine on the photographic image of that last exposure.[24]

However, neither Toma nor I were much concerned with looking at those images at the time (though some of them were digitally available to us). We were fully absorbed in enjoying the aesthetic experience of making the photograph, the dramatic play of photography as performative process.[25] Invited to write for the catalogue of a photography biennale,

---

[24] This complexity problematizes the conventional presumption of photography's transparency – its direct, veridical rendering of the person or object photographed. Toma's work challenges the common idea that photography – through its automatic mechanism – simply presents what that object is rather than creatively interpreting or representing it through a particular perspective or light. In Toma's photography, what is the photographed object? The person photographed; the person at a particular moment from a particular angle under certain conditions of light; that person's momentary changing (and normally invisible) aura; that person and her momentary aura along with the energy and movement traces that the artist has painted with light (which are visibly in the photographic image); or all of those things plus the invisible body and lamps of the artist who paints those traces (or also his visible body in those cases where the artist remains in one place too long to sustain his invisibility in the photographic image)?

[25] This dramatic performative process should be distinguished from the sort of theatricality that critics like Michael Fried criticize and oppose to absorption. Such theatricality involves a dominant orientation or appeal to an audience outside the dramatic scene or action, a desire to engage or interest that audience, instead of being fully absorbed in the action itself. Fried develops this line of thought from Diderot's views on theater and has applied them first to painting and then, more recently, to photography. See Michael Fried, *Absorption and Theatricality: Painting and Beholder in the Age of Diderot* (Chicago: University of Chicago Press, 1980); and *Why Photography Matters as Art as Never before*, cited earlier. But Toma and I were totally absorbed in our own dramatic interaction rather than thinking of playing to an audience, even an imagined one who might eventually look at the photographic images that emerged from our work of artistic exploration and communicative expression.

I initially produced an essay about this work that was so absorbed with the rich aesthetic experience of the photographic process that I failed to mention any of the images that resulted from it, until the curator asked me to refer to at least one of them.[26] I happily complied, realizing the error of neglecting the aesthetics of the photographic image because of the aesthetic appeal of its engendering process. I hope, however, this essay will convince readers that the latter should not be neglected because of our interest in the former. Photography is a mixed art, where aesthetic pluralism is advisable.[27]

---

[26] The biennale referred to is Le Mois de la Photo à Montréal 2011, and the essay, "A Philosopher in Darkness and in Light," is published (bilingually) in Anne-Marie Ninacs (ed.), *Lucidité. Vues de l'intérieur/Lucidity. Inward Views: Le Mois de la Photo à Montréal 2011* (Montréal: Le Mois de la Photo à Montréal, 2011), 210–219; 280–288. A few of Toma's photographs of our Royaumont session have also been published as part of a French interview article on my work in somaesthetics, see http://www.tales-magazine.fr/style-harmony-life-vision/richard_shusterman. Three other photographs and three short films of the Man in Gold, from my continuing collaboration with Toma, were exhibited at *Aesthetic Transactions: Pragmatist Philosophy through Art and Life*, an art show I curated at the Michel Journiac Gallery in Paris (May 24-June 6, 2012). For some of these images and further analysis of my work with Toma (and other artists in the show, including ORLAN, Carsten Höller, Tatiana Trouvé, Pan Gongkai, Luca Del Baldo, and Thecla Schiphorst), see the title essay I wrote for the show's catalogue, *Aesthetic Transactions: Pragmatist Philosophy through Art and Life* (Paris: Galerie Michel Journiac/L'éclat, 2012).

[27] I suspect that other arts are similarly mixed and invite an aesthetic experience of their creative process. Portrait painting, for example, should provide something analogous to the sort of performative process that I have described in photography.

12

Asian *Ars Erotica* and the Question of Sexual Aesthetics

I

On a recent visit to Vienna's opulent Kunsthistorisiches Museum, I unexpectedly encountered a genre painting that expressed, with art's most powerful immediacy, a central theme of this chapter. The theme is philosophy's persistent pose of resistance to the seductive aesthetics of sex, and the painting, *The Steadfast Philosopher* by Gerrit van Honthorst (1592–1656), depicts the attempted seduction of a diligent philosopher by a lovely young woman with fully exposed breasts.[1]

The philosopher in the painting is a manly, moustached figure in the prime of life, seated at his desk with a pile of books to his right and an open book directly in front of him. He has apparently been interrupted in the act of writing, since his right hand holds a feathered-quill pen, while his left arm is raised forward with its fingers spread in a gesture of "stop," as if to ward off both physically and symbolically the advances and attractions of the seductress who stands near the desk and seems to be removing the wrap covering his left shoulder and tugging gently on the upper sleeve of his shirt. The woman's blue dress and undergarments hang about her waist, while under a matching blue cap (whose feather corresponds nicely to the philosopher's quill), her open-mouthed smile and intent eyes are invitingly directed toward the philosopher, whose gaze is turned away, his lips pursed and his face flushed red (whether from mere embarrassment or other passions). In the chiaroscuro style of the painting, the woman's confident, open, naked posture is bathed in painterly light, while the philosopher's figure contrastingly shrinks defensively toward the shadows. Not only uninterested in engaging in the

[1] It was painted in 1623, and a digital image of it has been posted at http://www.fau.edu/humanitieschair/Steadfast%20Philosopher%20medium2.jpg.

pleasurable beauties of sexual seduction, he also seems, with his averted gaze, resolutely unwilling to face up to the reality of their attractions – personifying philosophy's willful, fearful blindness to the aesthetics of erotic experience, a blindness that the painter van Honthorst seems to portray with some critical irony.[2]

If the painting reminds us of the familiar ancient quarrel between philosophy and the mimetic arts, it should also recall philosophy's traditional hostility and neglect regarding erotic arts, extending back to Socrates' condemnation of sex as "a savage and tyrannical master," and despite his provocative self-definition as "a master of erotics."[3] Making a case for the aesthetic potential of lovemaking means confronting the problem that modern Western philosophy has tended to define aesthetic experience by contrast to sexual experience.[4] Consider this history in brief summary.

Shaftesbury defined the contemplation of beauty as disinterested and distanced by explicitly contrasting it to sexual feelings aroused by (and in) human bodies, "a set of eager desires, wishes and hopes; no way suitable... to your rational and refined contemplation of beauty." Although "wonderful as they are," sexually attractive bodies "inspire nothing of a studious or contemplative kind. The more they are viewed, the further they are from satisfying by mere view."[5] Kant made this notion of contemplative disinterestedness a cornerstone for defining aesthetic pleasure (and judgment) in opposition to the agreeable feelings of sensuality and the satisfactions of appetite that also give pleasure. Refining still further the notion of aesthetic disinterestedness and linking it to the perception of Platonic Ideas, Schopenhauer draws the contrast of sexual and aesthetic experience still more sharply and explicitly. In "aesthetic

---

[2] The resistance of philosophers to the beauties of erotic seduction is a classic theme in the arts, exemplified by John Keats's famous poem "Lamia," where the philosopher seeks to rescue his student from the wiles of a beautiful woman who is actually a lamia (a creature with the head and breast of a woman and the lower body of a serpent and that is said to suck the blood of those it seduces). The female figure depicted by Honthorst, with her head and breast exposed but her lower body concealed, could represent such a creature.

[3] See Plato's *Republic* 329c, where Socrates confirms this condemnation, originally attributed to Sophocles; *Symposium* 198d for his self-description as a master of erotics (δεινός τὰ ἐρωτικά) and 203c–212b for his account of the philosophical quest in the erotic terms of seeking and giving birth in beauty.

[4] See Richard Shusterman, "Aesthetic Experience: From Analysis to Eros," *Journal of Aesthetics and Art Criticism* 64 (2006): 217–229.

[5] Anthony Ashley Cooper, (Third Earl of Shaftesbury), *Characteristics of Men, Manners, Opinions, Times*, ed. Lawrence Klein (Cambridge: Cambridge University Press, 1999), 319.

pleasure," we enjoy the disinterested experience of "delight in the mere knowledge of perception as such, in contrast to the will"; "aesthetic contemplation" is "pure will-less knowing and with the knowledge, which necessarily appears therewith, of the Ideas." Sexual experience instead involves the "strongest" of life's interests – "the will-to-live" – and is cognitively deficient and distorted by this insistent will. For Schopenhauer, "the genitals are the real *focus* of the will, and are therefore the opposite pole to the brain, the representative of knowledge."[6]

We saw, in Chapter 7, how Burke is an exception to this antisexual aesthetic tradition, and how Nietzsche derided its prudish naïveté: "When our estheticians tirelessly rehearse, in support of Kant's view, that the spell of beauty enables us to view even *nude* female statues 'disinterestedly' we may be allowed to laugh a little at their expense. The experiences of artists in this delicate matter are rather more 'interesting'; certainly Pygmalion was not entirely devoid of esthetic feeling."[7] However, even if Nietzsche astutely admits "the possibility that the peculiar sweetness and richness proper to the esthetic condition may stem from its sensual ingredient," he still refuses to affirm that erotic experience of sexual activity can be aesthetic. Insisting that the "the emergence of the esthetic condition... transmutes [sexual feeling] in such a way that it is no longer experienced as a sexual incentive," he follows the antisexual aesthetic tradition by warning that actual sexual activity is detrimental for aesthetic creation and recommending "sexual continence" for artists and philosophers: "Every artist is familiar with the adverse effect which sexual intercourse has during times of great intellectual tension and preparation. The strongest and instinctually surest among them do not need to learn this by experience, since their 'maternal' instinct has from the start made its strict dispositions, putting all animal instincts at the service of that one great end, so that the lesser energy is absorbed by the greater" and directed to higher artistic goals.[8] The erotic play of human sexual behavior is thus relegated to the realm of mere animal instincts and deprived of aesthetic recognition.

Contrasting sexual and aesthetic experience has become so deeply entrenched in our Western philosophical tradition that the authoritative *Oxford Companion to Aesthetics* even insists that one of the four major

---

[6] Schopenhauer, *The World as Will and Representation*, trans. E.F.J. Payne, vol. 1 (New York: Dover, 1958), 200–202, 330–331.
[7] Friedrich Nietzsche, *The Genealogy of Morals in The Birth of Tragedy and The Genealogy of Morals*, trans. Francis Golffing (New York: Doubleday, 1956), 238–239.
[8] Ibid., 247.

desiderata for a theory of aesthetic experience is explaining the difference between such experience and the experience of sex and drugs.[9] But if we put aside philosophical prejudice and recall our most gratifying sexual performances, do we not recognize that some such experiences can be truly aesthetic? Many of us, I sincerely hope, have had experiences of lovemaking that are rich in beauty, intensity, pleasure, and meaning, that display harmonies of structure and developing form, and that deeply engage both thought and feeling, stimulating body, mind, and soul. The definition of aesthetic experience is, of course, very much contested, for there are divergent, competing conceptions of that rich and valued concept. But a careful analysis of the concept of aesthetic experience reveals that the most prominent features attributed to such experience seem also attributable to certain sexual experiences.

One famously defining feature of aesthetic experience is its intrinsic value, the appreciation of the experience for its own sake. Sexual experience can certainly be pursued, enjoyed, and highly valued for its own sake rather than for its role in producing children, in acquiring material or social gains, or for forging psychological bonds of intimacy. In this sense of being appreciated for itself rather than for its instrumentality in serving other interests or ulterior motives, lovemaking could even be said to exhibit disinterested albeit desiring enjoyment. (Disinterestedness, of course, is another feature traditionally attributed to aesthetic experience, though one increasingly contested). Another key feature of aesthetic experience is pleasure, which takes different forms. Sex is pleasurable both in the Aristotelian sense of enjoying a fulfilling, absorbing, undistracted activity and in the sense of the attendant pleasurable sensations that sexual activity gives. Just as aesthetic experience is often characterized by its firmly felt phenomenological quality, intentionality, and meaning, so lovemaking is subjectively savored for its phenomenological quality but also intentionally directed at an object (typically another human subject) that structures the erotic experience, shapes its quality, and gives it important dimensions of meaning commensurate with the properties and significance of that object.[10] Unity

---

[9] Gary Iseminger, "Aesthetic Experience" in Jerrold Levinson (ed.), *The Oxford Handbook of Aesthetics* (Oxford: Oxford University Press, 2003), 99–116.

[10] In some erotic experience, the intentional object might be more accurately defined not as simply the person with whom one is erotically engaged but rather (the more inclusive structure of) the erotic episode, drama, or interactive relationship that is being shaped through one's intentional activity and in which the "particularized" object of desire (e.g., the sexual partner) is embedded. In such cases where this sense of developing

and cognitive content are other key features of aesthetic experience that can be salient in lovemaking. Providing knowledge of one's own body and mind but also those of one's sexual partners, the sexual act typically displays a distinctive unity both of coherence and completion, a sense of things developing consistently and powerfully toward a fulfilling consummation, just as aesthetic experience. Like great aesthetic experiences, a peak sexual experience will stand out distinctively from the flow of ordinary humdrum experience and can involve a wide range of affect, some of which is unrivalled in its intensity. Moreover, as aesthetic experience involves not only dynamic doing but also more passive undergoing, so sexual experience displays both moments of active self-assertive grasping and self-surrendering absorption.

If human sexual performance can be significantly aesthetic, then we can think of the *ars erotica* as art in a truly aesthetic sense rather than simply in the general (nonaesthetic) meaning of the word "art" as any organized expertise, skill, or branch of learning. Such a reorientation not only has value in expanding our theoretical perspectives on aesthetics and erotics while challenging the presumption that art must be distinguished from performances in "real life," it could also enrich, in a most practical and pleasurable way, the actual aesthetic experience of our lives by enhancing the artistry and appreciation of our erotic activity. This in turn could deepen our appreciation of the aesthetic potential of other somatic practices, thus promoting further explorations in the emerging field of somaesthetics. As our Western intellectual tradition seems to offer very little guidance or encouragement in sexual aesthetics, it seems worth exploring the Asian tradition of *ars erotica*.

II

The erotic arts of ancient China and (especially) India form the core of this study, but their distinctive character can be brought into sharper focus by examining them against the background of two interesting contemporary exceptions to Western philosophy's resistance to the aesthetics of sex. The first is a short article by the distinguished Anglo-American analytic philosopher Ronald de Sousa, who "argue[s] for the rehabilitation of certain forms of imaginative rehearsals of love in 'casual,'

> drama is very much present to consciousness and influences our activity and enjoyment, the aesthetic character of erotic experience is more likely to be clearly exhibited and appreciated.

'uncommitted,' or even commercial sex."[11] His provocative claim is motivated by an equally bold assertion that "the project of romantic love is in essence incoherent or impossible" (LT, 483) because such love involves conflicting commitments to both consummation and the impossibility of possession, to Platonic idealization of what is loved and anti-Platonic affirmation that it is a concrete particular, to unique novelty and the desire for permanence that instead involves repetition of consummation with the beloved.

Given the alleged impossibility of realizing such romantic love, de Sousa argues that individuals committed to its ideal (and seeking consolation for its perceived impossibility) can seek satisfaction in what he calls "the theater of love," which "mixes real sex and aesthetic imagination" (LT, 489). In contrast to the theatrical traditions of marriage ceremonies (which de Souza claims are essentially opposed to erotic love because they highlight social and family relations), "the theatrical ceremonies" he recommends are sexual encounters that "consist in *staging the erotic gestures of love* with a view to pleasure and an *aesthetic* creation or re-creation of the poignancy of love, of the impossibility of possession and the irreplaceability of time" (LT, 485). "Such ceremonies," he insists, "require some of the same qualities of art and of the best kinds of nonerotic love – integrity, honesty, intense attention, generosity, imagination, and a capacity to take pleasure in the pleasure of the other. It can therefore be demanding in the sense in which all aesthetic experiences can be demanding. Nevertheless it can remain primarily an aesthetic experience, a piece of theater, a form of play, because both parties agree to keep the experience of romantic love confined inside a kind of frame isolated from the rest of their lives and expectations" (ibid.).

Unfortunately, de Souza does not adequately elucidate the dimensions in which such sexual experiences are aesthetic. The required qualities he mentions clearly refer to qualities demanded of the persons engaged in the ceremonies rather than aesthetic qualities of the experience of such ceremonies. His assertion of the aesthetic status of these sexual engagements seems to rest wholly on their theatrical nature, and their theatrical nature seems to rests almost entirely on the idea of some sort of fictionality of simulation and separation from life. The aesthetics of his theatre of love is constituted by "the self-conscious *playing out* of an

---

[11] Ronald de Sousa, "Love as Theater," in Robert Solomon and Kathleen Higgins (eds.), *The Philosophy of (Erotic) Love* (Lawrence: University of Kansas Press, 1991), 477–491; hereafter LT; this citation from 478.

emotion relatively insulated from the rest of reality" (LT, 486). Although such theatre is not explicitly and fictionally "scripted" as most plays are, de Souza argues it is implicitly scripted by our past performances – and, one could add, by our fantasies. Further its fictional, simulational essence, he assumes, is already established by the fact that the romantic love it expresses cannot be real. With an obliging nod "to the aesthetics and ethics of prostitution," de Souza concludes: "If the conscious simulation of love bolstered by the power of sex is a valuable form of theater, why should some people not make a profession of it?" (LT, 488).

I shall not pause here to examine the contested reality of romantic love as de Souza defines it, nor to insist that there are other notions of romantic love worth exploring that do not seem caught in the web of contradictions that make him think the whole notion is incoherent. Nor shall I belabor the point that reality need not imply permanence and consistency, so that romantic love can be real even if transient and conflicted. Instead, I wish to underline how his defense of the aesthetics of sex is essentially committed to the idea that sexual performance is aesthetic only insofar that it involves a theatrical fiction or simulation of something else (i.e., an impossible ideal or feeling of romantic love). It is not aesthetic because (or in terms) of the intentional and appreciated aesthetic qualities of the sexual performance as a real event that is deeply embedded in (rather than "isolated from") the rest of the lives and expectations of the performing lovers. This sexual aesthetics, with its double commitment to fictionality and isolation, reflects the old philosophical dogmas of contrasting art to reality and dividing aesthetics from the affairs of real life – whether practical, political, or sexual. In contesting these dogmas, pragmatist aesthetics not only makes a case for the robust role of the arts and aesthetics in the diverse currents of real life, it further argues that the very doctrine that relegates them to the realm of fictional simulations implies the regrettable counterpart and consequence that real life is robbed of artistry and beauty.[12]

A post-puritan pragmatism[13] and somaesthetics should recognize that sexual performance provides a realm of human artistry and aesthetic

---

[12] See, for example, John Dewey, *Art as Experience* (Carbondale: Southern Illinois University Press, 1987); and Richard Shusterman, *Pragmatist Aesthetics* (Oxford: Blackwell, 1992).

[13] There is not much emphasis on the erotic in the classical pragmatists, and William James even affirms, in *The Principles of Psychology* (Cambridge: Harvard University Press, 1983), 1053, the role of an "*anti-sexual instinct.*" Paul Taylor notes Dewey's neglect of the erotic and argues that Du Bois's frank recognition of sexual dimensions of self-realization usefully enriches the classical pragmatist notion of perfectionism. See Paul C. Taylor, "What's the Use of Calling Du Bois a Pragmatist?" in Richard Shusterman (ed.), *The Range of Pragmatism and the Limits of Philosophy* (Oxford: Blackwell, 2004), 95–111.

experience that can be practiced and enjoyed in real life and real love (marital or extramarital) without invoking the need for theatrical fictions. The rich potential of such real-life sexual aesthetics can be found in the ancient Asian traditions of *ars erotica*, which Michel Foucault (the second contemporary Western exception I shall consider) highlights and opposes to the *scientia sexualis* of modern Western culture.

Unlike de Souza's, Foucault's advocacy of sexual aesthetics has been extremely influential. His most prominent advocatory theorizing of sexual artistry concerns gay sex, and more particularly consensual homosexual S/M, which Foucault celebrates as "a whole new art of sexual practice which tries to explore all the internal possibilities of sexual conduct." This art, a "mixture of rules and openness," combines consensual codes (that significantly script sexual behavior) with experiments "to innovate and create variations that will enhance the pleasure of the act" by introducing novelty, variety, and uncertainty that otherwise would be lacking in the sexual act.[14] Moreover, despite its use of scripting and special fictional frames of performance (e.g., the sexual dungeon), this sexual activity is not portrayed by Foucault as isolated from the rest of one's life and subjectivity. One's formation as a sexual subject is an important part of one's thoughtful shaping of one's self in terms of one's "aesthetics of existence."[15]

Foucault's sexual theorizing was not principally inspired by the Asian erotic arts but rather by his study of ancient Greek and Roman literature on the erotic, and by his own erotic desires and activity. However, he

[14] Michel Foucault, "Sexual Choice, Sexual Act" in *Essential Works of Michel Foucault*, vol. 1 (New York: New Press, 1997), 151–152. In making his case for "aesthetic appreciation of the sexual act as such," Foucault praises gay S/M because "all the energy and imagination, which in the heterosexual relationship were channeled into courtship, now become devoted to intensifying the act of sex itself. A whole new art of sexual practice develops which tries to explore all the internal possibilities of sexual conduct." Likening the gay leather scenes in San Francisco and New York to "laboratories of sexual experimentation," Foucault claims such experimentation is strictly controlled by consensual codes, as in the medieval chivalric courts, "where strict rules of proprietary courtship were defined." "Experimentation is necessary," explains Foucault, "because the sexual act has become so easy and available... that it runs the risk of quickly becoming boring, so that every effort has to be made to innovate and create variations that will enhance the pleasure of the act." Foucault concludes, "This mixture of rules and openness has the effect of intensifying sexual relations by introducing a perpetual novelty, a perpetual tension and a perpetual uncertainty, which the simple consummation of the act lacks. The idea is also to make use of every part of the body as a sexual instrument" (ibid., 149, 151–152). For a critical analysis of Foucault's somaesthetics of sex as part of his idea of philosophy as an art of living, see Richard Shusterman, *Body Consciousness: A Philosophy of Mindfulness and Somaesthetics* (Cambridge: Cambridge University Press, 2008), ch. 1.

[15] Michel Foucault, *History of Sexuality*, vol. 2 (New York: Pantheon, 1986), 12, 89–93.

does enlist the Asian erotic arts to demonstrate the valuable importance of an alternative to our modern Western "*scientia sexualis.*"[16] In contrast to our sexual science whose discourse of truth combines the ancient tool of confession with the modern "imperative of medicalization" of sexual behavior and function, the erotic arts draw their truth "from pleasure itself, understood as a practice and accumulated as experience" (HS, 57, 68). In these arts, Foucault explains, the pleasure of erotic practice:

> is not considered in relation to an absolute law of the permitted and the forbidden, nor by reference to a criterion of utility, but first and foremost in relation to itself; it is experienced as pleasure, evaluated in terms of its intensity, its specific quality, its duration, its reverberations in the body and the soul. Moreover, this knowledge must be deflected back into the sexual practice itself, in order to shape it as though from within and amplify its effects. In this way, there is formed a knowledge that must remain secret, not because of an element of infamy that might attach to its object, but because of the need to hold it in the greatest reserve, since, according to tradition, it would lose its effectiveness and its virtue by being divulged. Consequently, the relationship to the master who holds the secrets is of paramount importance; only he, working alone, can transmit this art in an esoteric manner and as the culmination of an initiation in which he guides the disciple's progress with unfailing skill and severity. The effects of this masterful art, which are considerably more generous than the sparseness of its prescriptions would lead one to imagine, are said to transfigure the one fortunate enough to receive its privileges: an absolute mastery of the body, a singular bliss, obliviousness to time and limits, the elixir of life, the exile of death and its threats (HS, 57).

Refining, in a later interview, his views on *ars erotica* and summarizing the differences between Greek, Christian, and Chinese cultural attitudes to sexual practice in terms of the three factors of "act, pleasure, and desire," Foucault claims that in contrast to the Greeks, who focused on the act and its control as "the important element" by defining the quantity, rhythm, occasion, and circumstances of its performance, but also in contrast to the Christians who focused on desire in terms of how to fight it and extirpate its slightest roots while limiting or even avoiding pleasure when performing the act, the Chinese elevated pleasure as the highest, most valuable factor in sex. "In Chinese erotics, if one believes Van Gulik, the important element was pleasure, which it was necessary to increase,

---

[16] Michel Foucault, *History of Sexuality*, vol. 1 (New York: Pantheon, 1980), 57–71; hereafter HS.

intensify, prolong as much as possible in delaying the act itself, and to the limit of abstaining from it."[17]

As this interview indicates, Foucault's understanding of the Asian *ars erotica* rests largely on Chinese sources, particularly those compiled, translated, and analyzed by Robert van Gulik in his groundbreaking classic *Sexual Life in Ancient China*.[18] Unfortunately, he seems to have misconstrued the texts and gloss that Van Gulik provides in some important ways, which I shall presently demonstrate.

III

First, it is very misleading to characterize the classical Chinese texts of *ars erotica* in sharp contrast to sexual science and the medical approach to sex.[19] These writings (which the Chinese often described as treating "the Art of the Bedchamber" or as "handbooks of sex") were instead very much concerned and largely motivated by health issues; so much so, that when they are listed in the bibliographical sections of the anciently written histories of the various dynasties, they often appear under the heading of medical books or, when listed separately, after the medical books (SL, 71, 121, 193). Van Gulik himself repeatedly affirms that the "handbooks of sex... constituted a special branch of medical literature" because their two primary goals of sexual intercourse were focused on promoting health – that of the husband, his wife, and the child to be conceived (SL, 72).[20] "Primarily," he argues, "the sexual act was to achieve

---

[17] An English version of this interview, "On the Genealogy of Ethics: An Overview of Work in Progress," was first published in English in Herbert Dreyfus and Paul Rabinow (eds.), *Michel Foucault: Beyond Structuralism and Hermeneutics* (Chicago: University of Chicago Press, 1983), but I am citing (and translating) from the more complete French version that was revised by Foucault and published in his *Dits et Ecrits*, vol. 2: 1976–1988 (Paris: Gallimard, 2001), 1428–1450; quotations, 1441. In this interview, Foucault acknowledges that the ancient Greeks and Romans did not really have an elaborate *ars erotica* comparable to that of the Chinese (see 1434).

[18] R.H. van Gulik, *Sexual Life in Ancient China: A Preliminary Survey of Chinese Sex and Society from ca. 1500 B.C. till 1644 A.D.* (Leiden: Brill, 2003); hereafter SL.

[19] It is also worth noting that Chinese texts on the erotic arts are not a monolithic unity but rather display some variety in different historical periods and according to the different dominant philosophical ideologies that inspired their authors (for example, the more sexually liberal Daoist versus the more straight-laced Confucian). The classic texts of Indian *ars erotica* also display clear differences that reflect the different mores of different periods.

[20] Foucault's emphasis on the essential esoteric nature of these arts is also rather misleading. For many periods of China's long history, according to Van Gulik, the handbooks of sex, which were frequently illustrated, "circulated widely" and "were well known and the

the woman's conceiving," (preferably a male child) so as to perpetuate the family. "Secondly, the sexual act was to strengthen the man's vitality by making him absorb the woman's *yin* essence [held to be an invigorating power], while at the same time the woman would derive physical benefit from the stirring of her latent *yin* nature" (SL, 46).

This suggested the following twofold sexual economy: Since "a man's semen [where his *yang* force is concentrated] is his most precious possession, the source not only of his health but of his very life; every emission of semen will diminish this vital force, unless compensated by the acquiring of an equivalent amount of *yin* essence from the woman" (SL, 47). Therefore, a man's sexual activity should seek to ensure that his female partners be given full satisfaction so that he can absorb the *yin* essence that will flow from their multiple orgasms, "but he should allow himself to reach orgasm only on certain specified occasions," notably those most suitable for conceiving a child with his wife (ibid.). A plurality of wives and concubines was accordingly recommended to provide this abundance of *yin*, since relying on a single woman for multiple orgasms would eventually drain her of the *yin* essence needed both to maintain her own health (and consequent power to conceive) and to increase the health of her male partner.[21] By copulating with many women each night without reaching orgasm while saving his semen only for occasional ejaculations, the man not only increased his vitality and *yang* (i.e., male) essence, but also thereby raised the chances of conceiving a male child to perpetuate the family name.

These principles of sexual logic, explains Van Gulik, "implied that the man had to learn to prolong the coitus as much as possible without reaching orgasm; for the longer the member stays inside, the more *yin* essence the man will absorb, thereby augmenting and strengthening his vital force" (SL, 46). The sex handbooks therefore advise the man of methods to "prevent ejaculation either by mental discipline or by such physical means as compressing the seminal duct with his fingers.

---

methods given by them widely practiced" not only by esoteric specialists but "by the people in general." Handbooks began to fall into decline in the Sung period, and still more in the Ming period with its greater Confucian prudishness, but the handbooks' practices and "principles still pervaded sexual life" (SL, 79, 94, 121, 192, 228, 268).

[21] See SL, 138: "If a man continually changes the woman with whom he copulates the benefit will be great. If in one night one can copulate with more than ten women it is best. If one always copulates with one and the same woman her vital essence will gradually grow weaker and in the end she will be in no fit condition to give the man benefit. Moreover the woman herself will become emaciated."

Then his *yang*-essence, intensified by its contact with the woman's *yin* will flow upwards along the spinal column and fortify his brain and his entire system. If therefore the man limits his emissions to the days when the woman is liable to conceive, his loss of Yang [sic] essence on those occasions will be compensated by the obtaining of children perfect in body and mind" (SL, 47).[22]

Moreover, according to some of the radical Daoist-inspired texts, a man who thus preserves his semen through such *coitus reservatus* while absorbing the *yin* of many women that he brings to orgasm will not only sustain his health; he will become more youthful and age-resistant, even to the point of achieving immortality.[23] To quote one of the Tang Dynasty texts that Van Gulik supplies (whose title, *Fang-nei-pu-i*, is "freely translated as 'Healthy Sex life'"): "If one can copulate with twelve women without once emitting semen, one will remain young and handsome for ever. If a man can copulate with 93 women and still control himself, he will attain immortality" (SL, 194). Although most potent in the woman's genitalia, the invigorating flows of *yin* could also be drawn from the secretions of her mouth and breast, both in erotic foreplay and in the act of coitus itself. These secretions were often referred to as the "Medicine of the Three Peaks" (SL, 96, 283).

Coitus reservatus served another health-related function: the emotional stability and peace of mind that depends on a harmoniously managed and satisfied household of women. Already in the ancient Confucian *Book of Rites* (*Liji*), a man's sexual duty to both his wives and concubines was firmly asserted and even inscribed in strict protocols of sequence and frequency of intercourse, whose violation was "a grave offense." As the *Liji* states: "Even if a concubine is growing older, as long as she has not yet reached the age of fifty, the husband shall copulate with her once every five days. She on her part shall, when she is led to his couch, be cleanly washed, neatly attired, have her hair combed and properly done up, and wear a long robe and properly fastened house shoes" (SL, 60). These duties (apart from brief respites in periods of mourning)

---

[22] It followed from this logic that male masturbation was "forbidden [except for extreme occasions] ... and nocturnal emissions were viewed with concern." As long as it did not involve ejaculation, homosexuality was not condemned in classical Chinese culture, but nor did it form part of the ancient sexual handbooks (SL, 47, 48).

[23] In one document from the Later Han Period, we read of Daoist master who "lived to the age of over 150 years by practicing the art of having sexual intercourse with women," and that by such art "one's grey hair will turn black again and new teeth will replace those that have fallen out" (SL, 71).

only ceased when the husband "reached the age of seventy" (SL, 60). Without saving his *yang* through *coitus reservatus* and without the erotic ability to consistently give his wives and concubines real sexual (and emotional) gratification, a husband with a large household of women could easily exhaust himself without satisfying his females, thus creating a disgruntled, disorderly home whose ill repute as mismanaged "could ruin a man's reputation and break his career" (SL, 109).

It should already be clear from this brief account (and there is an overwhelming wealth of further evidence in Van Gulik) that, *pace* Foucault, the Chinese *ars erotica* were very deeply motivated by health issues and very much concerned with medical matters and sexual science (albeit not in the dominant forms of modern Western medical science). Foucault is thus wrong in highlighting pleasure as the most important aspect of China's erotic arts, since matters of health clearly trump it.[24] He is further confused in thinking that pleasure, for them, is more important than the sexual act because it is pleasure that they seek to prolong by delaying and even abstaining from the act. Instead, it is the act itself that the Chinese male seeks to prolong, so as to magnify his *yin* and *yang* powers and the salutary benefits these bring. Pleasure is indeed significant for Chinese sexual theory, but it is integrally bound up in the act and cannot be increased by being separated from it. Foucault's error seems to be in identifying the sexual act with the act of orgasm rather than the act of coitus or the broader act that we could call the entire erotic performance and that would include foreplay, coitus, and (when present) even postcoital play.

[24] Another passage from the *Fang-nei-pu-i* that emphasizes multiple partners clearly affirms that this multiplicity does not have pleasure as its highest end. "The method is to copulate on one night with ten different women without emitting semen even a single time. This is the essence of the Art of the Bedchamber. A man must not engage in sexual intercourse merely to satisfy his lust. He must strive to control his sexual desire so as to be able to nurture his vital essence. He must not force his body to sexual extravagance in order to enjoy carnal pleasure, giving free rein to his passion. On the contrary, a man must think of how the act will benefit his health and thus keep himself free from disease. This is the subtle secret of the Art of the Bedchamber." The text also discusses the method for controlling ejaculation and making its energy "ascend and benefit the brain" (SL, 193–194). A Sui Dynasty sex handbook, *Fang Nei Chi*, offers a health-oriented graduated schedule of ejaculations according to one's age and strength of constitution, ranging from strongly built fifteen year olds who can ejaculate twice a day to strong men of seventy who may ejaculate once a month; "weak ones should not ejaculate anymore at that age" (SL, 146). A different Sui Dynasty handbook, *The Ars Amatoria of Master Tung – Hsuan*, which also offers methods of controlling ejaculation, is less nuanced in prescriptions of frequency: "only emit semen two or three times in ten" acts of intercourse (SL, 132).

Though sometimes celebrating sexual pleasure as "the supreme joy" and "climax of human emotions," and affirming its embodiment of "the Supreme Way" (SL, 70, 203), classical Chinese sexual theory embedded it into the larger goals of health and good management (of self and household). The view was that sexual pleasure should be used to regulate and refine one's body, mind, and character through the ritual shaping of the rules of *ars erotica*. As one Former Han Dynasty document puts it: "'The ancients created sexual pleasure thereby to regulate all human affairs.' If one regulates his sexual pleasure he will feel at peace and attain a high age. If, on the other hand, one abandons himself to its pleasure disregarding the rules set forth in the above-mentioned treatises [i.e., the sexual handbooks] one will fall ill and harm one's very life" (SL, 70–71).

If the classical Chinese erotic arts were largely aimed at promoting practical matters such as health, does it then follow that we cannot speak of them as having aesthetic character? That misguided inference rests on the common error of assuming (because of the dogma of disinterestedness) that functionality and aesthetic quality are incompatible. The fact that religious paintings and sculptures have spiritual functions and that protest songs have political goals does not preclude them from having aesthetic value and being appreciated for their aesthetic qualities even while we appreciate their other functions. Such appreciation of functionality can even feed back into our aesthetic appreciation by adding dimensions of meaning to the aesthetic experience of these works. Intrinsic value is not inconsistent with instrumental value. We can appreciate the intrinsic taste of a meal we are eating even if we know that the meal is also nourishing us; likewise, our intrinsic enjoyment of good sex is no less in knowing that it is also good for us.

One can indeed make a case for the presence of aesthetic dimensions in the classic Chinese erotic arts, as these are described in the texts presented by Van Gulik. These aesthetic elements can be discerned in certain remarks relating to the cosmic meanings of the sexual relations between man and woman; to issues of harmonizing the couple's energies through foreplay; to the aesthetic arrangement of "the bedstead" as the stage of the erotic encounter; and to the blending of different erotic movements and pleasures, including the orchestration of different styles, depths, speed, and rhythms of the penetrating strokes of the penis. But since discussion of the aesthetic aspects of these elements is rather limited and is overwhelmingly overshadowed by the emphasis on health issues,

IV

My discussion of India's erotic arts is based on three classic texts from three different periods: the *Kama Sutra*, the *Koka Shastra*, and the *Ananga Ranga*, from, respectively, around the third, twelfth, and sixteenth centuries A.D.[25] The founding and most influential work of this tradition, the *Kama Sutra* was written in prose by a religious student, Vatsyayana, on the basis of more ancient texts (now lost) that, according to legend, stretch back to the God Shiva who, after falling in love with his own female emanation, discovered sexual intercourse and then celebrated its pleasures in many thousands of books. In contrast, the *Koka Shastra* and *Ananga Ranga* were shorter works composed in poetry; and because they were written in much later times, when Indian society was growing increasingly chaste and morally restrictive, they also differ from the *Kama Sutra* in some of their sexual attitudes or emphases. While the *Kama Sutra* was directed at a more promiscuous and wide-ranging population of lovers intent on engaging with multiple partners in both marital and extramarital sex, the *Koka Shastra* and *Ananga Ranga* were essentially addressed to husbands and their wives, aiming to promote couples' conjugal satisfaction so as to enable them to avoid the temptations of extramarital erotics. Therefore, they contain far more sexual prohibitions (relating to partners, times, and places) than the *Kama Sutra*.[26] Nonetheless, because these later works were substantially derived from the *Kama Sutra*, they

---

[25] See Richard Burton and F.F. Arbuthnot (trans.), *The Kama Sutra of Vatsyayana* (Unwin: London, 1988), hereafter KS. Besides this influential (and controversial) translation, I have consulted two others: Wendy Doniger and Sudhir Kakar (Oxford: Oxford University Press, 2003); and S.C. Upadya (Castle Books: New York, 1963). See also, Alex Comfort, (trans.), *The Koka Shastra*, with a Preface by W. G. Archer (Stein & Day: New York, 1965); hereafter KKS; and F.F. Arbuthnot and Richard Burton (ed. and trans.), *Ananga Ranga* (Medical Press: New York, 1964); hereafter AR. The dating of the *Kama Sutra* is particularly uncertain, ranging from 300 B.C. to 400 A.D., while that of the *Koka Shastra* (whose formal title is *Ratirahasya* or "Secrets of Rati") ranges from the eleventh to twelfth century, and *Ananga Ranga* from the sixteenth to the seventeenth. Besides these primary texts (and the commentary of the editions cited), my research also draws on J.J. Meyer, *Sexual Life in Ancient India*, 2 vols. (London: Kegan Paul, 2003); and S.C. Banerji, *Crime and Sex in Ancient India* (Calcutta: Naya Prokash, 1980).

[26] This is especially so with the *Ananga Ranga*, which, Archer notes, excludes more than thirty kinds of women as partners for sexual intercourse, while the *Kama Sutra* only lists two (KKS, 30–31).

essentially agree with its fundamental principles, including the aesthetic character of *ars erotica* as necessary for the proper realization of *kama* – a term that signifies not only sexual love but sensuality in general, and which together with *dharma* (connoting duty or right conduct) and *artha* (the acquiring of wealth and status through practical activity) constitute the traditionally requisite three-part way of life leading to the goal of *moksha* or liberation (KS, 102).

In making a case for the aesthetic character of Indian erotic arts, the first point to underline is that expertise in sexual artistry implies proficiency in the arts more generally. Although recognizing that brute animals have sex and that humans can also engage in it at this brute level, the *Kama Sutra* insists that human sexuality is motivated primarily by attractiveness and pleasures rather than dictated by the seasonal instincts of animals in heat. It claims that human sexual performance therefore can and should be rendered more enjoyable and rewarding through the application of knowledge, methods, and refinements introduced by learning, thought, and aesthetic sensitivity – exactly the sort of mastery "of proper means" that its erotic theory aim to promote (KS, 103). As the *Ananga Ranga* later laments, men typically neither give their wives "plenary contentment, nor do they themselves thoroughly enjoy their charms" because "they are purely ignorant" of the erotic arts "and, despising the difference between the several kinds of women [elaborated with colorful detail in the Indian texts of erotic theory], they regard them only in an animal point of view" (AR, xxiii).

The artistic training considered essential for mastering the erotic arts and perfecting sexual performance emphatically includes and highlights those arts that Western culture distinctively denotes as fine arts, although it ranges far wider. In urging that both men and women "should study the *Kama Sutra* and the arts and sciences subordinate thereto," Vatsyayana insists on the study of sixty-four arts through which it draws its skills: "Singing; playing on musical instruments; dancing; union of dancing, singing, and playing instrumental music; writing and drawing" are the first to be mentioned, but the list also includes other practices central to the Western fine arts tradition, such as "picture making... scenic representations, stage playing... architecture... composing poems... [and] ... making figures and images in clay." Other arts among the sixty-four also clearly have aesthetic character – from tattooing, working in stained glass, bed and flower arrangement, and the making of artificial flowers to the fashioning of jewelry and other ornaments and further to various cosmetic and culinary arts (KS, 107–111).

To regard these diverse arts as contributing to *ars erotica* is not, however, to assert that their highest purpose is sexual or sensual, for the expressed goal of even the *Kama Sutra* itself is not merely the satisfaction of erotic or more broadly sensual desire. It is rather to deploy and educate one's desires in order to cultivate and refine the mastery of one's senses so that one can emerge a more complete and effective person. Vatsyayana concludes his book by insisting it "is not intended to be used merely as an instrument for satisfying our desires," but to enable a person "to obtain the mastery over his senses" and thus obtain "success in everything that he may undertake" (KS, 292).

Aesthetic arts are not only included in the recommended training for Indian erotics but also in the conception of the erotic performance itself. This performance is not limited to the act of coitus, but includes an elaborate aesthetics of foreplay and postcoital entertainment. As described by Vatsyayana, "the beginning of sexual union" involves the gentleman receiving his lady love in an aesthetically arranged "pleasure room, decorated with flowers, and fragrant with perfumes," where he and his lover are "attended by his friends and servants... He should then seat her on his left side, and holding her hair, and touching also the end and knot of her garment, he should gently embrace her with his right arm.... They may then sing... and play on musical instruments, talk about the arts, and persuade each other to drink," until her loving feelings and desire for coitus are strongly aroused (KS, 167).

Then, when the other people are dismissed, more intimate foreplay ensues that leads to the consummation of "congress." But the end of coitus does not terminate the sexual performance, which instead continues into postcoital embraces, massage, sweet refreshments, and entertaining conversation, including the gentleman's pointing out the different celestial beauties of the night sky that his lady contemplates, lying "in his lap, with her face towards the moon." Only at this point does Vatsyayana demarcate "the end of sexual union" (KS, 168). The clear sense of a staged, choreographed structure of a beginning, middle, and end in the sexual performance suggests a dramatic, stylized mise-en-scène with aesthetic intent.

The aesthetically designed stage for the erotic event is reaffirmed in the *Koka Shastra* and elaborated most fully in the *Ananga Ranga*, whose recommended artistic furnishings include not only musical instruments but "books containing amorous songs" and "illustrations of love-postures" for "gladdening the glance," and "spacious and beautiful walls" decorated "with pictures and other objects upon which the eye may dwell with delight," such aesthetic delights enhancing those of sex by quickening our sensory imagination and pleasures (AR, 96–97).[27]

The staging of the sexual performance does not confine itself to aesthetic considerations of artfully organized space and artistic activities; temporal factors also need to be harmonized into the performance. According to the type of woman and the day of the (lunar) month, the woman lover will be best aroused in different parts of her body and by different forms of foreplay; in the same way, different kinds of women will enjoy sex at different times of the day. These different times, days, body parts, and modes of foreplay (involving different styles of embracing, kissing, biting, scratching, rubbing, sucking, stroking, squeezing, and the making of certain erotic sounds) are articulated in great detail, and the lover is instructed that by "varying the site of your caress with [the calendar], you will see her light up in successive places like a figure cut in moonstone when the moon strikes on it." In short, not only the setting and acts of sexual arousal but also the display of arousal itself is clearly aestheticized (AR, 6–14; KKS, 105–110, quotation 107).

If music, choreographed movement, artistic decorations of the erotic stage, and the lovers' aesthetic discourse form part of India's extended notion of sexual performance, there are also distinctly aesthetic dimensions in its aims, methods, and principles of sexual foreplay and coitus.[28]

---

[27] *The Koka Shastra* (KKS, 133) describes the staging of the act in an attractive room with flowers and incense and with the gentleman singing cheerful songs, while *Ananga Ranga* (AR, 96–97) describes the setting "best fitted for sexual intercourse with women" as follows: "Choose the largest, and finest, and the most airy room in the house, purify it thoroughly with whitewash, and decorate its spacious and beautiful walls with pictures and other objects upon which the eye may dwell with delight. Scattered about this apartment place musical instruments, especially the pipe and the lute; with refreshments, as cocoa-nut, betel leaf and milk, which is so useful for retaining and restoring vigour; bottles of rose water and various essences, fans and chauris for cooling the air, and books containing amorous songs, and gladdening the glance with illustrations of love-postures. Splendid Diválgiri, or wall lights, should gleam around the hall, reflected by a hundred mirrors, whilst both man and woman should contend against any reserve, or false shame, giving themselves up in complete nakedness to unrestrained voluptuousness, upon a high and handsome bedstead, raised on tall legs, furnished with many pillows, and covered by a rich *chatra* or canopy; the sheets being besprinkled with flowers and the coverlet scented by burning luscious incense, such as aloes and other fragrant woods. In such a place, let the man, ascending the throne of love, enjoy the woman in ease and comfort, gratifying his and her every wish and every whim."

[28] The methods and joys of foreplay and coitus are distinguished (in the *Koka Shastra* and *Ananga Ranga*) as "'outer' and ... 'inner' forms of lovemaking" (KKS, 125) or "external enjoyments" and "internal enjoyment[s]" (AR, 97, 115). The Indian classification recognizes that outer actions and pleasures (e.g., kissing) can continue well beyond foreplay.

Many of these methods and principles aim at both stimulating and harmonizing the energies of the lovers and ensuring that coitus brings fullness of pleasure to both man and woman. Hence, the intense concern with classifying male and female types in terms of size (and sometimes also texture) of the genitals, force of desire, and time required for its satisfaction, so that disparities between the lovers regarding these dimensions can be identified and then remedied through appropriate foreplay and coital positions that overcome such disproportions that impinge on the aesthetic harmony, graceful balance, and pleasurable ease of the union. Proportionate unions are deemed best, and the optimum desire cannot be the most intense because extreme intensity could so captivate the lovers that they would neither notice nor oblige the needs of each other nor have the patient presence of mind to stylize their sexual performance so as to maximize its beauties and draw out its pleasures to the fullest (AR, 21–24; KS, 127–130).[29]

Aesthetic intent is clearly displayed in the making of certain representational forms on the body of the lover through bites and nail markings, so that the sexual performance also becomes a performance of figurative art. Besides the tactile pleasures they give the lovers, these erotic figurations are aesthetically appreciated as artful representations.[30] One variety of nail marks made on the neck and breasts "resembles a half-moon" (AR, 105; cf. KS, 143), another "made on the breast by means of the five nails... is called the 'peacock's foot'" and "is made with the object of being praised, for it requires a great deal of skill to make it properly" (KS, 143). The varieties of bite marks include a special cluster of impressions on the woman's brow, cheek, neck, and breast that together form "the mouth-shaped oblong" of the mandala summarizing the different forms of biting, and, we are told, "it will add greatly to her beauty" (AR, 108). Such nail and bite markings also serve as symbols of affection that endure beyond the sexual performance but aesthetically document it, serving as a comforting "token of remembrance" that also rekindles love and desire between the lovers (AR, 106; KS, 144).[31] Such

[29] Nor can desire be too weak. Indeed, it is the proportionate fit of the organs and its production of sufficient enjoyment and desire that "enables the husband to turn his mind [away from problems of mechanics of penetration] towards the usual arts which bring women under subjection" to the enthralling pleasures of sexual love (AR, 22).
[30] Some styles of bitings and nail applications are not meant to leave marks, but simply to give more tactile pleasure.
[31] Indian erotic arts also deploy elements of symbolic action that leave no marks but refer suggestively to other elements of the sexual performance, thereby seeking to promote

markings are also appreciated by strangers who, when noticing them (on either the man or the woman), are "filled with love and respect" for them (KS, 144).[32]

Complementing the various styles of biting and use of the nails are varieties of embraces, kisses, love sounds, modes of erotic striking of the body, and ways of holding of the hair. Indian *ars erotica* is, however, probably most famous for its detailed articulation, classification, and colorful naming of a wide variety of coital positions. Variety here, as elsewhere, derives from the aesthetic impulse for the richness of diversity that renews interest, compounds pleasure, and prevents the boredom of monotony. As Vatsyayana argues, "if variety is sought in all the arts and amusements, ... how much more should it be sought after in the present case" (namely, the erotic arts)? For just "as variety is necessary in love, so love is to be produced by means of variety" (KS, 144).

That many of these coital positions (or *bandhas*) seem to somewhat overlap or blend into each other suggests that this variety is to be deployed within one act of coitus, rather than limiting the coital act to a single posture. In other words, in any particular coital event, a number of diverse *bandhas* can be aesthetically arranged as sequenced dance steps into a choreography of sexual performance. These postural changes not only add variety and can help prolong the act by delaying the male's ejaculation, they can also have special symbolic significance in terms of the names and associations they bear. Thus, for example, "by adopting successively the 'fish,' 'tortoise,' 'wheel,' and 'sea-shell' position (*mātsya, kaurma, cakra, śankhabandha*) one identifies oneself with the first four avatars of Vishnu."[33] Moreover, in such animal-named positions, the lover is encouraged to dramatize "the characteristics of these different animals ... by acting like them," thus adding a further dimension of artistic representation to the sexual performance (KS, 152).

---

them. The "transferred kiss" is one given not to the lover but to a child or object simultaneously viewed by the lover in order to suggest the desire to kiss the lover (KS, 141). The "Ghatika" kiss, designed to stimulate the man toward the act of coitus by also symbolizing it, is when the woman "thrusts her tongue into his mouth, moving it to and fro with a motion so pleasant and slow that it at once suggests another and a higher form of enjoyment" (AR, 102).

[32] Vatsyayana also cites some ancient verses on this matter: "The love of a woman who sees the marks of nails on the private parts of her body, even though they are old and almost worn out, becomes again fresh and new. If there be no marks of nails to remind a person of the passages of love, then love is lessened in the same way as when no union takes place for a long time" (KS, 144).

[33] Alex Comfort, "Introduction," KKS, 63.

The analogy of sexual performance to dance, although present in other cultures, is especially salient in the Indian tradition. Close affinities exist, for example, between its erotic texts and the twenty-fourth chapter of the *Bharata Natya Sastra* (the classic ancient text on drama, dance, and aesthetics), which, as one commentator notes, treats "the practice of harlotry... as part of the technique of dance. Not only did the virtuosi of one art practice the other, but judging from sculptural representations [often found in holy temples] it was in the spirit of a dance that ritual [notably Tantric], and possibly also secular, coition was undertaken."[34] In this cultural context, sexual union with its taste of heavenly pleasures and god-like feelings of radiating fulfillment could be seen both as an analogue and an instrument to the higher mystical union with God.[35]

Well beyond the sexually intense framework of Tantrism, Indian tradition regarded the proper pursuit of erotic arts as divinely inspired and leading toward religious progress. Vatsyayana insisted his *Kama Sutra* was "composed according to the precepts of the Holy Writ... while leading the life of a religious student... and wholly engaged in the contemplation of the Deity" (KS, 92), while the *Ananga Ranga* argues that having carefully studied the arts of carnal knowledge and being fulfilled and refined through their pleasures, a man "as advancing age cooleth his passions... learneth to think of his Creator, to study religious subjects, and to acquire divine knowledge" (AR, xxiii).

The religious significance of the sexual union – whether symbolized in terms of copulating deities (such as Shakti and Shiva) or in the more abstract terms of basic gender-related principles (such as Purusha and Prakriti or, in Chinese theory, *yin* and *yang*) – adds further richness of symbolic meaning to the erotic arts and encourages their ritualized aestheticization even in contexts that are not explicitly religious.[36] That such aesthetic ritualization can artfully transform the most basic functions of life is a crucial insight of Asian culture that could be therapeutic for our dominantly Platonic-Kantian aesthetic tradition grounded on

---

[34] Ibid., 49, 63.

[35] See the *Brihadaranyaka Upanishad*: "In the embrace of his beloved, a man forgets the whole world – everything both within and without; in the same way he who embraces the Self knows neither within nor without," cited in ibid., 28.

[36] Such ritualized aestheticization can be found in the Japanese tea-ceremony, which has its roots in ritual tea drinking in Zen monasteries (in China before Japan), but has long flourished beyond these religious contexts while still maintaining a strong sense of aesthetic ritual with a Zen-like devotion to harmony, gentleness of spirit, reverence, purity, and tranquility. See D.T. Suzuki, *Zen and Japanese Culture* (Princeton: Princeton University Press, 1989), 272–274.

the art/reality and aesthetic/functional dichotomies. Art's transfiguration of the commonplace need not require the production of fictional counterparts to the real world but simply a more intensified experience and mindfully stylized performance of the ordinary practices of living (whether having sex or taking tea) that renders those practices replete with special beauty, vividness, and meaning.[37] Such transfigured practices of the real can in turn inspire art's fictional figurations.

It is therefore not enough to insist that India's erotic arts deploy the objects and practices of fine art; we must acknowledge that its fine arts reciprocally draw on its *ars erotica*. The positions outlined in the *Kama Sutra* clearly helped inspire the sculptural depictions of sexual union in medieval Hindu temples, most notably in Konarak, Khajuraho, Belur, and Halebid, but also in Buddhist centers such as Nagarjunikonda, where many statues of sexual congress "could be identified as sculptural versions of Vatsyayana's sutras – sometimes as interpreted by poets."[38] His seminal text of *ars erotica* indeed became the main paradigm for literary depictions of love (and the characters of lovers) in Sanskrit poetry. Its influence was especially strong in epics and dramatic works (which traditionally included dance and music, as well), but extended to lyrics of love and even some religious poetry (for example, the *Gita Govinda*, which treats a girl cowherder's love for the god Krishna as analogical to the human soul's thirst for the ecstasy of union with the divine). This central role in literature and sculpture helped *ars erotica* further its influence also in other Indian fine arts.[39]

Unity in variety is among the most prominent of our traditional definitions of beauty. In Indian erotic arts, the richness of variety is found not only in the diversity of embraces, kisses, scratchings, bitings, strikings, hair fondlings, temporalities, love noises, coital positions (which include oral and anal sex[40]), and even different ways of moving the penis inside the vagina but also in the ways these several modes of variety are

---

[37] In Chapter 13, I explore further examples of such aesthetic transfigurations of everyday life.
[38] K.M. Pannikar, "Introduction," KS, 74.
[39] Painters thus came to deploy, as classical representations of love, the various female types and situations delineated by the erotic texts and by the literary works they inspired. See ibid., 75; Comfort, 70. Eight of these classical figures are described in AR, 113–114.
[40] The *Kama Sutra* devotes a chapter (ch. 9) to positions and methods of oral sex, but has nothing to say about methods of anal sex, merely noting that it is done (KS, 153). In the later, more straight-laced *Koka Shastra*, very little is said of oral sex and anal sex is not mentioned. Neither oral nor anal sex is discussed in the still more prudish *Ananga Ranga*, although later erotic writers recognize oral sex. See Comfort, KKS, 124.

combined into an aesthetic unity, achieving, in the words of one commentator, "the creation of an elaborate sexual sensation as a positive work of art."[41] Sexual performance is heightened and harmonized by paying careful attention to which elements of these various modes fit most successfully together to both stimulate and satisfy desire. An entire chapter of the *Kama Sutra*, for example, treats "the various modes of striking, and of the sounds appropriate to them," which should also appropriately vary according to whether the man or woman is striking or being struck, and according to the stage of foreplay or coitus in which the lovers find themselves (KS, 154–157). Guiding this aesthetic of dynamically harmonizing mixture is the recognition that these rules of art are not absolutely fixed prescriptions but rather need to be applied with a discriminating sense of the varieties of context, ranging from the contingencies of the individual lovers (their bodily condition, social status, habitual inclinations, and current feelings) to circumstances of time, place, and culture. "The various modes of enjoyment are not for all times or for all persons, but they should only be used at the proper time, and in the proper countries and places" (KS, 157).

In drawing on so many varieties of sensorial, formal, cognitive, cosmic, socio-cultural, and ethical aspects, the aesthetic variety of Indian *ars erotica* self-consciously served a variety of purposes. One purpose that became increasingly important was the sustaining of sexual attraction and sexual love between the married couple in order to preserve domestic harmony and through it social stability. "The chief reason for the separation between the married couple and the cause, which drives the husband to the embraces of strange women, and the wife to the arms of strange men, is the want of varied pleasures and the monotony which follows possession," concludes the *Ananga Ranga*. "There is no doubt about it. Monotony begets satiety, and satiety distaste for congress, especially in one or the other; malicious feelings are engendered, the husband or the wife yield to temptation, and the other follows, being driven by jealousy." From such monotony and discord "result polygamy, adulteries, abortions, and every manner of vice" that ruin the lives and reputations of couples and even "drag down the names of their deceased ancestors." The book's study of erotic arts is thus dedicated to showing "how the husband, by varying the enjoyment of his wife, may live with her as with thirty-two different women, ever varying the enjoyment of her, and rendering satiety

---

[41] Comfort, KKS, 49.

impossible," while also teaching the wife "all manner of useful arts and mysteries, by which she may render herself pure, beautiful and pleasing in his eyes" (AR, 128–129).

If Indian erotic arts strives both to give women "plenary contentment" and to "thoroughly enjoy their charms," such satisfactions are characterized in clearly aesthetic terms of the participatory enjoyment of sensorial harmonies of pleasurable perceptions and movements, replete with representational forms and complex meanings and carefully structured with dramatic self-consciousness and performative stylization. The aesthetic goal of artfully creating harmony and pleasure through skill in playing variations on an instrument of beauty is stated most explicitly in the *Ananga Ranga*: "all you who read this book shall know how delicious an instrument is woman, when artfully played upon; how capable she is of producing the most exquisite harmony; of executing the most complicated variations and of giving the divinest pleasures" (AR, xxiii). One might understandably baulk at objectifying woman as an aesthetic instrument for man's pleasure, but the sting is somewhat mitigated by Indian erotics insistent advocacy that women reciprocally play on male instruments, and sometimes even play the male by taking on his actions and coital positions. Here, in the different forms of Purushayita, the wife mounts the supine man, effects the penetration, initiates the rhythmic coital movement, and thus "enjoys her husband, and thoroughly satisfies herself" (AR, 126).

Besides the aims of conjugal happiness through the pleasures of love and the bonds of intimate friendship they can create, the aesthetic variety of the Indian erotic tradition has broader cognitive and ethical aims. Extending well beyond matters of sexual and sensual pleasure, *kama* concerns the whole domain of sensory cognition. *Ars erotica*'s rich stimulation and sophistication of the senses together with its mastery and refinement of a wide range of complex motor coordinations and bodily postures cannot help but bring significant cognitive enhancement to both sensory and motor abilities. Its cultivation of perception includes an education in recognizing the enduring dispositions but also changing thoughts and feelings of others, so that the lover can properly respond to them. Considerable attention is paid to discerning the movements and expressions that indicate a woman's character, erotic accessibility, interest, inclinations, changing moods, sexual passions, and the means and degrees to which her interests and passions are satisfied. Such perceptual training develops ethical sensitivity to others and to their diversity (reflected in the complex, multiple classifications of different types of lovers but also of go-betweens and courtesans).[42]

If such perceptual and ethical sensitivity is aimed at promoting sexual activity, then such activity is conversely applied to hone ethical self-knowledge and self-discipline through erotic practices that probe our desires and inhibitions as they reshape them, while also testing and refining our self-control through artful, pleasureful mastery of our senses and sensuality. As "Kama is the enjoyment of appropriate objects by the five senses of hearing, feeling, seeing, tasting and smelling, assisted by the mind together with the soul," so its practice in *ars erotica* aims at a varied "mastery of [one's] senses" (KS, 102–103, 292). These aims of masterful sensuous enjoyment remain aesthetic for all their practical, ethical, and cognitive value.

To conclude, ancient India (even more than ancient China) has much to teach the West about the aesthetic powers and possibilities of sexual activity. Because our culture is dominated by the model of *scientia sexualis* and the Cartesian notion of the body as machine, we are obsessively preoccupied with improving sex through mechanical, nonperceptual means (such as pills, lubricants, penis enlargements), thus neglecting the artistic techniques of enhancing erotic experience. While Indian erotic theory (including the three exemplary texts here discussed) likewise offers an abundance of mechanical devices (pharmacological, prosthetic, and even magical) for enhancing sexual performance and desirability, its dominant emphasis is on cultivating erotic artistry through aesthetic expertise and its perfection of sensorimotor skills relating to lovemaking. For the discipline of somaesthetics, proposed as a field of theory and practice devoted to the study and cultivation of our bodies as loci of aesthetic perception and self-fashioning, the Asian erotic arts, especially as formulated in classical Indian culture, constitute an exemplary resource and an invaluable inspiration.

If somaesthetics can likewise be construed as a pragmatist philosophy of education – a discipline concerned with improving our ability to learn

[42] The *Kama Sutra* also contains elaborate recommendations for the aesthetic stylization of life in general, not just for specifically erotic matters. See its chapter "On the Arrangements of a House, and Household Furniture; and about the Daily Life of a Citizen, his Companions, Amusements, etc.," which contains suggestions of how to aesthetically organize the living conditions and daily routines of a gentleman or man about town (the Sanskrit term is *nayaka*) These lifestyle recommendations range from ablutions, cosmetics, clothes, meals, and siestas to amusements such as festivals, drinking parties, discussions of the arts, and aesthetic pastimes (e.g., games of verse and decorating oneself with flowers).

by improving the use of the soma (in perception and performance) as the indispensable tool, general site, and subject of learning, then *ars erotica* – with its cultivation of sensory perception, sensuous mastery, psychological insight, ethical sensibility, and artistic and cognitive skills – can surely be recommended somaesthetically for its wide-ranging values of edification. Here we could find a promising concept of sex education that seems both radically new and authentically ancient – education through erotic desire and the arts of its shaping, pursuit, and fulfillment in practice.

13

Somaesthetic Awakening and the Art of Living

Everyday Aesthetics in American Transcendentalism and Japanese Zen Practice

I

Why have America's most important and inspirational transcendentalist thinkers, Ralph Waldo Emerson and Henry David Thoreau, been so neglected by academic philosophy and relegated to the status of merely literary figures? One reason for this marginalization may be their advocacy that philosophy is more importantly practiced as a deliberate way of life concerned with self-improvement than as a mere academic enterprise. As Thoreau most pointedly put it, "There are nowadays professors of philosophy, but not philosophers. Yet it is admirable to profess because it was once admirable to live."[1] Both New England thinkers resist the restriction of philosophy to a scholastic exercise of pure intellect that is essentially confined to the reading, writing, and discussion of texts. If Emerson affirms that genuine "life is not [mere] dialectics" and that "intellectual tasting of life will not supersede muscular activity,"[2] then Thoreau more specifically explains: "To be a philosopher is not merely to have subtle thoughts, nor even to found a school, but so to love wisdom as to live according to its dictates, a life of simplicity, independence, magnanimity, and trust. It is to solve some of the problems of life, not only theoretically, but practically" (W, 14).

This insistence on the practical dimension of philosophy was an inspiration for later pragmatists such as William James and John Dewey, whose exemplary path has guided my own efforts. While my books *Pragmatist Aesthetics*, *Practicing Philosophy*, and *Performing Live* offered

---

[1] Henry David Thoreau, *Walden*, in Brooks Atkinson (ed.), *Walden and Other Writings* (New York: Modern Library, 2000), 14; hereafter W.

[2] Ralph Waldo Emerson, "Experience," in *Ralph Waldo Emerson: Essays and Poems* (New York: Library of America, 1996), 478, hereafter RWE.

arguments for reintegrating aesthetic principles into the ethical and practical conduct of life, these ideas were already prefigured in Emerson and Thoreau.[3] "Art," says Emerson, "must not be a superficial talent" of "making cripples and monsters, such as all pictures and statues are," but must "serve the ideal" by remaking men and women of character (RWE, 437–439). Thoreau provides a still more explicit formulation: "It is something to be able to paint a particular picture, or to carve a statue, and so to make a few objects beautiful; but it is far more glorious to carve and paint the very atmosphere and medium through which we look, which morally we can do. To affect the quality of the day, that is the highest of arts. Every man is tasked to make his life, even in its details, worthy of the contemplation of his most elevated and critical hour" (W, 85–86).

In seeking to establish a field of somaesthetics that included practical bodily disciplines to enhance our experience and performance while increasing our tools for self-fashioning, I could again look to Thoreau as a prophetic forerunner:[4] "Every man is the builder of a temple, called his body, to the god he worships, after a style purely his own, nor can he get off by hammering marble instead. We are all sculptors and painters, and our material is our own flesh and blood and bones. Any nobleness begins at once to refine a man's features, any meanness or sensuality to imbrute them" (W, 209).

In this chapter, I consider another important way that Emerson and Thoreau portray embodied philosophical living, one that is easily overlooked because it seems so inconspicuously simple. The idea is that to live philosophically means living in a waking rather than sleeping state. To explore what this richly ambiguous idea signifies, I will focus on how Emerson and Thoreau apply it, while noting some of its other major expressions in the history of philosophy. But to give this idea (which is also an ideal) more concrete and contemporary exemplification, I then

---

[3] Richard Shusterman, *Pragmatist Aesthetics: Living Beauty, Rethinking Art* (Oxford: Blackwell, 1992); *Practicing Philosophy: Pragmatism and the Philosophical Life* (New York: Routledge, 1997); and *Performing Live: Aesthetic Alternatives for the Ends of Art* (Ithaca: Cornell University Press, 2000). Although Dewey was my primary American inspiration in pragmatist aesthetics, I have come to realize that many of his central ideas could already be found in Emerson, especially Emerson's essay on "Art." See Richard Shusterman, "Emerson's Pragmatist Aesthetics," *Revue Internationale de Philosophie* 207 (1999): 87–99. William James likewise adumbrates the major aesthetic insights that Dewey later, more systematically developed. See Richard Shusterman, "The Pragmatist Aesthetics of William James," *British Journal of Aesthetics* 51 (2011): 347–361.

[4] Richard Shusterman, *Body Consciousness: A Philosophy of Mindfulness and Somaesthetics* (Cambridge: Cambridge University Press, 2008), 47–48; *Practicing Philosophy*, 108–109, 176–177.

discuss how the discipline of awakened life can provide everyday experience with deep aesthetic enrichment and even spiritual enlightenment. Here I will draw on my personal experience of awakened living in a Japanese Zen cloister.

It is best, however, to frame our discussion of awakened life by first situating it among other influential models of philosophical living. We should recall at least three key Western conceptions of philosophical living that can be traced back to Plato. If the *Apology* presents Socrates' philosophical life in terms of the Delphic quest for self-knowledge and the right way to live an examined life that would benefit both self and society, Plato, in other dialogues, offers other models. In the *Crito, Gorgias,* and the *Republic*, he compares the philosopher's role to the physician's. As the latter cares for the body's health, the philosopher cares for the soul's. But if the soul is immortal and nobler than the body, then philosophy, Plato argues, should be seen as the superior practice. This medical or therapeutic model of caring for the soul's health was highly influential in ancient philosophy and has been convincingly explained by Pierre Hadot, who has also highlighted its use of spiritual exercises to serve the soul's health.[5]

In his *Symposium*, Plato sketches another model of the philosophical life that I have described as more aesthetic than therapeutic. Love's desire for beauty is claimed to be the source of philosophy, and the philosophical life is portrayed as a continuous quest for higher beauty that ennobles the philosopher and that culminates in the vision of the perfect form of beauty itself and the knowledge to give birth with beauty to "real virtue." This life of beauty Plato describes as "the only life worth living," and it makes the philosopher "immortal, if any man ever is" (198c–213d).[6] To recommend the philosophical life in terms of beauty, harmony, attractive nobility, or innovative creative expression is to advocate what I call the aesthetic model of philosophical living, and in *Practicing Philosophy* I have elaborated its contemporary expression in philosophers as diverse as Michel Foucault, Ludwig Wittgenstein, and John Dewey. From the passages cited at the outset of this chapter, we readily see Emerson and Thoreau as endorsing the idea of an aesthetically noble art of living in which the subject seeks to shape himself and his environment into an attractive form "worthy of the contemplation of his most elevated and

---

[5] Pierre Hadot, *Philosophy as a Way of Life* (Oxford: Blackwell, 1995). See also Martha Nussbaum, *The Therapy of Desire* (Princeton: Princeton University Press, 1994).

[6] John Cooper (ed.), *Plato: The Complete Works* (Indianapolis: Hackett, 1997), 481–495.

critical hour." This chapter, however, will focus instead on their cryptically simple-sounding injunction to live one's life in a waking state.

II

Emerson, the older mentor, leads the way with richly poetic suggestiveness, while Thoreau is more detailed and systematic in elaborating this model of philosophical living as wakefulness. Emerson's famous essay "Experience" opens with this theme. "Where do we find ourselves? In a series of which we do not know the extremes, and believe that it has none. We wake and find ourselves on a stair; there are stairs below us, which we seem to have ascended; there are stairs above us, many a one, which go upward and out of sight" (RWE, 471). Emerson's message is not addressed to the few literal sleepwalkers but to the vast majority of us normal men and women whose conduct of life (our "series" of steps or actions) is not pursued in a properly wakeful state; so when we suddenly do "wake" or become truly aware of ourselves at a particular step or stage in our lives, we do not really know where exactly we are and have come from and where we are going. Living in a state of sleep is a potent metaphor for the unexamined life that Socrates opposed to the life of philosophy. Even when we think we are awake "now at noonday" when the light is brightest, Emerson continues, "we cannot shake off the lethargy" of our somnolent consciousness (RWE, 471). "Sleep lingers all our lifetime about our eyes, as night hovers all day in the boughs of the fir-tree.... Our life is not so much threatened as our perception" (RWE, 307).

Thoreau echoes this complaint in his critique of common sense: "Why level downward to our dullest perception always, and praise that as common sense? The commonest sense is the sense of men asleep, which they express by snoring" (W, 304). We fail to see things as they really are with the rich, sensuous resplendence of their full being because we see them through eyes heavy with conventional habits of viewing them and blinded by stereotypes of meaning. Such habits of seeing, like other habits, have certain advantages of efficiency and are thus useful at certain times. But if we allow these habits to overwhelm and displace real seeing (as they will tend to do since habits are inclined to reinforce themselves), then they will miserably impoverish perception and experience while substituting our vision of the truth with illusory stereotypes that common sense takes for the ultimately real. "By closing the eyes and slumbering, and consenting to be deceived by shows," Thoreau complains, "men establish and confirm their daily life of routine and habit everywhere, which still is built on purely illusory foundations" (W, 91). Philosophy, however, can provide a means of reawakening us so that we can see things more clearly, experience them more fully than we can in sleep (real or figurative), when our eyes are closed, our senses dulled, and our minds either blank or obscured by dreams.

The concern with breaking us out of a slumbering dream state is a familiar topos in philosophy, both East and West. The ancient Chinese Daoist Zhuangzi famously wondered whether he was a philosopher who dreamed he was a butterfly or a butterfly dreaming he was the philosopher Zhuangzi. René Descartes just as famously (though very differently) invoked the illusion of dreams in the skeptical argument of his First Meditation, arguing that although seemingly awake and purposively moving his body parts, he has often been deceived by dreams to that effect and thus he feels "there are never any sure signs by means of which being awake can be distinguished from being asleep."[7] Still later, and in a different register than dreams, we find Immanuel Kant praising David Hume for arousing him from his dogmatic slumbers and thus prompting him to develop his critical philosophy. In Kant's usage here, sleep is not so much a dream state but a state of uncritical belief and action that is usually identified with a waking state, but which is not truly or fully awakened to a condition of perceptive, critical acuity. This metaphorical meaning of sleep as an uncritical waking state that needs a further, true awakening can be traced back to Socrates, who describes himself in the *Apology* as "a sort of gadfly, given to the state by the God," in order to ensure that people be "awakened" by his critical questioning, for without being so "irritated" they "would sleep on for the remainder of [their] lives" (30e).

The notion of awakening to a clearer, critical awareness of the nature of things is also extremely central to the philosophy of Buddhism. The name Buddha means "the awakened one" in Sanskrit (deriving from the root "*budh*," meaning to "awake," "arouse," or "know"), and it was given to Siddhārtha Gautama to express the fact that he, too, awoke from the dogma and illusions of our conventional beliefs to a clearer awareness of the human conditions of suffering, false ego consciousness, and impermanence but also of the ways to escape from such suffering through precisely such heightened awareness of those conditions. Here,

---

[7] René Descartes, *Meditations on First Philosophy*, in John Cottingham, Robert Stoothoff, and Dugald Murdoch (trans.), *The Philosophical Writings of Descartes*, vol. 2. (Cambridge: Cambridge University Press, 1984), 13.

being awake means being more aware than one normally is in one's waking hours, and the theme of mindfulness or intensified awareness remains extremely central to the Buddhist tradition.[8]

Thoreau pursues the same idea in his advocacy of early rising and his praise of morning because it is "the awakening hour" (W, 84). In morning, "there is least somnolence in us, and for an hour, at least, some part of us awakes which slumbers all the rest of the day and night" (W, 84). Awakening means waking up to a higher consciousness than that we have in ordinary daily and nightly thought and action; it is awakening "to a higher life than we fell asleep from" (W, 84–85). Night, Thoreau explains, has its value in preparing us for such awakening: "After a partial cessation of his sensuous life, the soul of man, or its organs, rather, are reinvigorated each day, and his genius tries again what noble life it can make. All memorable events, I should say, transpire in morning time and in a morning atmosphere" (W, 85). Quoting the Vedas that "All intelligences awake with the morning," Thoreau insists that this morning atmosphere of awakening is not a matter of chronological time, but should be kept in one's spirit at all times. For the mind "whose elastic and vigorous thought keeps pace with the sun, the day is perpetual morning. It matters not what the clocks say.... Morning is when I am awake and there is a dawn in me" (W, 85).

Praising the artist for "the power of awakening other souls" to higher life, Emerson affirms that ethically "nobler souls" perform the same function, because a noble character "awakens in us by its actions and words, by its very looks and manners, the same power and beauty that a gallery of sculpture or of pictures addresses" (RWE, 244). Thoreau likewise claims that, "Poetry and art, and the fairest and most memorable of the actions of men, date from" but also contribute to the awakening morning spirit. "All poets and heroes are the children of Aurora, and emit their music

---

[8] This can be traced, for example, from the Buddha's early lectures on "The Foundations of Mindfulness" to the Japanese Zen Master Dōgen's "The Eight Awarenesses of Great People." Although Emerson and Thoreau were avid readers of ancient Asian philosophy, I should also note a more local religious context for the notion of spiritual awakening. The religious movement known as the "First Great Awakening" (1730–1740s) was influential in New England (and elsewhere in the American colonies), finding forceful expression in the work of the influential Massachusetts theologian-philosopher Jonathan Edwards. The "Second Great Awakening" (1790–1840s) was also very influential in Emerson and Thoreau's New England, stimulating not only spiritual awakening but also social movements for reform in such areas as abolitionism and temperance that were important for Emerson and Thoreau.

at sunrise" in the spiritual rather than merely chronological sense that Thoreau urges (W, 85).

In maintaining that "Moral reform is the effort to throw off sleep" (W, 85), Thoreau is perhaps suggesting that awakening implies the ethical effort of overcoming the agreeable lethargy or comfortable laziness associated with sleep and its reclining position. Saint Augustine's *Confessions* highlight this point by likening his stubborn habit of fleshly lust to a seductively pleasurable sleepiness that is difficult to shake off, despite one's desire to awaken and rise (here to the higher life of communion with God). "I was held down as agreeably by this world's baggage as one often is by sleep; and indeed the thoughts with which I meditated upon You were like the efforts of a man who wants to get up but is so heavy with sleep that he simply sinks back into it again," writes Augustine. "There is no one who wants to be asleep always – for every sound judgment holds that it is best to be awake – yet a man often postpones the effort of shaking himself awake when he feels a sluggish heaviness in the limbs, and settles pleasurably into another doze though he knows he should not, because it is time to get up. Similarly I regarded it as settled that it would be better to give myself to Your love rather than go on yielding to my own lust; but the first course delighted and convinced my mind, the second delighted my body and held it in bondage."[9]

Intellectual achievement, Thoreau maintains, likewise requires awakening from our drowsiness: "The millions are awake enough for physical labor; but only one in a million is awake enough for effective intellectual exertion, only one in a hundred millions to a poetic or divine life. To be awake is to be alive. I have never yet met a man who was quite awake. How could I have looked him in the face" (W, 85)? Being awake is thus a special, critical, meliorative way of life, a path of self-improvement toward higher consciousness requiring a reflective self-disciplined askesis that is the hallmark of philosophical living as first sketched by Socrates. However, being critically disciplined and mindfully aware in one's intellect does not preclude practicing disciplined body consciousness; for Socrates was equally famous for his powers of physical discipline.

The sort of awakening we require, Thoreau insists, cannot rely on external means like drugs or other stimulants. "We must learn to reawaken and keep ourselves awake, not by mechanical aids, but by an infinite expectation of the dawn, which does not forsake us in our soundest sleep," if our dreams are also thoroughly shaped by the conscious meliorative

---

[9] Saint Augustine, *Confessions*, trans. F.J. Sheed (Indianapolis: Hackett, 1992), 135–136.

effort of our waking life. We must, in other words, apply "the unquestionable ability of man to elevate his life by a conscious endeavor." And Thoreau immediately connects this effort of heightened awareness with an aesthetic vision of awakened life that is worth quoting again because of its potent argument for an everyday aesthetics that also applies to philosophy's art of living:[10] "It is something to be able to paint a particular picture, or to carve a statue, and so to make a few objects beautiful; but it is far more glorious to carve and paint the very atmosphere and medium through which we look, which morally we can do. To affect the quality of the day, that is the highest of arts. Every man is tasked to make his life, even in its details, worthy of the contemplation of his most elevated and critical hour" (W, 85–86).

III

If Emerson and Thoreau celebrate awakened living as key to their ideal, then what characterizes such life apart from greater awareness? Disciplined effort driven by melioristic desire and guided by critical consciousness, self-probing, and self-cultivation that includes an unselfish openness to the vibrant energies of world is surely part of the awakened life they advocate. But what aims does such life serve that makes it desirable, and what methods are used to achieve awakening? Emerson and Thoreau commend awakening first for promoting genius in the fields of art, ethics, and spiritual character. If this requires sustained discipline and ascetic "elevation of purpose" (W, 87), there is also the paradox that genius is not entirely a matter of the individual's self-perfecting will but instead requires also a "letting go" or self-abandonment to forces greater and higher than the individual so that those superior forces can be expressed through the individual's genius (which, as Emerson emphasizes, is thus always more than merely individual).[11]

There is the further puzzle that while awakened life is recommended for the inspiring gifts of artistic, ethical, intellectual, and spiritual achievements that it generates, these very achievements (of beauty, virtue,

---

[10] For the democratic Emerson and Thoreau (just as originally for Socrates), the philosophical life is in principle open to anyone willing to make the required efforts of askesis, and making such efforts are incumbent on everyone who properly cares about himself. This democratic openness is why they rarely characterize such life as specifically, distinctively "philosophical," as that might suggest that poets, artists, heroes, and even humble farmers cannot lead that life but only professional (or at least self-professing) philosophers.

[11] See my essay on "Genius and the Paradoxes of Self-Styling," in *Performing Live*, ch. 10.

knowledge, and penetrating wisdom) are precisely what in turn awaken us to the awakened life. This reciprocal action or interdependence entails no vitiating circularity to frustrate renewed awakening and continuing creation, because past achievements in these fields of art, knowledge, and action have an enduring exemplary presence that can continuously prompt new individuals to awakened life and inspired achievement. The enduring inspiration of Emerson's and Thoreau's writings is decisive evidence of the present power of past awakenings.

Besides the creation of distinctive works of genius, awakening is praised for the more general value of promoting keener, more focused consciousness in our everyday living. We know from previous chapters that heightened consciousness is not always considered a good, even by philosophers. Many motor tasks are most effectively performed when done automatically with minimal awareness, whereas thinking about them with deliberative, heightened consciousness hinders their smooth flow. Even intellectual tasks involving motor control (such as playing the piano, responding impromptu to a philosophical question, or even orally reading a prepared lecture with proper intonation) are often done best without reflective awareness of what we are doing. However, we also know from previous chapters that heightened, critical awareness of our actions and feelings has its valuable uses for reforming bad habits, refining acquired skills, and learning new ones. Awakening to more explicit awareness of what we actually do contributes, moreover, to the aims of self-knowledge and self-improvement that are central to the idea of philosophy as an examined, critical, meliorative art of living. It provides a richer appreciation of meaning in what we do because we take the time to attend more explicitly to our thoughts, feelings, and actions. If we recall Montaigne's argument that heightened consciousness usefully augments our pleasures by letting us savor them with more attentive awareness, then we should also include here the pleasures of meaning.[12] Moreover, regardless of pleasure, there is value simply in an awakened appreciation of meanings (even painful ones), particularly if one is engaged in the cognitive, critical, meliorative pursuit of a philosophical art of living.

What, then, are the methods advocated for awakening? Two distinctive points the transcendentalists insist on are simplicity and slowness. The first Thoreau emphasizes paradoxically by repetition (rather than a

---

[12] See Michel de Montaigne, *The Complete Essays of Montaigne*, trans. Donald Frame (Stanford: Stanford University Press, 1965), 853.

simple single mention): "Simplicity, simplicity, simplicity," he demands, because our "life is frittered away" and our consciousness is hopelessly distracted by too much detail (W, 86). Awareness can be sharper, attention more concentrated, if focused on a more limited range of objects. A few lines later he repeats this message of economy: "Simplify, simplify. Instead of three meals a day, if it be necessary eat but one; instead of a hundred dishes, five; and reduce all other things in proportion" (W, 87). Emerson likewise affirms simplicity as a key to spiritual awakening since it puts us in touch with "the transcendent simplicity and energy of the Highest Law" (RWE, 386). He therefore urges that "the basis of character must be simplicity," which puts a man more in tune with "the simplicity of nature." "Nothing is more simple than greatness; indeed, to be simple is to be great."[13]

Slowness is another method Thoreau recommends for heightened awareness. Things that move quickly are harder to attend to with care and deliberation; they go by too fast for us to get a good grasp of them. Hence, Thoreau's critique of American culture that "lives too fast" (W, 87), exemplified by the railroad, a prime nineteenth-century symbol of rapid transit and the fast-moving life that it brings. The railroad example lets him elaborate the theme of sleep and awakening by exploiting the term "sleeper," which is also the name for the wooden planks on which the railroad rails are laid. "We do not ride on the railroad; it rides upon us. Did you ever think what those sleepers are that underlie the railroad?" asks Thoreau. "Each one is a man, an Irishman or a Yankee man [who spiritually slept while doing the railroad's labor]...and the cars run smoothly over them. They are sound sleepers, I assure you." It is only when trains run over another kind of sleeper – "a man that is walking in his sleep" – that anyone takes any notice or concern to "wake him up" (W, 87–88). Thoreau thus exhorts us to stop our rush on the narrow rails of business and instead take the time to awaken to the wonders of experience and creative living through higher consciousness.

For Emerson, the value of slowness as taking one's time is linked to the virtue of patience and the fact that nature typically works its wonders through slow evolution and maturation rather than hurried explosions. "The pace of nature is so slow," he writes in praise, not in complaint. Not only do fishing, yachting, hunting, or planting teach us to be patient

---

[13] Ralph Waldo Emerson, "The Superlative," in *Lectures and Biographical Sketches* (Boston: Mifflin, 1904), 174, 176; "Literary Ethics," in *Emerson: Essays and Poems* (New York: Library of America, 1996), 100.

in attending carefully to the slow "manners of Nature," the scholar too "must have a great patience" and examine his subject slowly so as not to overlook hidden dimensions or facts.[14] "Patience is the chiefest fruit of study," Emerson concludes, urging us to "Leave this military hurry and adopt the pace of Nature [whose] secret is patience."[15] The principle of slowness as a means to achieve clearer consciousness and greater control of what we do and feel is central to certain somaesthetic disciplines of heightened body awareness.[16]

Closely related to the methods of simplicity and slowness but worth articulating in its own right is the transcendentalist advocacy of focalizing attention on the here and now. Concentrating on the present moment heightens our attentive powers by avoiding their dispersal into the immense complexities of a past that extends unfathomably back behind us or into the vast incalculable vagaries of an undefined, unbounded future. Deliberate slowness helps us focus on the present moment by making it last longer, in the sense that the activity that occupies the present takes more time by being performed more slowly. Moreover, such slowness enables greater attentiveness to any activity by allowing attention to linger longer on each phase of that activity because each phase indeed lasts longer. Emerson and Thoreau thus insist on being focused on the here and now.

"We are always getting ready to live, but never living," complains Emerson in his journal, and thus boldly resolves: "With the past, I have nothing to do; nor with the future. I live now."[17] "Above all, we cannot afford not to live in the present," Thoreau echoes, in an extraordinary essay on walking. "He is blessed over all mortals who loses no moment of the passing life in remembering the past."[18] This focus on the now is immediately linked to Thoreau's philosophy of morning inspiration and its power of fresh presence to free us from the bonds of old habits of thought

---

[14] Ralph Waldo Emerson, "Farming," in Brooks Atkinson (ed.), *The Essential Writings of Ralph Waldo Emerson* (New York: Modern Library, 2000), 674; "Powers and Laws of Thought," and "The Scholar" in *The Complete Works of Ralph Waldo Emerson* (New York: Houghton Mifflin, 1904), vol. 7, 49; vol. 10, 286, respectively.

[15] Ralph Waldo Emerson, "Address at Opening of Concord Free Public Library," and "Education" in *The Complete Works of Ralph Waldo Emerson*, vol. 11. 505; vol. 10. 155, respectively.

[16] For details, see *Performing Live*, ch. 8.

[17] Ralph Waldo Emerson, entry April 13, 1834, in E. W. Emerson and R. W. Forbes (eds.), *Journals of Ralph Waldo Emerson* (Boston: Houghton Mifflin, 1910–1914), vol. 3, 276; and his later entry of September 18, 1839, vol. 5, 255.

[18] Henry David Thoreau, "Walking," in *Walden and Other Writings*.

and action. "Unless our philosophy hears the cock crow in every barnyard within our horizon, it is belated. That sound commonly reminds us that we are growing rusty and antique in our employments and habits of thought" (W, 662). Recognizing that the past and future (through the cultural richness of history and forward-looking hopes) may seem to dwarf the fleeting present in terms of narrative grandeur, Thoreau counters by affirming that the "true and sublime... are now and here. God himself culminates in the present moment.... And we are enabled to apprehend at all what is sublime and noble only by the perpetual instilling and drenching of the reality that surrounds us" in the here and now (W, 92).

Emerson likewise celebrates the sublimity of the present moment when the soul truly attends to it. Even when that here and now is only commonplace objects or trifling events, the attentive present moment is the window that opens us to reality in all its fullness and grandeur, both material and spiritual. Combining the themes of simplicity and thoughtful attention to the here and now, Emerson insists that "the soul that ascendeth... is plain and true; has no rose color; no fine friends; no chivalry; no adventures; does not want admiration; dwells in the hour that now is, in the earnest experience of the common day – by reason of the present moment, and the mere trifle having become porous to thought, and bibulous of the sea of light" (RWE, 397). Bemoaning that man has not yet awoken to attentive awareness of the present moment, "but with reverted eye laments the past, or heedless of the riches that surround him, stands on tiptoe to foresee the future," Emerson insists that man "cannot be happy and strong until he too lives with nature in the present, above time" (RWE, 270). This is because the present moment – although fleeting – is also, in a sense, beyond time, when it is appreciated in itself as fully present and thus outside the conceptual line of temporal extension that runs from past to future.

But apart from these sublime, quasi-mystical moments of grasping a timeless now, there is the simpler yet significant value of attentive awareness to our mundane experience, of being fully present in what we do and where we are so that we can more fully profit from what our surroundings actually offer. In his essay on walking, Thoreau provides an excellent example of how one can lose one's focus in the present moment and thus lose out on the meaning it has: "I am alarmed when it happens that I have walked a mile into the woods bodily, without getting there in spirit.... But it sometimes happens that I cannot easily shake off the village. The thought of some work will run in my head and I am not where my body is–I am out of my senses. In my walks I would fain return to my senses. What business have I in the woods, if I am thinking of something out of the woods?" (W, 632).

While we may regret Thoreau's rhetoric for too sharply contrasting body and spirit, we should surely appreciate his point that the senses are where the body is and that we should be appreciatively focused on what they could perceive in the here and now instead of filling one's mind and attention with absent, distant things. This idea of living in the here and now by appreciating the present moment with vivid attention and clear consciousness is central to the Zen tradition I encountered in Japan and will discuss in the concluding sections of this chapter.

Another of Thoreau's touted methods for spiritual awakening consists of mind-directed body disciplines involving ascetic austerity and purifying purpose. At one point, when discussing our habits of eating and drinking, he draws an inverse relationship between spiritual awakening and the animal consciousness of our typically sensuous culinary habits. In the "slimy, beastly life" of our customary "eating and drinking," Thoreau remarks, "We are conscious of an animal in us, which awakens in proportion as our higher nature slumbers. It is reptile and sensual, and perhaps cannot be wholly expelled" (W, 206).

However, evoking Mencius and the Vedas, Thoreau claims we can increase our measure of purity by mentally dominating our brutish appetites by channeling them into disciplined and ritual restraint: "'A command over our passions, and over the external senses of the body, and good acts, are declared by the Ved to be indispensable in the mind's approximation to God.' Yet the spirit can for the time pervade and control every member and function of the body, and transmute what in form is the grossest sensuality into purity and devotion. The generative energy, which, when we are loose, dissipates and makes us unclean, when we are continent invigorates and inspires us" (W, 207). Because, for Thoreau, "all purity is one," our conscious discipline of eating and drinking can guide us toward more mindful control of other appetites and to the rich fruits of spiritual awakening. "Chastity is the flowering of man; and what are called Genius, Heroism, Holiness, and the like, are but various fruits which succeed it. Man flows at once to God when the channel of purity is open" (W, 207–208).

Mindful somatic discipline is not meant to destroy the body but rather to raise it to a higher level; for the body is not simply flesh, bones, and skin, but a sentient soma that includes all the entrenched bodily dispositions that constitute our unreflective habits – what guides our unconscious "sleepwalking" through life. By making our somatic life more conscious, deliberate, and controlled, we are spiritualizing it. Once again, Thoreau turns to Indian philosophical culture, where every bodily "function was reverently spoken of and regulated by law." The "Hindoo lawgiver... teaches us how to eat, drink, cohabit, void excrement and urine, and the like, elevating what is mean" (W, 208–209). But he then evokes a mythical American everyman, John Farmer, whose only method to awaken the spiritual "faculties which slumbered in him" was "to practise some new austerity, to let his mind, descend into his body and redeem it" (W, 209). This dualistic contrast of body and mind is unfortunate from the point of view of somaesthetics, which prefers to speak of the soma as body-mind or embodied intentionality that can experience itself as both subject and object. Somaesthetics, however, shares Thoreau's important insight that feelings and actions that seem merely brutish and bodily can be significantly transformed in meaning and refined in quality through the greater cultivated consciousness we give them in our efforts to attend to them and reshape them in better ways.

Even the act of eating, which Thoreau portrays as lowly, "slimy, beastly," can be raised to spiritual value through enhanced attentive consciousness that carefully discriminates the qualities of flavor and meaning in what and how we eat, thus rendering our tasting also a mental act of cognitive appreciation. "Who has not sometimes derived an inexpressible satisfaction from his food in which appetite had no share? I have been thrilled to think that I owed a mental perception to the commonly gross sense of taste, that I have been inspired through the palate, that some berries which I had eaten on a hillside had fed my genius," he avows (W, 205). If heightened discriminating consciousness elevates tasting from crude sensuality to inspired spiritual refinement, then "he who distinguishes the true savor of his food can never be a glutton; he who does not cannot be otherwise" (W, 205). Eating with the proper attitude of mindfulness (rather than blind desire) allows us to sustain our purity while nourishing the body and inspiring the soul. "Not that food which entereth into the mouth defileth a man, but the appetite with which it is eaten. It is neither the quality nor the quantity, but the devotion to sensual savors; when that which is eaten is not a viand to sustain our animal, or inspire our spiritual life, but food for the worms that possess us" (W, 205–206).

Emerson likewise recognized that our most basic, humble, physical needs can be transformed through enhanced awareness into beautiful expressions of spiritual life and ideas. We should not simply eat and drink and breathe so that we can thereafter have the strength to create ideal works of artistic beauty that we then elevate (and isolate) as superior to life; we should instead "serve the ideal in [the very act of] eating and drinking, in drawing the breath, and in the functions of life" (RWE, 439). Through such heightened, appreciative awareness and the mindful movements and actions that emerge from it, one can achieve extraordinary aesthetic experience in everyday living, as I learned not so much from philosophical readings as from personal experience during my training with a Zen master at his dojo on Japan's Inland Sea, not far from Hiroshima, where I was a visiting professor in 2002–2003.

IV

The idea of philosophy as an embodied, enlightened, and highly conscious art of living (which I first discovered through my readings of the ancient Greeks, Montaigne, the transcendentalists, Nietzsche, and pragmatism) was what indeed initiated my encounter with Zen. Seeking to experience such living but finding no contemporary Western frameworks for it that attracted me, I hoped an interlude of Zen might provide it. I knew it would not be easy to find a genuine Zen dojo with an experienced Zen master who would take me on as a trainee, nor for me to find the time to train there.

I was therefore thrilled when Hiroshima University's Graduate School of Education invited me for the academic year 2002–2003 as a visiting research professor (with full salary but no teaching duties) to pursue my work in somaesthetics, whose project of cognitive enrichment through greater somatic consciousness and body-mind unity appealed to their interest in new ways of learning. While the study of actual Zen technique was surely pertinent to somaesthetic research (which touts the integration of theory and practice), my university hosts, however, seemed averse to my experimenting with Zen monastic life. They apparently worried I would not only be disappointed by not achieving enlightenment, but also be painfully distressed by the ascetic rigors of life in the Zen cloister. After more than six months of asking them if a suitable teacher and dojo could be found (I did not want a Disney Zen experience in a program designed for foreign tourists), I realized that I had to look elsewhere for help.

Fortunately, after giving a lecture at Tokyo University, I met a postdoctoral scholar, Kakutani Masanori, who was researching the concept of teacher in traditional Japanese culture. He found me a teacher whom he knew only by reputation, and then kindly arranged my first meeting with Zen Master (Roshi) Inoue Kido. Dr. Kakutani also generously instructed me on how to prepare for my period of training in the dojo, patiently translating for me the daily schedule (which was on the dojo's website but in a Japanese far beyond my primitive level of basic conversation). He further explained the articles of clothing I needed to buy for my training and where I could procure them. He even advised me on the appropriate sum of money I should give the Roshi as an introductory gift, explaining which sums involved numbers that were considered lucky rather than unlucky in Japanese culture while reminding me that I should provide only clean new bills in my gift envelope. His technical advice was wonderfully helpful, but far from enough to prepare me for the sort of everyday aesthetics of living that I would experience at the dojo under Roshi's guidance.

Before trying to articulate this aesthetics (whose lived quality resists rendition in clear conceptual language), I should note two very different conceptions of everyday aesthetics. Although both are concerned with appreciating ordinary objects or commonplace events, the first notion stresses the ordinariness of these everyday things, while the latter instead emphasizes how such things can be perceived through a distinctively focused aesthetic appreciation that transfigures them into a more richly meaningful experience. This second conception of everyday aesthetics emphasizes aesthetics' root meaning of perception but also the idea that aesthetic experience is a matter of conscious, concentrated attention that is essentially aware of itself as focused or heightened experience and that is appreciated as such. If the first conception of everyday aesthetics is resolutely focused on appreciating the ordinary as ordinary rather than as special, then the aesthetic quality appreciated in this first kind of everyday aesthetics would not call special attention to itself as an intense quality or powerful experience. It would instead be something like appreciating dull weather with an ordinary, dull appreciation of its dullness, rather than a sudden spectacular vision or special experience of its dullness. In contrast, the second conception of everyday aesthetics is about the transfiguration of ordinary objects or commonplace experience into a more intensified perceptual experience that is characterized by explicit, heightened, appreciative awareness.

I read Emerson as advocating this second view when he speaks of our appreciating "the sublime presence of the highest spiritual cause lurking" in the simple things of life ("the milk in the pan; the ballad in the street; the news of the boat; the glance of the eye; the form and the gait of the body"), so that "the world no longer lies a dull miscellany and lumber-room," but rather "every trifle" shines with "form and order" (RWE, 69). While recognizing the validity of the first conception of everyday aesthetics, I find the second more promising, especially when aesthetics is conceived melioristically as a field of study aimed at enriching our lives by providing richer and more rewarding aesthetic experience. From this perspective, aesthetic appreciation of ordinary objects and events serves to enhance and sharpen our perception of them so that we can derive from them the richest experience and most enlightened perception they can offer. If this approach seems paradoxical because its heightened perception renders the ordinary somehow extraordinary in experience, this paradox of awakened perception of the ordinary is less problematic for everyday aesthetics than a parallel paradox we can find in the first conception of ordinary aesthetics. Here the ordinary is experienced in the most ordinary, habitual, inattentive, or "slumbering" way, so that one risks not really perceiving anything aesthetically at all; we cannot savor the object, event, or experience without being aware of it as a special focus of attention.

The second conception is appealing because it offers an attractive alternative to contemporary art's principal method for achieving the similar goal of rendering our perception more attentively conscious or focused, and thus our experience both richer and more memorable. That method involves defamiliarization or "making strange," essentially by making more difficult. As the famous Russian formalist thinker Viktor Shklovsky formulates it, defamiliarization is a special "device of art" aimed at awakening us to a fuller perception of what we see and feel "by 'estranging' objects and complicating form." This technique purposely "makes perception long and 'laborious,'" because "the perceptual process in art has a purpose all its own [is an aesthetic end in itself] and ought to be extended to the fullest."[19] Underlying Shklovsky's argument is the modernist assumption that art's aesthetic forms must be difficult in order to compel prolonged attention needed to render our perception of things conscious and clear.

Developing a comment by Tolstoy echoing Emerson and Thoreau's complaint that habitualized modes of inattentive perception deprive us of the richness of meaning in everyday life, Shklovsky advocates art's estranging difficulty as a way to shock us into awakening by obliging us to

---

[19] Viktor Shklovsky, "Art as Device," in *Theory of Prose*, trans. Benjamin Sher (Normal, IL: Dalkey Archive Press, 1991), 6.

pay attention to things "in order to return sensation to our limbs,... to make us feel objects" more fully and perceive them more clearly than in our "habitual" perception and behavior that "function unconsciously – automatically."[20] One proven danger of this technique, however, is that such difficulty alienates art from the everyday lives of people, especially ordinary people who have neither the cultural education nor the leisure to learn and ponder the sophisticated difficulties that fine art imposes to make its perception "laborious." Such difficulty undemocratically confines art to a privileged elite, while also isolating it even from that elite's praxis of everyday living.

The awakened-consciousness version of everyday aesthetics offers the same sort of transfiguring intensity of awareness, perception, and feeling, but without high art's alienating difficulty and isolating elitism. Of course, it has its own challenges; for it requires some sort of discipline or askesis of perception, a special quality of attentive consciousness or receptive, caring mindfulness that discloses a vast domain of extraordinary beauty in the ordinary objects and events of everyday experience that are transfigured by such mindful attention.

I learned this lesson of discipline from Roshi Inoue Kido at his Shorinkutsu-dojo, situated on a hill looking down at the tiny town of Tadanoumi, in a tranquil rural and mountainous area on the coast of Japan's beautiful Inland Sea. The dojo belongs to the Soto school of Zen, established in Japan by Dōgen (1200–1253), who developed this school's teaching from his experiences of sitting meditation in China as a disciple of Tiantong Rujing. In contrast to the Rinzai school of Zen, which puts greater emphasis on literary texts and the study of *koans*, the Soto school is more strictly focused on the actual bodily practice of sitting meditation and on the strict, uncompromising discipline associated with teaching it, in which the teacher will sometimes resort to shouts or blows to impress his message on the student. Because my Japanese language skills were very limited and seemed far inferior to my skills of somaesthetic focusing (developed through my training as a professional Feldenkrais practitioner and my study of yoga and taijiquan), the body-centered Soto approach seemed best for me, despite its risk of auditory and corporeal violence.

Roshi, who had studied philosophy at Hiroshima University, was very eager to spread Zen teaching to a world he thought desperately needed it, and he warmly welcomed me; but his open, friendly personality did not

---

[20] Ibid., 5.

interfere with the strict disciplinary role he had to play as my teacher.[21] Roshi did not spare the rod on his students when he thought it would instruct them. If I somehow managed to avoid his instructive boxing of the ears (which he always delivered to his students with an affectionate smile), this was only because my Japanese was too feeble to formulate a stupid question (the most frequently punished offense) and because I was so earnest in my efforts of meditation. Once, however, he sharply reprimanded me for leaving three grains of rice in my bowl. If my misdeed was an obvious violation of the Zen commitment to abjure wastefulness, then it was also, I believe, a deplorable gaffe in terms of Roshi's standards in the art of eating, which formed an integral part of his everyday aesthetics of awakened mindfulness, an aesthetic he taught through action as much as through words.

I confine myself to three examples of the abundant lessons he taught me in the aesthetics of the ordinary: the first concerned with ordinary objects, the second with ordinary practices, and the third with the experience of ordinary biological functions. To put these examples in proper context, I should first outline the dojo's everyday training routine, to which I resolutely submitted myself, having relinquished on arrival the books, laptop, cell phone, and other personal belongings relating to my worldly activities that could distract me from Roshi's training. I also had to shed my street clothes for the required training outfit. Purchased online through the help of Dr. Kakutani, it consisted of a *dogi* (white shirt), a dark-colored kimono jacket, a black *hakama* (skirt), and a black *obi* (a cord-like belt) to hold the hakama and dogi in place. The obi was very difficult to tie in the appropriate way. It was first tied for me by Roshi's assistant priest, and I did my best to keep it tied, so I would not have to retie it myself when getting dressed in predawn darkness to start my day of meditation training, whose schedule was as follows.

At 5 A.M., a wooden drum sounded the wake-up call, and we hurried to dress and descend the path from our sleeping quarters to the *zendo* (meditation hall), where we started practicing *zazen* (seated meditation) and found either Roshi or his chief assistant already deep in practice. After an hour of meditation, Roshi usually performed a morning service at the adjacent Shounji temple, followed by another short service back at the dojo's main building, where we then breakfasted. Immediately after eating but before the post-meal prayers, Roshi would give a lecture

---

[21] Various texts of Roshi Kido (including translations into French and English) are available on the dojo's website: http://shorinkutsu.com/.

on Buddhist philosophy or Zen practice. He would sometimes lecture at other meals, although his breakfast lessons were the most formal and powerfully substantive ones, in keeping with the inspiring energy of morning freshness that Thoreau so celebrates.

After breakfast, novices like me would immediately go back to the *zendo* to continue practicing *zazen*, while more experienced trainees would do some light manual maintenance work in the dojo before joining us in the *zendo*. Lunch was at noon, followed by an immediate return to Zen practice for us tyros, until a 6 p.m. supper. In the afternoons, besides work and *zazen*, trainees would have a bath every other day (each member of the community taking his turn to prepare wood for the fire that kept the water hot), but newcomers would not be allowed to bathe for the first four days. Occasionally, a formal tea ceremony was offered by Roshi. The designated bedtime was 9 p.m., with lights out at 10 p.m., but the *zendo* was always open, and one could practice *zazen* there throughout the night, if one had the stamina and alertness.

Roshi insisted, however, that Zen discipline was not essentially a matter of physical endurance in sitting. He did not require new trainees to sit in the full lotus position (*kekkafuza*), but instead urged them to adopt a posture that allowed them to focus their mind on other things than physical discomfort in sitting. Convinced that the alert attentiveness of one's *kokoro* (the heart and mind) is much more important for meditation than one's precise sitting position, Roshi also realized that such focused concentration is very tiring for beginners and that there is no point in meditating when too tired to achieve mindful awakening. Analogizing that one cannot properly cut rice plants with a dull blade, he advised me to get up from my meditation cushion at the *zendo* whenever I felt tired and go back to the sleeping hut for a nap to refresh my soma and thus sharpen my consciousness. My powers of sustained concentration, he explained, would grow through enhanced mental acuity not through mere willful efforts of stubborn endurance in sitting. I followed Roshi's advice, and my attentive capacities indeed developed in ways that the following three examples should, I hope, make clear.

V

1. As a novice, I spent most of my time between the *zendo* and the trainees' sleeping quarters. There were two different paths between these locations, and near one of them I noticed a small clearing with an especially open and beautiful view of the sea, dotted with a few small islands of

lush, soft, bushy green. In the clearing was a primitive stool, rudely constructed from a round section of log on whose short, upright column (still adorned with bark) there rested a small rectangular wooden board to sit on, and with no nails or adhesive other than gravity to fix it to the log. A couple of feet in front of the stool stood two rusty old cast-iron oil barrels, the kind I had often seen used as makeshift open-air stoves by homeless people in America's poor inner city neighborhoods.[22] Sitting on the stool to look at the sea beneath the dojo, one's view was inescapably framed by the two corroding brownish barrels. I wondered why this ugly pair was left in such a lovely spot, spoiling the sublime natural seascape with an industrial eyesore.

One day I got the courage to ask Roshi whether I would be permitted to practice meditation for a short time in that spot overlooking the sea, although I dared not ask him why the hideous barrels (which the Japanese call "drum cans") were allowed to pollute the aesthetic and natural purity of that perspective. Permission was readily granted, since Zen meditation can, in principle, be done anywhere, and Roshi felt I had progressed enough to practice outside the *zendo*. So I sat myself down on the stool and, having directed my gaze above the barrels, fixed my contemplation on the beautiful sea while following Roshi's meditation instruction of focusing attention to my breathing and trying to clear my mind of all thoughts. After about twenty minutes of effective meditation, I lost my grip of concentration and decided to end this meditative session. Turning my glance toward the closest of the two barrels, I discovered that my perception had awakened to a more penetrating level in which the ordinary ugly object was transfigured into something of breathtaking beauty, just as beautiful as the sea; indeed, even more so. I felt I was now truly seeing that drum can for the first time, savoring the subtle sumptuousness of its coloring, the shades of orange, the tints of blue and green that highlighted its earthy browns. I thrilled to the richness of its irregular texture, its tissue of flaking and peeling crusts embellishing the hard iron shell, a symphony of soft and firm surfaces that suggested a delicious *feuilleté*.

In my awakened consciousness, the drum can glowed with the fullness of vivid presence. The rusty barrel had an immediate, robust, absolutely

---

[22] Readers more familiar with contemporary art might recognize them as the kind of barrels that Christo and Jeanne Claude painted and massively piled on their sides in two notable artworks – *Iron Curtain*, an installation that temporarily sealed the Parisian rue Visconti in 1962, and *The Wall* of 1999 that involved 1,300 brightly painted and monumentally stacked barrels.

absorbing reality that made my vision of the sea pale in comparison. The drum can's everyday proximity (in being perceived attentively as fully here and now) radiated the gleam and energy with which the wondrous flux of our immanent material world resonates and sparkles. Conversely, I realized that it was more *the idea* of the sea that I had been regarding as beautiful, not the sea itself, which I saw through a veil of familiar thoughts – its conventional romantic meanings and the wonderful personal associations it had for me, a Tel Aviv beach boy turned philosopher. In contrast, the barrel, without losing its status as everyday object, was grasped as a beauty of the most concrete and captivating immediacy. But to see that beauty required a sustained period of disciplined meditative awareness. Although the disciplined mindfulness was initially not directed at the drum can, this alone was what enabled the perception of its beauty in the immediate fullness of the present moment, and I could – on subsequent occasions – recover this vision of its beauty by foregoing the seascape and directing my absorbed contemplation at the barrels themselves.

2. From the vision of ordinary objects transfigured through awakened perception, I turn to the transformation of everyday practices into performative arts of living beauty through awakened attentiveness of mindful action. My example of such artistry was the eating of meals at the dojo. On the one hand, such meals were paradigms of ordinary simplicity. The stage was bare and humble. We sat on the floor, in the kitchen, around a low wooden table with no one formally serving us. The food was very plain and was presented with no garnish or visual adornment. The crockery and cutlery were equally humble, the kind one could find in a *hyaku yen* shop (or Japanese dollar store); and they were old with use and sometimes even slightly chipped or damaged. But emerging in vivid contrast from the lowly stage and shabby props, the actual action of the meal was extraordinary in performative grace and thoughtful elegance, as each movement was meant to be executed and experienced as the focus of careful, mindful, loving attention.

Rather than functioning simply as breaks for necessary physical nourishment and relief from the trainee's essential activity of meditation, the dojo meals were in fact an important extension of our training in awakened awareness, but by other means than sitting meditation and in other venues than the *zendo*. (Indeed, even in the *zendo* we were sometimes told to practice walking meditation or *kinyin* as a break from constant *zazen*.) Meals were a place where we could demonstrate awakened mindfulness in active everyday movement, and do so in a challenging context where our appetites and unconscious habits were fully aroused and thus especially potent for distracting us from focused attention to the movements we performed and the feelings we experienced in this communal act of dining.

As we ate in silence, Roshi's penetrating and authoritative gaze would gauge our progress in mindful awareness from the quality of our eating style, from the focused grace of our movements – the way we handled our bowls and chopsticks, how we tasted, chewed, and swallowed our food, how we passed food to our eating companions, whether we noticed (from their gaze or postural orientation) when our companions were interested in receiving a dish that was in our reach. Knowing Roshi was judging our mindfulness in eating, we trainees would also critically examine each others' dining performance while seeking to maximize the mindful grace of one's own eating style. The result was that everyday ordinary meals became an extraordinary experience of mindful, coordinated action, a sophisticated, elegant choreography of dining movement pursued with heightened attentiveness to graceful movement and careful respect for one's comrades and one's food as well as for one's self and one's teacher.

For me, meals posed a special challenge. This was not because of the dojo's cooking, which differed from typical restaurant food and had its funky aspects. Having married into a Japanese family that cherished all varieties of Japanese cuisine, I was fortunately able to enjoy the dojo's rustic fare. Otherwise, my experience would have been a nightmare, as one was forced to eat all that one was served. (One trainee who did not finish his raw squid at dinner found the remains on his plate the following breakfast.) My special dining challenge, however, was to eat with graceful, mindful elegance. Knowing my habitual manners of eating were rather careless, casual, and often sloppy, I also knew that Roshi would be paying close attention to my eating style. For at our very first meal together, he stunned me by his brutally frank critique of it. "You are technically quite skillful at using chopsticks," he noted, "perhaps because your wife is Japanese. But for a professor of aesthetics you eat in a most ugly manner. You have a lot more than *zazen* to learn here!" I felt my breath stop and my face flush red. I did not know what to say or do.

Roshi, fortunately, continued by explaining that my technical competence in using chopsticks was ruined by the sloppily thoughtless manner in which I picked them up and set them down, but also by the graceless way I handled my rice bowl and tea cup – the inelegant positioning of my hands on these vessels and the ungainly postural manner in which I brought their contents to my mouth. He then patiently showed me what he considered the aesthetically proper way to pick up and put down one's chopsticks and to hold one's rice bowl and cup. When I tried to emulate his method, inaccurately at first, he demonstrated and explained again, until I grasped the principles and method, which I subsequently applied in actual practice.

Everyday dining thus became a challenging dramatic performance of mindful grace in movement, of aesthetically elegant eating through awakened appreciative awareness of all one's actions and feelings (including one's interactions with one's companions) in partaking of food and drink. At first, I was terrified. If my days were full of meditation, then my nights were sometimes troubled by nightmarish images of soiling my new white *dogi* with food dropping clumsily from my chopsticks or dripping sloppily from my careless slurping mouth. With no other *dogi* to change into, the shameful stain of my ugly, mindless eating would always remain exposed to Roshi's scornful condemnation and the ridicule of my fellow trainees. I thus resolved to eat as carefully, deliberately, and mindfully as I could, despite being haunted by the worry that my actions of eating would in fact be rendered more awkward precisely by thinking about them while performing them. For I knew how theorists of body consciousness repeatedly insist that explicit, focused attention to the details of motor action impedes its smooth and graceful execution by destroying the effective spontaneity of our habits of coordinated movement that perform our ordinary desired actions with such marvelous yet thoughtless efficacy.

But after all my efforts to find a true Zen teacher, it seemed foolish to ignore his instruction while training with him, so I took the path of explicit attentiveness in action, and I was not disappointed in the results. My *dogi* remained spotlessly white. Still more rewarding was the way awakened awareness enriched the satisfaction of eating. With skillfully focused purpose, my consciousness would smoothly shift attention from the pickled plum, seaweed, or clump of sticky rice and fermented soy beans on the tips of my chopsticks and direct it to the opening of my mouth and then to the diverse feelings of tasting and chewing the food, before I would swallow with similarly heightened awareness. As this attention to savoring, chewing, and swallowing enhanced the sensory pleasures of these activities, so my focused awareness of the hand and body movements (and attendant feelings) involved in taking or passing the plates of food made these movements likewise more enjoyable and graceful. Coordinating these movements and feelings with those of my companions further enriched the dining experience with valuable harmonies of collaborative interaction. Mealtime anxiety soon diminished, displaced by burgeoning gratification from this simply staged but exquisitely transfigured communal choreography. This lived experience of improved action through greater consciousness of movement so clearly contradicted the prevailing philosophical arguments against heightened body consciousness that I came to suspect the limits of those arguments, and subsequently articulated them in *Body Consciousness* and in this book.

3. My third Zen example of aesthetically transfiguring everyday life concerns the basic function of breathing. Its being an instinctive biological necessity does not preclude also constituting an aesthetic pleasure enhanced through artistry. As Thoreau highlights the simple yet captivating pleasure of breathing, "Of all ebriosity, who does not prefer to be intoxicated by the air he breathes?" (W, 205), so Zen advocates focused concentration on breathing as a tool that can bring not only pleasures of awakened somatic awareness but also the bliss of enlightenment or *satori*, through greater mindfulness of the concrete reality of the present moment (what Roshi, following Dōgen, calls "the now"). Since breathing is always in the present moment, concentrating on the breath helps break the habits of thought that take us away from "the now" through chains of associations that distract the mind with thoughts of past events and future projects, concealing the truth of the present with a veil of images ranging from regrets of earlier actions to worries about what lies ahead.

The importance of focusing on the moment is why Roshi Kido, unlike many teachers of meditation, does not recommend the technique of counting breath (*sosokukan*), because its serialization tempts the mind to past and future. If we are counting our third breath, we are implicitly looking back to the second and ahead to the fourth. One reason why Zen meditation finds it useful to focus on a somatic feature like breathing is because the soma is always present in the here and now of real experience, even though it is typically absent from explicit consciousness and not (as perceptive subjectivity) defined in terms of mere physical place.

In concentrating on my breathing, I became gradually aware of many previously unappreciated aspects of my bodily experience. I noticed more precisely how my breathing changes when attention is directed to it. I discerned a difference, hard to capture in words, between thinking of my breathing (where I felt totally absorbed in its presence) and thinking of my "breathing" in a less complete way where it seemed more like thinking about the idea of breathing or thinking *about* breathing. I felt a difference between focusing my concentration fiercely (as if gripping something tightly) and attending more tenderly (as if gently holding a delicate flower or welcoming the soft, soothing kiss of a lover's lips on my own). I found that the latter way of following my breath proved better for sustaining my focus and generating pleasure, making each breath taste cleaner, sweeter, and fresher than I had ever previously experienced. I could appreciate the different rhythms of my breathing and the different parts of my body in which they resonated; I also learned to discern those parts of me in which each breath was initiated. By directing attention to these different aspects of my breathing and then noticing the changes this attention introduced to it, I was able to sustain a longer, clearer focus on my breath and resist the tendency for my mind to wander elsewhere.

On the sixth day of meditation, I suddenly felt a thrilling sensation of "breathing through my ears," an experience I had never even imagined and still cannot properly understand conceptually, but which I repeatedly achieved in my meditation and which Roshi clearly recognized. While attending to such breathing the following day, I felt a whole symphony of movement in my head, neck, shoulders, chest, and abdomen. At the center of it all were the very clear sound of my heart and the feeling of its quiet rhythm as I sat tranquilly. I could hear its double beat and feel its different places (and directions) of contraction, sensing the flow of blood that was pumped out the aorta. The heartbeat was clearest at my pauses in breathing, and I therefore lingered and prolonged those pauses, especially as it seemed to make the subsequent breath even more deliciously fresh and fragrant. The pleasures of this somatic symphony were so overwhelming that I felt my eyes streaming with tears of joy. I was convinced that every impulse of greed, violence, and jealousy would evaporate in anyone who experienced such simple, pure, but potent somatic happiness. Here, it seemed, was more than a method for everyday aesthetics but also perhaps a program for world peace.

Roshi was neither surprised by my discoveries nor pleased by my somatic manipulations. Once the mind is no longer distracted by its familiar habits of dwelling on images of the outside world, he explained, the phenomena of one's inner bodily life manifest themselves much more clearly to consciousness. But the aim of meditation, he continued, is not somatic introspection in itself nor the intensification of everyday pleasures through such tricks as holding the breath (which he argued was unnatural). The aim instead is a mindful consciousness that is so fully absorbed in the reality of the moment that it no longer feels itself as separate from that reality. My breathing tricks and somaesthetic diagnoses, Roshi cautioned, were vestigial intellectualist handicaps to my progress, drawing me to experience my body as an object to be explored and manipulated by a distinct, critical, scopic consciousness. Though initially useful in strengthening my concentration on breathing, this analytic, manipulative consciousness of somatic introspection, Roshi said, had to be transcended in order for me to make further progress, to achieve a more complete experience of nondualism where there was no longer a consciousness of self and breath but simply an overwhelming impersonal perception of breathing that pervaded all my consciousness and carried the breathing forward on its own accord.

By the end of my stay at the dojo, I occasionally seemed to reach this state, accompanied by an intense feeling of profound fulfillment, enhanced by the delicious pleasures of fresh air and rhythmic respiratory motion. Although I experienced this pleasure somatically, the body's sense of being a distinct place with well-defined borders (whether physical or phenomenological) dissolved into an expansively flowing field of experience, pulsating with joy and a sense of unbounded wholeness whose fullness is also an emptiness of distinctions between consciousness and its different objects and places. The now of the moment is no enduring place, but by its essence vanishes into the next moment. So, too, the Zen soma, although initially the salient site of meditative practice, is ultimately experienced as a no-place when that practice is successful, exemplifying (albeit in a more blissfully powerful form) the way that the body tends to efface itself into the wider field of action when it is functioning at its happy best.

14

Somatic Style

I

Style is a crucial feature in the arts; not only the fine arts but also in the practical arts of fashion, jewelry, fragrance, cuisine, and product and graphic design. To appreciate how the body is likewise central to the arts, we need only to recognize its crucial role in style. Yet one of America's greatest minds and finest stylists, Ralph Waldo Emerson, has affirmed, "A man's style is his mind's voice. Wooden minds have wooden voices."[1] If Emerson here defines style through the notion of mind, it is not to deny the somatic dimension of style. Style is essentially embodied, as Emerson's reference to voice clearly implies. Vocalization is clearly a bodily act, involving one's breath, vocal chords, and mouth. Moreover, the materiality of the mind's expression in style is further suggested in Emerson's reference to wooden minds and wooden voices. If we look at the concept of style through etymology, however, we find its somatic roots not in the orality of voice but rather in the bodily gesture of inscription. The word derives from the Latin word *stylus*, one of whose primary meanings was a sharp instrument used by the Romans for writing and engraving on wax tablets. It thus came, by implication, to convey more generally the method of writing or engraving with any sharp or pointed instrument, such action involving some somatic skill.

From a particular physical tool or method of writing (one notably different from the traditional Chinese use of a soft brush), style's primary meaning has evolved into a more abstract, literary, and lofty sense. Not merely a *means* of writing or making other kinds of signs, style has become an aesthetic quality whose creation and appreciation forms part of the

---

[1] Ralph Waldo Emerson, "Journal 67" in E. W. Emerson and R. W. Forbes (eds.), *Journals of Ralph Waldo Emerson* (Boston: Houghton Mifflin, 1910–1914), vol. 10, 457.

end of writing and is indeed sought and cherished for its own intrinsic value. Some theorists, however, appeal to style's homely instrumental origin in order to insist that we should confine its role to a practical means for conveying thoughts, so as to ensure that style will not distract from clarity and honesty of communication. This is the view of Emerson's friend and transcendentalist fellow traveler, Henry David Thoreau. "Who cares what a man's style is, so [long as] it is intelligible," he argues. "Literally and really, the style is no more than the *stylus*, the pen he writes with; and it is not worth scraping and polishing, and gilding, unless it will write his thoughts the better for it. It is something for use, and not to look at."[2]

Without endorsing Thoreau's view of style as a mere physical means for mental ends (and pending subsequent critique of that view through Thoreau's own writing), we can affirm its recognition of the basic somatic nature of style. If a person's style of mind and thought is in some way bodily – whether through voice or writing (as these two famous transcendentalists insist) – then it would seem that all human style is in some way somatic. What then is a specifically somatic style? What are its distinctive components or dimensions? What features or uses of the body are especially formative or expressive of somatic style? Which senses and modalities of perception are engaged in our appreciation of somatic style?

Before engaging such questions directly, we should frame them by considering five important distinctions that inhabit and structure the general concept of style and also inform its more specific somatic version. This quintet of contrasting senses of style are the honorific versus merely descriptive; the generic versus the personal; the explicitly conscious or reflective versus the merely spontaneous or unconscious; the voluntary versus involuntary; the permanent versus the contextual. Before explaining these distinctions, let me offer here two largely neglected and perhaps surprising reasons why a philosopher should be interested in somatic style, even if they do not share my own special commitment to the field of somaesthetics.[3]

---

[2] Henry David Thoreau, "Thomas Carlyle and His Works," in *Miscellanies by Henry David Thoreau* (Boston: Houghton, Mifflin and Co., 1894), 99.

[3] Style is, of course, central to the project of somaesthetics, whose initial definition as "the critical, meliorative study of the experience and use of one's body as a locus of sensory-aesthetic appreciation (aesthesis) and creative self-fashioning" could also have been formulated in terms of "creative self-stylization." See Richard Shusterman, "Somaesthetics: A Disciplinary Proposal," *Journal of Aesthetics and Art Criticism* 57:3 (1999): 302.

II

Although it seems to have nothing to do with intellectual thought or reasoning, somatic style can be very effective in communicating a philosopher's views and rendering them convincing. William James apparently believed that one could not fully understand a philosopher until one met him in person, because philosophy, for James, was ultimately an expression of the philosopher's personality, which would be more completely displayed in a full-bodied encounter.[4] Such real-life encounters could reveal aspects of the philosopher's basic attitude toward life and society that his texts concealed. If philosophy is also conceived as a way of life, then seeing the philosopher in a real-life context could likewise reveal whether he practiced what he seemed to preach; it is easier to say things than to do them; easier to lie in words than in one's body language. But somatic style can conversely give greater force to one's words and philosophical ideas.

We learn from G.E. Moore's distinguished colleagues from Bloomsbury and Cambridge that his "sublime beauty" and vehement body language gave him tremendous powers of persuasion in philosophical discussion and debate. "Still slim in those days, Moore seemed indeed not of this miserable planet, but a prophet nourished with wisdom and goodness from some far-off mysterious source, enhaloed with transcendental illumination." His teachings were "branded into the consciousness of his students by a variety of forensic devices (opening wide his eyes, raising his eyebrows, sticking out his tongue, wagging his head in the negative so violently that his hair shook)." The inspirational power of Moore's ideas were thus enhanced by a somatic style that even the logical Bertrand Russell described as exuding "a kind of exquisite purity," "beautiful and slim, with a look almost of inspiration," that enabled him to embody Russell's "ideal of genius."[5]

---

[4] James occasionally makes this point in his correspondence. See, for example, his letter to Bergson of May 13, 1905, where he requests to meet the French philosopher, explaining that to "see [Bergson] face to face" could give him "a little better understanding of some of the points in [Bergson's] philosophy," even if they did not spend the time of their meeting discussing these points. James adds, "I think it must always be good for two philosophers who are *near* each other to come into personal contact. They will understand each other better, even if they should only gossip away their hour." I quote from the letter as reproduced in Ralph Barton Perry, *The Thought and Character of William James* (Boston: Little, Brown, 1935), vol. 1, 613. James first met Bergson shortly thereafter, on May 28, 1905.

[5] See, respectively, Michael Holroyd, *Lytton Strachey: A Biography* (London: Penguin, 1971), 199, 201; G. Spater and I. Parsons, *A Marriage of True Minds: An Intimate Portrait of Leonard*

Somatic style likewise contributed to the communicative power of Ludwig Wittgenstein, another of Russell's renowned Cambridge philosophical colleagues. It helped endow him with an inspiring aura of intellectual brilliance that made his views and arguments more compelling through the power of his commanding personality. "His face was lean and brown, his profile was aquiline and strikingly beautiful... His look was concentrated, he made striking gestures with his hands.... His face was remarkably mobile and expressive when he talked. His eyes were deep and often fierce in their expression. His whole personality was commanding, even imperial."[6]

One's personality is indeed expressed in somatic style. A meek or shy individual can often be recognized by a stooped posture, a lowered gaze that fails to make eye-contact, a hesitant walk, and restrained or inhibited

---

and Virginia Woolf (London: Hogarth, 1972), 32; and Bertrand Russell, *The Autobiography of Bertrand Russell, 1872–1914* (London: Allen & Unwin, 1967), 90. Consider also the direct written testimony of Leonard Woolf, who regarded Moore as "the only great man" he ever met: "When I first knew him, his face was amazingly beautiful, almost ethereal, and, as Bertrand Russell has said, 'he had, what he retained throughout his life, an extraordinarily lovable smile.' But he resembled Socrates in possessing a profound simplicity, a simplicity which Tolstoy and some other Russian writers consider to produce the finest human beings.... It showed itself perhaps in such simple, unrestrained, passionate gestures as when, if told something particularly astonishing or confronted by some absurd statement at the crisis of an argument, his eyes would open wide, his eyebrows shoot up, and his tongue shoot out of his mouth. And Bertrand Russell has described the pleasure with which one used to watch Moore trying unsuccessfully to light his pipe when he was arguing an important point. He would light a match, hold it over the bowl of his pipe until it burnt his fingers and he had to throw it away, and go on doing this – talking the whole time or listening intently to the other man's argument – until the whole box of matches was exhausted." Leonard Woolf, *Sowing, An Autobiography of the Years 1880 to 1904* (New York: Harcourt, Brace, 1960), 144, 151. Another Cambridge admirer, the famous Nobel Prize economist John Maynard Keynes, explains how Moore used his somatic style to win his arguments, where "victory was with those who could speak with the greatest appearance of clear, undoubting conviction and could best use the accents of infallibility. Moore at this time was a master of this method – greeting one's remarks with a gasp of incredulity – Do you *really* think *that*, an expression of face as if to hear such a thing said reduced him to a state of wonder verging on imbecility, with his mouth wide open and wagging his head in the negative so violently that his hair shook. *Oh!* He would say, goggling at you as if either you or he must be mad; and no reply was possible." J.M. Keynes, "My Early Beliefs," in *Essays and Sketches in Biography* (New York: Meridian, 1956), 243–44. Leonard Woolf confirms this use of somatic style through forceful yet appealing gesture: "When Moore said: 'I simply don't understand what he means,' the emphasis on the 'simply' and the 'what' and the shake of his head over each word gave one a glimpse of the passionate distress which muddled thinking aroused in him" (Woolf, *Sowing*, 149).

[6] Norman Malcolm, *Wittgenstein: A Memoir* (Oxford: Oxford University Press, 1985), 23–24.

gestural movement. Wittgenstein surely knew this, as he affirmed not only that "The human body is the best picture of the human soul," but also "that a man's style is [the] *picture* of him."[7] Although the famous historian Edward Gibbon made the similar remark that "Style is the image of character,"[8] we could, I think, go further by arguing that the relationship is even closer than these picturing and image metaphors suggest. For they still imply a dualism of soma and psyche that could allow cases like the portrait of Dorian Gray, in which the visible portrait or image of character remains eminently attractive although the character has become hideously corrupt. Somatic style, then, is not simply an external image of character but an integral expression or aspect of it, because character is not merely a secret inner essence but rather something intrinsically expressed or constituted through somatic behavior, demeanor, and attitude.

This key Confucian doctrine that one's character and somatic comportment are essentially indivisible explains why Confucius insists so much on the importance of countenance or demeanor in the practice of ethical virtues. The key virtue of filial piety, he tells us, requires "showing the proper countenance" rather than merely performing the dutiful action, since one's somatic expression shows that one is doing the act with the proper feeling. Exemplary persons therefore insist on "maintaining a dignified demeanor... [t]o keep violent and rancorous conduct at a distance" and "maintaining a proper countenance... [to] keep trust and confidence near at hand."[9] The essential connection of somatic and ethical style is also why Confucianism sees ritual and the fine arts (especially music, poetry, dance, and calligraphy) as the two main pillars of ethics. Ritual, by stylizing our bodily actions and gestures, also shapes and harmonizes our character, both in terms of self-unity and in coordination with others in the social context. By developing the individual's sense of harmony, grace, and beauty, the arts thereby enhance his ability to express these qualities in his conduct and in his rapport with others;

---

[7] Ludwig Wittgenstein, *Philosophical Investigations*, trans. G.E.M. Anscombe (Oxford: Blackwell, 1968), II, 178; *Culture and Value*, trans. Peter Winch (Oxford: Blackwell, 1980), 78.

[8] Edward Gibbon, *Memoirs of My Life and Writings*, in *Miscellaneous works of Edward Gibbon, Esquire. With memoirs of his life and writings, composed by himself: illustrated from his letters, with occasional notes and narrative by John Lord Sheffield* (Basel: J.J. Tourneisen, 1796), vol. 1, 1.

[9] I quote from Roger Ames and Henry Rosemont, Jr. (trans.), *The Analects of Confucius: A Philosophical Translation* (New York: Ballantine, 1998), 78, 121.

playing music or dancing together creates harmonious habits that are both somatic and social.[10]

Because of the firm Confucian faith in the unity of the mental and somatic, a teacher can teach without words, but instead by his embodied example of behavior. Confucius therefore once proposed to "leave off speaking" and teach wordlessly as nature does through somatic expression both in action and in rest (*Analects* 17:9). Thus, his disciple Mencius could write: "His every limb bears wordless testimony."[11] This crucial role of somatic style in ethical instruction is why so much of Book Ten of the *Analects* is devoted to describing Confucius's somatic comportment (the different ways he ate, dressed, bowed, walked, and so on as fitting the different contexts in which his action was situated). The corollary of this idea is that one cannot hide one's moral character, even if one wants to because it is wicked. "How," asks Mencius, "can a man conceal his true character," when not only "his words" but also "the pupils of his eyes" reveal it?[12] These Confucian ideas of style and character are not without their echoes in the West, where we have Buffon's famous epigram, "*Le style c'est l'homme même*" ("Style is the man himself"), which Wittgenstein unfortunately glosses in terms of a picturing metaphor that paradoxically divides or distances what Buffon was trying to bring together.

The distinction of style (whether literary or otherwise) from the essence of a person's character and thought finds expression in other metaphors than picturing or imaging. One such distancing metaphor is that of clothes, which merely dress the body rather than being part of it. Typical here is Lord Chesterfield's remark: "Style is the dress of thoughts; and let them be ever so just, if your style is homely, coarse, and vulgar, they will appear to as much disadvantage, and be as ill received, as your person, though ever so well proportioned, would, if dressed in rags, dirt, and tatters."[13] As clothes dress the body to make it appear less coarse and more cultured, so style renders our thoughts less crude, more cultured,

---

[10] The crucial Confucian concept of developing, refining, or cultivating one's character or self is explicitly described (in *The Great Learning* and in Xunzi's essay "On Self-Cultivation") in terms of *xiu shen* 修身, *shen* being the word for "body" and "person." Art and ritual are crucial ways of cultivating the *shen*, so that ritual bodily action or labor with its characteristic bowing of the body is sometimes conveyed with the *shen*-deploying character of "*gong*" (躬).

[11] See W.A.C.H. Dobson (trans.), *Mencius: A New Translation* (Toronto: University of Toronto Press, 1963), 181.

[12] Here I cite D.C. Lau (trans.) *Mencius* (London: Penguin, 1970), 124.

[13] Earl of Chesterfield, *Letters to His Son: On the Fine Art of Becoming a Man of the World and a Gentleman* (New York: Tudor, 1937), 245.

hence superior. But this metaphor can be turned around to style's disadvantage. As clothes conceal or disguise the body, so style can obscure or distort one's thoughts. Style here becomes an artificial dressing that hides the real substance of one's thoughts or distracts attention from even seeing that those thoughts have no real substance worth communicating, that they are full of manner but empty of matter. Style here becomes synonymous with artifice, pretension, gratuitous ornament, feigning, and falseness.

Thoreau's critique of style for its fuss of "gilding and polishing" is a response to such artificiality of style that, rather than humbly serving the matter of thought, calls excessive attention to itself in the way that impractical fancy clothes often do. In advocating style that is simple, clear, practical, and sincere, he echoes the ideal of natural style praised by Blaise Pascal as delighting us through its refreshingly candid communication of the human soul rather than the artificial posturing of an artist. "When we see a natural style, we are quite amazed and delighted, because we expected to see an author and find a man."[14]

This praise of natural style implies an endorsement of the intimate connection of style with character or personality. Though Pascal here is obviously referring to a style of writing, we could surely apply the notion of natural style also to a person's somatic rather than literary expression. For we often conversely criticize people for affectation in their style of bodily comportment and gesture or for artificiality in stylizing their physical appearance and attire. But the notion of natural style raises some interesting questions: What makes a style natural, and why should its being natural imply that it is also good? How does having a natural style differ from having no distinctive style at all or no style worthy of the name but instead merely acting in the most natural way available or in an instinctive, thoughtless, uncultivated manner? How can a person develop or work on one's natural style without turning it into something affected or unnatural? As such questions reflect the ambiguities of the concept of style, we should now turn to an analysis of its fivefold complexity.

III

1. Style is a term that is often used in an evaluative sense to praise someone or something, as when one commends a person by saying she has style. In such locutions and in describing someone as stylish, the implication is

---

[14] Blaise Pascal, *Pensées*, trans. A.J. Krailsheimer (London: Penguin, 1966), 242.

that the manifested style is good. But in another, non-evaluative, sense of the term, everyone has his or her style (of speech, writing, comportment, clothing), even if that style is unattractive, outmoded, or lacking in style in the honorific sense. When we say something like "That's John's style," the term means the distinctive way the person has of presenting herself or behaving. We could call this non-evaluative meaning of style "descriptive," as long as we recognize that it does not really describe very much. Saying "That's John style" or "He has this style" may be a placeholder for further descriptions of John's way of acting or speaking or dressing, but it may simply be used on its own to note or indicate ostensively that way, which may seem to the speaker indescribable in further terms or simply not worth describing further. If clothing belongs to somatic style, as it surely seems to, then somatic style also involves this ambiguity. But even excluding attire from the notion of somatic style, we can look at ways of walking, gesturing, eating, getting in and out of one's seat, which are more or less stylish in the honorific sense but which, no matter how unstylish, will exemplify style in the descriptive sense – an awkwardly unattractive yet idiosyncratic style of eating or walking, for example.

2. Style can be generic or personal. In painting, we can speak of a Baroque style or a Cubist style, but we can also speak of the individual styles of particular Baroque painters. To be a memorable painter (or significant artist in other genres), one should have a distinctive personal style rather than simply exhibit a generic style. Developing such a signature style is part of what it is to be a successful artist. Of course, an artist might deploy a variety of styles (cubism, surrealism, abstract expressionism), but we still look for a signature personal style in the different generic styles that the artist uses, a stylistic unity beneath those differences that expresses the individual's particular genius. We sometimes distinguish between the early style of an artist and his style at a later period. The same sort of distinction can sometimes be made between a philosopher's different styles. For instance, not only did the ideas of Wittgenstein's later philosophy diverge significantly from that of his early Tractarian period, the style of his philosophical writing was also very different; so different that it serves to magnify the difference of content. But again, we can see both periods as in some way expressing, despite their difference, an underlying style or quality that expresses Ludwig Wittgenstein's unique and remarkable philosophical personality. Although the contrast between generic and individual style is helpfully clear, it is worth noting that an individual's style may become so distinctive, influential, and recognizable that it can also function in a more generic way in which it can be applied to other persons than the individual who defined it, though usually with the suggestion that those others suffer from not developing their own signature style. (We can thus speak of someone having a philosophical style that is late Wittgensteinian or a writing style that is Hemingwayesque.)

Somatic styles can likewise be generic and personal. Obviously, there are generic dressing styles. These include the classificational styles of dress code (such as formal, semiformal, business informal, smart casual, business casual, and so forth). Others are ethnic genre styles (such as Japanese, Indian, Hasidic, Scottish, etc.), while still others involve taste-group styles (such as preppie, grunge, corporate, hip hop, etc.). But within each genre of clothing style, an individual can still strive to find a personal style of his own. Somatic styles of movement can also be generic. A military drill sergeant walks and gestures differently than a sommelier, a nun differently than a runway model or a hooker. Their different generic somatic styles are incorporated habits instilled through practicing their professions. Sports can also create different generic somatic styles, and so we speak of a surfer's or swimmer's or sumo wrestler's bodily style. Musical subcultures likewise generate somatic styles that go beyond mere clothes: for instance, in hip-hop culture the b-boy's way of walking and gesturing.

Other generic somatic styles relate to age groups: we sometimes describe a grown man's looks, body, or style of movement as being boyish; or an adult woman's somatic style as being girlish or contrastingly matronly or elderly beyond her years. Perhaps the most generic of somatic styles is that of gender itself: a feminine way of looking, walking, gesturing, sitting, and so on as opposed to a manly appearance, posture, or style of movement. But alongside such generic styles, each individual in these professions, subcultures, or age groups may have his or her own personal style of movement, a recognizable gait and manner of gesture. That particular personal style may be so distinctive and influential that it constitutes a generic style (e.g., the Twiggy look); but also when it is far less distinctive, a somatic style can still be very evident to observers, even if the person herself does not consciously try to develop or display it – indeed, even if she does not even know she manifests it.

3. This raises a third distinction within the concept of style: its conscious, deliberate formation through explicit stylization versus its spontaneous, unreflective expression. Just as writers often strive consciously to develop or improve their literary style, many people devote considerable conscious thought and effort to stylizing themselves somatically. Somatic self-stylization generates an enormous commercial market that feeds the cosmetic, fashion, dieting, exercise, and plastic surgery industries, along with the advertising industry that supports them by stimulating our desire to stylize ourselves somatically. This desire typically takes the paradoxical form of wanting to fit in yet also to stand out as distinctive. In other words, self-styling involves conforming in some way to the norms of some social taste group (which could be a subculture that resists mainstream taste), yet not allowing such conformity to generic style to preclude one's own individual expression.

Within the realm of voluntary stylizing, we can distinguish between self-conscious, deliberative efforts to stylize and spontaneous choices of style that are more or less unconscious expressions of personality or taste. In the former case, these conscious, calculating efforts of self-styling may become evident also to those who regard that style. If they find it too self-conscious and effortful, they are likely to criticize the style as affected, forced, or artificial. In contrast, one might point to the unreflective spontaneity of style in the latter case as exemplifying natural style. But we must be careful to recognize that we are dealing here with a form of spontaneity that is not instinctive but rather very much culturally conditioned. The individual simply absorbs a preference for certain somatic modes or models from the surrounding human environment (which is always already also a social environment) and then unreflectively expresses such preference by spontaneously emulating them in her voluntary somatic behavior: how she walks, eats, dresses, combs her hair, and so on.

In such cases, it is one's habits rather than one's deliberative consciousness that performs one's self-stylization, and as habits recursively reinforce themselves, this form of self-stylization – even if implicit and unplanned – can be extremely powerful. So if we speak of natural style here, it is the second nature of habit (with its inevitable penumbra of the social world which shapes it) that one has integrated into one's character or personality. Style (including somatic style) is a disposition or habit to perform or appear in a certain manner or set of ways. Although they involve automatic mechanisms and can lead to ruinous routines, habits can also be creative in adapting themselves to new conditions and incorporating new elements and applications to improve their utility. Indeed, the power of habit depends on such creative adaptation, which ensures its reinforcement in a wide range of different conditions and uses.

4. As somatic style can be acquired and displayed unreflectively without conscious choice, so it can also be acquired and displayed without

our choosing at all. This involuntary form of style can result, for example, from the way we were trained to walk or eat or from bodily habits developed through our occupations, but also from the ways our genetic makeup shaped our bodies and appetites. Here again, we could distinguish between involuntary expressions of somatic style of which one is not aware and those of which one has explicit consciousness but cannot control. I may not be aware that I have a crude, unattractive manner of eating or that I have a particular posture or gait, and that may be the main reason I cannot choose or change them. But even if I were aware that I have a tendency to blush, stutter, or sweat profusely, or to overeat, laugh too loudly or cry too easily, I still might not be able to change these dimensions of somatic style.

Some theorists, however, might protest that we cannot truly think of involuntary somatic features as dimensions of style. Does not having a particular style, they might argue, essentially entail the possibility of choice? Does it not necessarily imply that there exist other styles, other ways of behaving and presenting oneself somatically, from which to choose? Yes, but this does not imply that those other styles (or stylistic choices) are available to the person in question; and so in that sense there can be involuntary aspects of a person's style. Likewise, even if every style allows some degree of free choice among elements or modes of action and display, this does not preclude that other aspects of a person's style are imposed on the person. That we commonly use the term "free style" to designate a special stylistic form should clearly imply that other styles are more constrained and thus lack complete freedom of choice. And even so-called free styles are not fully free, if the stylizing person wants to do a good job.

5. Through its association with fashion, style is often seen as ephemeral. But having a personal style cannot be a mere momentary affair; it implies a tendency to behave or appear in a certain way (or range of related ways). It thus involves dispositions or habits that imply repetition and enduring over time. For a personal style to be recognized, individuated, and re-identified over time, it must to some extent be durable and lasting. Yet style also has its contextual or temporal dimension; one's basic style of writing or dress may be essentially permanent, yet certain contexts (whether of extreme formality and importance or of urgency, intimacy, or informality) will demand variations of style. However casual or grungy one's normal style of dress, the context of attending a wedding or other formal affair will dictate a different sartorial style. One's style

in writing a job application letter will be different from that of one's intimate cell-phone texting. Somatic style likewise inhabits this general distinction between the permanent and the contextual. The same person may have a morning somatic style – brimming with extremely brisk and energetic movement (often exacerbated by too much caffeine) – that differs significantly from his evening style of motion and gesture (slower, wearier) and posture (considerably more saggy and slumping if not also more relaxed) after a long day at the office. I witnessed this metamorphosis (and its sartorial accompaniments of loosened or absent tie and disheveled hair) when I used to ride the commuter trains between New York City and Philadelphia. As we know from other contexts, someone may be a somatic lamb in the classroom and a lioness in the bedroom, or vice versa.

IV

As a bodily expression, somatic style should be formed and expressed through the body's various elements and should be appreciated through our bodily senses. What then are the elements of somatic style, and what are the sense modalities for its perception? Beginning with the latter question, we should recognize that though it may seem synonymous with bodily looks, somatic style involves much more than visual appearance. Although sight may be preeminent for appreciating somatic style, other senses are decidedly involved. After vision, philosophy generally honors hearing as the next most cognitively and aesthetically refined sense, partly because it similarly provides perception from a distance. But in what ways does hearing perceive somatic style? In the first place, voice – a product of modulating breath's passage through our bodies – functions as an aspect of someone's somatic style. If someone we know with a deep throaty voice suddenly addresses us with a thin falsetto or a hesitant whisper, we will wonder whether he is joking by departing from his familiar style or whether something is somatically ailing him. Generically, certain body styles are associated with certain styles of voice, so we inwardly smile on hearing a burly heavyweight wrestler with a shrill squeaky voice (or a tiny nymphet with a booming baritone) because of the incongruity of somatic style. The generic somatic style of the homosexual queen is expressed equally in certain styles of voice (typically high-pitched, lilting, or lisping) as in clothes and gestural mannerisms. Persistent stuttering or shouting can contribute to someone's somatic style, and we often first notice the auditory aspect of this style before recognizing the visual expression of this somatic behavior that transforms not only the person's facial gestures but typically her posture, as well.

Our auditory appreciation of somatic style goes beyond the voice of speech. There are styles of laughing – like the deep and easy full-bodied guffaw or the tense yet uncontrollably explosive and repetitive high-pitched giggle – and ways of crying or sighing that contribute to a person's somatic style; they have their visual counterparts in the ways that laughing, crying, and sighing transfigure our bodily movement and facial and postural expression. The sounds of somatic style include also ways of coughing, gasping, sneezing, grunting, burping, and snoring. From a woman of dainty, gentle, and refined somatic style, we do not expect raucous sneezes or ear-splitting snores, not to mention thunderous burps or blaring farts. Their repeated production would mean revising our judgment of her somatic style from the delicate and demure toward the boisterous or vulgar.

The sounds of somatic style are not only those of air passing through our bodies apertures but also of the sounds the body makes with its limbs or members. We can hear the exuberant somatic style of someone who slaps his thighs in enthusiasm or wonder, or the flashy style of the woman with noisy, jangling jewelry. We recognize an awkward lumbering somatic style through the heavy-footed thud of its footsteps, while the soft pitter-patter sound of little feet expresses a somatic style of gentle lightness and ease. We often recognize a person by his or her distinctive style of walking; usually it is a visual recognition of the gait, but if we are close enough (or in a room immediately below) we can identify it by hearing. I have a university colleague who is heavy and unsteady on his feet and thus uses a large wooden stick for walking. We can easily recognize his presence even when he is out of view by the rhythmic sound of feet and wood meeting the floor or sidewalk. More could surely be said about these and other sounds of somatic style, such as the different sounds made in various styles of eating (loud chewing or gulping, lip smacking, and so on) or the different noises people make in sitting down from a standing position or, conversely, standing up from sitting. But we should move on to other sense modalities.

Smell could logically be considered next, not only because like sight and hearing it is a distance sense that requires no direct contact with the object whose odor it perceives, but also because of the power and pervasiveness of scent in our reactions to other people's bodies and in our own somatic self-styling. Some somatic styles are unintentionally expressed through distinctive odors. As we easily identify the smoker without his cigarettes by the stale smoky stench that pervades his clothes and pores, so the heavy drinker has his own distinctive aroma that can be very penetrating and unpleasant. The somatic style of the rugged, woodsy non-bather or of the urban tramp likewise imposes itself through its foul fragrance. Styles of diet are likewise recognized not only through the smell of the food itself but through the odiferous traces they leave on our skin and breath. I remember arriving in my mother-in-law's small town in rural Japan and being told that I smelled like a Korean, because the garlicky food I had consumed the night before in Seoul was still producing its somatic scent. (Is it too vulgar and obvious to note that burps and farts, earlier described as auditory elements, can be transmodal and thus also form part of the olfactory dimension of someone's somatic style?)[15]

More agreeable fragrances, however, deserve special attention because they play a crucial role in conscious efforts of somatic self-styling. Achieving a body with the desired olfactory style means more than simply eliminating unpleasant body odors. A totally odorless body, if indeed possible, would be unattractively bland, antiseptically devoid of character. A merely pleasant scent will also not suffice. The serious self-stylizer instead seeks a fragrance that goes beyond the scent's intrinsic allure but also expresses the particular character, personality, or style that the person in question wants to convey – and through which she seeks to become more attractive (to herself or to others), whether in a particular context (a special event, a job interview, or romantic dating) or in general.

One's choice of fragrance is not simply a choice to attract others by satisfying their tastes. Like clothes fashion, it is an assertion of one's own taste and an appeal to be appreciated not just sensually but also cognitively for expressing one's singular taste in style. This is one reason why the most successful clothes designers are also perfume designers. Moreover, the style expressed is more than a mere superficial matter of surface body scent or olfactory connoisseurship but also an expression of one's deeper character or ethical style. Consider the recent testimony of Anjelica Huston who glowingly praises her chosen fragrance, Jean Patou's Mille, not only for expressing her own unique personality

---

[15] For clarity of exposition, I discuss the senses individually, but it should be clear that our sensory experience is typically transmodal or multimodal, with different sensory inputs finely integrated by the brain. Somatic style is usually appreciated through different senses simultaneously in such integrated multimodal sensory perception.

but also for being so difficult to procure that it heightens still further the distinction of she who wears it.

> Joy never did it for me. My friend Joan Juliet Buck, then the rédactrice en chef of French Vogue – and what's known in the business as a very good nose – showed me Mille when I was visiting in Paris and said, "This would be great for you." From the moment I smelled it, it was mine in a way that no other perfume had been since Blue Grass, which my mother first gave me when I was a child. It's round and floral and warm, with just a hint of spice without being too hippie, and just floral enough without being too sweet. It smells like midnight in the Bois de Boulogne – sexy and mysterious. I think it creates a mood. It's alluring. It says, "I'm interested in life, in olfactory senses as well as visual ones." It says, "I'm in the mood for something." It also says, "I'm feminine, I'm complete." It stands to exist with my mother's perfume, Shalimar, which haunts me to this day. I even wear it to go to bed: I spray it behind my ears, old style. (Unless I'm wearing pearls.) People really like it. Even when I was a smoker, they told me I smelled good – which is saying something! When you find yourself in an embrace and someone tells you that you smell good, it's wonderful and unexpected. Mille is rare, hard to find, which I like about it. It means I don't bump into many people who smell like me.[16]

The art and appreciation of bodily fragrance styles should not be mistaken as the product of modern capitalist consumption, for we find them most powerfully present in medieval Japan, where the blending of scents was enthusiastically cultivated as a fine art and aesthetic aristocrats would compete with respect to their skill both in creating complex fragrances and in tastefully discriminating them and recognizing their components. In the classic *Tale of Genji*, we read of such "competition to be pleasantly scented," and indeed the two male heroes of the book's final part are particularly distinguished by their differently exquisite styles of fragrance – Prince Niou, known as "His Perfumed Highness" because "the blending of perfumes would become his work for days on end" and his rival Kaoru, called "the fragrant captain" because his body had the knack to collect good ambient aromas and thus exude a perfumed scent without his even making the effort to perfume himself.[17]

---

[16] Anjelica Houston (as told to Christine Mulke), "1001 Nights," *New York Times*, Style Magazine, Women's Fashion Summer 2010, Sunday, April 25, 58.
[17] Murasaki Shikibu, *The Tale of Genji*, trans. Edward Seidensticker (New York: Knopf, 2001), 739, 740. Earlier we read that when Genji met "the Akashi lady. He was greeted by the perfume from within her blinds, a delicate mixture that told of the most refined tastes" (412).

Intimately linked to the sense of smell is that of taste, which is indeed significantly dependent on the former, so that when our olfactory powers are hindered by a cold in our nose, our capacities to taste are likewise diminished. Smell and taste also overlap in vocabularies; we speak of both tastes and fragrances as fruity or spicy, fresh, stale, or pungent. Do we also appreciate somatic style through our sense of taste? We certainly taste people considerably less than we see, hear, or smell them, but in our most intimate personal contact with others, we sometimes can appreciate somatic style through taste. The fresh, minty, garlicky, wine-steeped, or stale-cigarette taste of one's lover's mouth can be an unforgettable mark of somatic style, for better or for worse, as can the distinctive flavor of one's lover's skin, saliva, or other fluids that our taste buds encounter.

Touch presents a twofold sense for appreciating somatic style: the way that bodies (as objects) feel to our touch when we touch them and the way that bodies as active subjectivities touch us – the feel of someone's touch as it expresses her somatic intentionality in feeling us. These two different forms of touch – how people feel when we touch them versus how they feel when they touch us – need not be perfectly congruent in the somatic style of a person. A man can have a sinewy, muscular body with a bristly beard, rough skin, and coarse hair, all of whose tactile roughness suggests a tough or rugged somatic style. Yet that same person could have a manner of touching others that is so skillfully subtle and gentle that we could nonetheless describe his somatic style as ultimately sophisticated and tender, despite the coarseness of his body surfaces. Someone may feel distinctly cold when we touch her skin, yet still express warmth in the way she touches us. As with fragrances, conscious cultivators of somatic style are likely to prefer combining different tactile qualities in an attractive blend connoting an interestingly complex personality rather than presenting a one-sided somatic tactility – a body that is all soft, spongy, tenderness or coarse, abrasive hardness.

Although all five traditional senses can thus be used to appreciate somatic style, they do not exhaust the sensory modes through which the soma is perceived. Proprioception, kinesthesis, and other distinctively bodily senses related to the somaesthetic nervous system provide further ways. Proprioception concerns the inner sensations and resulting cognition of the position, posture, weight, orientation, balance, and internal pressures of one's body, while kinesthetic perception more specifically relates to perceived changes in such feelings of posture, orientation, pressure, and equilibrium that arise through bodily movement. Other specifically somaesthetic sensations are feelings of body temperature and feelings of one's internal organs (often associated with pain). Could any of these distinctively somaesthetic senses also play a role in appreciating somatic style, and if so, in what way?

Proprioception and kinesthesis clearly seem to do so in two different ways: first, in the subject's own sense of her somatic style. When one's movements are full of vibrant energy, power, and grace or, conversely, awkward, imbalanced, hesitant, and heavy, one can feel it proprioceptively and kinesthetically in one's muscles, joints, and bones. Proprioception (which literally connotes self-perception) can also be used for perceiving the somatic styles of others. For example, someone with an aggressive style of movement who tends to come too close to people with whom he converses will tend to cause those people to react somatically by leaning away, moving back, cringing, or stiffening when that person penetrates their more personal space. By attending to the proprioceptive or kinesthetic feelings of their own defensive postural reactions, these people can recognize the person's aggressive style that generated those reactions.

A further way that proprioception or kinesthesis may help us perceive another person's somatic style is through our empathetic appreciation of that person's movement or posture. Part of our appreciation of watching dance and sports seems to be based on our empathetically imagining the feel of the movements that the dancers and athletes make. Such movements essentially involve proprioceptive and kinesthetic feelings, so our empathetic watching of these movements will include those kinds of feelings (though they will not be strictly identical to the feelings experienced by the actual performers themselves). The mirror neuron system (already discussed in earlier chapters) could provide a neurological basis for such empathetic experience, as seeing the movement would activate not only the relevant visual neurons but also motor neurons associated with performing that action. Such mirror neurons help explain why a neonate can imitate facial gestures he sees without any protracted learning process of trial and error. Merely in seeing those gestures, he also experiences in some way the proprioceptive motor feelings of those movements (the feelings of the orientation and muscular pressure of one's lips, mouth, tongue, nose, etc.), which enables him to mimetically reproduce those movements. In the same way, when we see behavior expressive of somatic style (energetic movement and dynamic gesture or awkward, sagging posture), our mirror neurons can yield a proprioceptive or kinesthetic appreciation of such style that may be just as powerful and discriminating as our visual perception of it.[18]

V

As more than all the five senses contribute to appreciating somatic style,[19] so are more than all the body's parts involved in constituting it. There is no point belaboring this in detail, once we recognize that the clothes, cosmetics, and jewelry we use to cover and adorn the body help shape and express one's somatic style. But besides such material somatic accessories of fashion, should we recognize other elements or qualities of somatic style that go beyond the body's parts and surfaces and that are more ethereal in character? We sometimes speak of someone's having a special aura that makes that person's physical presence particularly charismatic, compelling, or captivating and that does not reduce to mere good looks. This aura appears not as an ordinary physical property but more as an energetic quality, radiating out from the person's body (as the German term *Ausstrahlung* suggests) but not reducible to its parts. It seems partly a function of the body's ways of moving, of taking or making its place, and of interacting in both the spatial and social kinesphere. This contextual dimension suggests that somatic style also depends on environmental factors beyond the self. The radiance of dazzling hair depends also on the conditions of light; the moisture of succulent lips and skin rely on other environmental factors, just as an imperiously commanding somatic style depends on a social world with creatures to impress and command.

Some body parts are more stylistically important than others. If the face seems paramount, this is not only because of its prominent visibility but also because of our ability to move it in so many clear and subtle ways to express our personality and feelings, our desires and moods. If our hands and other bodily limbs also seem especially important for conveying style, this is likewise due to the fact that we can articulate

---

[18] For more details on these points, see A.N. Meltzoff and M.K. Moore, "Imitation of Facial and Manual Gestures by Human Neonates," *Science*, New Series 198 (1977): 75–78; "Imitation, Memory, and the Representation of Persons," *Infant Behavior and Development* 17 (1994): 83–99; Barbara Montero, "Proprioception as an Aesthetic Sense," *Journal of Aesthetics and Art Criticism* 64 (2006): 230–242; and Chapter 9 of this volume.

[19] In elaborating the ways our different senses appreciate somatic style, I do not preclude other ways of perceiving it. We can sometimes feel a person's somatic style (say, a fierce or aggressive one) through our general emotional reaction to it, before distinguishing any particular sense through which it has impressed us. Of course, as emotions are essentially embodied, so is such affective appreciation of style.

them with far greater visibility, skill, and, hence, expressive power than we can articulate our torso and pelvis. Are there some body parts that in principle play no significant role at all, such as inner organs that are normally invisible to observers? It might seem dogmatic to insist categorically that every organ or body part is significant for somatic style without arguing the case for each and every item. On the other hand, surely the loss or malfunction of an otherwise stylistically insignificant organ would indeed significantly influence a person's somatic style. It is neither uncommon nor unreasonable for people who have suffered a heart attack to modify (deliberately or unconsciously) their somatic style. Bladder problems obviously heighten nervous agitation and other changes in somatic behavior that yield stylistic effects, just as hormonal or blood problems can alter one's style of bodily comportment.

Beyond the body's material parts (though somehow present and active in them), scientists and philosophers distinguish what they call body schemata. Such schemata involve entrenched habits, dispositional mechanisms, or tendencies of movement, feeling, and attitude that are incorporated in our bodies and enable us to act skillfully and intelligently without having to think about what we are doing with our limbs. They are what guide the great bulk of our everyday activity that flows successfully and spontaneously without the need of explicit reflection of how we are using our bodies to perform what we need and want to perform in perception and action. By governing so much of our behavior, these entrenched body schemata or habitual dispositions of behavior and experience inevitably also shape somatic style. Indeed, if habits constitute so much of the self, then such somatic schemata of perception, action, and feeling should be central to one's personality rather than being a superficial adornment. The upshot is not that such basic body schemata do not belong to one's somatic style but rather that somatic style is not a merely superficial adornment to the self but a core dimension of one's personality. This returns us to the Confucian doctrine of somatic style as intrinsic to character and to further arguments for a notion of somatic style that goes deeper than the familiar metaphors of clothes and pictures suggest.

VI

As form is contrasted with content, style is often opposed to substance, and identified with the external and inessential. It is thus associated with surface rather than depth, with appearance not reality, with artificial technique rather than with authentic soul. But if somatic style, through our body schemata, extends into the deepest habits of feeling, perception, and action that constitute the self, then it should be seen as an integral dimension of the individual, the expression of her particular spirit. Spirit indeed seems fundamental to the notion of style. If style is the man himself, then it includes his spirit. As Emerson spoke of style as expressing the mind's voice, so Wittgenstein insists that the creation or improvement of an artistic style is essentially different from mere improvements in technique or technology because "spirit plays no part" in these latter.[20]

Somatic style also implies spirit. We distinguish a person's somatic style from her looks not simply because it involves more than visual aspects but also because it connotes more than mere physical qualities in general. Style implies an intentionality that animates the various ways the person acts, feels, thinks, and desires – an animating spirit that underlies her looks and other somatic dimensions of sensory appearance and that helps define a person's character or personality.

The famous American prose stylist H.L. Mencken expresses this notion of style in the somatic terms of breath (a common metaphor for life and spirit), skin, and blood, through which the individual always lives and cannot live without: "The essence of a sound style is that it cannot be reduced to rules – that it is a living and breathing thing with something of the devilish in it – that it fits its proprietor tightly and yet ever so loosely, as his skin fits him. It is, in fact, quite as securely an integral part of him as that skin is. It hardens as his arteries harden."[21] Although Mencken is speaking here of prose style, his points have even clearer pertinence and validity for somatic style, which cannot be a mere externality of personhood – no more than the body itself can exist as a mere outside without its innards of organs and fluids.

If style and self are so intimately related, then the way to develop or create a style is through self-development or self-creation. As the novelist Katherine Anne Porter explains, "You do not create a style. You work, and develop yourself; your style is an emanation from your own being."[22] But since emanation is another distancing metaphor, I prefer to reformulate her point as affirming that style is simply an integral part of one's own

---

[20] Ludwig Wittgenstein, *Culture and Value*, trans. Peter Winch (Oxford: Blackwell, 1980), 3.
[21] H.L. Mencken, "Literature and the Schoolm'am," in *Prejudices: Fifth Series* (New York: Octagon Books, 1977), 197.
[22] Katherine Anne Porter, interview with Barbara Thompson, 1963, reprinted in George Plimpton (ed.), *Women Writers at Work: The Paris Review Interviews* (New York: Modern Library, 1998), 53.

being, so that changing one's style means in some way changing one's self.

We should not be troubled here about the logical issues of self-transformation, questions such as how one can change in a significant way and still be identified as the same person rather than an altogether different individual. Such formal issues of reference, individuation, and re-identification have various formal solutions.[23] We all know, of course, that people can change or develop without entirely losing their identity as the persons they already are. When there is a significant change of style, we can always point to other continuities of behavior, appearance, and cognition that justify our ascribing the same logical identity to the person, even if we feel there has been an important change in that self.

More important is the practical issue of how to work on oneself to create or improve one's style. Although the question is too complex to be adequately addressed here, surely part of this work on the self is an effort of self-knowledge, including an examination of our strengths, weaknesses, and proclivities. But it also involves a critical study of inspiring exemplars, theories, and methods of self-cultivation that can help us to transform ourselves stylistically in the ways we judge desirable. In what remains of this essay I will merely suggest how work on somatic self-transformation of style may be pursued through two complementary directions whose collaborative interaction reveals in yet another way that somatic style transcends the simplistic distinction of inner soul or substance and outer form or manner.

To do so, I return to Thoreau, in a passage from *Walden* where he seems to regard style as much more important and integral to character than the mere external tool for writing with which he elsewhere identified it. "Every man is the builder of a temple, called his body, to the god he worships, after a style purely his own, nor can he get off by hammering marble instead. We are all sculptors and painters, and our material is our own flesh and blood and bones. Any nobleness begins to refine a man's features, any meanness or sensuality to imbrute them."[24]

This argument seems to combine two different somatic directions of self-stylizing or self-creation. The first is that of working on the body's outside form in the way that a painter or sculptor would give an attractive

---

[23] For more detailed discussion of these matters, see Richard Shusterman, *Pragmatist Aesthetics: Living Beauty, Rethinking Art* (Oxford: Blackwell, 1992), 93–94; and *Practicing Philosophy: Pragmatism and the Philosophical Life* (New York: Routledge, 1997), 37–42.

[24] Henry David Thoreau, *Walden*, in Brooks Atkinson (ed.), *Walden and Other Writings* (New York: Modern Library, 2000), 209; hereafter W.

aesthetic form to an artwork that also expresses his distinctive personality. If this suggests practices like cosmetics or bodybuilding that are focused on representational somaesthetics and external somatic forms and images, we should remember that Thoreau insists this shaping is not to serve the body for itself but to transform it into a temple to serve the god one worships, to express one's deepest values. In other words, somatic stylization of the outside is a means for spiritual ends, indeed a work of askesis to purify or strengthen the spirit, an askesis that can be punishing to the body as the image of hammering clearly suggests.

The often painful difficulty of transforming the body into a "temple of God" is a core dimension of Christian asceticism and celibacy that goes back to Saint Paul, if not even further back to Christ himself, whose somatic incarnation, temptation, and suffering provide the means of spiritual salvation for the entire world. But the idea of somatic askesis for spiritual ends was already salient in the Greek philosophical tradition, particularly in the line of idealism that can be traced to Plato's *Phaedo* and to Plotinus, whose notorious distaste for the body (which he refused to bathe) was nonetheless combined with a sculptural image of beauty in stylizing the self toward pure virtue. As the sculptor, "cuts away here and polishes there and makes one part smooth and clears another till he has given his statue a beautiful face," Plotinus exhorts, "so you too must cut away excess and straighten the crooked and clear the dark and make it bright, and never stop 'working on your statue' till the divine glory of virtue shines out on you" (*Enneads*, I.vi.9).[25]

In highlighting the sculpting acts of purifying simplification, Plotinus certainly resonates with Thoreau's ardent exhortation to "Simplify, simplify" (W, 87). But the particular ideological context from which Thoreau's affirmation of somatic self-sculpting here emerges is neither Christian nor Greek philosophy but rather Asian thought. Nor does he seem to be maintaining a one-sided idealism where the body is despised and punitively worked on so as to raise the spirit and where there is no reciprocal work of the spirit serving to beautify the body. In the lines immediately preceding his body-temple-sculpture remarks (and in words already cited in Chapter 13), Thoreau praises "the Hindoo lawgiver" for dealing "reverently" with even the most basic bodily functions. "He teaches us how to eat, drink, cohabit, void excrement and urine, and the like, elevating what is mean, and does not falsely excuse himself by calling these things trifles." In other words, the style in which we do

---

[25] Plotinus, *The Enneads*, trans. A.H. Armstrong (Cambridge, MA: Harvard University Press, 1966), vol. 1, 259.

these bodily things can raise them from mere baseness if that style has the right spirit, expressing proper respect and in the manner "regulated by [ritual or] law (W, 208–209)."

The idea that spirit refines one's bodily style suggests a second direction for stylistic self-transformation in Thoreau's compressed remarks on the discipline of self-sculpting. Just as working on the body's surface can lead to the beauty of virtue, so working on one's inner spiritual virtues can render the body more beautiful. "Any nobleness begins at once to refine a man's features, any meanness or sensuality to imbrute them." As G.E. Moore's pure passion for truth and sincerity gave him an angelically beautiful look, so we can also imagine how a man's lecherous thoughts could bring a leer that disfigures such beauty.

If one's moral attitudes, sentiments, and qualities shape our physical features, then this should not be seen as a mysterious link or interaction between two distinct orders of existence – one inner and spiritual, the other material and external. Rather, our moral feelings and dispositions are always already somatic, just as our somatic style is always already shaped by the spirit and ethical norms of the social world. The soma – as lived, sentient, intelligent human body – is intrinsically character as well as corpuscles; it is inner subjectivity as well as outer form. Working on its outside can be a means of working on inner virtues and attitudes, just as working on the inside (through meditative practices) can improve the way we look. As bodybuilding enthusiasts assert the moral value of their practice for building also character (by instilling discipline and confidence), so ancient writings on yoga affirm that its meditative inner work of concentration yields remarkable external benefits in making its practitioners look not only much healthier and more attractive but even giving them a more appealing fragrance. While somatic style remains a perceptible aspect of body surface, it also goes all the way down into the depths of self and character. It is far too deep to disregard as a trivial matter of taste, far too central to neglect its cultivation and analysis.

Select Bibliography

Abrams, J.J. "Pragmatism, Artificial Intelligence, and Posthuman Bioethics: Shusterman, Rorty, and Foucault." *Human Studies*, 27 (2004): 241–258.
———. "Shusterman and the Paradoxes of Posthuman Self-Styling." In *Shusterman's Pragmatism: Between Literature and Somaesthetics*. Edited by Dorota Koczanowicz and Wojciech Małecki. Amsterdam: Rodopi, 2012.
Aeschylus. *Prometheus Bound*. Translated by Arthur S. Way. London: MacMillan and Co. 1907.
Ames, Roger, and H. Rosemont Jr. (translators). *The Analects of Confucius: A Philosophical Translation*. New York: Ballantine, 1998.
Ames, Roger, and David Hall (translators). *Daodejing: "Making This Life Significant": A Philosophical Translation*. New York: Ballantine, 2003.
Ando, Tadao. "Shintai and Space." *Tadao Ando: Complete Works*. Edited by Francesco Dal Co. London: Phaidon, 1995.
Arbuthnot, F.F. and Richard Burton (translators). *Ananga Ranga*. New York: Medical Press, 1964.
———. *The Kama Sutra of Vatsyayana*. London: Unwin, 1988.
Arnold, Peter. "Somaesthetics, Education, and the Art of Dance." *Journal of Aesthetic Education*, 39 (2005): 48–64.
Augustine. *Confessions*. Translated by F.J. Sheed. Indianapolis: Hackett, 1992.
Austin, J.L. *How to Do Things with Words*. Oxford: Oxford University Press, 1962.
Baird, George. "Criticality and its Discontents." In *Crossover: Architecture, Urbanism, Technology*. Edited by A. Graafland, L. Kavanaugh, G. Baird. Rotterdam: 010 Publishers, 2006.
Barthes, Roland. *Camera Lucida: Reflections on Photography*. Translated by Richard Howard. New York: Hill and Wang, 1981.
Bataille, Georges. *Inner Experience*. Translated by L.A. Boldt. Albany: SUNY, 1988.
Baudelaire, Charles. "The Salon of 1859." In *Art in Paris, 1845–1862*. Translated by Jonathan Mayne. London: Phaidon, 1965.
Baumgarten, Alexander. *Theoretische Ästhetik: Die grundlegenden Abschnitte aus der "Aesthetica" (1750/58)*. Translated by H.R. Schweizer. Hamburg: Felix Meiner, 1988.

Beardsley, Monroe C. *Aesthetics*. New York: Harcourt, Brace, 1958.
―――. *The Possibility of Criticism*. Detroit: Wayne State University Press, 1970.
Benjamin, Walter. "A Short History of Photography." Translated by Stanley Mitchell. *Screen*, 13 (1972): 5–26.
―――. "The Work of Art in the Age of Mechanical Reproduction." In *Illuminations*. Translated by Harry Zohn. New York: Schocken, 1969.
Ford, Anna, et al. "Treatment of Childhood Obesity by Retraining Eating Behaviour: Randomized Controlled Trial." *British Medical Journal*, 2010. doi: 10.1136/bmj.b5388. Web.
Berthoz, Alain. *The Brain's Sense of Movement*. Translated by Giselle Weiss. Cambridge, MA: Harvard University Press, 2000.
Bielefeldt, Carl (translator). *Dōgen's Manuals of Zen Meditation*. Berkeley: University of California Press, 1988.
Böhme, Gernot. "Atmosphere as the Fundamental Concept of a New Aesthetics." *Thesis Eleven*, 36 (1993): 113–126.
Bourdieu, Pierre. *Distinction: A Social Critique of the Judgment of Taste*. Translated by Richard Nice. Cambridge, MA: Harvard University Press, 1984.
―――, and Loic Wacquant. *An Invitation to Reflexive Sociology*. Chicago: University of Chicago Press, 1992.
―――. *The Logic of Practice*. Translated by Richard Nice. Stanford: Stanford University Press, 1990.
―――. *Pascalian Meditations*. Translated by Richard Nice. Stanford: Stanford University Press, 2000.
Bressler, Liora. "Dancing the Curriculum: Exploring the Body and Movement in Elementary Schools." In *Knowing Bodies, Moving Minds*. Edited by Liora Bressler. Dordrecht: Kluwer, 2004.
Burke, Edmund. *A Philosophical Enquiry into the Origin of our Ideas of the Sublime and Beautiful*. London: Penguin, 1998.
Caillet, Aline. "Émanciper le corps: Sur Quelques applications du concept de la soma-esthétique en art." In *Penser en Corps: Soma-esthétique, art et philosophie*. Edited by Barbara Formis. Paris: L'Harmattan, 2009: 99–132.
Camus, Albert. "The Myth of Sisyphus." Translated by Justin O'Brien. In *The Myth of Sisyphus and Other Essays*. New York: Random House, 1955.
Carlyle, Thomas. *Past and Present*. 2nd edition. London: Chapman and Hall, 1845.
―――. *Sartor Resartus*. London: Chapman and Hall, 1831.
Chan, Wing-tsit (translator). "The Great Learning." In *A Source Book in Chinese Philosophy*. Edited by Wing-tsit Chan. Princeton, NJ: Princeton University Press, 1963.
Chevrier, Jean-Francois. "The Adventures of the Picture Form in the History of Photography." Translated by Michael Gilson. In *The Last Picture Show: Artists Using Photography, 1960–1982*. Edited by Douglas Fogle. Minneapolis: Walker Art Center, 2003.
Cicero. *Letters to Quintus and Brutus*. Translated by D.R. Shackleton Bailey. Cambridge, MA: Harvard University Press, 2002.
―――. *On the Laws (De Legibus)*. In *On the Republic, On the Laws*. Translated by C.W. Keyes. Cambridge, MA: Harvard University Press, 1928.

Cohen, Ted. "Aesthetic/Non-aesthetic and the Concept of Taste: A Critique of Sibley's Position." *Theoria*, 39 (1979): 113–152.
Cole, Jonathan, and Barbara Montero. "Affective Proprioception." *Janus Head*, 9 (2007): 299–317.
Coleridge, Samuel T. *Aids to Reflection*. New York: Stanford and Swords, 1854.
———. *Biographia Literaria*. London: J.M. Dent & Sons, 1975.
Comfort, Alex (translator). *The Koka Shastra*. New York: Stein & Day, 1965.
Cooper, Anthony Ashley (Third Earl of Shaftesbury). *Characteristics of Men, Manners, Opinions, Times*. Edited by Lawrence Klein. Cambridge: Cambridge University Press, 1999.
Croce, Benedetto. *Aesthetic*. Translated by D. Ainslie. London: MacMillan and Co., 1922.
Dahms, Hans-Joachim, et al. "Editorial: Neuer Pragmatismus in der Architektur." *ARCH+*, 156 (2001): 26–29.
D'Avila, Juan. *Epistolario Espiritual*. Madrid: Espasa-Calpe, S.A., 1962.
Danto, Arthur. *After the End of Art*. Princeton: Princeton University Press, 1997.
———. *The Madonna of the Future*. New York: Farrar, Straus, and Giroux, 2000.
———. "Minding his A's and E's: How Saul Steinberg defined aesthetics in a nutshell." *Art News*, November 2006: 112–114.
———. "The Naked Truth." In *Aesthetics and Ethics: Essays at the Intersection*. Edited by Jerrold Levinson. Cambridge: Cambridge University Press, 2001.
———. *The Transfiguration of the Commonplace*. Cambridge, MA: Harvard University Press, 1981.
Davidson, Richard J. "Well-Being and Affective Style: Neural Substrates and Biobehavioural Correlates." *Philosophical Transactions of the Royal Society*, Series B, 359 (2004): 1395–1411.
———, et al. "Alterations in Brain and Immune Function Produced by Mindfulness Meditation." *Psychosomatic Medicine*, 65 (2003): 564–570.
Descartes, René. *Meditations on First Philosophy*. In *The Philosophical Writings of Descartes*, 2 vols. Translated by John Cottingham, Robert Stoothoff, and Dugald Murdoch. Cambridge: Cambridge University Press, 1984–1985.
Dewey, John. *Art as Experience*. Carbondale: Southern Illinois University Press, 1987.
———. "Body and Mind." In *John Dewey: The Later Works*, vol. 3. Carbondale, Southern Illinois University Press, 1988.
———. *Ethics*. Carbondale: Southern Illinois University Press, 1985.
———. *Experience and Nature*. Carbondale: Southern Illinois University Press, 1988.
———. *Freedom and Culture*. Carbondale: Southern Illinois University Press, 1988.
———. *Human Nature and Conduct*. Carbondale: Southern Illinois University Press, 1983.
———. "Introduction." in F.M. Alexander. In *Constructive Conscious Control of the Individual*, 1923; reprinted in *John Dewey: The Middle Works*, vol. 15. Carbondale: Southern Illinois University Press, 1983.

———. "Introduction." in F.M. Alexander. In *The Use of the Self*, 1932; reprinted in *John Dewey: The Later Works*, vol. 6. Carbondale: Southern Illinois University Press, 1985.
———. "Introductory Word." in F.M. Alexander. In *Man's Supreme Inheritance*, 1918; reprinted in *John Dewey: The Middle Works*, vol. 11. Carbondale: Southern Illinois University Press, 1982.
———. "Philosophy and Civilization." In *Philosophy and Civilization*. New York: Capricorn, 1963.
———. "Qualitative Thought." Reprinted in *John Dewey: The Later Works*, vol. 5. Carbondale: Southern Illinois University Press, 1984.
———. *The Quest for Certainty*. Carbondale: Southern Illinois University Press, 1988.
Dickie, George. *Aesthetics*. Indianapolis: Bobbs-Merrill, 1971.
———. *Art and the Aesthetic: An Institutional Analysis*. Ithaca: Cornell University Press, 1974.
Dobson, W.A.C.H. (translator). *Mencius: A New Translation*. Toronto: Toronto University Press, 1969.
Doidge, Norman. *The Brain That Changes Itself*. New York: Viking, 2007.
Draganski, B. and A. May. "Training-induced Structural Changes in the Adult Human Brain." *Behavioural Brain Research*, 192 (2008): 137–142.
Driskell, J., et al. "Does Mental Practice Enhance Performance?" *Journal of Applied Psychology*, 79 (1974): 481–489.
Durkheim, Émile. *Pragmatism and Sociology*. Translated by J.C. Whitehouse. Cambridge: Cambridge University Press, 1983.
Ebisch, S.J.H., et al. "The Sense of Touch: Embodied Simulation in a Visuotactile Mirroring Mechanism for Observed Animate or Inanimate Touch." *Journal of Cognitive Neuroscience*, 20 (2008): 1–13.
Eisenman, Peter. "En Terror Firma: In Trails of Grotexts." *Architectural Design*, 1–2 (1989): 41.
Eliot, T.S. *The Use of Poetry and the Use of Criticism*. London: Faber, 1964.
Emerson, Ralph Waldo. "Address at the Opening of Concord Free Public Library." In *The Complete Works of Ralph Waldo Emerson*, vol. 11. New York: Houghton Mifflin, 1904.
———. "Education." In *The Complete Works of Ralph Waldo Emerson*, vol. 10. New York: Houghton Mifflin, 1904.
———. "Farming." In *The Essential Writings of Ralph Waldo Emerson*. Edited by Brooks Atkinson. New York: Modern Library, 2000.
———. *Journals of Ralph Waldo Emerson*, vols. 3, 5. Edited by E.W. Emerson and R.W. Forbes. Boston: Houghton Mifflin, 1910–1914.
———. "Literary Ethics." In *Emerson: Essays and Poems*. New York: Library of America, 1996.
———. "Powers and Laws of Thought." In *The Complete Works of Ralph Waldo Emerson*, vol. 12. New York: Houghton Mifflin, 1904.
———. "The Scholar." In *The Complete Works of Ralph Waldo Emerson*, vol. 10. New York: Houghton Mifflin, 1904.
———. "The Superlative." In *Lectures and Biographical Sketches*. Boston: Mifflin, 1904.

———. "Works and Days." In *Society and Solitude, Works of Ralph Waldo Emerson*, vol. 2. Boston: Houghton, Osgood Company, 1880.

Engel, Lis. "The Somaesthetic Dimension of Dance Art and Education: A Phenomenological and Aesthetic Analysis of the Problem of Creativity in Dance." In *Ethics and Politics Embodied in Dance: Proceedings of the International Dance Conference, December 9–12, 2004*. Edited by E. Anttila, S. Hämäläinen, T. Löytönen & L. Rouhiainen. Helsinki: Theatre Academy, 2005: 50–58.

Feldenkrais, Moshe. *Awareness Through Movement*. New York: Harper and Row, 1972.

Formis, Barbara (editor). *Penser en corps : Soma-esthetique, art, et philosophie*. Paris: L'Harmattan, 2009.

Frampton, Kenneth. *Modern Architecture: A Critical History*, 4th edition. London: Thames and Hudson, 2007.

Foucault, Michel. *Dits et Ecrits*, 2 vols. Paris: Gallimard, 2001.

———. *History of Sexuality*, 2 vols. New York: Pantheon, 1980, 1986.

———. "How an 'Experience-Book' is Born." In *Remarks on Marx: Conversations with Duccio Trombadori*. Translated by R.J. Goldstein and J. Cascaito. New York: Semiotext, 1991.

———. "On the Genealogy of Ethics: An Overview of Work in Progress." In *Michel Foucault: Beyond Structuralism and Hermeneutics*. Edited by Herbert Dreyfus and Paul Rabinow. Chicago: University of Chicago Press, 1983.

———. "Sexual Choice, Sexual Act." In *Essential Works of Michel Foucault*, vol. 1. New York: New Press, 1997.

———. *Technologies of the Self*. Amherst: University of Massachusetts Press, 1988.

Freud, Sigmund. *Introductory Lectures on Psycho-analysis*. Edited by James Strachey. New York: Norton, 1966.

———. *The Interpretation of Dreams*. Translated by James Strachey. New York: Avon, 1965.

Fried, Michael. *Why Photography Matters as Art as Never Before*. New Haven: Yale University Press, 2008.

Gallagher, Shaun. *How the Body Shapes the Mind*. Oxford: Oxford University Press, 2005.

———. "Somaesthetics and the Care of the Body." *Metaphilosophy*, 42 (2011): 305–313.

Gallese, V., et al. "Action Recognition in the Premotor Cortex." *Brain*, 119 (1996): 593–609.

Goethe, Johann Wolfgang. "Allgemeine Naturwissenschaft." In *Goethes Werke*. Hamburg: Christian Wegner Verlag, 1955.

———. "Baukunst." In *Ästhetische Schriften 1771–1805. Sämtliche Werke*, vol. 8. Edited by Friedmar Apel. Frankfurt: Deutscher Klassiker Verlag, 1998.

———. *Conversations of Goethe with Eckermann and Soret*, vol. 2. Translated by John Oxenford. London: Smith, Elder & Co., 1850.

———. *Maxims and Reflections*. Translated by Elisabeth Stopp. London: Penguin, 1988.

———. "Sprichtwörtlich." In *Goethes Werke*. Edited by Eduard Scheidemantel. Berlin: Deutsches Verlagshaus Bong & Co., 1891.

Goodman, Nelson. *Languages of Art*. Oxford: Oxford University Press, 1969.

Graham, A.C. (translator). *The Book of Lieh-tzu.* New York: Columbia University Press, 1990.
Granger, David. "Somaesthetics and Racism: Toward an Embodied Pedagogy of Difference." *Journal of Aesthetic Education,* 44 (2010): 69–81.
———. "Review Essay of *Pragmatist Aesthetics.*" *Studies in Philosophy of Education,* 22 (2003): 381–402.
Gropius, Walter. "Grundsätze der Bauhausproduktion." In *Programme und Manifeste zur Architektur des 20. Jahrhunderts.* Edited by Ulrich Conrad. Braunschweig: Bauwelt Fundamente, 1975.
Guerra, Gustavo. "Practicing Pragmatism: Richard Shusterman's Unbound Philosophy." *Journal of Aesthetic Education,* 36 (2002): 70–83.
Hadot, Pierre. *Philosophy as a Way of Life.* Oxford: Blackwell, 1995.
Hampshire, Stuart. "Logic and Appreciation." In *Aesthetics and Language.* Edited by William Elton. Oxford: Blackwell, 1967.
Haskins, Casey. "Enlivened Bodies, Authenticity, and Romanticism." *Journal of Aesthetic Education,* 36 (2002): 92–102.
Hays, Michael K. "Critical Architecture Between Form and Culture." *Perspecta: The Yale Architectural Journal,* 21 (1984): 15–29.
———. "Wider den Pragmatismus." *ARCH+,* 156 (2001): 50–51.
Hegel, Georg Wilhelm Friedrich. *Introductory Lectures in Aesthetics.* Translated by Bernard Bosanquet. London: Penguin, 1993.
———. *Hegel's Philosophy of Mind.* Translated by William Wallace. Oxford: Clarendon, 1894.
———. *Lectures on the History of Philosophy: Medieval and Modern Philosophy.* Translated by E.S. Haldane. Lincoln: University of Nebraska Press, 1995.
Heyes, Cressida. "Somaesthetics for the Normalized Body." In *Self-Transformations: Foucault, Ethics, and Normalized Bodies.* Oxford: Oxford University Press, 2007.
Heynen, Hilde. "A Critical Position for Architecture?" In *Critical Architecture.* Edited by Jane Rendell and Jonathan Hill. London: Routledge, 2007.
Higgins, Kathleen. "Living and Feeling at Home: Shusterman's Performing Live." *Journal of Aesthetic Education,* 36 (2002): 84–92.
Hipple, Walter J. Jr. *The Beautiful, the Sublime, and the Picturesque in Eighteenth-Century British Aesthetic Theory.* Carbondale Southern Illinois University Press, 1957.
Holroyd, Michael. *Lytton Strachey: A Biography.* London: Penguin, 1971.
Huang, Liqiang, and Harold Pashler. "Attention Capacity and Task Difficulty in Visual Search." *Cognition,* 94 (2005): B101–B111.
Ioakimidis, I., M. Zandian, C. Bergh, and P. Södersten. "A Method for the Control of Eating Rate: A Potential Intervention in Eating Disorders." *Behavioral Research Methods,* 41 (2009): 755–760.
Iseminger, Gary. "Aesthetic Experience." In *The Oxford Handbook of Aesthetics.* Edited by Jerrold Levinson. Oxford: Oxford University Press, 2003.
Knoblock, John. *Xunzi: A Translation and Study of the Complete Works,* 3 vols. Stanford: Stanford University Press, 1988–1994.
James, William. *The Correspondence of William James,* vols. 1, 4, 8. Charlottesville: University Press of Virginia, 1992–2000.
———. *Essays in Radical Empiricism.* Cambridge, MA: Harvard University Press, 1976.

———. *Talks To Teachers on Psychology and To Students on Some of Life's Ideals*. New York: Dover, 1962.

———. *The Principles of Psychology*. Cambridge, MA: Harvard University Press, 1983.

Jay, Martin. "Somaesthetics and Democracy: John Dewey and Contemporary Body Art." In *Refractions of Violence*. New York: Routledge, 2003.

Jowitt, Deborah. *Time and the Dancing Image*. Berkeley: University of California Press, 1989.

Kabat-Zinn, Jon. "The Relationship of Cognitive and Somatic Components of Anxiety to Patient Preference for Alternative Relaxation Techniques." *Mind/Body Medicine*, 2 (1997): 101–109.

———, et al. "Effectiveness of a Meditation-Based Stress Reduction Program in the Treatment of Anxiety Disorders." *American Journal of Psychiatry*, 149 (1992): 936–943.

Kahneman, Daniel. "Objective Happiness." In *Well-being: the Foundations of Hedonic Psychology*. Edited by D. Kahneman, E. Diner and N. Schwartz. New York: Russell Sage, 1999.

Kallio, Titti. "Why We Choose the More Attractive Looking Objects: Somatic Markers and Somaesthetics in User Experience." *Proceedings of the 2003 International Conference on Designing Pleasurable Products and Interfaces*. New York: ACM (2003): 142–143.

Kandel, Eric R. *In Search of Memory*. New York: Norton, 2006.

Kant, Immanuel. *Anthropology from a Pragmatic Point of View*. Translated by V. Dowdell. Carbondale: Southern Illinois University Press, 1996.

———. *The Conflict of the Faculties*. Translated by Mary Gregor. Lincoln: University of Nebraska Press, 1992.

———. *The Critique of Judgment*. Translated by J.C. Meredith. Oxford: Oxford University Press, 1986.

———. *The Metaphysics of Morals*. Translated by Mary Gregor. Cambridge: Cambridge University Press, 1996.

———. *Reflexionen Kants zur Kritischen Philosophie*. Edited by Benno Erdmann. Stuttgart: Frommann-Holzboog, 1992.

Keynes, J.M. "My Early Beliefs." In *Essays and Sketches in Biography*. New York: Meridian, 1956.

Kierkegaard, Soren. *The Sickness unto Death*. In *Fear and Trembling and The Sickness Unto Death*. Translated by W. Lowrie. New York: Anchor, 1954.

Knoblock, John (translator). *Xunzi*, 3 vols. Stanford: Stanford University Press, 1988–1994.

Koczanowicz, Dorota, and Wojciech Małecki (editors). *Shusterman's Pragmatism: From Literature to Somaesthetics*. Amsterdam: Rodopi, 2012.

Koolhaas, Rem. "What Ever Happened to Urbanism?" In *S,M,L,XL*. Edited by Rem Koolhaas and Bruce Mau. New York: Monacelli Press, 1995.

Kristeva, Julia. *Black Sun: Depression and Melancholia*. Translated by L. Roudiez. New York: Columbia University Press, 1989.

Krüger, Hans-Peter. *Zwischen Lachen und Weinen*, 2 vols. Berlin: Akademie Verlag, 1999, 2001.

Lackner, J.R. and Paul Zio. "Aspects of Body Self-Calibration." *Trends in Cognitive Science*, 4 (2000): 279–282.

———. "Vestibular, Proprioceptive, and Haptic Contributions to Spatial Organization." *Annual Review of Psychology*, 56 (2005): 115–147.
Laertius, Diogenes. *Lives of Eminent Philosophers*, 2 vols. Translated by R.D. Hicks. Cambridge, MA: Harvard University Press, 1991.
Lau, D.C. (translator). *Lao Tzu*. London: Penguin, 1963.
——— (translator). *Mencius*. London: Penguin, 1970.
Leddy, Thomas. "Shusterman's *Pragmatist Aesthetics*." *Journal of Speculative Philosophy*, 16 (2002): 10–15.
Leypoldt, Gunther. "The Pragmatist Aesthetics of Richard Shusterman: A Conversation." *Zeitschrift für Anglistik und Amerikanistik: A Quarterly of Language, Literature, and Culture*, 48 (2000): 57–71.
Libet, Benjamin. "Do We Have Free Will?" *Journal of Consciousness Studies*, 6 (1999): 47–57.
———. "Unconscious Cerebral Initiative and the Role of Conscious Will in Voluntary Action." *Behavioral and Brain Sciences*, 8 (1985): 529–66.
Lim, Youn-Kyung, Erik Stolterman, et al. "Interaction Gestalt and the Design of Aesthetic Interactions." *Proceedings of the 2007 Conference on Designing Pleasurable Products and Interfaces*. New York: ACM (2007): 239–254.
Loland, N.W. "The Art of Concealment in a Culture of Display: Aerobicizing Women's and Men's Experience and Use of Their Own Bodies." *Sociology of Sport Journal*, 17 (2000): 111–129.
Lopes, D.M. "The Aesthetics of Photographic Transparency." *Mind*, 36 (2003): 335–348.
Malcolm, Norman. *Wittgenstein: A Memoir*. Oxford: Oxford University Press, 1984.
Małecki, Wojciech. *Embodying Pragmatism: Richard Shusterman's Philosophy and Literary Theory*. Frankfurt: Peter Lang, 2010.
Maynard, Patrick. *The Engine of Visualization: Thinking Through Photography*. Ithaca: Cornell University Press, 1997.
Meltzoff, A.N. and M.K. Moore. "Imitation of Facial and Manual Gestures by Human Neonates." *Science*, New Series 198 (1977): 75–78.
———. "Imitation, Memory, and the Representation of Persons." *Infant Behavior and Development*, 17 (1994): 83–99.
Mencken, H.L. "Literature and the Schoolm'am." In *Prejudices: Fifth Series*. New York: Octagon Books, 1977.
Merleau-Ponty, Maurice. *In Praise of Philosophy and Other Essays*. Translated by John Wild, James Edie, and John O'Neill. Evanston: Northwestern University Press, 1970.
———. *The Phenomenology of Perception*. Translated by Colin Smith. London: Routledge, 1962.
———. *Signs*. Translated by R.C. McCleary. Evanston: Northwestern University Press, 1970.
———. *The Visible and the Invisible*. Translated by A. Lingis. Evanston: Northwestern University Press, 1968.
Miller, James. *The Passion of Michel Foucault*. New York: Simon and Schuster, 1993.
Moholy-Nagy, Laszlo. *Painting, Photography, Film*. Translated by Janet Seligman. Cambridge, MA: MIT Press, 1987.
Monk, Ray. *Ludwig Wittgenstein: The Duty of Genius*. London: Penguin, 1990.

Montaigne, Michel de. *The Complete Essays of Montaigne*. Translated by Donald Frame. Stanford: Stanford University Press, 1965.

Montero, Barbara. "Proprioception as an Aesthetic Sense." *Journal of Aesthetics and Art Criticism*, 64 (2006): 230–242.

Morrow, Jannay. "Effects of Rumination and Distraction on Naturally Occurring Depressed Mood." *Cognition & Emotion*, 7 (1993): 561–570.

Mullis, Eric. "Performative Somaesthetics: Principles and Scope." *Journal of Aesthetic Education*, 40 (2006): 104–117.

———. "Review of *Body Consciousness: A Philosophy of Mindfulness and Somaesthetics*." *Journal of Aesthetic Education*, 45 (2011): 123–127.

Needham, Joseph. *Science and Civilisation in China*, vol. 2. Cambridge: Cambridge University Press, 1956.

Nehamas, Alexander. "Richard Shusterman on Pleasure and Aesthetic Experience." *Journal of Aesthetics and Art Criticism*, 56 (1998): 49–51.

Nielsen, H.S. "The Computer Game as a Somatic Experience." *Eludamos. Journal for Computer Game Culture*, 4 (2010): 25–40.

Nietzche, Friedrich. *The Birth of Tragedy and The Genealogy of Morals*. Translated by Francis Golffing. New York: Doubleday, 1956.

———. *Ecce Homo*. Translated by R.J. Hollingdale. London: Penguin, 1992.

———. *Friedrich Nietzsche: Sämtliche Werke*, 5 vols. Edited by G. Colli and M. Montinari. Berlin: de Gruyter, 1999.

———. *Human, All Too Human*. Translated by R.J. Hollingdale. Cambridge: Cambridge University Press, 1996.

———. *Nietzsche: Untimely Meditations*. Translated by R.J. Hollingdale. Cambridge: Cambridge University Press, 1983.

———. *Thus Spoke Zarathustra*. In *The Portable Nietzsche*. Translated by Walter Kaufmann. New York: Penguin, 1976.

———. *The Will to Power*. Translated by Walter Kaufmann and R.J. Hollingdale. New York: Random House, 1967.

Nolen-Hoeksema, Susan. "Responses to Depression and Their Effects on the Duration of Depressive Episodes." *Journal of Abnormal Psychology*, 100 (1991): 569–582.

———, et al. "Explaining the Gender Difference in Depressive Symptoms." *Journal of Personality and Social Psychology*, 77 (1999): 1061–72.

Nussbaum, Martha. *The Therapy of Desire*. Princeton: Princeton University Press, 1994.

Ockman, Joan. *The Pragmatist Imagination*. New York: Princeton Architectural Press, 2000.

Pascal, Blaise. *Pensées*. Translated by A.J. Krailsheimer. London: Penguin, 1966.

Pascual-Leone, A., et al. "Modulation of Muscle Responses Evoked by Transcranial Magnetic Stimulation during the Acquisition of New Fine Motor Skills." *Journal of Neurophysiology*, 74 (1995): 1037–1045.

Passmore, John. "The Dreariness of Aesthetics." In *Aesthetics and Language*. Edited by W. Elton. Oxford: Blackwell, 1954.

Perry, Ralph Barton. *The Thought and Character of William James*, 2 vols. Boston: Little, Brown and Company, 1935.

Plato. *Plato: Complete Works*. Edited by John Cooper. Indianapolis: Hackett, 1997.

Plotinus. *Enneads.* Translated by A.H. Armstrong. Cambridge, MA: Harvard University Press, 1966.
Plessner, Helmuth. *Macht und menschliche Natur: Ein Versuch zur Anthropologie der geschichtlichen Weltansicht.* In *Helmuth Plessner Gesammelte Schriften,* vol. 5. Frankfurt am Main: Suhrkamp, 1982.
Plutarch. "Tranquility of Mind." In *Plutarch's Moralia,* vol. 6. Translated by W.C. Helmbold. Cambridge, MA: Harvard University Press, 1939.
Porter, Katherine Anne. "Interview with Barbara Thompson, 1963." Reprinted in *Women Writers at Work: The Paris Review Interviews.* Edited by George Plimpton. New York: Modern Library, 1998.
Price, Uvedale. "An Essay on the Picturesque, as Compared with the Sublime and Beautiful." In *The Sublime: A Reader in British Eighteenth-century Aesthetic Theory.* Edited by Andrew Ashfield and Peter de Bolla. Cambridge: Cambridge University Press, 1996.
Rahula, Walpoa (editor). *What the Buddha Taught,* 2nd edition. New York: Grove Press, 1974.
Rhees, Rush (editor). *Recollections of Wittgenstein.* Oxford: Blackwell, 1984.
Ricket, W.A. (translator). *Kuan-Tzu.* Hong Kong: Hong Kong University Press, 1965.
Rimer, J.T., and Masakazu Yamazaki (translators). *On the Art of the Nō Drama: The Major Treatises of Zeami.* Princeton: Princeton University Press, 1983.
Rizzolati, Giacomo, and Laila Craighero. "The Mirror Neuron System." *Annual Review of Neuroscience,* 27 (2004): 169–192.
Rorty, Richard. *Achieving Our Country.* Cambridge, MA: Harvard University Press, 1999.
———. "Afterword: Intellectual Historians and Pragmatism." In *A Pragmatist's Progress?* Edited by John Pettegrew. Lanham, MD: Rowman & Littlefield, 2000.
———. *Consequences of Pragmatism.* Minneapolis: University of Minnesota Press, 1982.
———. *Contingency, Irony, and Solidarity.* Cambridge: Cambridge University Press, 1989.
———. *Essays on Heidegger and Others: Philosophical Papers,* vol. 2. Cambridge: Cambridge University Press, 1991.
———. "The Fire of Life." *Poetry,* 191 (November 2007): 129.
———. "Inquiry as Recontextualization: An Anti-Dualist Account of Interpretation." In *The Interpretive Turn: Philosophy, Science, Culture.* Edited by David Hiley, James Bohman, and Richard Shusterman. Ithaca: Cornell University Press, 1991.
———. "The Inspirational Value of Great Literature." In *Achieving Our Country.* Cambridge, MA: Harvard University Press, 1999.
———. "The Intellectuals at the End of Socialism." *Yale Review,* 80 (April, 1992): 1–16.
———. "Intellectuals in Politics: Too Far In? Too Far Out?" *Dissent,* 38 (1991): 483–490.
———. *Objectivity, Relativism, and Truth: Philosophical Papers,* vol. 1. Cambridge: Cambridge University Press, 1991.
———. *Philosophy as Cultural Politics: Philosophical Papers,* vol. 4. Cambridge: Cambridge University Press, 2007.

———. "Response to Richard Shusterman." In *Richard Rorty: Critical Dialogues.* Edited by Matthew Festenstein and Simon Thompson. Cambridge: Polity Press, 2001.

———. "Thugs and Theorists." *Political Theory,* 15 (1987): 564–580.

———. *Truth and Progress: Philosophical Papers,* vol. 3. Cambridge: Cambridge University Press, 1998.

Roth, Harold. *Original Tao: Inward Training (Nei-yeh) and the Foundations of Taoist Mysticism.* New York: Columbia University Press, 1999.

Rousseau, Jean-Jacques. *Émile: Or, on Education.* Translated by Allan Bloom. New York: Basic Books, 1979.

Ruskin, John. "Of Wisdom and Folly in Science." In *The Eagle's Nest: Ten Lectures on the Relation of Natural Science to Art, given before the University of Oxford in Lent Term, 1872.* London: Smith, Elder & Co., 1872.

Russell, Bertrand. *The Autobiography of Bertrand Russell 1872–1914.* London: Allen & Unwin, 1967.

Säätelä, Simo. "Between Intellectualism and 'Somaesthetics'." In *Filozofski Vestnik,* 2 (1999): 151–162.

Schiphorst, Thecla. "soft(n): Toward a Somaesthetics of Touch." *Proceedings of the 27th International Conference Extended Abstracts on Human Factors in Computing Systems,* New York: ACM (2009): 2427–2438.

———, Jinsil Seo, and Norman Jaffe. "Exploring Touch and Breath in Networked Wearable Installation Design." *Proceedings of the International Conference on Multimedia,* New York: ACM (2010): 1399–1400.

Schopenhauer, Arthur. *The World as Will and Representation,* 2 vols. Translated by E.F.J. Payne. New York: Dover, 1958.

Schwartz, Barry. *The Paradox of Choice.* New York: Harper Collins, 2004.

Scruton, Roger. "Photography and Representation." In *The Aesthetic Understanding.* London: Methuen, 1983.

Searle, John R. *The Construction of Social Reality.* New York: Free Press, 1995.

———. *Intentionality: An Essay in the Philosophy of Mind.* Cambridge: Cambridge University Press, 1983

———. *Rationality in Action.* Cambridge, MA: MIT Press, 2001.

———. *The Rediscovery of the Mind.* Cambridge, MA: MIT Press, 1992.

———. *Speech Acts.* Cambridge: Cambridge University Press, 1969.

Shechner, Stanley and Judith Ronin. *Obese Humans and Rats.* New York: Wiley, 1974.

Shikibu, Murasaki. *The Tale of Genji.* Translated by Edward Seidensticker. New York: Knopf 2001.

Shklovsky, Viktor. "Art as Device." In *Theory of Prose.* Translated by Benjamin Sher. Normal, IL: Dalkey Archive Press, 1991.

Shusterman, Richard. "Aesthetic Experience: From Analysis to Eros." *Journal of Aesthetics and Art Criticism,* 64 (2006): 217–229.

——— (editor). *Analytic Aesthetics.* Oxford: Blackwell, 1989.

———. "Analytic Aesthetics, Literary Theory, and Deconstruction." *The Monist,* 69 (1986): 22–38.

———. "The Anomalous Nature of Literature." *British Journal of Aesthetics,* 18 (1978): 317–329.

———. *Body Consciousness: A Philosophy of Mindfulness and Somaesthetics*. Cambridge: Cambridge University Press, 2008.
———. "Bourdieu and Anglo-American Philosophy." In *Bourdieu: A Critical Reader*. Edited by Richard Shusterman. Oxford: Blackwell, 1999.
———. "Croce on Interpretation: Deconstruction and Pragmatism." *New Literary History*, 20 (1988): 199–216.
———. "Deconstruction and Analysis: Confrontation and Convergence." *British Journal of Aesthetics*, 26 (1986): 311–327.
———. "Discussion with Peng Feng." *Art Press*, 379, Venice Biennale Supplement (June 2011): 24–25.
———. "Emerson's Pragmatist Aesthetics," *Revue Internationale de Philosophie*, 207 (1999): 87–99.
———. "Entertainment: A Question for Aesthetics." *British Journal of Aesthetics*, 43 (2003): 289–307.
———. "Interpretation, Pleasure, and Value in Aesthetic Experience." *Journal of Aesthetics and Art Criticism*, 56 (1998): 51–53.
———. "Le corps en act et en conscience." In *Philosophie du corps*. Edited by Bernard Andrieu. Paris: Vrin, 2010.
———. "The Logic of Evaluation." *Philosophy Quarterly*, 30 (1980): 327–341.
———. "The Logic of Interpretation." *Philosophy Quarterly*, 28 (1978): 310–324.
———. *Performing Live: Aesthetic Alternatives for the Ends of Art*. Ithaca: Cornell University Press, 2000.
———. "A Philosopher in Darkness and in Light: Practical Somaesthetics and Photographic Art." In *Lucidité. Vues de l'intérieur / Lucidity. Inward Views: Le Mois de la Photo à Montréal 2011*. Edited by Anne-Marie Ninacs. Montréal: Le Mois de la Photo à Montréal, 2011.
———. *Practicing Philosophy: Pragmatism and the Philosophical Life*. New York: Routledge, 1997.
———. "Pragmatist Aesthetics and East-Asian Thought." *The Range of Pragmatism and the Limits of Philosophy*. Edited by Richard Shusterman. Oxford: Blackwell, 2004.
———. *Pragmatist Aesthetics: Living Beauty, Rethinking Art*. Oxford: Blackwell, 1992. 2nd edition. New York: Rowman & Littlefield, 2000.
———. "Pragmatist Aesthetics: Between Aesthetic Experience and Aesthetic Education." *Studies in Philosophy and Education*, 22 (2003): 403–412.
———. "Pragmatism and Criticism: A Response to Three Critics of Pragmatist Aesthetics." *Journal of Speculative Philosophy*, 16 (2002): 26–38.
———. "Regarding Oneself and Seeing Double: Fragments of Autobiography." *The Philosophical I: Personal Reflections on Life in Philosophy*. Edited by George Yancey. New York: Rowman and Littlefield, 2002.
———. "Soma and Psyche." *Journal of Speculative Philosophy*, 24 (2010): 205–223.
———. "Soma, Self, and Society." *Metaphilosophy*, 42 (2011): 314–327.
———. "Somaesthetics: A Disciplinary Proposal." *Journal of Aesthetics and Art Criticism*, 57 (1999): 299–313.
———. "Somaesthetics and Care of the Self: The Case of Foucault." *Monist*, 83 (2000): 530–551.
———. *Surface and Depth*. Ithaca: Cornell University Press, 2002.

———. *T.S. Eliot and the Philosophy of Criticism.* London and New York: Duckworth and Columbia University Press, 1988.

———. *Vor der Interpretation.* Wien: Passagen Verlag, 1996.

Sibley, Frank. "Aesthetic Concepts." *Philosophical Review,* 68 (1959): 421–450.

Skowronski, K.P. *Values and Powers: Re-reading the Philosophical Tradition of American Pragmatism.* Amsterdam: Rodopi, 2009.

Smith, S.J. and R.J. Lloyd. "Promoting Vitality in Health and Physical Education." *Qualitative Health Research,* 16 (2006): 249–267.

Sommer, Deborah. "Boundaries of the *Ti* Body." *Asia Major,* 21 (2008): 293–324.

Somol, Robert, and Sarah Whiting. "Notes Around the Doppler Effect and Other Moods of Modernism." *Perspecta,* 33 (2002): 72–77.

Sontag, Susan. *On Photography.* New York: Farrar, Straus and Giroux, 1977.

Soulez, Antonia. "Practice, Theory, Pleasure, and the Problems of Form and Resistance: Shusterman's *Pragmatist Aesthetics.*" *Journal of Speculative Philosophy,* 16 (2002): 1–9.

Sousa, Ronald de. "Love as Theater." In *The Philosophy of (Erotic) Love.* Edited by Robert Solomon and Kathleen Higgins. Lawrence: University of Kansas Press, 1991.

Spater, George, and Ian Parsons. *A Marriage of True Minds: An Intimate Portrait of Leonard and Virginia Woolf.* London: Hogarth, 1972.

Stanhope, Philip Dormer, Fourth Earl of Chesterfield. *Letters to His Son: On the Fine Art of Becoming a Man of the World and a Gentleman.* New York: Tudor, 1937.

Stern, Daniel N. *The Interpersonal World of the Infant.* New York: Basic Books, 1985.

Styron, William. *Darkness Visible: A Memoir of Madness.* New York: Random House, 1990.

Sullivan, Shannon. "Transactional Somaesthetics." In *Living Across and Through Skins: Transactional Bodies, Pragmatism, and Feminism.* Bloomington, IN: Indiana University Press, 2001.

Sundström, P., K. Höök et al. "Experiential Artifacts as a Design Method for Sómaesthetic Service Development." *Proceedings of the 2011 ACM Symposium on the Role of Design in UbiComp Research.* New York: ACM (2011), 33–36.

Surbaugh, Michael. "'Somaesthetics,' Education, and Disability." *Philosophy of Education,* (2009): 417–424.

Suzuki, D.T. *Zen and Japanese Culture.* Princeton: Princeton University Press, 1989.

Taine, Hippolyte. *History of English Literature.* Translated by H. van Laun. New York: Holt and Williams, 1886.

Taylor, Paul C. "The Two-Dewey Thesis, Continued: Shusterman's *Pragmatist Aesthetics.*" *Journal of Speculative Philosophy,* 16 (2002): 17–25.

———. "What's the Use of Calling Du Bois a Pragmatist?" In *The Range of Pragmatism and the Limits of Philosophy.* Edited by Richard Shusterman. Oxford: Blackwell, (2004): 95–111.

Thoreau, Henry David. "Thomas Carlyle and His Works." In *Miscellanies by Henry David Thoreau.* Boston: Houghton, Mifflin and Co, 1894.

———. *Walden and Other Writings.* Edited by Brooks Atkinson. New York: Modern Library, 2000.

Thorold, Algar Labouchere (translator). "A Treatise of Discretion." In *Dialogue of St. Catherine of Siena.* New York: Cosimo Classics, 2007.

Tolstoy, Lev Nikolayevich. *Confession.* Translated by David Patterson. New York: Norton 1983.
Tononi, Giulio, and Christof Koch. "The Neural Correlates of Consciousness: An Update." *Annals of the New York Academy of Science,* 1124 (2008): 239–261.
Trapnell, P., and J. Campbell. "Private Self-Consciousness and the Five-Factor Model of Personality: Distinguishing Rumination from Reflection." *Journal of Personality and Social Psychology,* 76 (1999): 284–304.
Tupper, Ken. "Entheogens and Education." *Journal of Drug Education and Awareness,* 1 (2003): 145–161.
Turner, Bryan. "Somaesthetics and the Critique of Cartesian Dualism." *Body and Society,* 14 (2008): 129–133.
Tversky, Barbara. "Remembering Spaces." In *The Oxford Handbook of Memory.* Oxford: Oxford University Press, 2000.
Urmson, J.O. "What Makes a Situation Aesthetic?" In *Proceedings of the Aristotelian Society,* supplementary vol. 131 (1957): 72–92.
Van der Kolk, B.A., J. Hopper, and J. Osterman. "Exploring the Nature of Traumatic Memory: Combining Clinical Knowledge with Laboratory Methods." In *Trauma and Cognitive Science: A Meeting of Minds, Science, and Human Experience.* Edited by J. Freyd and A. DePrince. Philadelphia: Haworth Press, 2001.
Van Gulik, R.H. *Sexual Life in Ancient China: A Preliminary Survey of Chinese Sex and Society from ca. 1500 B.C. till 1644 A.D.* Leiden: Brill, 2003.
Verhaeghen, P., J. Joormann, and R. Kahn. "Why We Sing the Blues: The Relation Between Self-Reflective Rumination, Mood, and Creativity." *Emotion,* 5 (2005): 226–232.
Vitruvius. *The Ten Books on Architecture.* Translated by M.H. Morgan. Cambridge, MA: Harvard University Press, 1914.
Vogt, Stefan. "On Relations between Perceiving, Imagining, and Performing in the Learning of Cyclical Movement Sequences." *British Journal of Psychology,* 86 (1995): 191–216.
Voparil, Christopher, and Richard Bernstein (editors). *The Rorty Reader.* Oxford: Blackwell, 2010.
Watson, Burton (translator). *The Complete Works of Chuang Tzu.* New York: Columbia University Press, 1968.
Walton, Kendall. "Transparent Pictures: On the Nature of Photographic Realism." *Noûs,* 18 (1984): 67–72.
Weston, Edward. "Photography – Not Pictorial." *Camera Craft,* 37 (1930): 313–20.
Whitman, Walt. "Song of Myself." In *Whitman: Poetry and Prose.* Edited by Justin Kaplan. New York: Library of America, 1996.
Wilkins, E.G. *The Delphic Maxims in Literature.* Chicago: University of Chicago Press, 1929.
Wimsatt, W.K., Jr. *The Verbal Icon: Studies in the Meaning of Poetry.* Lexington: University of Kentucky Press, 1967.
Wittgenstein, Ludwig. *Culture and Value.* Translated by Peter Winch. Oxford: Blackwell, 1980, revised edition 1998.
———. *Denkbewegungen: Tagebücher 1930–1932, 1936–1937.* Edited by Ilse Somavilla. Innsbruck: Haymon, 1997.

———. *Philosophical Investigations*. Translated by G.E.M. Anscombe. Oxford: Blackwell, 1968.
———. *Zettel*. Translated by G.E.M. Anscombe. Oxford: Blackwell, 1967.
Wolfe, Leonard. *Sowing: An Autobiography of the Years 1880 to 1904*. New York: Harcourt, Brace, 1960.
Wotton, Henry. *The Elements of Architecture*. London: Longmans, Green, and Co., 1624.
Xenophon. *Conversations of Socrates*. Translated by Robin Waterfield. London: Penguin, 1990.
Yasuo, Yuasa. *The Body: Towards an Eastern Mind-Body Theory*. Albany: SUNY Press, 1987.
Young, Edward. *Night Thoughts*. Holborn, London: C. Whittingham for T. Heptinstall, 1798.
Yue, Guang, and Kelly Cole. "Strength Increases from the Motor Program. Comparison of Training with Maximal Voluntary and Imagined Muscle Contractions." *Journal of Neurophysiology*, 67 (1992): 1114–1123.
Zandian, Modjtaba, et al. "Decelerated and Linear Eaters: Effect of Eating Rate on Food Intake and Satiety." *Physiological Behavior*, 96 (2009): 270–275.
Zerbib, David. "Soma-esthétique du corps absent." In *Penser en corps. Soma-esthétique, art, et philosophie*. Edited by Barbara Formis. Paris: L'Harmattan, 2009.

Index

abilities, 31, 51, 52, 94, 147, 165, 211, 225, 285, 319, 332
Abrams, Jerrold, 12
accident, 101, 105, 177, 208
accuracy, 207, 234
aches. *See* pain
acting, 9, 37, 50, 135, 169, 211, 212, 281, 321, 322
action, 2, 4, 15, 16, 17, 26, 32–34, 38–42, 47, 49, 50, 54–56, 58, 60–66, 78, 81, 84, 91, 95, 96, 99, 108, 109, 140, 141, 174, 183, 192, 193, 199, 201–210, 213–215, 238, 293, 296, 301, 306, 309–312, 316, 319–320, 325, 331, 333
activism, 138, 169, 178, 186
actor, 210–214, 249
acuity, 84, 111, 113, 120, 148, 292, 307
Adorno, Theodor W., 127, 164, 165
advertising, 109, 183, 239, 244, 324
Aeschylus, 68
aesthesis, 103, 111, 113, 141, 183, 188
aesthetic attitude, 2, 133
aesthetic experience, 2, 3, 5, 6, 8, 19, 21, 45, 133, 135, 138–140, 143, 145, 147, 148, 150, 161, 163–165, 171, 176, 181, 241–244, 246, 251, 252, 256, 258–267, 269, 275, 302–304
aesthetic judgment, 2, 132, 162
aesthetics 3, 145
   analytic, 19, 125–127, 128, 130, 131, 134, 135, 139
   appreciation, 1, 14, 27, 46, 133, 176, 182, 183, 259, 275, 303–304
   everyday, ordinary, 295, 303–306, 313
   history of, 128

affect, 64, 82, 85, 133, 147, 151, 153, 159, 190
age, 273–275, 323
agent, 16, 53
Alexander, Frederick Matthias, 11, 14, 37, 43, 56, 62–64, 87, 89, 205
America, 110, 128, 168, 180, 186, 288, 297, 301, 308, 315
amusements, 281
Ananga Ranga, 276–278, 282, 284–285
anatomy, 42, 142
Ando, Tadao, 227
angle, 15, 49, 112, 116, 251
animals, 29, 30, 96, 152, 191, 277, 281
Apollo, 68, 69, 86
appearance, 5, 7, 11, 15, 27, 44, 86, 132, 133, 140, 149, 210–212, 214, 233, 236, 321, 323, 326, 333–335
appetite, 109, 263, 300–301
Arbus, Diane, 81, 245
archery, 206
architecture, 20, 219–238, 277. *See also* building
arm, 97, 98, 108, 112, 117, 262, 278
aroma, 109, 328, 329
arousal, 164, 279
ars erotica, 262–287
art, 9, 10, 15, 140
   concept of, 134, 137, 140
   contemporary, 10, 137, 139, 164, 171, 304
   definition and theories of, 2, 134–135, 137, 139, 171, 233, 241
   fine, 2, 3, 20–22, 130, 140, 171, 226, 277, 283, 305, 315, 319, 329
   identity and authenticy of, 126, 135
   institutional theory of, 135–136

355

Index

art (cont.)
  of living, 3, 5, 21, 141, 171, 185, 189, 288–314
  popular, 139, 141, 171, 182
art world, 134–137
artha, 277
artificiality, 321
artist, 9–10, 21, 37, 45, 131, 145, 165, 241, 243, 254, 260, 264, 293, 321–322
artistry, 21, 140, 193, 266, 268–269, 277, 286, 309, 312
artwork, 133–135, 336
Asia, 11, 20–22, 34, 84, 115, 190, 200, 227–228, 262–287, 336
Asian *ars erotica*, 269–271, 286
askesis, 17, 71, 257, 294, 305, 336
association (of ideas), 59–60, 81, 121, 159, 160
athletics, 45–46, 140, 192
atmosphere, 20–21, 210, 220, 223, 226, 229, 231–238, 257, 289, 293, 295
attention, 3, 17–18, 38–44, 49, 56, 61–65, 74, 77–78, 84, 87–89, 95, 99, 103, 107–109, 115–121, 147, 149, 164–165, 198, 200, 203–210, 215, 231, 234–238, 245, 250, 297–300, 303–313, 321
attitude, 89, 107, 145, 214, 228–230, 258, 301, 317, 319, 333
audience, 105, 131, 136, 165, 175, 193, 210–213
auditory, 109, 305, 326–328
Augustine, Saint, 294
aura, 25, 233, 234, 236, 253–260, 318, 332
Austin, John Langshaw, 53, 256
authority, 96, 98, 167, 236
Avedon, Richard, 246
awakening, 21, 288–314
awareness, 3, 15–16, 18, 20, 28, 30, 34, 37–39, 43, 46, 61, 63, 86, 92, 105–107, 111, 113–118, 144, 158, 165, 187–191, 194, 197–199, 204, 214, 235, 237–238, 292–293, 295–299, 301–305, 309–312
axis, 47, 95, 102

back, 95, 98, 101, 103, 105, 108, 112, 115–120, 161, 211, 212
background, 47–67
  environing conditions, 55, 65
  fringe, 57–58
  qualitative, 57–58, 61

balance, 6, 40, 43, 133, 147, 178, 181, 198, 210, 213, 226, 235, 244–245, 280, 330
Balanchine, George, 99
Barthes, Roland, 240, 247–248, 251, 257, 258
Bataille, Georges, 143, 192
Baudelaire, Charles, 251–252
Bauhaus, 220
Baumgarten, Alexander, 1, 2, 7, 19, 129, 140, 141, 148
Beardsley, Monroe, 131, 132, 134, 135
beauty, 2, 3, 5, 14, 21, 22, 27, 42, 129–130, 133, 145–146, 148, 151–152, 155–158, 163–165, 189, 263–265, 268, 280, 283, 290, 293, 305, 309, 317, 319, 336–337
  bodily, 5, 152, 189
Beethoven, Ludwig van, 192
behavior, 4, 17, 18, 27, 29–30, 57, 61, 113, 141, 156, 162–163, 174–175, 191, 200, 205–206, 208–209, 235, 237, 305, 319–320, 324, 327, 331, 333
belief, 19, 51, 53, 147, 164, 166, 172, 190–191, 194, 292
Benjamin, Walter, 164, 233, 234, 236–238, 240, 252–254
Bergson, Henri, 35, 194
Bharata Natya Sastra, 282
bias, 26, 105, 138, 145
blood, 46, 89, 147, 204, 289, 313, 333–335
Bloom, Harold, 177–178, 181
body. *See also* somaesthetics
  ambiguity, 16, 28, 32, 35, 173, 222
  as background, 47–67
  as center, 33, 94, 305
  contextuality, 17, 50, 52, 58–59, 96, 325, 332
  as distraction, 38, 150, 209, 310
  as expression, 15, 35, 151, 326
  as external form, 44, 50, 111, 113
  feeling of continuity, 93
  and freedom, 16, 32, 35
  as instrument or medium, 1, 3, 9, 16, 26, 28, 31–37, 41–43, 45, 63, 108, 149, 156, 164, 203, 227, 265, 275, 277–278, 282, 285, 289, 295, 315, 316
  as intentionality or subjectivity, 5, 28, 141, 160–161
  as machine, 161, 286
  norms, 5, 9, 32, 42

as physical object, 1, 4, 6, 16–17, 28, 32–33, 35, 111, 313
as point of view, 33, 94, 224
role in aesthetic experience, 1, 19, 147–148, 161–165
role in cognition, 15, 41, 92, 140
role in emotion, 147
role in ethics, 32
role in perception, 7, 8, 14
body parts, 16, 27, 28, 43–44, 101, 119, 120–122, 205, 207, 244, 279, 292, 332
body scan, 13, 114–117, 120–122
seated, 18
bodybuilding, 14, 43–44, 336, 337
bones, 43, 58, 89, 164, 289, 300, 331, 335
boundary, 74, 127–133, 143
Bourdieu, Pierre, 17, 31, 48, 53–54, 56, 127–128, 140, 178, 185
brain, 27, 52, 53, 85, 91, 102, 207, 208, 213–215, 264, 273
breasts, 262, 280
breathing, 12, 27, 32, 34, 38–39, 43, 61, 65, 87–88, 101–102, 106, 112, 115, 118, 121, 143, 157, 161, 165, 197, 198, 206, 226, 234, 235, 259, 308, 312–314, 334
Buddha, 89, 292
Buddhism, 89, 283, 293–294, 306
Buffon, Georges-Louis Leclerc, Comte de, 320
building, 60, 72, 186, 187, 226, 228, 230, 232, 236
Burke, Edmund, 19, 145–165, 264
buttock, 64, 116, 120

calligraphy, 319
Cambridge University, 317–318
camera, 10, 239–261
Campanella, Tommaso, 149–150
Camus, Albert, 185
Carlyle, Thomas, 78–79
Catherine, Saint of Siena, 71
ceremony, 253, 267, 307
change, 82, 98, 102, 117–118, 130, 166, 169, 186, 335
chest, 74, 118, 313
chewing, 108–109, 311, 327
child, 31, 97, 244, 259, 265, 271–273
China (and Chinese Culture), 10, 20–21, 200–209, 227, 266, 270–271, 274–275, 282, 292, 305

choice, 32, 153, 249, 324–325, 328
chopsticks, 207, 310, 311
Christianity, 36, 47, 70, 71–78, 88, 184, 270, 336
Cicero, 70
clothes, 98, 256, 259, 303, 306, 320–323, 326, 328, 332–333
cognition, 11, 14, 15, 21, 26, 73, 87, 92, 97, 99, 106, 121, 129, 143, 148, 150, 157, 159, 163, 173–174, 182, 236, 266, 284–287, 296, 301, 302, 330, 335
coitus, 272–281, 284
reservatus, 273–274
Coleridge, Samuel, 75
common sense, 291
commonplace, the, 251, 283, 299, 303
communication, 243, 258, 260, 316, 321
community, 169, 184, 307
computer. *See* human computer interaction
concentration, 11, 38, 88, 108, 150, 210, 236, 241, 245, 307, 308, 312, 314, 337
concubine, 272, 273
conditioning, cultural, 29
conduct, 277, 319
of life, 3, 150, 289, 291
confession, 83, 270
Confucius, 4, 20, 22, 31, 141, 168, 190, 200, 273, 319–320, 333
consciousness, 73, 78, 198, 251
body consciousness, 9, 11, 15, 18, 20, 22, 48, 62, 86–89, 93, 114, 122, 183, 197, 200, 208, 294, 311–312
explicit, 18, 30, 51, 57, 64, 99, 100, 108, 189, 235, 238, 312, 325
reflective, 18, 86, 161, 199, 208, 251
stream of, 57
constipation, 74
consummation, 171, 266, 267, 278
contemplation, 2, 46, 71, 78, 203, 236, 237, 263, 282, 289, 290, 295, 308, 309
content, 50–52, 57, 59, 76, 113, 133, 147, 164, 266, 322, 333
context. *See* background
contingency, 137, 177, 178, 284
contraction, 38–41, 102–104, 108, 119, 144, 154, 155–163, 313
contrast, 3, 5, 21, 73, 119, 152, 174, 200, 234, 257, 270, 301, 322
conversation, 169, 183, 188
coordination, 209, 231, 319

cosmetics, 332, 336
countenance, 151, 319
creativity, 82, 208, 222, 243
criticality, 219, 222–223, 228, 229–231, 233–236
  critical distance, 20, 222, 229
  immanent critique, 20, 221, 231
  post-critical, 221–223, 228–230, 233
criticism
  art, 131
  literary, 131–132, 185
Croce, Benedetto, 130–131
cultivation, 4, 16, 36–37, 45, 111, 113, 166, 189, 202–203, 227, 285–287
cultural politics, 18, 20, 166–196
culture. *See also* cultural politics
  high, 10, 25, 182
  popular, 25, 182

dance, 8–9, 14, 43, 45, 107, 211, 226, 255–259, 281–283, 331
danger, 149–160, 165
Dante (Durante degli Alighieri), 185
Danto, Arthur C., 7, 127, 134–137, 140
Daodejing, 201, 203
Daoism, 20, 200–204, 273, 292
darkness, 160, 257
d'Avila, St. Juan (St. John of Avila), 71
death, 30, 32, 251
deconstruction, 131
defamiliarization, 304
definition, 3, 84, 129–140, 171, 188, 219, 223, 224, 234, 248, 263, 265
Deleuze, Gilles, 192
deliberation, 91, 92, 109, 174, 297
delight, 2, 22, 147, 151–158, 165, 264, 279
Delphi, 68–78, 86, 90, 290
demeanor, 31, 34, 96, 246, 319
democracy, 10, 141, 171, 179, 219, 221
depression, 17, 39, 62, 70, 71, 75, 76, 80–89, 111
Derrida, Jacques, 178
Descartes, René, 72, 292
design, 8, 9, 11, 12, 221, 224–226, 233, 236, 238, 315
desire, 21, 30, 43, 49, 56, 71, 106, 140, 145, 146, 161, 247, 248, 267, 270, 278, 280, 284, 287, 290, 294, 295, 301, 324
despair, 71, 75, 76, 154
Dewey, John, 7, 10, 54–64, 86–89, 92, 139, 168, 170, 171, 176–178, 180, 182, 183, 185–188, 192, 204, 205, 229, 288, 290
dharma, 277
Dickie, George, 135, 140
diet, 27, 43, 44, 175, 324, 328
difference, 7, 28, 29, 35, 156, 170–172, 179, 181, 192, 265, 270, 277, 312, 322
dignity, 30, 35, 157
Diogenes the Cynic, 190
disability (and dysfunction), 37, 101
discipline, 17, 27, 44, 85, 272, 286, 290, 294–295, 300, 305, 307, 337
discomfort, 8, 44, 65–66, 74, 97, 101, 103, 106, 109, 110, 115, 153, 161, 207, 235, 247, 307
discourse, 4, 176, 192, 193, 195, 232, 270, 279
discursive, the 3, 27, 30, 142, 163, 176, 192–195, 229, 230, 234. *See also* discourse
disinterestedness, 2, 138, 145, 148, 152, 229, 230, 263–265
disposition, 63, 74, 149, 324
distance, 30, 107, 222, 224, 229–230, 237, 245, 251, 325–327, 333, 337
distinction, 5, 13, 43, 44, 59, 60, 65, 131–133, 136–137, 142, 173–174, 178–180, 192, 227, 242, 316, 320, 322, 323, 326, 329, 335
diversity, 5, 16, 70, 155, 158, 159, 228, 240, 243, 281, 283, 285
Dōgen, Zenji, 305
domination, 5, 9, 32, 180
dramatization, 139, 241, 249, 281
dream, 100, 174, 224, 292, 294
dress, 22, 98, 99, 262, 306, 320–325
Dreyfus, Hubert, 48
drink, 6, 101, 108–110, 278, 300–302, 311, 328
drugs, 8, 11, 150, 192, 265, 294
dualism, 5, 164, 193, 237, 314, 319
Duchamp, Marcel, 136
Durkheim, Émile, 54
duty, 31, 73, 75, 86, 177, 241, 251, 273, 277

ear, 102, 117
eating, 108–111, 162, 275, 300–302, 306, 309–311, 322, 325, 327
economics, 7, 38, 168, 272, 297
education, 4, 7, 8, 9, 37, 99, 191, 237, 285, 286, 302, 305

effort, 37, 49, 73, 91, 95, 107, 108, 118, 119, 150, 160, 235, 244, 246–247, 249, 259, 294–295, 323–324, 328
Eisenman, Peter, 222, 230, 233
ejaculation, 272, 281
Eliot, T.S., 126–127, 141
embodiment, 3, 5, 6, 11, 21, 29, 32, 36, 46, 47, 98, 111, 141, 197, 200, 275, 288
Emerson, Ralph Waldo, 5, 22, 36, 62, 185, 288–304, 315–316, 334
emotion, 2, 3, 14, 39, 46, 49, 76, 81, 97, 147, 149, 150, 152, 155, 156, 164, 168, 181, 207, 268, 273, 275
emptiness, 136, 314
ends, 2, 16, 28, 36–38, 40, 41, 44–46, 61, 64, 73, 77, 114, 152, 183, 205, 209, 316, 336
energy, 9, 15, 27, 33, 35, 43, 44, 46, 141, 254–256, 258–260, 264, 297, 300, 307, 309
enjoyment, 2, 109–110, 151, 193, 265, 275, 284–286
enlightenment, 290, 302, 312
entertainment, 72, 182, 278
environment, 27, 29, 39, 55, 63–66, 121, 134, 162, 184, 189, 205, 210, 219, 226, 290, 324
epistemology, 16, 17, 32, 172, 194, 219
equilibrium, 35, 225, 226, 331
eroticism, 21, 43, 140, 193, 262–287
essence, 28, 129, 132, 135–138, 154, 177, 187, 195, 240, 257, 267, 268, 272, 314, 319, 320, 334
essentialism, 5, 126, 131, 156, 158, 173, 175, 188
ethics, 16, 19, 32, 41, 172, 219, 268, 295, 319
ethnicity, 5, 179
evaluation, 126, 130, 142
Evans, Walker, 246
evolution, 12, 256, 297
excrement, 301, 336
exercise, 4, 27, 36, 39, 46, 72–74, 88, 114, 141, 147–149, 154–155, 159, 161, 167, 175, 190, 236, 288, 290
experience. *See* aesthetic experience
limit-experience, 143–144, 192
nonlinguistic, 19
expression, 31, 81, 97, 130–131, 150–151, 156, 243, 245–247, 257, 318–321, 323–324, 326–328, 334
eye, 15, 32, 38–39, 41, 42, 105, 154, 160, 212–214, 241, 278, 318

face, 28, 33, 71, 117, 149, 230, 237, 262, 278, 294, 310, 318, 332, 336
faith, 71, 75–76, 87, 184, 320
fallibilism, 78, 172
fashion, 8, 254, 315, 324–325, 328, 332
fatigue, 37, 38, 61, 88, 108, 111, 165, 207, 257
feeling, 1, 3, 21, 30, 31, 38–41, 44, 45, 49, 57–58, 61, 64–66, 74, 81, 93, 96, 97, 101–104, 106, 109–112, 115, 117–121, 145–147, 150–159, 188–191, 226, 234–235, 237, 238, 248, 259, 263–265, 319, 330–334
feet, 38, 40, 43, 64, 65, 101, 118, 198, 202, 210, 235, 308, 327
Feldenkrais, Moshe, 11, 15, 43–44, 86, 115, 127, 205, 305
fetishism, 138–139
fiction, 6, 164, 268
film, 21, 236–237, 239, 244, 255. *See also* movie
fingers, 28, 98, 108, 201, 207, 209, 230, 244, 250, 262, 272
fist, 119
fixity, 131, 248
flatulence, 74
flavor, 301, 330
flesh, 5, 27, 30, 58, 88, 89, 141, 147, 164, 197, 235, 289, 294, 300, 335
flexibility, 42, 143
floor, 44, 45, 88, 112, 114, 119, 120, 309, 327
focusing, 15–16, 39, 44, 55, 60, 84, 87–88, 120, 122, 191, 200, 207, 237, 248, 252, 305, 308, 312
food, 101, 109–110, 134, 230, 301, 309–311, 328
foreplay, 273–275, 278–279, 284
form, 2, 17, 29, 111, 129, 148, 225, 232, 233, 265, 303–304, 333, 335–337
Foucault, Michel, 31, 79, 80, 127, 143, 178, 185, 192, 269–271, 274, 290
foundationalism, 4, 93, 172–177, 191, 194, 195
fragrance, 10, 315, 328–330, 337
frailty, 16, 30, 35, 36
frame, 39, 248, 253
France (and French culture), 127–128, 168, 222, 256
freedom, 2, 16, 32, 35, 63, 99, 141, 190, 220, 221, 325
Freud, Sigmund, 100, 224

Fried, Michael, 261
function, 18, 35, 51–52, 59, 65, 142, 176, 219, 231–232, 253, 270, 273, 283, 293, 300–301, 312

gain (versus loss), 153, 238
gait, 29, 98, 107, 235, 303, 323, 325, 327
Gallese, Vittorio, 214
gender, 5, 11, 25, 32, 36, 42, 169, 179, 282, 323
generalization, 97, 126, 132
genitals, 264, 280
genius, 293, 295, 301, 317, 322
genre, 7, 130, 131, 239, 243, 254, 262, 322, 323
Germany, 168, 172, 179
gesture, 14, 21, 48, 107, 149, 151, 157, 175, 210, 211, 225, 245, 262, 267, 315, 318, 319, 321, 323, 326, 327, 331
Gibbon, Edward, 319
God, 70–71, 75–76, 78, 276, 282, 292, 294, 299, 300, 336
Goethe, Johan Wolfgang van, 77–79, 226
Goodman, Nelson, 127, 135
government, 167, 169, 211, 214
grace, 6, 17, 71, 165, 210, 255, 309–311, 319, 331
Graham, Agnus Charles, 202
gravity, 115, 161, 308
Greece (and Greek Culture), 1, 4, 5, 7, 25, 34–36, 68–69, 184, 190, 223, 229, 231, 233, 255, 269, 270, 302, 336
Guanzi, 203

habit, 15–18, 31–32, 37–38, 40–41, 43, 46, 50, 54–57, 60–66, 72, 73, 79, 82, 88, 92, 96–97, 103–105, 108–111, 143, 147, 161–163, 174, 192–193, 199, 205–209, 236–238, 291, 294, 298–301, 304, 310–313, 320, 323–325, 333–334
habitus, 53–54, 107, 128
Hadot, Pierre, 290
hair, 29, 43, 89, 273, 278, 281, 283, 317, 324, 326, 330, 332
Hampshire, Stuart, 132
Han Dynasty, 275
happiness, 46, 85, 111, 197, 285, 313
harmony, 28, 34, 43, 58, 171, 203, 205, 280, 284–285, 290, 319
Hays, Michael K., 222–223, 230
head, 14, 32–33, 37–38, 40–42, 95, 102–103, 105, 120, 150, 202, 208, 213, 225, 313

health, 8, 26, 33, 42, 45–46, 72, 74, 76, 85, 86, 153, 154, 161, 190, 271–275, 290
hearing, 6, 14, 102, 121, 128, 202, 236, 286, 326, 327
heart, 49, 100, 157, 202–204, 313
    heart and mind, 204, 307
heaven, 201, 206
hedonics, 153
Hegel, Georg Wilhelm Friedrich, 2, 74, 127, 129–130, 180, 183
Heidegger, Martin, 48
Hemingway, Ernest, 323
hermeneutics, 14, 126, 139, 172, 178, 181
Heyes, Cressida, 11
hip hop (and rap), 9, 15, 127, 137, 139, 141, 182, 323
Hipple, Walter, 146, 164
Hiroshima, 302, 305
history, 25, 74, 128, 136–138, 142, 169, 175, 184, 188, 194, 251, 252, 263, 289, 299
Hobbes, Thomas, 138
holiness, 71, 300
homosexuality, 179, 269, 273
horror, 151–152, 154–155, 165
house, 220, 224, 226
human nature, 29, 162, 175, 177
human-computer interaction, 12, 101
humanities, 7, 16, 25, 26, 28, 35, 37, 42
Hume, David, 159, 292
hunger, 44, 110, 144
Husserl, Edmund, 48
Huston, Anjelica, 328
hypertension, 104, 161
hypochondria, 17, 39, 62, 73, 80, 83–84, 86–87

idea, 99, 183, 312, 317. *See also* association of ideas
idealism, 3, 19, 130, 336
identity, 7, 93, 101, 104, 134, 248, 256–259, 335
    of artwork, 126, 135
identity politics, 168–169, 178–179
ideology, 13, 32, 98, 126, 167–168, 188, 192, 228, 232
ignorance, 16, 30, 32, 35, 42, 69, 77, 79, 146
image, 29, 57, 70, 162, 169, 179, 184, 207, 209
    of actor in performance, 210–214
    photographic, 240, 247, 250, 260, 261

imagination, 51, 148, 153, 168, 169, 178, 183, 191, 213, 257, 267, 279
immediacy, 231, 262, 309
immediate quality, 58–59
immortality, 71, 77, 88, 273
incarnation, 54, 228, 336
incorporation, 31, 53, 56, 103, 106, 107
independence, 133, 229, 231, 288
India (and Indian culture), 21, 276–286, 301
individual, 53, 78, 89, 161, 184, 189, 295–296, 322–324, 334
individuality, 89, 155, 166, 182, 184, 196, 226, 234
infancy, 29, 97
information, 11, 95, 168, 213
inhibition, 63, 64
injury, 40, 44, 65, 78, 108, 150, 205
inner/outer, 44, 77, 210, 335, 337
insomnia, 144
inspiration, 170, 178, 181, 288, 296, 298, 317
installation, 10, 257
instinct, 88, 108, 152, 161, 164, 245, 257, 264, 277, 312, 321, 324
institution, 20, 135, 136, 167, 177–179, 186–188, 222, 228
instruction, 112–115, 122, 193, 308, 311, 320
instrument, 1, 16, 26, 28, 33, 35–37, 41–43, 45, 108, 203, 278, 282, 285, 315
  instrumentality, 16, 28, 36, 37, 63, 265
intelligence, 36, 92, 107, 175, 221
intensity, 51, 139, 140, 143, 155, 235, 246, 270, 280, 305
intention (and the intentional), 50–52, 63, 131
interaction, 11, 12, 21, 33, 55, 66, 97, 106, 185, 243, 244, 311, 312, 335, 337
intercourse. See lovemaking
interdisciplinarity, 1, 7, 8, 25–27, 92, 111, 140, 142, 184, 186, 188
interest, 2, 17, 33, 75, 80, 88, 117–121, 138, 144, 145–146, 152, 229, 245, 264–265, 281, 285
internet, 239
interpersonal, the, 18, 21, 96–98, 106–107
interpretation, 14, 19, 29, 50–52, 65, 66, 70, 125, 126, 136, 172–175, 181, 182, 224, 234
intersomatic, the, 96–97
intimacy, 58, 93, 102, 246, 265, 325

introspection, 38, 39, 61–62, 72–73, 87, 117–122, 150, 313–314
intuition, 130–131
Israel, 98, 107, 115, 128, 170

James, Henry, 182
James, William, 5, 33, 38–41, 48, 49, 54–58, 61–64, 78–82, 87, 88, 92, 93, 101–102, 118, 121, 149, 164, 185, 191–192, 204, 207, 288, 317
  The Principles of Psychology, 55, 57, 79, 80, 93, 102
Jameson, Fredric, 165
Japan, 9, 15, 20, 22, 88, 128, 201, 227, 253, 288, 290, 300, 302–314, 328, 329
Jay, Martin, 9–10
jewelry, 277, 315, 327, 332
Jews, 128, 179
joy, 187, 192–193, 202, 275, 314
judge, 116, 151, 158, 229, 335
  judgment, 1, 2, 19, 33, 58–60, 106, 126, 129, 132, 148, 153, 162, 229, 263, 294, 327
justice, 141, 197

Kakutani, Masanori, 302, 306, 313
Kama Sutra, 276–286
Kant, Immanuel, 1, 2, 38–39, 48, 62, 73–74, 84, 86, 87, 140, 145, 159, 187–188, 219, 263–264, 282, 292
Keaton, Buster, 244
Kido, Inoue (Roshi), 303–314
Kierkegaard, Søren, 76
kinesthesis, 6, 259, 330–331
kiss, 281, 283, 313
knee, 28, 101, 112, 116
knowledge, 16–17, 26–27, 30, 32–35, 42, 46, 54, 69, 71–72, 106, 129, 133, 138, 147, 166, 172, 174, 176, 183, 194, 197, 201, 264, 266, 270, 282. *See also* self-knowledge
Koka Shastra, 276–278, 280–284, 286
Koolhaas, Rem, 230
Kristeva, Julia, 76

language, 17, 19, 27–29, 37, 50–51, 121, 122, 130–131, 173–176, 180, 303
  body, 39, 107, 122, 245, 317
Laozi, 202
law, 31, 78, 110, 143, 168, 301, 337
leg, 112, 116
Leib, 17
Libet, Benjamin, 63–64
Liezi, 201–206

life, 288–314. *See also* art of living
  philosophical, 11, 45, 80, 290–291
light, 157, 160, 202, 220, 233, 235, 239,
  249, 252, 255, 256, 257, 259, 260,
  262, 291, 332
Liji (Li-chi), 273
Lim, Youn-Kyung, 12
limit-experience, 143–144, 192
lips, 109, 230, 247, 262, 313, 327, 331,
  332
literature, 7, 37, 81, 84, 125–126, 140,
  169, 171, 173, 178, 181–182,
  184–185, 187, 191, 228, 269, 271, 283
Locke, John, 138, 160
locomotion, 14, 32, 35, 94, 224–225
logic, 18–20, 34, 41, 66, 71, 73, 74, 117,
  125–126, 129, 132, 142, 219, 272
looks. *See* appearance
love, 31, 46, 107, 140, 152, 155, 156,
  262–287, 290, 294
lovemaking, 16, 21, 262–287
lover, 36, 69, 96, 107, 121, 175, 268–285,
  313
Lucretius, 185
lust, 152, 294
lying, 96, 112, 114–115, 120, 137, 189,
  226, 278

magic, 252–253
magnitude, 154, 156–157
martial arts, 8, 34, 45, 142
Marx, Karl, 219
massage, 43, 278
mastery, 3, 26, 50, 63, 84–85, 98–99, 165,
  203, 209, 211, 270, 277–278,
  285–287
material, 3, 5, 16, 22, 37, 46, 56, 133, 174,
  189, 220, 225, 227, 233, 235, 265,
  289, 299, 309, 315, 332–333, 335,
  337
  materiality, 225, 233, 315
meals, 275, 297, 306, 309–312
meaning, 3, 29, 33, 50–53, 55, 57, 100,
  130, 133, 134, 139, 174–175, 211,
  242, 249, 257, 265, 275, 282, 296,
  299, 301
means, 16, 28, 32, 36–38, 40–41, 45–46,
  60, 64, 150, 168–169, 183, 190–191,
  199, 205–207, 209, 272, 294,
  315–316
mechanism, 150, 156–159, 163
media, 11, 27, 137, 229, 232, 258
medicine, 10, 273

meditation, 34, 85–88, 121, 185, 201, 292,
  305–314
medium, 3, 9, 31, 164, 227, 289, 295
melancholy, 17, 76, 80, 89, 154
meliorism, 3, 8, 19, 20, 21, 27, 35, 41, 79,
  106, 111, 113, 150, 167, 182, 193,
  220, 229, 294–296, 299, 304
memory
  implicit, 18, 91–111
  motor, 91–92
  muscle, 18, 46, 64, 91–111
  procedural, 91, 98, 108, 205
Mencius, 34, 141, 190, 200, 300, 320
Mencken, Henry Louis, 334
Merleau-Ponty, Maurice, 3–4, 48–50, 52,
  92, 99, 195, 198, 207, 208, 256
metaphysics, 3, 19, 171, 172, 177, 219
method, 8, 42, 72, 117, 200, 203,
  296–298, 311, 313
Mili, Gjon, 255
mind, 26–27, 33, 35, 36, 38, 47, 55–56,
  72–75, 84, 86–89, 91, 147–150, 197,
  200–208, 211, 213–214, 227
  body-mind, 27–28, 34, 42–43, 62, 74,
    115, 150, 164, 188–189, 301–302
  philosophy of, 3, 5, 7, 16, 54–55, 61,
    66–67
mindfulness, 21, 89, 92, 293, 300–302,
  305–307, 309–313
minorities, 169, 178–179
mirror, 71, 75, 137, 213–214, 247, 331
mise-en-scène, 243, 246, 249, 250, 253,
  256, 257, 259
modernism, 219, 222
moksha, 277
monotony, 118, 131, 281, 284
Montaigne, Michel de, 36, 72, 78, 79, 86,
  87, 147, 153, 185, 296, 302
mood, 79, 84, 191, 193, 232, 235, 329,
  332
moon, 278–280
Moore, G.E., 317, 337
morality, 30–31, 73, 190. *See also* ethics
morbidity, 74, 76–77, 81–82, 84, 86, 88,
  114
morning, 293, 298, 307, 326
mortality, 35, 69, 74–75, 251
mouth, 4, 32, 108–109, 117, 118, 235,
  273, 280, 301, 311, 315, 330, 331
movement, 8–9, 15, 29, 32, 35, 37, 39–40,
  46, 49–51, 59, 61–64, 87, 95, 98, 103,
  108, 162, 175, 190, 202–203,
  206–211, 213–214, 226, 235, 238,

248, 257, 259, 275, 279, 285, 302, 309–313, 319, 323, 326, 331, 333
movie, 104, 168. *See also* film
Mullis, Eric, 8
muscle, 6, 14–15, 18, 37–39, 42–44, 46, 64, 91–111, 119, 121, 154, 156, 160–162, 164, 210
music, 9, 14, 15, 31, 45, 50–51, 135, 139, 182, 187, 193, 277–279, 283, 319–320
myth (of the given), 19–20, 176

nails, 43, 89, 280, 281
namelessness, 18, 34. *See also* nonlinguistic
narrative, 52, 93, 100, 137, 299
neck, 37, 102–104, 108, 117, 280, 313
nerves, 146, 154–160
nervous system, 27, 29, 38, 53, 91, 208, 330
neuron, 213, 214, 238, 331
neuroscience, 6, 20, 63, 85, 142–143, 164, 212
New York, 15, 244, 246, 326
Nietzsche, Friedrich, 19, 42, 78–79, 83, 86, 87, 100, 127, 145–146, 172, 230, 264, 302
Nō Theater, 9, 20, 209, 212
Noelen-Hoeksema, Susan, 84
noise, 154, 249
nonlinguistic (and nondiscursive), 14, 19, 141, 158, 175–176, 187, 193–195, 320
norms, 5, 9, 30–32, 53, 113, 143, 177, 179, 188, 222, 324, 337
novelty, 181, 240, 267, 269

obesity, 109–111, 144
object, 16–17, 28, 77, 117–118, 131, 134, 139, 157, 173, 197–198, 234, 241–242, 247–252, 265, 301, 303–305, 309
objectivity, 54, 57, 93, 126, 134, 173, 223, 229, 234, 248
odor. *See* scent
ontology, 3, 16–17, 126, 139, 148, 194
orality 125, 174, 283, 315. *See also* voice
order, 20, 54, 168, 229, 304
organ, 35, 94, 333
orgasm, 272, 273, 274
orientational bias, 104–105
Oxford University, 125–126, 128, 132, 170–171

pain, 6, 18, 37, 38, 40–41, 44, 48, 88, 99–101, 103, 108, 144, 149–161, 165, 207, 230, 235, 237, 331
painting, 1, 15, 43, 45, 134, 187, 193, 236, 251–252, 255, 262–263, 322
Paris, 10, 21, 29, 104, 136, 168, 252, 254, 256, 329
Pascal, Blaise, 72, 321
passion, 149–150, 152, 154, 337
passivity, 55, 78, 84–86, 114, 149, 266
Passmore, John, 132
past, the, 240, 251, 296, 298–299, 312
pathology, 103–110
Patou, Jean, 328
pattern, 29, 91, 97, 102, 157, 163, 208
Paul, Saint, 30, 223–224, 336
peace, 37, 85, 273, 275, 313
Peng, Feng, 10
performance, 8–10, 13, 14, 17, 20, 26, 27, 28, 61, 91–92, 99, 142, 169, 185, 188, 193, 199–216, 233, 238, 239–261, 268–270, 274, 278–284, 289, 310–311
perfume, 328–329. *See also* scent
person, 29, 30, 43, 93–94, 101–102, 200, 227, 320, 334–335
personality, 97, 107–108, 187, 305, 317–322, 324, 328, 330, 332–333, 334, 336
persuasion, 191, 317
phenomenology, 17, 48, 194
Philadelphia, 326
philosophy
   analytic, 2, 17, 48, 49, 53, 125–128, 130–135, 139, 170–171, 186, 247, 256
   of art 131, 176. *See also* aesthetics
   continental, 126–127
   as cultural politics, 166–196
   of language, 3, 131
   of mind, 3, 5, 7, 16, 54–61, 66
   pragmatist. *See* pragmatism
   as a way of life, 140–142
photography
   as performative process, 10, 239–261
   versus photograph, 21, 240–244, 248–253
   techniques, 239, 244, 255
physiology, 18, 19, 42, 53, 142, 157, 161, 163, 188
piano, 91, 99, 296
Picasso, Pablo, 255

picture, 168, 244, 250, 254, 277, 289, 293, 295
Plato, 33, 69, 70, 138, 141, 185, 223–224, 282, 290, 336
  Alcibiades, 69
  Apology, 69, 290, 292
  Charmides, 69
  Crito, 290
  Gorgias, 290
  Phaedo, 33, 141, 336
  Phaedrus, 69
  Republic, 290
platonism (and neoplatonism), 71, 73, 75, 86
play (an instrument), 205, 277, 285
pleasure, 1–2, 6, 10, 14, 16, 21, 27, 43, 48, 72, 85, 87, 107, 113, 143, 145, 148–153, 155–156, 158, 162, 237, 259, 263–264, 265, 267, 269–270, 274–282, 284–286
  positive versus relative, 151–153, 156
Plessner, Helmuth, 162
Plotinus, 71, 336
pluralism, 13, 128, 172, 181, 261
poet, 75, 81, 89, 283, 293
poetry, 125, 276, 283, 319
politics, 9, 10–11, 138, 139, 141, 166–172, 178–190, 219, 221–222, 229, 236, 268, 275
  cultural versus real, 178–179
polygamy, 284
Pope, Alexander, 76
Porter, Katherine Anne, 334
portrait, 21, 239, 253, 319
pose (posing), 245–249, 254, 256, 258, 260
positivism, 130
postmodernism, 165, 171, 221
posture, 8, 14, 40–41, 66, 87, 96, 98, 102–108, 112, 206, 212, 214, 225, 229, 230, 235, 244, 245, 250, 257–259, 262, 281, 307, 318, 323, 325–331
power, 30, 35, 50, 56, 84–85, 130, 147, 148, 152–153, 156, 157, 163, 167–169, 178–179, 199, 235, 272, 318, 331
pragmatism, 37–38, 48, 54–55, 61, 65–67, 137, 138–140, 166–196, 204, 268, 286
  and meliorism, 3, 35, 167
  and pluralism, 173
  and somaesthetics, 3, 42–45, 140, 142, 188–196

Prakriti, 282
praxis, 185–187, 305
prejudice, 11, 30, 66–67, 97, 106, 179, 189, 265
preperception, 121
present, the, 298–299, 309–312
pressure, 102, 103, 108, 116, 120, 248, 330, 331
Proclus, 71
progress, 28, 79, 183, 191, 219, 222, 270, 282, 310, 313
properties, 12, 133–136, 157, 160, 265
propositions, 56, 60, 234
proprioception, 6, 40–41, 46, 110, 112, 115, 120, 147, 210, 212–215, 224, 226, 235–236, 238, 247, 259, 330–331
prostitution, 268
protest, 9, 32, 275
psychology, 19, 57, 66, 70, 81, 85, 142–143
public, the, 168, 187, 237, 248
  versus the private, 179–180, 184
purification (and purity), 71, 74, 88, 300, 301, 308, 317, 336
purpose, 60, 173
Purusha, 282

quality, 27, 55, 58–60, 66, 119, 148, 153, 231–235, 245, 252, 255, 260, 265, 275, 289, 295, 301, 303, 305, 315, 332
quantity, 82, 270, 301

race, 11, 25, 66, 130, 179, 189
rap. *See* hip hop
rationality, 30, 138, 158, 190, 192, 219, 220
Ray, Man (Emmanuel Radnitzky), 255
reading, 37–38, 45, 99, 140, 181, 187, 192, 288, 296
reality, 74, 89, 136–137, 166, 175, 177, 194, 249, 268, 283, 299, 309, 312, 313, 333
reasoning, 7, 126, 127, 158–159
reflection, 14, 18, 33, 38, 45, 49, 50, 61–65, 70–90, 92, 94–95, 137–138, 158, 163, 174, 182, 198–211, 227, 231, 294, 296
rehearsal (mental or imaginative), 208, 213, 266
relation, 58–60, 66, 77, 97, 118, 225, 270
relaxation, 104, 106, 119, 121, 154–158, 163, 165

religion, 178, 184–185, 187–188, 224
Renaissance, 42, 72, 142, 223
reproduction, 35, 237, 240, 249, 252, 253
resilience, 85, 87, 104
resistance, 28, 30, 221, 228, 233, 262, 266
respect, 30–31, 310
rest, 154, 155, 320
revolution, 129, 137, 220
rhetoric, 131, 300
rhythm, 109, 147, 162, 210, 235, 270, 275, 313
  breathing rhythm, 27, 31, 50, 51, 107, 121, 143
ribcage, 40, 42, 103, 108
ritual, 31, 34, 140, 168, 233, 240, 247, 252, 253, 258, 275, 282, 300, 319
robotics, 11
Rohe, Ludwig Mies van der, 220, 223
role playing, 248, 259
Rome, 4, 25, 68, 223, 269
Rorty, Richard, 19–20, 127, 167–196
rotation, 42, 142, 238
Rousseau, Jean-Jacques, 36
routine, 54, 66, 246, 292, 306, 324
Royaumont Abbey, 256–258
rules, 50, 130, 133, 179, 226, 269, 275, 284, 334
rumination, 17, 81–87
running, 99, 192
Ruskin, John, 76
Russell, Bertrand, 317–318
Russia, 168

sadomasicism (S/M), 269
satisfaction, 51, 87, 110, 151, 189, 263, 267, 272, 276, 278, 280, 285, 301, 311
scent (smell), 6, 96, 235, 259, 327–330
schema, motor, 91, 96, 97, 199, 333
Schiphorst, Thecla, 12
Schlemmer, Oskar, 220
Schopenhauer, Arthur, 78, 140, 145, 176, 263–264
science, 1, 2, 7, 25–26, 42, 63, 129, 142, 148, 177–179, 183–188, 270, 271, 274, 277
screen, 101, 209, 245
script, 18, 114, 250, 268, 269
sculpture, 1, 9, 15, 275, 283, 293, 336
Searle, John, 49–53
seduction, 262–263

self, the, 40, 55, 68–90, 94, 113–115, 143, 155, 177, 189–190, 201–209, 247–248, 258, 267, 332–336
self-care, 18, 40, 72, 113
self-consciousness, 74, 81, 85, 87, 201, 211, 246, 248, 285
self-control, 68–69, 86, 89, 286
self-cultivation, 11, 21–22, 34, 69–83, 113–114, 180, 295, 335
self-examination, 17, 68–90, 112, 200–204, 231
self-fashioning, 21, 27, 41, 83, 111, 113, 142, 182–183, 188, 258, 286, 289
selfishness (and self-absorption), 17, 75, 86, 90, 180, 190, 201
self-knowledge, 17–18, 68–90, 106, 113–114, 143, 197, 199, 202–203, 266, 286, 290, 296, 335
self-loathing, 70, 73, 75, 88, 104
self-preservation, 152–155, 164
self-stylization, 11, 13, 21, 285, 323–324, 336
self-use, 34, 37, 41–42, 62, 89, 165, 197, 199, 204, 244
semen, 272–273
sensation, 2, 148, 150–151, 160, 226, 235, 259, 265, 284, 305, 313
senses, 1, 6, 10, 16, 22, 33–34, 36, 46, 77, 87, 136, 149, 164, 226–227, 235–236, 257, 278, 285–286, 292, 300, 316, 326–332
sensibility, 28, 38, 46, 129, 148, 191, 233, 238, 260, 287
sensuality (and the sensual), 145, 187, 192, 237, 263–264, 277–278, 285–286, 289, 300–301, 335, 337
Seoul, 328
sex (and sexuality), 146, 152–153, 179, 187, 191, 193. *See also* eroticism
sexual performance, 265, 266, 268, 277–282, 286
Shaftesbury, Anthony Ashley-Cooper, 3rd Earl of, 140, 148, 263
Shakti, 282
shintai, 227
Shiva, 276, 282
Shklovsky, Viktor, 304
Shorinkutsu, 305
shoulder, 103–104, 108, 112, 117–120
Sibley, Frank, 133
simplicity, 220, 288, 296–299, 309
simulation, 213, 267–268
simultaneity, 33, 43, 120–121, 209, 236

sitting, 18, 64, 104–105, 114, 115, 201, 305–309. *See also* zazen
situation, 12, 58–60, 231, 234, 243–245, 248–249, 255–258
size, 133, 175, 280
skill, 1, 34, 42, 45, 61, 63, 64, 91–92, 99, 101, 109, 165, 193, 205–212, 244–246, 249, 266, 270, 280, 285, 315
skin, 6, 29, 43, 235, 237, 328, 330, 332, 334
sleep, 101, 121, 231, 197–198, 289–294, 297
slowness, 37, 296–298
smell. *See* scent
social hope, 183, 189, 191
social roles, 18, 98, 107
social status, 36, 86, 128, 169, 284
society, 31, 54, 56, 152, 155, 159, 169, 180, 182, 184, 188–191, 196, 220, 222, 230–231, 290
Socrates, 17, 33, 68–72, 82, 219, 263, 290–294
solidarity, 15, 190
soma, 3, 5, 6, 8, 9, 12, 16, 18, 28, 33, 35, 46, 47, 62, 65, 92, 94, 96, 106–107, 111, 141, 188, 189, 198, 223–227, 230, 235, 259, 287, 300, 307, 312, 314, 319, 330, 337
somaesthetic perception, 92, 105, 111, 199
somaesthetic reflection, 61, 88, 118, 199–200
somaesthetic system, 6
somaesthetics
　analytic, 42, 142, 188
　branches and dimensions, 5, 8, 13–15, 20, 22, 41–45, 111, 141–142
　critiques of, 6, 13–15, 19, 169–170, 194
　experiential, 44–45, 113–115
　genealogy, 125–128
　origin of, 5, 6, 125
　performative, 45
　practical, 45, 113, 142, 188, 256
　pragmatic, 42–43, 45, 142, 188
　representational, 44, 336
　as theory and practice, 3, 10, 27, 67, 111, 113, 115, 227, 286, 302
somatic cultivation, 4, 14–16, 33, 140
somatic style, 4, 14, 22, 315–338
Sontag, Susan, 242, 245–246, 249, 251
soul, 16, 36, 69–88, 283, 286, 290, 293, 299, 301, 319, 321, 333, 335
sound, 284, 313, 327
　love sounds, 279, 281. *See also* noise
Sousa, Ronald de, 266–268

space, 94–96, 104–106, 220, 224–226, 232, 234–235
　verus place, 94–96
Speaks, Michael, 221
species, 28, 29, 162
speech, 31, 46, 92, 192, 322, 327
speed, 38, 109
spine, 40, 42, 103, 238
spirit, 22, 26, 74, 76, 87, 201, 206, 210, 227, 293, 299–301, 334, 336–337
sports, 8, 15, 101, 168, 175, 323, 331
stage
　temporal, 20, 99, 197, 204–205, 208–209, 221, 223, 284, 291
　theatrical, 8, 249, 258, 275, 277–279, 309
stairs, 235, 259, 291
Stanhope, Philip Dormer (Lord Chesterfield), 320
statue, 206, 289, 295, 336
Steinberg, Saul, 7
stereotypes, 5, 14, 183, 291
Stern, Daniel, 97
stimulation, 110, 115, 143–144, 213–215, 245, 285
Stolterman, Erik, 12
stress, 11, 33, 96, 103, 115
　posttraumatic stress disorder, 100
structure, 29, 41, 48, 52–54, 55–58, 66, 125, 128, 132, 136, 142, 147, 158, 179, 188, 210, 222–224, 231–232, 250, 265, 278
struggle, 125, 130, 138, 244
style. *See also* somatic style
　ambiguities of, 22, 321
　and character, 319–321, 324, 328, 333–337
　and spirit, 334, 336–337
Styron, William, 81, 84
subject, 28, 35, 46
　photographic, 21, 241–260
subjectivity, 4–6, 10, 15, 16, 22, 28, 45, 94, 143, 161, 250, 257, 269, 330, 337
sublime, 19, 83, 145–165, 233, 299, 303, 317
substance, 22, 73, 231, 234, 321, 333, 335
suffering, 29, 149, 153–154, 179, 292, 336
suicide, 76, 80–81
Sullivan, Shannon, 10
surface, 22, 43–44, 50, 132, 328, 330, 332, 333, 337
surgery, 43, 324
survival, 155, 162–163
swallowing, 101, 108–109, 310, 311

sweating, 100, 325
symbol, 30, 32, 35, 50, 75, 223–224, 227, 262, 280, 282, 297
symmetry (and asymmetry), 95, 153, 224, 225, 227

tactile, the 12, 112, 215, 224, 235–238, 330. *See also* touch
Tadanoumi, 305
Taine, Hippolyte Adolphe, 130
Tale of Genji, 329
target, 38, 61, 88, 205–206, 209, 242–244, 260
taste, 1–2, 6, 102, 109–110, 129, 133, 148, 159, 162, 198, 275, 301, 323–324, 328, 330
teaching, 10, 16, 18, 44, 113–115, 122, 215, 302, 305
technology, 8, 11–12, 232, 244
tectonics, 223, 232
teeth, 51, 156, 230
Tel Aviv, 107, 309
temple, 68, 86, 224, 225, 282, 283, 289, 306, 335–336
tennis, 101
tension, 39–40, 43–44, 103–105, 117, 119, 152–164, 210–211, 259
terminology, 5–8
terror, 149–159, 163, 165
textualism, 166, 175–176, 178, 185
texture, 109, 110, 308
theatre, 8–9, 20, 168, 209–215, 252, 267
theory, 126–127, 137, 139
 transformational, 139–140
 wrapper, 134, 139
therapy, 11, 100, 125, 282, 290
Thoreau, Henry David, 5, 22, 288–314, 316, 321, 335–337
throat, 61, 102
Tiantong Rujing (T'ien-t'ung Ju-ching), 305
Tokyo, 302
tolerance, 30, 97, 166, 196
Tolstoy, Leo, 76, 304
Toma, Yann, 10, 21, 243, 254–260
tone (of muscle), 104, 144, 154, 160, 161
tongue, 101, 108, 207, 226, 230, 317, 331
tool, 26, 31, 33, 36, 41–45, 62–63, 224, 315, 335
touch, 6, 12, 235–238, 259, 330
tranquility, 37–38, 151, 155, 157, 165, 203

transcendentalism, 22, 58, 61, 79, 296, 316–317
transgression, 128, 143, 192
transition, 59, 98, 118–119
transmodal perception, 10, 212–213, 238, 259, 328
trauma, 99–100
truth, 2, 134, 138, 147, 164, 270, 291
Twiggy (Lesley Lawson), 323

understanding
 non-linguistic, 174–175
 versus interpretation, 173–175
union. *See also* unity
 of body and mind, 27, 188, 227
 of human with divine, 71, 73, 282–283
 sexual, 278, 280, 282–283
unity, 27, 58–61, 93, 102, 149, 266, 283–284, 319, 320, 322
urbanism, 230
Urmson, James Opie, 132, 256
utopianism, 184, 220–221, 299

value
 aesthetic, 135, 147, 171, 242, 275
 cult, 240, 252–253
 exhibition, 240, 252–253
Van Gogh, Vincent, 81
Van Gulik, Robert, 270–275
Van Honthorst, Gerrit, 262–263
variety, 8, 13, 16, 150, 156–157, 281–285, 322
Vatsyayana, 276, 281–283
Venice, 10
vertebra, 102–103, 120
verticality, 225
vestibular system, 102, 213
Vienna, 262
violence, 143, 155
violin, 108
virtue, 31, 32, 34, 206, 290, 295, 319, 336–337
Vishnu, 281
vision, 15, 33, 42, 102, 212, 213, 237–238, 257, 326
visuality, 7–9, 10, 15, 115, 120, 212–214, 235–237, 254, 326–327
vitality, 272
Vitruvius, 223–225
voice, 315–316, 326–327
volume, 94, 225
voluntary action, 32, 49–50, 56, 63, 95, 316, 324, 325

walking, 64, 91, 99, 105, 198, 225, 235, 297–299, 300, 309, 322–323, 327
Warhol, Andy, 135–137
weakness, 16, 30, 35, 71, 73–75, 83–87, 114
Weber-Fechner law, 110, 143
weight, 64, 116
Whiting, Sarah, 230, 233
whole/part, 12–14, 43, 49, 58–60, 101–102, 118–119, 136, 155–157, 162, 176, 196, 224, 225, 227, 268–269, 285, 313, 318
will. *See* voluntary action
wisdom, 34, 69
Wittgenstein, Ludwig, 31, 37, 49–53, 79–81, 83, 225, 323, 318–320, 322, 334

woman, 36, 227, 262, 272–273, 275, 279–280, 285, 327
Wotton, Henry, 223

Xenaphon, 33
Xunzi, 200, 205

Yeats, William Butler, 45
yoga, 11, 43, 44, 87, 337
Young, Edward, 75

zazen, 87, 201, 306–307, 309–310
Zeami, Motokiyo, 20, 209–215
Zen, 22, 34, 88, 212, 288, 290, 300, 302–303, 305–307, 308, 311–312, 314
Zeus, 68
Zhuangzi, 201–203, 206, 292